Gilded Splendor

GILDED SPLENDOR

TREASURES OF CHINA'S LIAO EMPIRE (907–1125)

Edited by

Hsueh-man Shen

Published on the occasion of the exhibition
"Gilded Splendor: Treasures of China's Liao Empire (907–1125),"
organized by Asia Society.

Asia Society and Museum
New York, New York
October 6 through December 31, 2006

Museum für Ostasiatische Kunst
Cologne, Germany
January 26 through April 22, 2007

Museum Rietberg Zurich
Zürich, Switzerland
May 13 through July 15, 2007

Asia Society gratefully acknowledges
the support of John H. J. Guth.

Critical support for this project comes from our lead
corporate sponsor, Morgan Stanley, as part of the
Morgan Stanley Innovators Series.

Morgan Stanley

We also appreciate the support of the
National Endowment for the Arts,
the National Endowment for the Humanities,
and the E. Rhodes and
Leona B. Carpenter Foundation.

40th
ANNIVERSARY
NATIONAL
ENDOWMENT
FOR THE ARTS
Established 1965

NATIONAL
ENDOWMENT
FOR THE
HUMANITIES

Any views, findings, conclusions, or recommendations
expressed in this book do not necessarily reflect those
of the National Endowment for the Humanities.

© Asia Society, 2006

ISBN-10 Asia Society: 0-87848-105-2
ISBN-13 Asia Society: 978-0-87848-105-7

Library of Congress Control Number: 2006931305

Project Manager
Marion Kocot

Coordinator and In-house Curator
Adriana Proser

Copyeditors
Caroline Herrick and Mary Chou

5 Continents

Project Manager
Marco Jellinek

Art Director
Lara Gariboldi

Colour Separation
Eurofotolit, Cernusco sul Naviglio (Milan)

Printed in August 2006
by Conti Tipocolor, Calenzano (Florence), Italy

info@5continentseditions.com

© 5 Continents Editions srl, Milan, 2006

ISBN 5 Continents Editions : 88-7439-332-6

Frontispiece
Silk gauze fan (detail); Liao dynasty,
early or mid-tenth century; From Tomb Number 3,
Daiqintala Township, Keyou Central Banner,
Xing'an League; Bamboo, silk gauze, pigments,
gilding; Length of fan surface: 27 cm;
width of fan surface: 18.7 cm; total length: 46 cm;
Museum of the Inner Mongolia Autonomous Region;
Courtesy of the Cultural Bureau of Inner Mongolia
Autonomous Region.

Front Cover
Crown (detail); Liao dynasty, 1018 or earlier;
From the tomb of the Princess of Chen and Xiao
Shaoju at Qinglongshan Town in Naiman Banner;
Gilded silver; Height: 30 cm; diameter: 19.5 cm;
Research Institute of Cultural Relics and Archaeology
of Inner Mongolia; Courtesy of the Cultural Bureau
of Inner Mongolia Autonomous Region.

Back Cover
Burial mask with head netting (detail); Liao dynasty,
1018 or earlier; From the tomb of the Princess
of Chen and Xiao Shaoju at Qinglongshan Town
in Naiman Banner; Mask: gold; netting: silver;
Length: 21.7 cm; width: 18.8 cm; Research
Institute of Cultural Relics and Archaeology
of Inner Mongolia; Courtesy of the Cultural Bureau
of Inner Mongolia Autonomous Region.

Table of Contents

Foreword

The rise of China is a common enough epithet today. It is clear that the country's economic and political presence has increased dramatically in the past five years to attract this kind of attention. Yet to focus solely on these recent developments is to deny 5,000 years of great cultural achievement. The exhibition "Gilded Splendor: Treasures of China's Liao Empire (907–1125)" offers a more complex understanding of China's history. By bringing together extraordinary cultural objects that have only come to light during the last three decades through archaeological discoveries in Inner Mongolia, most of which have never left China before, the exhibition offers us a rare glimpse into the Liao dynasty, a little-known dynasty founded by the Khitan people. The Liao dynasty ruled northern China during much of the same period as the better-known Song dynasty. Until recently the Liao dynasty was considered by many Chinese scholars as a barbarian culture, an impression conveyed primarily through a Chinese bias in writings of their time. With these objects we are able to better understand the complex relationship and cultural exchange between these two substantial empires from the tenth to twelfth century, adding to our knowledge of China's history during this period.

Many people have played key roles in the development and successful realization of this exhibition and catalogue. I would like to thank the exceptional group of curators and catalogue authors of *Gilded Splendor: Treasures of China's Liao Empire (907–1125)*. The groundbreaking nature of this project owes much to the vision of curator Dr. Hsueh-man Shen and her scholarship and intimate knowledge of Liao history, religion, art, and archaeology. Dr. Adriana Proser, Asia Society's John H. Foster Curator for Traditional Asian Art, shepherded both the book and exhibition through every step from curatorial premise and website development to the exhibition design and the editorial process over the last two years. I would also like to thank Colin Mackenzie, former Associate Director and Curator at Asia Society, who first breathed life into the project and saw that it had a solid foundation from which to grow. My profound gratitude goes to the members of the scholarly advisory committee and catalogue contributors—Emma C. Bunker, Nicola Di Cosmo, Lothar von Falkenhausen, Lynette Sue-ling Gremli, Marilyn Leidig Gridley, Valerie Hansen, Hiromi Kinoshita, Dieter Kuhn, François Louis, Nancy S. Steinhardt, Sun Jianhua, Ta La, Chün-fang Yü, and Zhang Yaqiang.

Asia Society offers its profound thanks to the many Chinese officials and scholars who have supported the project: Sun Jiazheng, Minister of Culture, People's Republic of China; Shan Jixiang, Director, State Administration of Cultural Heritage, People's Republic of China; Zhang Jianxin, Section Chief, Section of International Affairs, State Administration of Cultural Heritage; Gao Yanqing, Director, Department of Culture, Inner Mongolia Autonomous Region, People's Republic of China; Liu Zhaohe, Deputy Director of the Department of Culture and Director of the Bureau of Cultural Heritage, Inner Mongolia Autonomous Region, People's Republic of China; and at the Inner Mongolia Autonomous Region Historic Relics Archaeological Studies Research Institute, Ta La, Director; Liu Laixue, Vice Director; Huang Xueyin; and Sun Jianhua.

"Gilded Splendor: Treasures of China's Liao Empire (907–1125)" and its associated programs would not have been possible without the support of a large group of generous donors. I would like to make special mention of John Guth who provided seed money without which the exhibition never would have been possible. His enthusiasm and support for the project early in its conception was integral to the realization of this exhibition. Critical support for this project from our lead corporate sponsor, Morgan Stanley, is part of the *Morgan Stanley Innovators Series* and marks the beginning of a multi-year collaboration. We also appreciate the support of the National Endowment for the Humanities, the National Endowment for the Arts, and the E. Rhodes and Leona B. Carpenter Foundation.

Among the many members of Asia Society staff who contributed to the success of this exhibition are: Marion Kocot, Assistant Director; Amy McEwen, Collections Manager and

Senior Registrar, Clare McGowan, Associate Registrar and Exhibitions Coordinator; Nancy Blume, Head of Museum Education Programs; Clay Vogel, Installation Coordinator and the designer of the exhibition; Mary Chou, Museum Associate; and Hannah Pritchard, Administrative Assistant. The project also could not have done without the assistance of a wonderful group of interns, including Michele Chase, Katherine Stuart, and Alia Swastika.

Yang Yingshi and Andy Liu Yong provided able assistance with travel and other arrangements for curators and delegates. Juliet Yung-Yi Chou used her creative and critical talents to develop a website that will prove valuable well beyond the life of the exhibition. Gratitude goes to Nancy Steinhardt and Tina Thomason of the University of Pennsylvania and Cary Y. Liu and Caroline Cassells of the Princeton University Art Museum, all of whom worked with Asia Society to create programs focused on their institutions' Liao collections to coincide with the exhibition. Special thanks go to Caroline Herrick for her meticulous attention to detail in editing the catalogue and her dedication in the development and realization of this scholarly text.

Rachel Cooper, Linden Chubin, and La Frances Hui of Cultural Programs and Performing Arts at Asia Society have organized a wonderful program including a symposium featuring an international group of scholars, performances, and lectures to complement and enhance the exhibition and book. I also want to thank Elaine Merguerian and the staff in Marketing and Communication for working so creatively to engage exhibition and related program visitors. The Development staff of Asia Society who secured the financial support for this project includes Todd Galitz, Julie Lang, Alice Hunsberger, and Sharon Fennimore.

Finally, I would like to express my gratitude to Vishakha N. Desai, President of Asia Society; Nicholas Platt, former President of Asia Society; and Jamie Metzl, Executive Vice President of Programs for their enthusiastic and crucial support for this compelling and important project.

We have been very pleased to be able to work collaboratively on this exhibition, and to make it possible for "Gilded Splendor: Treasures of China's Liao Empire (907–1125)" to have a life beyond its presentation in New York and travel to Museum für Ostasiatische Kunst in Cologne and Museum Rietberg in Zurich.

Special mention must be made of the efforts of Dr. Albert Lutz, Director Museum Rietberg Zurich, Switzerland and Dr. Adele Schlombs, Director Museum für Ostasiatische Kunst, Cologne, Germany. We also appreciate and acknowledge the contributions of Alexandra Von Przychowski, Assistant Curator of Chinese Art, Museum Rietberg Zurich, who coordinated the German edition of the catalogue, and of Dr. Martina Wernsdörfer and Dr. Khanh Trinh, who translated the essays for the German edition.

Our international colleagues, organizers, exhibitors, and contributors have shown a continued enthusiasm for the material and commitment to the project and tour that has made our work together truly memorable.

Melissa Chiu
Museum Director
Asia Society

Foreword

The Khitan were one of the northern minority peoples of ancient China. They were first mentioned in historical records during the Northern Wei dynasty (386–534), and they ascended in power and importance during the Sui (581–618) and Tang (618–907) dynasties. During the time of the Five Dynasties (907–979) and the Song dynasty (960–1279) in the south, the Khitan founded the powerful Liao dynasty (907–1125) in the north. As a result, historians referred to this period as, "the second Northern and Southern Dynasties." (In Chinese history, the period from 222 to 589 is referred to as the Northern and Southern Dynasties.) It was during the Jin (1115–1234) and Yuan (1279–1368) dynasties that the Khitan were assimilated with other peoples and disappeared from the pages of history. The Khitan dominated northern China for more than two hundred years, and the Liao culture they created became known throughout the world.

The Khitan made significant contributions to the structure of Chinese national pluralism. Politically, during the Liao dynasty the Khitan established a method of ruling different populations with different policies, integrating the nomadic and agricultural economies that existed in northern China, putting an end to the disputes that existed among peoples of different ethnic groups, and laying the foundations for governing China as an ordered, harmonious whole. The national culture produced by the double political system linked the characteristics of different peoples, areas, and eras and resulted in the remaking and the raising to a higher level of both northern and southern culture. The Khitan revealed the elegant demeanor of the nomadic peoples of northern China, and long ago Liao culture was fused into the broader Chinese national culture.

After the Liao dynasty, the word *Khitan* became known all over the world, and came to represent China, thus showing the broad influence of the Khitan. The history of the Khitan is very important in understanding the development of the northern ethnic groups of ancient China. Recent research into and revelations about Liao dynasty culture represent a breakthrough in our knowledge of the history of the peoples of northern China and is an important platform from which to expand our knowledge of Chinese civilization.

The grasslands of eastern Inner Mongolia were the cradle of Khitan civilization, as well as the political, economic, and cultural center of the Liao dynasty. The rich variety of material culture created by the Khitan, like an auspicious gem set in China's northern grassland, dazzles the eyes. Historical sites like the Liao-dynasty Supreme Capital (Shangjing) and Middle Capital (Zhongjing) and the Zuzhou, Songzhou, and Huaizhou are all located in this area. In recent years, important new archaeological finds have been made, including the tomb of the Princess of Chen, the tomb of Yelü Yuzhi, the Liao tomb on Baoshan Mountain, and the Liao tomb on Tuerji Mountain. Special mysterious funerary practices and myriad precious burial objects are, like the door to Ali Baba's treasures, gradually being opened up to the people of the world.

The 120 groups of items from the Liao dynasty in this exhibition include sparkling gold and silver wares, translucent jades, and fine ceramics as well as significant Buddhist objects; all reflect the politics, economy, and culture of the Khitan. This exhibition presents an unprecedented, magnificent array of cultural relics. Through the show, foreign friends can gain an understanding of the long-standing history and all-inclusive culture of China.

Liu Zhaohe
Deputy Director of the Cultural Bureau of Inner Mongolia
December 2005

Asia Society is proud to present "Gilded Splendor: Treasures of the Liao Empire (907–1125)," on the occasion of the 50th anniversary of Asia Society's founding by John D. Rockefeller 3rd. In this exciting year, Asia Society continues to celebrate the vision of its founder by promoting greater knowledge and understanding of Asia with groundbreaking programming as well as an expanded presence throughout the United States and Asia.

"Gilded Splendor: Treasures of the Liao Empire (907–1125)" provides greater insight into the culture of the Liao dynasty and goes far to amend a previous distorted image of Liao civilization. The exhibition and book assign a framework for serious consideration alongside their contemporaries. We are grateful to the government of the People's Republic of China, and representatives of the Bureau of Cultural Heritage of Inner Mongolia Autonomous Region for agreeing to lend these rare and beautiful works of art, most of which have never been seen outside of China, for this exhibition. Our thanks go to many individuals and organizations for their continued involvement with the mission of Asia Society, and whose support of the project is acknowledged elsewhere. We are especially indebted to Asia Society Trustee, John Guth, who inspired us to undertake the project and whose enthusiasm for it is deeply appreciated.

We hope that a greater awareness of the histories and cultures of earlier centuries will contribute to our deeper understanding of China's continuing and developing role in the twenty-first century.

Vishakha N. Desai
President
Asia Society

Message from the Sponsor

Morgan Stanley is proud to be the global sponsor of **"Gilded Splendor: Treasures of China's Liao Empire (907–1125)"** at the Asia Society. The beautiful objects in this exhibition—most on view for the first time outside of China—have come to light through archaeological excavations in the last decade and are causing a reassessment of this complex period in Chinese history. Long in the shadow of the great Tang and Song dynasties, the Liao dynasty is now revealed to have been stunningly sophisticated and cosmopolitan.

This exhibition and catalog represent the first part of **The Morgan Stanley Innovators Series**, our multi-year collaboration with the Asia Society celebrating Asian innovation, both ancient and contemporary. Morgan Stanley, a pioneer in financial services in China and worldwide, is honored to partner with the Asia Society in its 50th year of path-breaking exhibitions and performance programs that foster mutual understanding between Asia and the rest of the world.

Morgan Stanley

Curator's Foreword and Acknowledgments

The notion of the art and material culture of the Liao is difficult to define, for several reasons. Traditional Sinocentric opinion, which considered the Liao dynasty (907–1125) a barbarian state, contributed to a biased view against the culture created by the Liao people. For a long time, the Liao dynasty was considered nothing more than an inferior copy of the supreme models, the preceding Tang (618–907) and parallel Song (960–1279) dynasties. That the Liao borrowed a number of traditional Chinese elements from the Tang and Song further reinforced this way of thinking. For the same reason, studies of Liao art and material culture have focused on the exotic appeal associated with the Khitan nomads who founded the Liao empire, neglecting the fact that Liao territory encompassed an enormous landmass, stretching from Manchuria to Inner Asia, which was inhabited by peoples of a number of different ethnic origins, including the Jurchens, Han Chinese (the majority ethnic group of China), and Uighurs of Turkish descent.

Archaeology conducted in China in the past few decades has uncovered large quantities of artifacts that challenge the traditional Sinocentric view of Liao culture. Major finds have been discovered in Liaoning Province, Hebei Province, and the Inner Mongolia Autonomous Region, with the largest concentration in Inner Mongolia. Among the excavations of Liao sites in Inner Mongolia, the most well known are the tomb (dated 942) of Yelü Yuzhi and his wife, the tomb (dated 959) of the Prince of Wei and his wife, the tomb (dated 1018) of the Princess of Chen and her husband, and the relic deposit (dated 1049) inside the White Pagoda in Balin Right Banner. Objects from all of these finds are featured in the exhibition "Gilded Splendor: Treasures of China's Liao Empire (907–1175)."

Archaeological evidence shows that the fusion of ideas and styles of different origins was one of the major features of Liao culture, thanks to the multiethnicity of the Liao people and the broad contacts the Liao had with their neighbors. The hybridity of Khitan and Han Chinese traditions is most obvious in such areas as the Liao bureaucracy, writing system, and mortuary practices. A large number of foreign goods and ideas were brought into Liao territory via various routes, both overland and via the sea. There were also Song Chinese artisans working in Liao territory, producing artifacts that combined features of Liao and Song Chinese cultures. In their religious life, Liao Buddhists developed a unique interest, based on both Chinese and Korean Buddhist practices, in preserving and venerating Buddhist sacred texts.

As the first major exhibition in the West to explore the art and material culture of the Liao, this exhibition presents 120 groups of objects, comprising more than 200 individual artifacts, all of which are from Inner Mongolia. It is hoped that this pioneer exhibition will encourage more interest in, research on, and appreciation of the culture of the Liao dynasty. This exhibition would not have come into being without the commitment and support of the Asia Society Museum. My gratitude goes to Dr. Vishakha Desai, Dr. Melissa Chiu, and the members of the museum staff who contributed to the organization and realization of the exhibition and the catalogue. I should like to thank, in particular, Dr. Adriana Proser; her careful management of the project from New York has enabled me to concentrate on the content of the exhibition and the catalogue. Caroline Herrick has done an excellent job in carrying out the daunting task of editing the exhibition catalogue. I thank her especially for her diligence, patience, and interest. I am grateful to the Advisory Board members—professors Nicola Di Cosmo, Valerie Hansen, Nancy S. Steinhardt, Chün-fang Yü, and Lothar von Falkenhausen—for their kind and sound advice. I would like to thank Emma Bunker, Lynette Sue-ling Gremli, Dr. Marilyn Gridley, Dr. Hiromi Kinoshita, Professor Dieter Kuhn, Dr. François Louis, Professor Sun Jianhua, Professor Ta La, and Zhang Yaqiang for contributing the catalogue essays and entries. My thanks are due to Dr. Colin Mackenzie, former associate director of the Asia Society Museum, who generated the idea of an archaeological exhibition from Inner Mongolia in the first place. The Seattle Art Museum was generous in supporting my participation in this project during my tenure there from 2003 to 2005. Anke Hein and Yang Li helped with the compilation of the bibliography; their assistance is appreciated.

Hsueh-man Shen
University of Edinburgh

諸天童子　以為給使
若人惡罵　口則閉塞
智惠光明　如日之照
見諸如來　坐師子座
又見其身　阿僧羅等
自見其身　而為說法
教充量光　照於一切
佛為四眾　說充上法
閻浮嚴喜　而為供養
佛知其心　深入佛道
汝善男子　當從來世
國土嚴淨　廣大充化

Liao History and Society

An Introduction to Chinese Archaeology of the Liao

Temple Architecture and Tomb Architecture

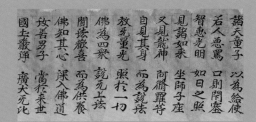

Praying for Eternity:
Use of Buddhist Texts in Liao Buddhist and Funerary Practices

Nicola Di Cosmo

Liao History and Society

The Liao dynasty takes its name from the Liao River region of northeastern China, homeland of the ruling clan of the Khitan people.[1] At the time of its greatest territorial expansion, the Liao empire extended from Manchuria to northern and southern Mongolia and included the northeastern part of what had been Tang China. The Khitan appear in Chinese sources from the fourth century AD as the descendants of a branch of the Xianbei, the powerful northeastern people who founded the Northern Wei dynasty (386–534). The Khitan spoke an Altaic language whose exact nature has yet to be fully identified but was probably Mongolic with a large Tungusic component.

The history of the Liao empire begins in 907, the year of the fall of the Tang dynasty in China, when dynastic founder Abaoji (Taizu, 872–926) assumed the title of *kaghan* (supreme ruler) (see chart 1).[2] He was formally enthroned in 916, after he had "pacified" pastoral peoples who lived in today's northern Mongolia and had resisted challenges to his authority from within his own ruling clan. According to Khitan custom, the ruler had to be reelected every three years, but Abaoji refused to give up his position in 910 and again in 913.[3] Unrest ensued from within his own family, some of whose members expected to challenge his reelection. Disputes over leadership succession were eventually put down after some of the challengers were executed and after Abaoji took measures to consolidate his own power as permanent ruler. One of these measures was the construction, ordered in 918, of the imperial capital Huangdu, later renamed Shangjing (Supreme Capital), located in today's Inner Mongolia, north of the Shira Mören River. This was a Chinese-style city, endowed with palaces, temples, ministry buildings, and merchant quarters; it was the administrative center of the kingdom. By the time construction began, Abaoji had already envisioned one of the trademark features of Khitan rule, namely, an imperial administration that comprised a northern division responsible for tribal peoples and pastoral areas and a southern division responsible for sedentary peoples and agricultural areas. This dual structure was formally established in 947.

Although Abaoji launched several campaigns against China, he did not conquer any Chinese territory but he did expand the area under Khitan rule extensively, into northern Mongolia and west to the Ordos region and the Gansu corridor. One of the most spectacular feats of his reign came just before he died in 926; this was the conquest of the southern Manchurian kingdom of Bohai,

Personal name		Temple name	Regnal title	
Abaoji	(907–26)	Taizu	Shence	916
			Tianzan	922–26
			Tianxian	926
Deguang	(927–47)	Taizong	Tianxian	926–38
			Huitong	938–47
			Datong	947
Yuan	(947–51)	Shizong	Tianlu	947–51
Jing	(951–69)	Muzong	Yingli	951–69
Xian	(969–82)	Jingzong	Baoning	969–79
			Qianheng	979–83
Longxu	(982–1031)	Shengzong	Tonghe	983–1012
			Kaitai	1012–21
			Taiping	1021–31
Zongzhen	(1031–55)	Xingzong	Jingfu	1031–32
			Chongxi	1032–55
Hongji	(1055–1101)	Daozong	Qingning	1055–65
			Xianyong	1065–75
			Taikang	1075–85
			Da'an	1085–95
			Shoulong	1095–1101
Yanxi	(1101–25)	Tianzuo	Qiantong	1101–11
			Tianqing	1111–21
			Baoda	1121–25
(Chun, emperor of Bei Liao, 1122)		(Xuanzong)	Jianfu	1122

Chart 1. Liao Emperors
This table is based on Fig. 2 and Table 1 in Herbert Franke and Denis Twitchett, eds., *Alien Regimes and Border States, 710–1368*, vol. 6 of *The Cambridge History of China*, pp. XXI–XXII.

a rich and populous agricultural area that Abaoji turned into a strictly controlled vassal state.[4]

In 936, Abaoji's successor, Deguang (Taizong, r. 927–47), favored the rise of Shi Jingtang as emperor of the ephemeral northern Chinese Later Jin dynasty (936–46) and in exchange, in 938, received an area of northern China known as the Sixteen Prefectures, which included today's Beijing. In 947, Deguang invaded northern China and installed himself in Kaifeng, where he proclaimed a name for the new dynasty, which was to be known as the Great Liao (Da Liao). But because of Chinese resistance, he eventually had to withdraw. This is but one example of the great difficulties the Khitan encountered as they tried to incorporate a large Chinese population under their rule.

In 960, most of China was reunified by Zhao Kuangyin (r. 960–76), founder of the Song dynasty (960–1279). Gaining control of the northern region, then under the pro-Liao Later Han (947–50) and Northern Han (951–79) dynasties, however, proved difficult. The Liao continued to lend military support to the Han royal family and it was only in 979 that the Song finally conquered this region. In the wake of this victory, the Song tried to conquer the Sixteen Prefectures, which were under Liao rule, but they were disastrously defeated and the emperor himself fled in a donkey cart. Tensions over territorial claims, which dominated the following years, led to a state of uneasy equilibrium and ineffective wars. In 1004, a new invasion by the Liao forced the Song to negotiate a peace treaty. On the surface, the treaty seemed to be humiliating and financially draining for the Song, but it was, in effect, extremely beneficial. The payments to the Khitan constituted only a tiny fraction of the total revenues produced by the burgeoning Song economy and were largely offset by commercial profits and savings in military expenses. The peace achieved with the Treaty of Shanyuan in 1005, by and large, held nearly until the collapse of the Liao dynasty, although in 1042 another treaty was signed and diplomatic negotiations were required at other times as well.

The decline of the Khitan began when endemic court factionalism weakened the central government to the point that it was no longer able to deal effectively with rebellions and uprisings from subject peoples that, in turn, grew ever more virulent and destructive. An attempted coup d'état by the emperor's uncle Zhongyuan in 1063 was probably motivated by a Khitan nativist reaction against Chinese influences; the coup's failure resulted in mass executions of its conspirators.[5] Troubles continued with the rise to power of Yelü Yixin in 1065. He was a courtier who gained control of the government and is recorded as having been responsible for the promotion of evil ministers, the murder of political opponents (including the heir apparent), corruption, violence, and intimidation. He was finally removed from power in 1081 and died in 1083. While the Liao court was rocked by internal struggles, a major rebellion broke out in the north, among the Zubu, a Mongolian nomadic people akin to the Tatars. In 1092, they invaded and occupied the Liao pasturelands in the northwestern part of the empire. It was only from 1100 to 1102 that the Liao managed to recover these areas and force the Zubu tribes to submit.

The Jurchen were in a position of vassalage to the Liao and thus were obliged to present them with tribute—in particular, special hunting birds (gyrfalcons). In 1112, the Jurchen chief Aguda defied Liao authority by refusing to dance at a ritual ceremony attended by the emperor. Moreover, the Jurchen accused the Liao local officials who came to exact tribute of behaving haughtily, of cheating them, and of abusing their women. At the root of Aguda's rebellion, which began in 1113, not long after the tribal leaders chose him as their chief, was a long-smoldering resentment against the Liao. Shrewdness and ferocity characterized the military operations that Aguda's much smaller Jurchen forces conducted against the Liao. In 1115, after a number of victories, Aguda declared himself emperor of the Jin dynasty and free from the yoke of Khitan rule. As the Liao amassed a large army to cross into Jurchen territory, another court conspiracy broke out, aimed at dethroning the emperor. No sooner was this conspiracy put down, with a purge of hundreds of aristocrats, than the Bohai people rebelled in the Eastern Capital. The Bohai leader requested Jurchen assistance against the Liao, which he received, but he himself was subsequently killed by the Jurchen, who annexed the entire region east of the Liao River. Aguda's preposterous requests, which included the areas surrounding the Supreme Capital and the Central Capital—the ancestral homeland of the Liao—in addition to princesses, silver, and silk, were not acceptable to the Liao, and in 1120 negotiations broke off and Aguda struck at the heart of the Liao, storming and destroying the Supreme Capital. The incompetent Liao Emperor Tianzuo (r. 1101–25) was unable to rise to the challenge, and infighting at court caused a general collapse of Liao political and military leadership. In 1122, the emperor ran away in the face of advancing Jurchen armies and the court appointed Prince Chun as an alternate emperor. Meanwhile, the Song tried to take advantage of the Liao's weakness; they established diplomatic relations with the Jurchen while also sending an army against the Liao, who, even though they were weakened, were able to repel the attack.[6]

With the death of Prince Chun in 1122, the situation rapidly deteriorated. In 1125, the Jurchen captured the old and still formally ruling Emperor Tianzuo, who died in captivity shortly thereafter, and completed the conquest of the Liao. A small number of Khitan and loyal Mongolian tribesmen, led by a member of the imperial clan, Yelü Dashi, fled westward to establish the Qara-Khitai dynasty in 1132. This comprised the territory of modern Xinjiang west of the Altai Mountains and Transoxiana as far as the Amu Darya and the Aral Sea, and centered in the Chu River valley. The dynasty, which is known in Chinese sources as Xi Liao, lasted until 1211 when it was overrun by the Mongol conquest.[7]

Dual Administration

The Khitan system of rule worked on a principle of dual administration, with its nomadic, pastoral, and mostly Khitan subjects in the north under the northern government and its agricultural, sedentary, and largely Chinese and Bohai subjects in the south under the southern government. The northern administration had greater power than the southern, and consisted predominantly of Khitan officials, the most important of whom were the commissioners for military affairs, the prime ministers of the northern and southern administrations, the northern and southern great kings (members of the royal clan), and the commander in chief. Below them were a number of tribal offices, military offices, imperial household agencies, and various commissioners in charge of the Chinese, Bohai, and Uighur populations living in the north.

The central offices of the southern administration, also based in the Supreme Capital, were deliberately modeled after the Tang government. This administration evolved over time and included, among other offices, a Chinese commission for military affairs, five executive boards, a secretariat, a chancellery, a Censorate, a Hanlin Academy, and an office of historiography. Many aspects of the two administrations were fashioned along ethnic lines; the northern maintained Khitan dress and traditions and used the Khitan language, while the southern was Chinese in style, language, and dress and was staffed mostly by Chinese government officials from northern Hebei captured in raids in 947.

Over time, the central administration was supplemented by provincial administrations in auxiliary capitals. An Eastern Capital was established in 938 in today's Liaoyang to control Bohai and the eastern part of the empire while a Southern Capital was established in what is now Beijing for the administration of the Sixteen Prefectures, acquired in 938. A Central Capital was added in 1007, located in the former capital of the Xi people, near today's Laoha River. Finally, a Western Capital was created at Datong in 1044.[8]

Foreign Relations

In the system of multistate relations that was established during the Liao period, we can distinguish between relations with the Song, which were regulated mainly by treaties, and relations with tributary states, which resulted from the formal acceptance of the Liao's superior status. Furthermore, tributary status varied from that accorded to subject or vassal peoples and tribes, such as the Jurchen and Zubu (Tatars), and that accorded to what were, in effect, independent states. Goryeo, the state that ruled Korea between 918 and 1392, became a tributary state of the Liao in 994 after Khitan military operations in the region. No longer a tributary of China, Goryeo began presenting tribute to the Liao court instead; it also adopted the Liao calendar. Goryeo followed a policy of convenience, staying loyal to the Liao as long as the Liao remained a regional power; the Liao put down Goryeo's few attempts to return to the Chinese fold. It was not until 1116 that the Goryeo court discarded the Liao calendar to assert its own independence.[9] Faraway countries such as Persia and Japan, as well as Khotan and Kucha in the Tarim Basin, also presented tribute to the Liao.

The Liao's relationship with the Tangut state of Xi Xia, to the west, was marked by military clashes alternated with long periods of peace during which the Tangut accepted a tributary position. During these periods of peace, particularly during the reign of the Tangut ruler Li Deming (r. 1004–32), commercial interests prevailed as Uighur merchants traveled across Tangut lands to reach Chinese and Khitan markets.

Much of the diplomatic and political history of Liao relations with the Song dynasty hinged on territorial, economic, and defense issues. The Treaty of Shanyuan, negotiated after the 1004–05 war and decades of intermittent warfare, established that the Song would pay the Liao a yearly "indemnity" of two hundred thousand bolts of silk and one hundred thousand taels of silver. It also called for a careful demarcation of the border between the two states and prohibited the violation of that border or the harboring of fugitives. In addition, it prohibited the construction of new frontier fortifications. The treaty allowed both sides to overcome the military deadlock, and peaceful relations fostered commercial relations, which were particularly profitable for the Chinese side while providing revenues and stability to the Liao.

In 1042 the Khitan made territorial demands on the Song, taking advantage of the weakness of the Song at the time of a particularly disastrous war against the Tanguts. These territorial demands were dropped in the course of negotiations, but the yearly payments of the Song court were raised to three hundred thousand bolts of silk and two hundred thousand taels of silver.

Another diplomatic crisis occurred from 1074–76, again triggered by territorial claims advanced by the Liao, this time in the Hedong region, east of the Yellow River. The Liao, who favored the concept of a border defined by natural topographic features, aimed to annex areas of strategic and economic importance.[10] The Song court was divided over how to respond, but the "appeasement" policy championed by the reformist statesman Wang Anshi (1021–86) prevailed and after two years of tough negotiations a new border was drawn. The negotiations included several joint inspections of the border zone, which resulted in substantial progress in cartography and geographic survey.[11]

Liao Society

Liao society can be defined as a multiethnic, polyglot pyramid, headed by two ruling exogamous clans, namely, the Yelü, the imperial family, and the Xiao, the consort family. They were constituted as actual kin-based clans and practiced ancestor worship even though the common members of Khitan traditional society, by and large, did not have clan names (*zu*) but were grouped in larger territorial units, ruled by aristocratic families, usually referred to as tribes.

These tribes and their aristocracies, with their extended and fluid kin groups, constituted the foundation of Khitan society, and it was from them that troops, military commanders, and civil administrators were recruited. Tribal composition changed over time, but the nucleus was the eighteen tribes unified by Abaoji, to which thirty-three tribes were added under Emperor Shengzong (r. 982–1031). Although the Liao emperors had capitals and palaces, their courts and entourages were often on the move between camps (*nabo*). During these migratory movements, the emperor set up hunting encampments whose locations changed according to the season.[12] He was accompanied by Khitan dignitaries and military commanders and ran governmental affairs from these camps. Each year, all the officials would be summoned to the summer *nabo* in the sixth month and to the winter *nabo* in the tenth month.[13]

Within Liao society, four systems of belief prevailed: Confucianism, Daoism, Buddhism, and Khitan shamanism. The first two were mostly limited to the Chinese territories and to some state rituals.[14] The Liao rulers were great patrons of Buddhism, favoring its spread in the northern regions, printing scriptures, and building temples and monasteries. As a result, the number of monks and nuns increased and they formed a substantial component of society. Most members of Khitan tribal society, however, continued to worship local spirits and supernatural powers and to practice shamanism and divination using animal bones. State shamanic ceremonies and sacrifices, among which the most important were those at Muye Mountain, were performed by special court officials.[15]

The material culture of the Liao court was, at its highest levels, distinctive and exquisite. Archaeological investigation of Liao royal tombs reveals the great wealth accumulated by the aristocracy in the form of precious gold and silver objects of superb workmanship. These objects were probably made either by Chinese artisans working for the Khitan or, in the context of tribute and trade relations, by Chinese workshops according to Liao specifications. They reveal not only the lavish lifestyle of the ruling class but also the development of a distinctive taste and "national" culture consciously distinct from China's.[16]

The Khitan script provides another example of the development of a "national" imperial culture. The Khitan adopted a so-called large script in 920 and a small script in 924 or 925. Both resemble Chinese: the first is made of simple characters written in a vertical line; the second is made of small characters assembled, usually in pairs, into a composite block that can contain from two to seven characters. The large characters were sometimes borrowed from Chinese but were more often coined anew, and each of them represents a single word (logogram). The assembled script is made of characters that represent sounds (phonograms) which, taken together, form a word. To date, some 370 small-script characters have been distinguished but only partially deciphered.[17]

The population of the empire included peoples of Mongol, Tungus, Chinese, and Korean origin, among whom members of the Khitan, Xi, Shiwei, Jurchen, Zubu, Bohai, and Chinese (Han) ethnic groups were the most numerous.[18] The most sizable portion of the Liao population was the sedentary, agricultural Chinese population of the Southern and Western capital circuits, that is, the areas within the jurisdiction of the two capitals' administrations. This, according to estimates, was about five times larger than the sparse nomadic population of the three northern areas. In addition, about half of the subject Bohai people continued to live in their original homeland on the eastern seaboard while the other half or more moved to the northern part of the empire or to the *ordo*. The *ordo* was a distinctive Liao institution and the central structure of the Liao military system. Originally, it was an extensive military camp around the imperial palace. Later, it developed into a much larger standing army with a separate administrative structure. At the death of the emperor, the *ordo* troops were assigned to guard his mausoleum. In all, twelve *ordos* were created over time with the growth of entitlements within the ruling clans.[19]

The Khitan engaged in trade with all their neighbors and were active participants in a commercial network that extended across Asia.[20] Abaoji understood the importance of trade and as early as 909 established trading posts and began developing a commercial network that expanded along with the territorial growth of his domain. Trade with China was conducted by land and by sea, through a port at the estuary of the Liao River, which connected the Khitan to the main ports of the eastern Chinese seaboard, on the Shandong Peninsula and in the Yangtze Delta. The presence of Khitan merchants in northern China must have been substantial since they had a commercial representative in Kaifeng, the capital of the short-lived Later Jin dynasty.[21]

Song China, notwithstanding frequent outbreaks of conflict with the Khitan, continued to trade with them. Although the Song were especially interested in horses, they also imported sheep, furs, woolen cloth, carpets, brocade, silver and gold ornaments, suits of armor, lumber, and slaves. The Liao imported from China silk, tea, weapons, ginger, medicines, and also silver and gold ornaments.[22] Markets flourished in the capitals, and the Liao expanded their reach by controlling the lucrative export of goods such as horses, pearls, ginseng, and furs from the Koreans and the Jurchen. The commercial economy of the Khitan empire was also enriched by tribute goods—jade, amber, agate, frankincense, carpets, cotton cloth, and gold and silver bullion—that arrived from dependent and foreign peoples and states, such as the Uighur, Khotan, and Kucha.[23]

Empresses played a particularly important role in Khitan history and society, as "king makers," regents, and military commanders. Abaoji's wife, Empress Chunqin, was a talented political adviser and military commander in charge of an army of two hundred thousand. After Abaoji's death, she assumed control over all civil and military matters, effectively resolving the succession. She is said to have volunteered (or perhaps to have been "invited") to follow her husband in death, together with many others who were sacrificed; but instead of killing herself, she cut off her right hand and threw it in the burial chamber.[24] Empress Dowager Ruizhi, the widow of Emperor Jingzong (r. 969–82), in effect held the reins of the state as regent from 982 until her death in 1009, although her son Shengzong (r. 982–1031), the actual emperor, was twenty-seven years old at the time of her death. In 1063, the mother of Emperor Daozong (r. 1055–1101) personally led a military expedition to put down a rebellion, and in 1122 the widow of the Liao "alternate" emperor, Prince Chun, fought victoriously against invading Song armies.

The Legacy of the Liao

The Liao were not a "conquest dynasty" since, strictly speaking, they did not conquer any part of China nor were they replaced by a native Chinese dynasty. As important as its relationship with China was, the genesis and demise of the Liao dynasty, as well as its culture, traditions, and place in history, cannot be fully appraised without considering the web of relations that linked the Khitan to the other non-Chinese peoples who were co-protagonists of this history. The legacy of the Liao, as a multiethnic empire, is especially relevant to the history of other dynasties of Inner Asian origin (the Jurchen Jin, Mongol Yuan, and Manchu Qing) that followed and to a large extent built on the Liao empire as they ruled over parts or the whole of China for over five centuries.

Indeed, the Liao can be seen as part of an Inner Asian continuum that shaped China's institutional and social history.[25] Within this dynamic continuum (rather than within the distorting notion of dynastic cycles), we can find positive innovation and radical changes that literally transformed China's (and Inner Asia's) history. The most important of these changes was the government's effort to combine a system of rule derived from and based on Inner Asian principles and one based on Chinese bureaucratic and administrative practices. The weaknesses inherent in the political traditions of the Inner Asian steppe nomads—a result of a scarcity of resources needed to support a centralized and highly militarized state, and the difficulty of holding together a union of independent-minded tribal leaders—were counterbalanced by the adoption of institutional practices derived from China. With the ability to tax a large base of sedentary agriculturalists, in addition to tribute from the dependent tribes and trade revenues, the government acquired the means to support its widespread needs, including the aristocracy, the military, and the court. It was able to command enough resources to retain and reinforce its position at the center of the political system.

The Liao system of dual administration, as rudimentary as it may appear to have been, constituted a giant step forward in the history of the Inner Asian peoples. Previously, peoples such as the Xiongnu, Turks, and Uighurs had been unable to extend their rule over Chinese territory while the non-Chinese dynasties that did rule in northern China, such as the Northern Wei, were forced to shift to a system of government steeped in Chinese tradition. In contrast, the Liao made the first conscious effort to combine Chinese and non-Chinese systems, and the institutions they devised formed the basis of a political system that was transferred to later dynasties.[26]

The first instance of such a transfer was effected by urban, acculturated Khitan administrators who remained in northern China to serve the Jurchen and, later, the Mongols as members of what has been defined as a *steppe intelligentsia*.[27] Among the most notable Khitan who served the Mongols were the brothers Yelü Ahai and Yelü Tuhua.[28] Ahai, who was thoroughly acculturated as a Chinese administrator, joined the Mongols in the early stage of their conquest and eventually became *daruγaci* (governor) of the former Jin capital Yanjing and of Bukhara after the Mongol invasion of Central Asia. His brother was one of the main military commanders in northern China. But the most celebrated of the Khitan advisers to the Mongols was Yelü Chucai (1189–1243), the architect of the administrative reforms that were carried out under Ögödei (r. 1229–41).[29] After having served under Chingghis Khan as astrologer, secretary, adviser, and administrator in charge of Chinese documents, Yelü Chucai took charge of the establishment of administrative districts and of the tax-collection bureau during the consolidation of Mongol rule in northern China from 1229–30. The bureaucratic staff consisted primarily of administrators who had formerly served under the Jin dynasty. The Mongols' creation of a rational fiscal policy was the first step toward the adoption of financial and administrative practices that rested on a tradition that had begun with Yelü Chucai's ancestors and continued with the same group of acculturated steppe administrators through the thirteenth century.

The continuing use of the name Khitan in Western languages—from the Catai of Marco Polo to the Russian Kitai to indicate China—is residual evidence of the prestige and renown that the Khitan once commanded in the world.

1. In English, these people are usually called Khitan and Kitan. Qidan, the pinyin romanization of the two-character modern Mandarin Chinese pronunciation of their name, is also used by scholars. Throughout this catalogue, they are referred to as Khitan.

2. For a concise general history of the Liao, see Denis Twitchett and Klaus-Peter Tietze, "The Liao," in Herbert Franke and Denis Twitchett (eds.), *Alien regimes and border states, 907–1368*, vol. 6 of *The Cambridge History of China*. The indispensable English-language tool for the study of Liao history is Karl Wittfogel and Fêng Chia-Shêng, *History of Chinese Society: Liao, 907–1125*.

3. Twitchett and Tietze, "The Liao," pp. 62–63.

4. Johannes Reckel, *Bohai: Geschichte und Kultur eines mandschurisch-koreanischen Königreiches der Tang-Zeit* [*Bohai: History and culture of a Manchu-Korean kindgom of the Tang period*], in *Aetas Manjurica* 5, pp. 485–87.

5. Twitchett and Tietze, "The Liao," pp. 127–28

6. Jingshen Tao, *Two Sons of Heaven: Studies in Sung-Liao Relations*, pp. 87–97.

7. Wittfogel and Fêng, *History of Chinese Society*, pp. 619–74. On the cultural features of the Qara-Khitai, see Michal Biran, "Sinicization Out of China? The Case of the Western Liao (Qara Khitai)."

8. Twitchett and Tietze, "The Liao," p. 79.

9. Wittfogel and Fêng, *History of Chinese Society*, pp. 318–19.

10. K. Tietze, "The Liao-Sung Border Conflict of 1074–1076," in Wolfgang Bauer (ed.), *Studia Sino-Mongolica: Festschrift für Herbert Franke*, pp. 127–51.

11. Christian Lamouroux, "Geography and Politics, The Song-Liao Dispute of 1074–75," in Sabine Dabringhaus and Roderich Ptak (eds.), *China and Her Neighbours: Borders, Visions of the Other, Foreign Policy, 10th–19th Century*, pp. 1–28.

12. Wittfogel and Fêng, *History of Chinese Society*, p. 436.

13. Wittfogel and Fêng, *History of Chinese Society*, pp. 131–34.

14. Wittfogel and Fêng, *History of Chinese Society*, p. 214.

15. Wittfogel and Fêng, *History of Chinese Society*, pp. 213–18.

16. François Louis, "Shaping Symbols of Privilege: Precious Metals and the Early Liao Aristocracy," *Journal of Song-Yuan Studies* 33 (2003), pp. 71–109.

17. György Kara, "Kitan and Jurchin," in Peter T. Daniels and William Bright (eds.), *The World's Writing Systems*, pp. 230–31; Herbert Franke, "The Forest Peoples of Manchuria: Khitans and Jurchens," in Denis Sinor (ed.), *The Cambridge History of Early Inner Asia*, p. 408.

18. Wittfogel and Fêng, *History of Chinese Society*, pp. 52–58.

19. Wittfogel and Fêng, *History of Chinese Society*, pp. 508–17.

20. Shiba Yoshinobu, "Sung Foreign Trade: Its Scope and Organization," in Morris Rossabi (ed.), *China Among Equals: The Middle Kingdom and Its Neighbors, 10ᵗʰ–14ᵗʰ Centuries*, pp. 89–115.

21. On that occasion in 942, the Jin general Jin Yanguang, angry at the Khitan, threatened to kill all the merchants in his realm. See Lien-sheng Yang, "A 'Posthumous Letter' from the Chin Emperor to the Khitan Emperor in 942," *Harvard Journal of Asiatic Studies* 10.3/4 (1947), p. 425.

22. Shiba Yoshinobu, "Sung Foreign Trade," p. 97.

23. Shiba Yoshinobu, "Sung Foreign Trade," p. 98.

24. Wittfogel and Fêng, *History of Chinese Society*, p. 254, n. 27.

25. Pamela Crossley, "The Rulerships of China," *American Historical Review* 97.5 (1992), pp. 1472–73.

26. Nicola Di Cosmo, "State Formation and Periodization in Inner Asian History," *Journal of World History* 10.1 (1999), pp. 1–40.

27. Igor de Rachewiltz, Hok-lam Chan, Hsiao Ch'i-ch'ing, and Peter W. Geier (eds.), *In the Service of the Khan: Eminent Personalities of the Early Mongol-Yüan Period*, pp. xx–xxi, 95–96.

28. P. D. Buell, "Yeh-lü A-Hai (ca. 1151–ca. 1223), Yeh-lü T'u-hua (d. 1231)," in Rachewiltz et al. (eds.), *In the Service of the Khan*, pp. 112–21.

29. Igor de Rachewiltz, "Yeh-lü Ch'u-ts'ai (1189–1243), Yeh-lü Chu (1221–1285)," in Rachewiltz et al. (eds.), *In the Service of the Khan*, pp. 136–75.

Dieter Kuhn

An Introduction to Chinese Archaeology of the Liao

The archaeological finds of innumerable excavations conducted during the twentieth century in the provinces of North China and Inner Mongolia have provided us with unexpected insights into the culture of the ethnic Khitan people and their Liao dynasty (916–1125). We not only have gained a new understanding of Liao culture but also are able to reposition the Liao in Chinese history and to explain how these archaeological finds have changed our view of material culture and daily life in the China of one thousand years ago.

But before becoming immersed in the history of twentieth-century Liao archaeology, introducing some of the finds, and drawing conclusions, we should examine the place of the "barbarian" Liao dynasty in Chinese history and how a distorted picture of Liao history and civilization came into being. The feat of archaeology providing entirely new insights, and thus widening our historical horizon, cannot be fully appreciated unless we have an idea of the historical framework for an interpretation of the Liao that existed until the early decades of the twentieth century—a framework that was developed on the basis of one-sided Chinese literary sources.

The Missing Liao Perspective in Liao History

The founding emperors of the Qing dynasty (1644–1911), which was established almost five hundred years after the Jin defeated and thus sealed the fate of the Liao in 1125, viewed themselves as the dynastic heirs of the two earlier alien regimes.[1] What all three of the dynasties had in common, and what set them apart from their Han Chinese subjects, was their complex tribal structure, their foreign ethnicity, their nomadic or semiagricultural lifestyle, and their origins in northeastern China, formerly known as Manchuria. In 1635, one year before he proclaimed himself emperor and changed the name of the pre-dynastic Jin (Gold) to Qing, the Manchu ruler Abahai (1592–1643) ordered a translation of an abridgement of the official histories of the Song (960–1279), Liao, Jin (1115–1234), and Yuan (1260–1368) dynasties from Chinese into Manchu. He emphasized the moral principles that should be adhered to in the passages deemed worthy of translation, and thought those parts confirming that welfare flourished in the nations should be selected for translation.[2] Abahai was already thoroughly steeped in the Chinese understanding of history: according to the imperial reading, that which deserved to be called history was to be official history; only official historians could know the facts and have the Confucian morals essential for producing a presentation of them that would be of lasting historical relevance. When one reads the *Geschichte der Großen Liao* (the German translation of the History of the Great Liao), translated from the Manchu and published in 1877, one realizes that the translators unmistakably and unwaveringly followed the imperial order: the whole *Geschichte* is a collection of political and military factual events and their dates interwoven with explanatory stories of decision making.[3] This history book does not contain a single sentence about the tribal structure of the Liao or the cultural affairs or material culture of the Liao dynasty, not to mention the burial sites of the Liao emperors. It presents a rather narrow view of history that probably reflects the Manchu warriors' state of mind in the 1630s. They were about to conquer China and thus could not help but imagine the history of their northern predecessors as an endless sequence of struggles, fights, and military campaigns. However, it would be unfair to blame the early Manchu emperor and his scholars for the deficiencies of the abridged Liao history in Manchu, for they were only pursuing an established and in their eyes legitimate method of presenting history. The real problem of grasping Liao history as a historical and cultural entity in its own right is that the Khitan's own perspective in written form is missing from the very beginning:[4] Chinese historians composed the official and private histories of the Khitan and of the Liao dynasty, as in, for example, the *Qidan guozhi* (History of the Khitan)[5] of 1247 and the *Liaoshi* (History of the Liao)[6] of 1344. Thus, Chinese sources determine our views of the Khitan. There are several reasons for this essential shortcoming: first, little of "the documentation of the Liao survived the fall of the dynasty, and nothing remains today";[7] second, it took more than two hundred years after the fall of the dynasty before the *Liaoshi* was hastened to completion within one year, in 1344;[8] and third, a history of a legitimate dynasty could only be compiled according to the standards of Chinese models of composition.[9]

Although the *Liaoshi* is renowned among the dynastic histories for its infelicities and deficiencies, its completion, during the Yuan dynasty, may be regarded as an acknowledgment of the Liao dynasty's legitimate status in Chinese history. But the dynastic legitimacy conceded to the Liao dynasty by the Mongol Yuan dynasty should not be regarded as being on par with Chinese cultural and intellectual values, which were deeply rooted in a cumulative tradition and the legacy of antiquity, as identified in the understanding of participating in what Confucius referred to as "this culture of ours."[10]

The Chinese Depreciation of Liao Civilization

Indecision about how to deal with the Khitan's military superiority, on the one hand, and its own deficiencies in military prowess, on the other, caused the Song dynasty to sign bilateral agreements with the Liao in 1005 and 1042.[11] The agreements secured a peaceful coexistence along the northern border of the Song empire for almost one hundred years, at easily affordable conditions. But such political concessions did not mean that the Song accepted the Liao as their equals in terms of civilization. Officially, the Liao dynasty was called the Khitan or the Northern dynasty after 1005; in private, however, the Han Chinese scholar-officials continued to refer to the Khitan as the "northern barbarians" or "caitiffs" (*lu*). The eminent Song scholar Su Che (1039–1112) did not hesitate to describe their nature as that of "animals," and almost eight hundred years later, in his political program of 1905, Sun Yatsen (1866–1925), the father of the Republic of China, referred to the Manchus, who also hailed from the northeast, as "caitiffs."[12] The Liao emperors were well aware that their "southern" brothers were convinced of their cultural superiority over the tribal Khitan. The Liao ruler Daozong (r. 1055–1101) criticized the Chinese deprecation of Khitan culture as inferior. In 1057, he presented to the Liao empress dowager a poem entitled "Princes and ministers share the same determination: Chinese and barbarians share the same customs."[13] And when a Chinese official expounded the *Lunyu* (Analects) of Confucius to him, he retorted that although the ancient Xunyu and Xianyu peoples were without good laws and manners and thus were called barbarians, his country had a civilization that was not inferior to that of the Chinese.[14] But all attempts to defend the achievements of Khitan civilization must have been in vain when confronted with the Confucian understanding that there was only one civilization, and that it was Chinese. Thus, only the use of Chinese doctrines was regarded as sufficient to change the barbarians; such changes could never happen the other way around. And, anyway, the Song scholars may have asked what sort of civilization the Khitan had, since at the time of the founding of their dynasty they did not even have family names; they lived in a tribal system with only two clans (the Yelü imperial clan and the Xiao consort clan); their emperor was peripatetic, touring the empire all year round on horseback, followed by an entourage of huge carts drawn by camels and ox-drawn wagons bearing a portable city of tents and pavilions; they had five capitals but preferred to live in yurts instead of residences; their marriage system was immoral, if not incestuous; they followed strange and bloody burial customs; they performed strange ceremonies, dressed in an uncivilized (non-Chinese) way, and wore their hair in an exotic fashion. The list continues. The Chinese could not imagine, nor did they see any need for finding a way to, becoming accustomed to or overcoming these fundamental cultural differences.

The Archaeological Discovery of Liao Civilization

In their still unsurpassed magnum opus on the Liao dynasty, Karl-August Wittfogel and Fêng Chia-shêng comment on the importance of archaeological finds for the interpretation of history: "Archaeological remains, other than inscriptions, are not distorted by the subjective factors that influence the written records."[15] In the period of the most fruitful archaeological expeditions in China before World War I, it was Peter Kozloff of Russia, Aurel Stein of the United Kingdom, and other non-Chinese who made the first spectacular archaeological finds in the steppes and deserts of Xinjiang. In 1908, the Japanese archaeologist and anthropologist Torii Ryūzō started his field research on the Liao dynasty with a visit to the deserted ruins of the walls of the former Supreme Capital (Shangjing) of the Liao, in present-day Balin Left Banner in Inner Mongolia.[16]

The French missionary Joseph Mullie passed through the same region in 1912 and 1920, and shortly thereafter published his research on the historical geography of the area, leading to the identification of a number of places and locations. He included a description of the ruins of the Supreme Capital, which he compared with historical records.[17] The division of the walled Supreme Capital into Huangcheng, the imperial city of the Khitan rulers, and Hancheng, the Han Chinese city bordering Huangcheng on the south but separated from it by the Bayanguole (Bayan-gol) River, was only brought to light by excavations in the 1960s.[18] Mullie also identified the remains of a wall in the narrow Bayanguole River valley, southeast of the former Supreme Capital, as the city of Zuzhou (literally "ancestral prefecture"), the ancestral home of the founder of the Liao dynasty, Abaoji (Taizu, 872–926).[19] Chinese archaeologists assume that Zuzhou was the city Abaoji built as a center for future Khitan ancestor worship.[20] He was buried not far away, at a place called Zuling (ancestor's mausoleum).[21]

Japanese scholars conducted archaeological fieldwork in the Qingling burial ground of the Liao emperors Shengzong (r. 983–1031), Xingzong (r. 1031–55), and Daozong in the 1930s, in what was formerly Qingzhou, after local warlord Tang Zuorong, son of General Tang Yulin, in search of burial treasures, had broken down the massive wooden doors of the tombs.[22] Emperor Shengzong chose his burial site himself, after having sojourned at the place, and is reported to have said: "After my ten thousand years, I will be buried here."[23] Torii's photographic documentation of the ruined tombs shows the lamentable condition they were in when he investigated them.[24] Only the tomb of the emperor Daozong could be identified without difficulty, by a monument with Chinese and Khitan inscriptions bearing his name.[25]

It was not until the 1950s, more than eight hundred years after the collapse of the Liao dynasty, that archaeological finds began to contribute to a completely new picture of Liao cultural achievements and civilization. The excavations of the 1950s and 1960s are linked to the names and works of Bian Chengxiu,[26] Feng Yongqian,[27] Li Wenxin,[28] Li Yiyou,[29] Su Tianjun,[30] Zheng Long,[31] and Zheng Shaozong,[32] to mention only some of the best-known authors of the Liao archaeological literature written in those decades. Hundreds of archaeological excavation reports brought a wide range of Liao sites and objects of material culture, such as stone reliefs and burial inscriptions, to light. Tombs are by far the most informative archaeological source. By 1986, more than three hundred stand-alone Liao graves had been discovered—not all of them have been written about[33]—and the number of tombs and graves discovered in cemeteries was in the thousands.[34] In 1987, Feng Yongqian listed seventy tombs that had identified owners.[35] Forty-seven of the seventy, or two-thirds, belonged to Han Chinese. Forty tombs, or nearly 60 percent, date from the late Liao period (1055–1125), and, among the forty, twenty-six belonged to Han Chinese. As a rule, only well-preserved, comparatively elaborate, dome-shaped chamber tombs featuring bracket sets and other richly decorated architectural elements, mural paintings, and inscriptions were excavated and written about. Most of them, however, had previously been illegally opened and looted. From the more than two hundred dome-shaped chamber tombs described in excavation reports, more than fifty can be typologically defined and dated by year or decade. More than fifty chamber tombs contained mural paintings of extraordinary quality.[36] They all belonged to members of the ruling Khitan clans or to Han Chinese who served the Khitan as high officials.[37] The dome-shaped chamber tombs were more prevalent in Liaoning Province and Inner Mongolia, which together account for more than forty of the fifty tombs (80 percent), than in Hebei Province and the Beijing region.[38] Thus, Inner Mongolia, where the objects in this exhibition come from, was not only a region with a great number of towns and administrative centers but also an area preferred by the Khitan for burials.[39] Although the structures, interior furnishings, wall paintings, personal outfits of the deceased, and burial objects found in many of the tombs can only be described as breathtakingly spectacular, it took quite a number of years before some of the finds were presented to the public, either in China or abroad.[40]

Changing Views: Khitan Burial Traditions and Cultural Adoptions from China

As stated above, political parity between the Song and the Liao did not mean that the Song accepted the Liao as their equals in terms of civilization. The recent archaeological finds do nothing to change what is known about the Song's historical evaluation of Liao civilization; they only help us to reevaluate the Khitan's relation to and appreciation of Chinese culture. Our questions can only be: What is the nature of the archaeological finds? And how do they affect our view of Liao civilization?

Most Khitan were pastoral, moving from place to place in search of water and grazing land, and made a living from herding, fishing, and hunting. They raised sheep, horses, and cattle, and in their ox-drawn carts covered the long distances between the areas inhabited by the camel-breeders of the northern and western steppes and the pig-breeders of the more southern and eastern agricultural regions. Some of them may have tilled the soil, but most farmers in the Liao empire were Han Chinese or other people of non-Khitan ethnic origin. Like most nomadic peoples—for whom garments made of leather, wool, felt, and fur were indispensable—the Khitan engaged in barter trade for textiles, especially silks, which were regarded as one of the most valuable commodities. The nomadic lifestyle of the Khitan was beyond the comprehension of the average educated Chinese of the time, who could not imagine leading a life, not to mention a refined and fashionable life, under conditions other than those of a sedentary society based on agriculture. Before the archaeological findings of Liao materials, our knowledge of the life the Liao nobles led, their activities and festivities, and the way they buried their dead, depended entirely on biased Chinese written sources that emphasize the social mechanisms of the Khitan; their tribal structure and lineages; political events, territorial divisions, rebellions, and warfare; and tribal religion, as practiced in the worshipping of the sun on the first day of every month and at the winter solstice, the veneration of the tribal ancestress and the spirits of the ancestors, the rebirth ceremony (*zaisheng yi*),[41] the generous sacrifices of horses, oxen, sheep and geese, and the ceremonial gatherings and hunts. In the following pages, how the Liao materials discovered in the archaeological finds correlate with the Chinese understanding of Liao culture will be explored.

The most abundant and best-suited materials for this exploration come from the Liao-dynasty tombs.[42] But before discussing the burial customs of the Khitan as described in Chinese sources and examining Liao-dynasty tombs, one needs to look at the early decades of Liao rule in order to understand the cultural context in which aristocratic Chinese tomb architecture influenced the tomb building of the Khitan. After Abaoji, following Chinese custom, assumed the title of emperor in 916, he built a Confucian temple, thus advocating the acceptance of Confucianism rather than Buddhism as the state creed.[43] In 937, his successor, Deguang (Taizong, r. 927–47), donned Chinese-style attire decorated with the Chinese dragon and the twelve insignia known from the Tang (618–907) and earlier Chinese dynasties as symbols of the Son of Heaven.[44] During these early decades of the Liao dynasty, when the leading Khitan clans aspired to a dynastic identity better suited to imperial and national demands than to a tribal alliance, they started to foster a sense of ancestor-consciousness, which led to the building of impressive Chinese-style underground tombs, each equipped with several chambers, for the deceased emperors and their wives.[45]

The Khitan Burial Tradition

Karl A. Wittfogel and Fêng Chia-shêng have observed that "the funeral customs of the Ch'i-tan [Khitan] changed greatly from pre-dynastic to dynastic times."[46] In the early years of the dynasty, the Khitan followed the ancient customs as described in the *Qidan guozhi* (History of the Khitan) and in the *Xin Wudai shi* (New Historical Records of the Five Dynasties). Traditionally, the Khitan "placed their dead in trees in the mountains. After three years the relatives returned, gathered the bones and cremated them."[47] A Khitan man who wailed over the death of his parents was considered a weakling, whereas the Chinese would have condemned a man who did not wail as someone lacking filial piety. The treatment of people in the Liao state who

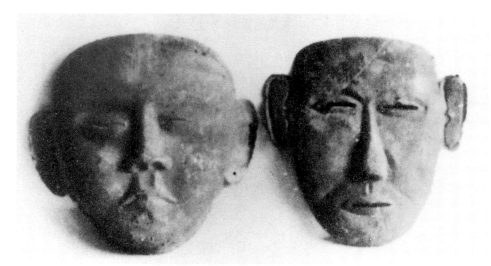

fig. 1

fig. 2

did not belong to the two Khitan clans or to the upper echelons of Chinese society did not differ very much from that of their counterparts in Song China. They were cremated or buried without much ado. It is not possible to determine whether cremation, which was widely practiced during the Liao dynasty, became more prevalent due to the influence of Buddhism or was just a continuation of tribal customs.[48] In addition to cremation, the Khitan aristocracy practiced other methods of preparing corpses for burial. One method, dating from 1055, consisted of hanging a corpse by the feet and then piercing the skin with sharp straws to drain the bodily fluids, leading to desiccation. The corpse was then treated with alum, which caused the body to shrink so that only the bones remained. The dressed-up bodily remains were placed in a tomb.[49] Another method of embalmment also was in use.[50] The abdomen of the deceased was cut open with a knife, the intestines were removed, and the area was cleansed and filled with aromatic herbs, salt, and alum; it was then sewn up, with a thread of five colors, in order to preserve the corpse. The face was covered with a mask made of gold or silver, and the hands and feet with a netting made of copper wire.[51]

The traditional Khitan dressing of a corpse changed according to the rank of the deceased. The body of the second Liao emperor, Deguang, was most probably prepared according to a method called "the salted meat emperor" (*diba*).[52] The face of

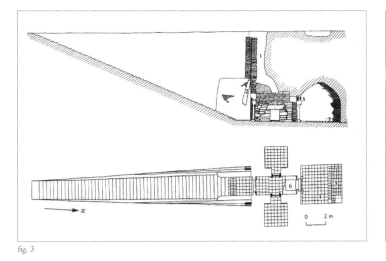

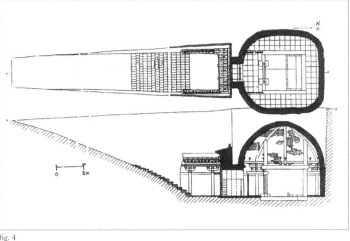

fig. 3

fig. 4

Fig. 3. Longitudinal section and outline of the complex tomb, with antechamber and side chambers, of Yelü Yuzhi (890–941)—a cousin of Liao-dynasty founding emperor Abaoji—and his wife, Chonggun; Aluke'erqin Banner, Inner Mongolia, 941.
1. Tunnel dug by looters
2. Stone slab sealing the entrance
3. Coffin stand
4. Coffin stand
5. Niche above the entrance
6. Epitaph

Fig. 4. Outline and longitudinal section of the tomb of Qinde (910–23), a son of Abaoji, furnished with a stone house (*shifang*); Aluke'erqin Banner, Inner Mongolia, 923

the deceased was covered with an individually fashioned mask (*mianju*) of gold, silver, or copper (see fig. 1), and the corpse was dressed in a special garment—a suit made of gold, silver, or copper metal wire (*tongsi luo*) (see fig. 2).[53] To dress the deceased in a metal-wire suit, a custom that first appeared in the mid-Liao era, was most probably not a Khitan tradition; the practice may have derived either from the jade burial suits used by the Chinese of Han (206 BC–AD 220) times or from the metal burial attire found in steppe burial customs.[54] Metal facial masks have a long history in central Asia, as, for example, has been documented from the fifth century onward in the Kirghiz Republic.[55] Western Asian influences are visible in Liao tombs in depictions of gowns with non-Chinese and non-Khitan backward-folded collars.[56]

To Chinese contemporaries, the burial customs of the Khitan must have been incomprehensible and revolting. According to Chinese tradition, the corpse had to be in unsullied physical condition when buried; cremation was unacceptable in all quarters of society. The Khitan's treatment of the dead and their methods of preparing corpses for interment may seem strange to us today, due to our general lack of knowledge of their ideas about death and their relationship to the dead. And yet Khitan practices, which displayed a need for reduction and not complete conservation of the corpse, were not so far removed from burial practices in Europe several centuries ago. From the fourteenth century onward, it was quite usual in central Europe to prepare the corpses of important people for burial. One method consisted of dissecting the corpse like a piece of game. "The remains were boiled so that the flesh could be peeled off the noble part, the bones."[57] Also, in central Europe the entrails were often removed before burial. Only in the second half of the eighteenth century, when a new desire to keep the corpse intact gained ground, did these practices gradually decline.[58]

Cultural Adoptions from Chinese Neighbors and Liao Peculiarities

At present, the earliest identifiable subterranean complex Khitan tomb of the imperial Yelü clan is the tomb of Yelü Yuzhi (890–941), a powerful aristocrat and official, and his wife, Chonggun.[59] Like most of the later tombs of this type, it is characterized by an axially symmetrical layout (fig. 3). The long approach ramp leads to the rectangular antechamber, and from there one enters into the square-shaped burial chamber, which has a corbeled dome. On each side of the antechamber are square side-rooms built on the same level.[60] The earliest date ever found in a Liao-dynasty tomb was discovered on a mural in the single-room, corbeled-dome tomb of Qinde (910–23), the second son of the emperor Abaoji,

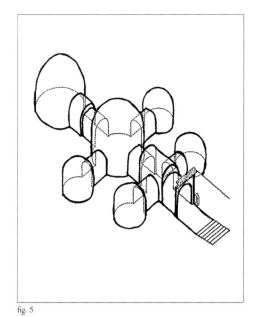

fig. 5

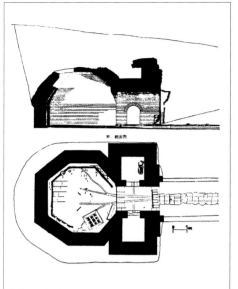

fig. 7

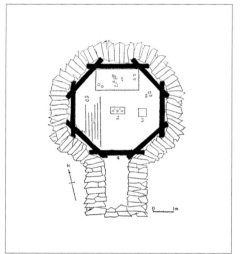

fig. 6a

fig. 6b

Fig. 5. Perspective drawing of the east mausoleum of the tomb of the emperor Shengzong (r. 983–1031); Balin Right Banner, Inner Mongolia

Fig. 6a–b. Stone tomb of an unknown person, furnished with a wooden octagonal interior tent (*muzhang*) built in log-cabin fashion; Chifeng, Inner Mongolia, before 1070. Height of interior tent, 160 cm
a. Plan of stone tomb
b. Photograph of wooden octagonal interior tent

Fig. 7. Longitudinal section and outline of the complex tomb of Xiao Paolu (1015–1088/89), with side chambers, an entrance corridor, a wooden interior tent (*muzhang*), and water-drainage channels; Faku District, Liaoning Province, 1090

which was furnished with a stone house (*shifang*) serving the dead as a burial room (fig. 4). The ink inscription reads "second year of the Tianzan reign," which corresponds to the Western year 923.[61]

The members of the Khitan Yelü and Xiao clans and of the Zhang, Han, and Ma families—privileged upper-class Han Chinese families in the service of the Liao dynasty—built two types of tombs in various layouts and on various scales: the complex multichamber tomb with a corbeled dome, and the single-room, corbeled-dome tomb.[62] The chambers could be round, square, rectangular, hexagonal, or octagonal, with domed ceilings in either corresponding or combined forms. In comparing the main features of Liao and Song tombs, it becomes obvious that members of the Khitan clans and upper-class Chinese families in the service of the Liao did not join in the rediscovery of simplicity in tombs and graves that was advocated by the scholar-official elite of the Song dynasty. Instead, they adopted and modified the traditional aristocratic and imperial Chinese tomb architecture style that had existed in northern China from the Han to the Five Dynasties (907–60) eras. These tombs—which were constructed not just for the burial of the dead but also for public functions, such as the performance of libation ceremonies (*dianli*)[63]—were manifestations of the status of the deceased in Liao society and thus preserved the social hierarchy of the living among the dead. A tomb was the

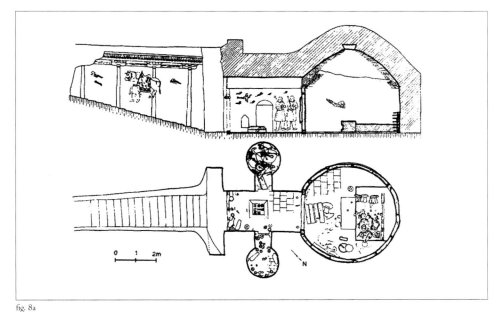

fig. 8a

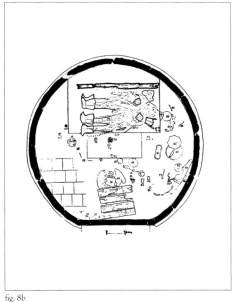

fig. 8b

Fig. 8a–b. The tomb of the Princess of Chen (1001–18) and her husband, Xiao Shaoju, Naiman Banner, Inner Mongolia, 1018.
a. Longitudinal section and outline of the complex tomb, furnished with side chambers and a wooden interior tent (*muzhang*)
b. Detail of the burial chamber and the fully dressed couple

deceased's reinsurance for the afterlife. The multichamber, corbeled-dome style of tomb construction reached its high point with the three imperial Qingling tombs of the emperors Shengzong, Xingzong, and Daozong.[64] The tomb of Emperor Shengzong consisted of seven rooms (fig. 5). It was made of brick and was 21.2 meters long, 15.5 meters wide, and 6.5 meters high. The three main rooms were arranged on a central axis, beginning with a rectangular antechamber that led to an almost round central chamber. Both the antechamber and the central chamber had two side-rooms, one to the left and one to the right. In the rear was the burial chamber. The tombs of emperors Xingzong and Daozong are similar in structure, but in them the antechamber has become a corridor and most of the chambers are octagonal in layout. The number of tombs with polygonal and octagonal chambers increased beginning in the middle of the eleventh century, and eventually these types of tombs superseded all other shapes; this may be interpreted as a reverence for the Khitan Octagonal Hall (*bajiao dian*),[65] which was used for performing the official ceremony of congratulations on the birth of the emperor's son.[66] The octagonal shape may be an architectural reference to the eight tribes in the Khitan's tribal origin legend and to ceremonial tasks that were performed by the elders of the eight tribes in the firewood investiture ceremony. The elders invested the emperor in the northeastern corner of the Rebirth Hall (*zaisheng shi*).[67]

Interestingly enough, the interiors of many corbeled dome-shaped tomb chambers were furnished with an additional architectural structure, made of wood and stone, that served as a room or coffin in which the dead were placed.[68] Several of these structures are unique to the Liao dynasty in their construction and use. The wooden interior tent (*muzhang*), which has been documented in fewer than a dozen tombs so far, is a structure without doors or windows; it has a domed roof, very often built in log-cabin fashion of *Thuja orientalis* (Oriental arborvitae) inside a burial chamber made of brick or stone.[69] Its floor plan and walls closely follow those of the burial chamber, so that the structure measures several meters in both height and diameter (figs. 6, 7). In this inaccessible wooden room, the remains of an individual or a couple were interred. The deceased, in full attire, lay inside the interior tent, generally not in a coffin but on a coffin platform or a sort of bed pedestal surrounded by curtains. The earliest datable wooden interior tent was discovered in the tomb of Xiao Qulie (908–59), a son-in-law of the emperor Abaoji.[70] All later

fig. 9

fig. 10

fig. 11

Fig. 9. A wooden coffin, fashioned as a wooden coffin housing (*xiaozhang*), of an unknown person; Wengniute Banner, Inner Mongolia, most probably tenth century. Length, 275 cm; height, 160 cm

Fig. 10. The condition of the wooden coffin housing (*xiaozhang*) with sarcophagus when it was discovered in the complex tomb of an unknown person; Tomb Number 7, Yemaotai, Faku, Liaoning Province, 959–86. Length, 259 cm; width, 168 cm; height, 220 cm

Fig. 11. Sarcophagus depicting the symbolic animals of the four directions; Tomb Number 7, Yemaotai, Faku, Liaoning Province, 959–86. Length, 215 cm; width, 124 cm; height, 88 cm

wooden interior tents unearthed so far are octagonal in shape, except for the round interior tent fashioned for the Princess of Chen (1001–18) and her husband, Xiao Shaoju (fig. 8). The royal couple was dressed in death garments made of silver wire, and their faces were covered with individually modeled masks made of pure gold.[71] We can only speculate about the Liao custom of placing an interior tent in a tomb. Perhaps it has to be viewed in the context of honoring the burial site of the emperor (or one of his family members). In the case of the tombs, long-lasting materials were chosen. Inside interior tents, neither a sarcophagus nor other architectural structures have been found.[72]

The idea of burying a man and his wife together, placing their remains on a bed pedestal, as the Liao did, was unimaginable, and from a moral point of view unacceptable, to the contemporaneous Song Chinese. We do not know whether the Han Chinese families in the service of the Liao dynasty who were honored by being allowed to erect a wooden interior tent inside their tombs followed the Khitan custom of burying a husband and wife side by side on a bed pedestal. Most probably they chose another option, as Zhang Guan (1048–1113) and her husband did. She ranked among the elite of the empire, her father was the Duke of Jin; her husband, Ma Zhiwen, held the title of Dynasty-founding Duke of the Great Liao. Their bodies were cremated, and the ashes were deposited in the rib cage of a life-size mannequin made of *Thuja orientalis*.[73] In a letter to Zhang Qiao, his brother-in-law who composed the epitaph for Zhang Guan, Ma Zhiwen described his desperate situation after his wife had died:

On the sixth day of the fourth month, your sister, my wife, passed away. I'm 72 years old; my teeth are shaky, my ears can't hear clearly, and my eyes can't see distinctly. I'm gradually becoming weaker. My hair is thinning out day by day. I'm chronically sick. How long can I bear up? Now my wife has passed away before me. That is what you call "the young one goes, the old one stays," and "the strong one is dead, the weak one is alive" . . . Last winter I met you at Yanjing. I asked you to write the epitaphs for me and my wife. We know—there is life, and there is death. So we had our grave built in advance.[74]

Apart from the wooden interior tents, there are also various types of sarcophagi, often stone housings (*shifang*) built or placed in the burial chamber of the tomb (fig. 4).[75] Furthermore, there were wooden housings (*xiaozhang*) that served as coffins or coffin housings (fig. 9).[76] The deceased lay inside the stone or wooden housing on a platform or bed. The wooden housings clearly mark the complete transition from traditional Tang burial style to the specific Liao-dynasty style. The most well known of the wooden housings discovered so far has enough space for a sarcophagus and could thus function as a coffin housing. The structure was excavated from the Yemaotai Tomb Number 7, which dates from between 959 and 986. It reflects the three-bay by two-bay[77] structure of Tang architecture, with walls made of planks, a main entrance, two windows, and a hip-gable roof (fig. 10).[78] Inside stood the richly engraved sarcophagus, on which the animals of the four directions, or the four supernatural creatures of heaven, were depicted: the green dragon (east), the white tiger (west), the vermillion bird (south), and the tortoise with snake (north). Around the coffin lid, which is decorated with peony ornaments, are the twelve Chinese symbolic animals (*shier shengxiao*) representing the Earthly Branches (fig.11).[79] The coffin housing, the sarcophagus, and the decorative motifs are, once more, adoptions from Tang China.

Conclusions

The archaeological finds dating from the Liao dynasty that were discovered and excavated in the twentieth century have immensely enhanced our knowledge about the Khitan and the Han Chinese in their service. Prior to these discoveries, our knowledge of Liao civilization was limited to the biased accounts of Chinese historians. From the archaeological finds, we have learned that the Yelü and Xiao clans of the Liao dynasty were deeply rooted in predynastic, nonsedentary tribal ways and customs but that they also adopted Chinese ideas and models, even if those ideas and models could be distinguished from those of the previous Tang and the contemporary Song dynasties. Two main types of archaeological finds help us to delineate prominent Liao features: the first is the remnants of the Liao capitals, in particular, the Supreme Capital and the Central Capital (Zhongjing), and the second is the graveyards, tombs, and mausoleums, and the burial objects found in them. Tombs are by far our most important source of archaeological information.[80] The structures and furnishings of the tombs, the use of epitaphs (*muzhiming*) and other stone inscriptions, the wall paintings, the method of the burial of the dead and their attire, and the rich variety of burial objects provide a reliable source for, as well as a vivid impression of, everyday life in the higher echelons of Liao society.

It was certainly no coincidence that Abaoji established the Khitan khanate in 907, the very year that the Tang dynasty came to an end. As soon as he had consolidated his power, he started to create political unity within his empire and continued his advances on Chinese culture by taking the Tang dynasty and Confucianism as models. In 918, he ordered the Chinese specialist in ritual affairs and architects Kang Moji and Han Yanhui to plan and build the August Capital (Huangdu) near Linhuang in Inner Mongolia; it was to be furnished with palaces, temples, educational institutions, and guesthouses.[81] The city was renamed in 938[82] by Abaoji's successor, Deguang, and became known as the Supreme Capital. It remained the most important capital until the end of the dynasty. Today, the remains of the Supreme Capital are about three meters underground. Nevertheless, it is possible to tell that the capital was divided into a northern part, reserved for the Khitan, and a southern part, where the Han Chinese, Bohai, Uighurs, and other non-Khitan people lived and their merchants and diplomatic envoys were received. Although the emperor of the Khitan had a palace in the Supreme Capital, there is little doubt that he and the Khitan nobles continued their nomadic lifestyle of touring their territory, living in yurts, and ruling from seasonal, temporary residences. "During the autumn and winter they shunned the cold; during the spring and summer they avoided the heat . . . For each of the four seasons [the emperor] had a temporary place as residence."[83] This place was called a *nabo*, which was probably a word borrowed from Mongolian meaning "a camp in the wilderness." The archaeological remains that help to identify the region of the Supreme Capital as the homeland, the ancestral prefecture (*zuzhou*) of Abaoji, are more important for the khanate or dynasty than the relics of the Central Capital, near present-day Dading, established about ninety years later, between 1003 and 1007.[84] Originally, each of these early capitals served the purpose of administering the indigenous population in the circuits. In the case of the Central Capital, the city planners strictly followed a Chinese layout by building a walled outer city, with a walled inner city in the center; the palace was situated inside the inner city. Datong was selected as the Western Capital (Xijing) in 1044, the last of the five capitals of the Liao empire to be determined.

The Khitan aristocracy tried to maintain their traditional tribal burial customs, but as early as the mid-tenth century, their tomb architecture and the motifs on their coffins and sarcophagi, as well as the murals on the walls of the long ramps leading to the underground tombs, revealed cultural adoptions from the Tang. The refined lifestyle of the Tang capital, Chang'an, as well as the mausoleums to the north of the city, were familiar to the Khitan and must have served as standards of Chinese civilization to be emulated. When the emperor of the Khitan "barbarians" succeeded in establishing political parity with the Song by the Treaty of Shanyuan of 1005, the Khitan aristocracy, we learn from the archaeological finds, had already made cultural concessions in their burial practices, diverging from tribal customs and thus beginning what was to become an unstoppable disintegration of their traditional tribal culture. By the time of the treaty, they had already adopted from the Chinese the custom of composing epitaphs, which were cut in stone and placed in burial chambers; these epitaphs serve as original Liao sources offering interesting insights and first-hand information about Liao culture. Two archaeological finds, hanging scrolls of a "Landscape with architecture" (fig. 12) and "Bamboo, birds, and rabbits," both painted in the Chinese fashion, are the earliest indubitably tenth-century hanging scrolls in the history of Chinese painting.[85] The Khitan also adopted from the Chinese, as an artistic and literary motif, filial piety, the most important Chinese cultural tradition of all, depicting sons and daughters in self-sacrificing service on behalf of the well-being and comfort of their parents. The scenes were depicted not only on stone reliefs in tombs[86] but also on a parcel-gilded silver vessel excavated

fig. 12

Fig. 12. Hanging scroll depicting "Landscape with architecture"; excavated from Tomb Number 7, Yemaotai, Faku, Liaoning Province, 959–986. Length, 174.2 cm; width. 54.5 cm

from the tomb of Yelü Yuzhi (cat. 95).[87] The admiration for Chinese traditional subject matter, however, was not limited to moralizing biographical stories. The Daoist immortals were used as decorative motifs to embellish the crowns of the Princess of Chen and her husband. Khitan aristocrats followed the Tang model of decorating their tombs with murals; they depicted various kinds of guardians at the doorways, and on the walls, colorful illustrations of scenes from their everyday life, their travels on horseback and in ox-drawn carts, their banquets and musical entertainments, and their favorite pastimes, such as hunting and horsemanship. The murals confirm that Khitan men wore not only the national garment (*guofu*), with a round collar that was fastened on the left side, in what the Chinese considered the "barbarian" way, but also Han Chinese garments that were similar to Tang clothing in cut and style. Khitan women dressed in colorful coats with tight sleeves and wore extravagant headgear. Leather boots and shoes complemented the wardrobes of both men and women. As far as the technical execution of woven and embroidered silk textiles is concerned, the finds excavated from the tombs of Yelü Yuzhi and others are of superb quality, their colors and designs of extraordinary freshness.[88] Breathtaking wall paintings, in colors enriched with gold on stone, were recently discovered in the tomb of an unknown aristocratic Khitan lady (who was buried after 923). The ladies depicted in the paintings are dressed in glamorous Tang-style attire. Some of them are shown in a southern landscape composed of bamboo, banana trees, palm trees, and a rock from Lake Taihu,[89] although in the territory of the Liao empire neither bamboo nor palm trees grew, thus revealing Liao enthusiasm for the beauty of the landscape of southern China. In a similar vein, the Khitan did not hesitate to extol the virtues of a mythical Chinese cultural hero. A tomb inscription of the military commissioner Xiao Jin (981–1028)—who after the death of his first wife, from the Yelü clan, married her younger sister, thus following the Khitan tradition of the sororate—states: "His virtue was like a solitary pine on Hua Mountain. His character was as green as the bamboo on the shores of the Xiang River."[90] And about the benevolent and virtuous Princess Supreme of Qin and Jin, Yelü Guanyinnü (970–1045), who was the oldest daughter of Emperor Jingzong (r. 969–82), elder sister to Emperor Shengzong, and aunt to Emperor Xingzong, we learn: "Her virtue can be compared to that of Shun."[91] In the epitaph of the Supreme Pillar of State and Acting Grand Preceptor Xiao Yi (1040–1112), sentences from the Chinese classics *Shijing* (Book of Poetry), *Liji* (Book of Rites), and *Yijing* (Book of Changes) are quoted to praise his virtue.[92]

The archaeological finds from the Liao dynasty give evidence of the great effort the Khitan made to establish a long-lasting, powerful empire. They founded capitals after the Chinese model and perpetuated the glorious aristocratic tomb architecture of the Tang, which they adapted in such a way that Chinese burial customs merged with their own predynastic, tribal customs. At the same time, contemporaneous Song officials and aristocrats were turning away from the Tang model and embracing the ideal of returning to antiquity (*fugu*), adopting the Confucian principles of simplicity, which they applied in burying their dead in mostly simple tombs or graves, so different from the extravagant architectural structures of the Liao-dynasty tombs. The impressive and clearly structured, yet still in many ways mysterious, multichamber Liao tombs, with their corbeled domes and remarkable interior furnishings, undoubtedly represent a high point of aristocratic tomb architecture in China, and thus a high point in the history of Chinese archaeology.

1. The chronology of the Khitan before 930 is contradictory. See Denis Twitchett and Klaus-Peter Tietze, "The Liao," in Herbert Franke and Denis Twitchett (eds.), *Alien Regimes and Border States, 907–1368*, vol. 6 of *The Cambridge History of China*, p. 60. Here, the year 907 is given as the date when Khitan rule started. It was the year when the Khitan chieftain Abaoji (872–926), from the Yila tribe, established his Khitan khanate, a dynasty of his own. In 916, when Abaoji secured his position as khan for the fourth time, he assumed the title of emperor in a formal ceremony of the Chinese fashion. The dynastic title of Khitan was changed to Liao sometime between 926 and 947, depending on which source is consulted.

2. Walter Fuchs, *Beiträge zur Mandjurischen Bibliographie und Literatur* [*Contributions to Manchu bibliography and literature*], pp. 42–43.

3. *Geschichte der Großen Liao*, translated from the Manchu by H. Conon von der Gabelentz.

4. For a short description of the historiographical situation, see also Yang Shusen, "Liaodai shixue shulue" [*A brief summary of Liao-dynasty historiography*], in Chen Shu (ed.), *Liao Jin shi lunji* [*Collection of articles on the history of the Liao and Jin*].

5. *Qidan guozhi* of 1247 by Ye Longli.

6. *Liaoshi*, compiled by Tuo Tuo.

7. Franke and Twitchett, *The Cambridge History of China*, vol. 6, p. 665.

8. Hok-lam Chan, "Chinese Official historiography at the Yüan Court: The Composition of the Liao, Chin, and Sung Histories," in John D. Langlois, Jr. (ed.), *China under Mongol Rule*, pp. 78–79.

9. Chan, "Chinese Official Historiography at the Yüan Court," pp. 77–78.

10. Peter K. Bol, *"This Culture of Ours": Intellectual Transitions in T'ang and Sung China*, p. 1.

11. Tao Jingshen, "Barbarians or Northerners: Northern Sung Images of the Khitans," in Morris Rossabi (ed.), *China among Equals: The Middle Kingdom and Its Neighbors, 10th to 14th Centuries*, pp. 68–69.

12. Dieter Kuhn, *Die Republik China von 1912 bis 1937. Entwurf für eine politische Ereignisgeschichte* [*Republican China from 1912 until 1937: Draft for a narrative history of political events*], vol. 1, p. xxxi, fig. 6.

13. *Liaoshi*, juan 21, p. 255.

14. *Songmo jiwen* [*Records of hearsay on the pine forests north of the desert*], p. 9a. For the full context, see Karl A. Wittfogel and Fêng Chia-shêng, *History of Chinese Society: Liao, 907–1125*, p. 236, n. 65.

15. Wittfogel and Fêng, *History of Chinese Society*, p. 30.

16. The date of 1908 is given in Torii Ryūzō, *Ryō no bunka: zufu*, vol. 1, pl. 7; he published the results of later expeditions in the journal *Kokka* in 1931; a description of the Supreme Capital can be found in Nancy S. Steinhardt, *Chinese Imperial City Planning*, pp. 123–24.

17. Joseph Mullie, "Les anciennes villes de l'empire des grands Leao au Royaume Mongol de Bârin" [*On the ancient cities of the Great Liao empire in the Mongol kingdom of Bârin*], *T'oung Pao* 21 (1922), pp. 156–61.

18. See the monograph on the Supreme Capital *Liao Shangjing yizhi jianjie* [*Brief introduction to the remains of Liao Supreme Capital*]; Li Yiyou, "Liao Shangjing yizhi" [*The remains of the Liao Supreme Capital*], in *Zhongguo dabaike quanshu: kaoguxue* 1986.1, pp. 277–78.

19. Mullie, "Les anciennes villes de l'empire des grands Leao," p. 139.

20. Zhang Songbai and Feng Lei, "Zuzhou shishi tansuo" [*An inquiry into the stone houses at the Zuzhou site*], quoted in Adam T. Kessler (ed.), *Empires Beyond the Great Wall: The Heritage of Genghis Khan*, p. 94.

21. *Liaoshi*, juan 2, p. 24.

22. Professor Tamura Jitsuzo started his scientific research on the site in 1939; see Tamura Jitsuzo and Yukio Kobayashi, "Tombs and Mural Paintings of Ch'ing-ling Liao Imperial Mausoleums of 11th Century A.D. in Eastern Mongolia," *Japan Quarterly* 1954.1, pp. 34–45; for bibliographical information, see Nancy S. Steinhardt, *Liao Architecture*, pp. 256–63.

23. *Liaoshi*, juan 37, p. 444.

24. See the description of the burials of emperors Shengzong and Xingzong in Steinhardt, *Liao Architecture*, p. 257–58; Wittfogel and Fêng, *History of Chinese Society*, pp. 278–83.

25. Torii, *Ryō no bunka: zufu*, vol. 3 (unidentified tombs of the emperors Shengzong and Xingzong); vol. 4 (Emperor Daozong).

26. Publishing on finds in the region of Datong; *Wenwu* 1959.7, p. 73; *Kaogu* 1960.10, pp. 37–42; *Kaogu tongxun* 1958.6, pp. 28–36.

27. Working in Liaoning Province and publishing on the tomb of Xiao Paolu (ca. 1015–1088/89), *Kaogu* 1983.7, pp. 624–35.

28. Publishing on tombs excavated in Liaoning Province; *Kaogu xuebao* 1954.8, pp. 163–202; *Kaogu* 1962.9, pp. 479–83.

29. Publishing on finds excavated mainly in Inner Mongolia; *Wenwu congkan ziliao* 1958.4, pp. 72–73; *Wenwu* 1959.7, pp. 63–64; *Wenwu* 1961.9, pp. 30–33, 40–44, 44–49, and many later articles.

30. Publishing on Liao tombs in Beijing; *Kaogu* 1959.2, pp. 89–93; *Kaogu* 1962.5, pp. 246–53 (the excellent tomb of Zhao Dejun, d. 937); *Kaogu* 1963.3, pp. 145–46.

31. Publishing on finds in Inner Mongolia; *Kaogu* 1959.1, pp. 47–48; *Wenwu* 1961.9, pp. 50–51 (tomb of Shang Wei, 1031–1096).

32. Publishing on Liao tombs excavated in Liaoning and Hebei provinces; *Kaogu xuebao* 1956.3, pp. 1–26; *Kaogu* 1962.8, pp. 429–35; and many later articles.

33. Xu Pingfang, "Liaodai muzang," in *Zhongguo dabaike quanshu: kaoguxue*, 1986, p. 274.

34. In 1975 at Xiawanzi in Aohan Banner, a Liao cemetery containing more than one hundred tombs was discovered; forty of the tombs had already been illegally opened, and only seven were archaeologically excavated; see Shao Guotian, "Aohanqi Xiawanzi Liao mu faxian jianbao" [*A brief report on the excavation of Liao tombs at Xianwanzi in Aohan Banner*], *Neimenggu wenwu kaogu* 1999.1, pp. 67–84. In various years, beginning in 1953, greater numbers of tombs were discovered at different cemeteries near Yemaotai Village in Faku County, Liaoning Province. In several excavations after 1974, twenty-one Liao tombs were excavated, among them the famous Yemaotai Tomb Number 7 of an anonymous noble lady and the tomb of Xiao Yi (1040–1112), see Xu Zhiguo and Wei Chunguang, "Faku Yemaotai di 22 hao Liao mu qingli jianbao" [*Brief report on the clearing of Tomb Number 22 at Yemaotai, Faku County*], *Beifang wenwu* 2000.1, pp. 48–51.

35. Feng Yongqian, "Jianguo yilai Liaodai kaogu de zhongyao faxian" [*Important archaeological discoveries of the Liao dynasty since the founding of the People's Republic China*], in Chen Shu (ed.), *Liao Jin shi lunji* [*Collection of articles on the history of the Liao and Jin*], vol. 1, pp. 295–334; see also Xiang Chunsong, *Liaodai lishi yu kaogu* [*History and archaeology of the Liao dynasty*]; for descriptions of the tombs in Western publications, see Steinhardt, *Liao Architecture*, pp. 285–304, 307–14; Kuhn, *Die Kunst des Grabbaus: Kuppelgräber der Liao-Zeit (907–1125)* [*The art of tomb building: Dome-shaped tombs of the Liao period (907–1125)*], pp. 148–70; Reckel, "Das Kitan-Volk im Spiegel seiner Gräber" [*The (Material) Culture) of the Khitan people as mirrored in the findings from their tombs*], *Zentralasiatische Studien des Seminars für Sprach- und Kulturwissenschaft Zentralasiens der Universität Bonn* 22 (1989/1991), pp. 18–141.

36. Dieter Kuhn, *Die Kunst des Grabbaus*, pp. 225–46; for the mural paintings excavated from more than fifty tombs in Liaoning Province, Hebei Province, Beijing, and Inner Mongolia since the 1930s, see Luo Shiping, "Liao mu bihua shidu" [*A tentative understanding of the murals in Liao tombs*], *Wenwu* 1999.1, pp. 76–85.

37. Dieter Kuhn, *How the Qidan Reshaped the Tradition of the Chinese Dome-shaped Tomb*, pp. 25–28.

38. Kuhn, *How the Qidan Reshaped the Tradition*, pp. 14–18.

39. Kessler, *Empires Beyond the Great Wall*, p. 93.

40. In autumn 1992, for example, the superb relics excavated from the tomb of the Princess of Chen (1001–18) and her husband, Xiao Shaoju, were displayed in an exhibition at the Historical Shaanxi Provincial Museum in Xi'an. Meanwhile, the Beijing Liao Jin Changyuan Bowuguan (City Wall Museum) opened its doors in 1995 at Fengtai, Beijing. An excellent exhibition on the material culture of tribal federations and alien dynasties in China, including the Khitan, and the material culture of the Liao dynasty, which toured several museums in North America in 1994 and 1995, was organized by the archaeological institutions of Inner Mongolia and the Natural History Museum of Los Angeles County in 1993; see Kessler, *Empires Beyond the Great Wall*, pp. 89–120. Christian Deydier organized two exhibitions, in 1990 and 1991, in London with outstanding, partly inscribed and thus datable objects, but, regrettably, the provenance of the objects remains a secret; see Christian Deydier, *Imperial Gold from Ancient China*. On the gold and silver artifacts in the Deydier exhibitions that have been smuggled out of China, see also Li Jinyun, "Liushi haiwai de yipi Liaodai jinyin qi" [*A group of gold and silver artefacts of the Liao dynasty now scattered abroad*], *Shoucangjia* 1999.14, pp. 12–15.

41. The rebirth ceremony was performed by the emperor himself every twelve years, in the last month of the winter preceding the year (of the duodenary cycle) of the emperor's birth, on an auspicious day. It took place in the Rebirth Hall (*zaisheng shi*), which were erected especially for that purpose. A young boy, an old man, an old midwife, shamans, and a group of seven selected additional old men took part in the ceremony, in which the emperor was symbolically reborn. The rebirth served the purpose of reconfirming the emperor's right to rule; the Khitan tribal aristocracy renewed its confidence in him for another twelve years. *Liaoshi*, juan 53, p. 879–80.

42. Feng Yongqian, "Jianguo yilai Liaodai kaogu de zhongyao faxian," pp. 295–296.

43. Wittfogel and Fêng, *History of Chinese Society*, p. 221.

44. Wittfogel and Fêng, *History of Chinese Society*, p. 143.

45. Wittfogel and Fêng, *History of Chinese Society*, p. 207.

46. Wittfogel and Fêng, *History of Chinese Society*, p. 280, n. 215.

47. *Xin Wudai shi* [*New historical records of the Five Dynasties*], juan 72, p. 888; see Xiang Chunsong, "Neimenggu Wengniuteqi Liaodai Guangde gong mu" [*The tomb of Guangde gong of Liao times in Wengniute Banner, Inner Mongolia*], *Beifang wenwu* 1989.4, pp. 41–44.

48. Kuhn, *How the Qidan Reshaped the Tradition*, p. 21.

49. *Xiari ji* [*Days of leisure record*], in *Wuchao xiaoshuo* [*Novels of the Five Dynasties*], juan 93:2a; *Huaman lu* [*Record of Zhang Shunmin*], in *Shuofu* [*Florilegium of (unofficial) literature*], edited by Tao Zongyi, juan 18:33b. Citations in this essay are to the Shanghai edition of *Shuofu*.

50. *Luting shishi* [*Facts from the caitiffs' court*], in *Shuofu*, juan 8:49b.

51. Wittfogel and Fêng, *History of Chinese Society*, p. 280, n. 215; they interpreted the sentence describing the use of the netting as "hands and feet were tied together with copper wire." The Chinese character given in the text (*luo*) can be translated both ways.

52. *Luting shishi*, in *Shuofu*, juan 8:49a.

53. Comprehensive lists of metal facial masks and metal wire clothing excavated from archaeological sites can be found in Kuhn, *How the Qidan Reshaped the Tradition*, p. 22, n. 19; see also the discussion in Kuhn, *Die Kunst des Grabbaus*, pp. 207–15.

54. See Hiromi Kinoshita, "Hybridity and Conquest: Patterns of Liao (AD 907–1125) Khitan Tomb Burial," in Michael Gervers, Uradyn E. Bulag, Gillian Long (eds.), *Cultural Interaction and Conflict in Central and Inner Asia*, pp. 129–44. Kinoshita prefers the burial customs of the steppes to those of the Han Chinese as an explanation for the origins of the metal wire suits used by Khitan aristocrats in their burials. She, however, concedes that "Han and Liao suits are similar in construction," but due to the eight hundred years that separate the Han and the Liao "a connection does not seem likely" (p. 138). Another reason she favors the steppe burial custom as an explanation for the Khitan custom of dressing their dead in metal-wire suits is the widespread use of metal masks in steppe burials (pp. 141–44). To my knowledge, there is so far no convincing archaeological evidence allowing the conclusion that the metal-wire suits used in Khitan burials are part of a common steppe burial tradition. The dressing and wrapping up of the dead with silk fabrics of various makes and cuts was quite common in China. In my opinion, it is too early to decide about the origins of this burial custom practised by the Khitan.

55. Namio Egami, *The Grand Exhibition of Silk Road Civilizations: The Oasis and the Steppe Routes*, p. 260, pl. 158, p. 258, pls. 150, 151; Kuhn, *Die Kunst des Grabbaus*, pp. 207–11. On the still earlier gold mask tradition in the Near East, see Kinoshita, "Hybridity and Conquest," pp. 138–40.

56. Torii Ryūzō, *Sculptured Stone Tombs of the Liao Dynasty*, pp. 66–70.

57. Philippe Ariès, *Geschichte des Todes* [History of Death], p. 461.

58. Kuhn, *How the Qidan Reshaped the Tradition*, p. 23.

59. Gai Zhiyong, "Yelü Yuzhi muzhiming kaozheng" [Some remarks on the memorial tablet inscription of Yelü Yuzhi], *Beifang wenwu* 2001.1, pp. 40–48.

60. Qi Xiaoguang and Wang Jianguo, "Liao Yelü Yuzhi mu fajue jianbao" [Short report on the tomb of Yelü Yuzhi of Liao times], *Wenwu* 1996.1, pp. 74–84; Kuhn, *Die Kunst des Grabbaus*, pp. 156–57.

61. Qi Xiaoguang et al., "Neimenggu Chifeng Baoshan Liao bihuamu fajue jianbao" [Brief report on the wall paintings from a Liao tomb in Baoshan, Chifeng, Inner Mongolia], *Wenwu* 1998.1, p. 82; Kuhn, *How the Qidan Reshaped the Tradition*, pp. 26, 31; see also Yang Xiaoneng, *New Perspectives on China's Past: Chinese Archaeology in the Twentieth Century*, vol. 2 of *Major Archaeological Discoveries in Twentieth Century China*, pp. 448–49.

62. Steinhardt presents the tombs in strict chrono-logical order, *Liao Architecture*, pp. 285–304, 307–14; Kuhn prefers a typological arrangement, *Die Kunst des Grabbaus*, pp. 148–70.

63. A libation was an alcoholic drink that was offered in a ceremony to the ancestors. *Liaoshi*, juan 50, pp. 839–40.

64. Jitsuzō Tamura and Yukio Kobayashi, *Keiryō* [*Qingling*], vol. 1, pp. 19, 31, 159, 174; Li Yiyou, "Liao Qingling," in *Zhongguo dabaike quanshu: kaoguxue* 1986.1, p. 277; Steinhardt, *Liao Architecture*, pp. 258–63.

65. Dieter Kuhn, "Liao Architecture: Qidan Innovations and Han-Chinese Traditions?" *T'oung Pao* 2000.86, pp. 348–51.

66. *Liaoshi*, juan 53, p. 872.

67. *Liaoshi*, juan 49, p. 836.

68. Other architectural structures erected in tombs that did not, however, serve to house the coffin or the dead are also documented; see Sun Jianhua et al., "Balinyouqi Zhuangjingou 5 hao Liao mu fajue jianbao" [Brief report on the Liao Tomb Number 5 at Zhuangjingou in Balin Right Banner], *Wenwu* 2002.3, p. 53, fig. 3.

69. The Chinese archaeologist Zhao Xiaohua describes an architectural structure of unknown provenance now preserved in the Museum of Liaoning Province as a *muguo* (wooden outer coffin). The wooden outer coffin, or coffin chamber, as it is sometimes called, clearly displays the features of a wooden interior tent. It is a large octagonal structure, 178 centimeters high and 427 centimeters in diameter, with a domed roof built in log-cabin fashion from the wood of *Thuja orientalis* (*baimu*). Seven of its eight sides are decorated with colorful scenes of a feast, picturing altogether fourteen life-size human figures. However, conclusions about such a structure can only be made when its in situ condition and placement are known. Zhao Xiaohua, "Liaoningsheng bowuguan zhengji rucang yitao Liaodai caihui muguo" [A painted wooden coffin chamber of the Liao dynasty preserved in the Museum of Liaoning Province], *Wenwu* 2000.11, pp. 61.

70. See *Kaogu xuebao* 1956.3, p. 2, fig. 1.

71. *Liao Chenguo gongzhu mu*, pp. 25–26, 31–37.

72. Kuhn, "Liao Architecture: Qidan Innovations and Han-Chinese Traditions?" pp. 356–57.

73. *Wenwu* 1980.12, p. 31; Dieter Kuhn, *Die Kunst des Grabbaus*, pp.120–23, 204–7.

74. Dieter Kuhn, "Liao Architecture: Qidan Innovations and Han-Chinese Traditions?" p. 358.

75. Compare *Kaogu* 1984.11, p. 996, fig. 8, pl.5.5.

76. Compare *Wenwu* 1979.6, p. 29, fig. 8.

77. A bay (*jian*) is the distance between two pillars. All houses of officials in traditional China built of wood were measured in the number of bays, e.g., three-bay front, five-bay front.

78. Cao Xun, "Yemaotai Liao mu zhong de guanchuang xiaozhang," [The small-scale "container" and coffin-bed in a Liao tomb at Yemaotai], *Wenwu* 1975.12, pp. 49–62; see also Yang Xiaoneng, *Chinese Archaeology*, p. 465.

79. The twelve Chinese symbolic animals correspond to the Western signs of the zodiac: rat (Aries), ox (Taurus), tiger (Gemini), hare (Cancer), dragon (Leo), snake (Virgo), horse (Libra), sheep (Scorpio), monkey (Sagittarius), cock (Capricornus), dog (Aquarius), boar (Pisces).

80. Feng Yongqian, "Jianguo yilai Liaodai kaogu de zhongyao faxian," pp. 295–96.

81. See Li Yiyou, "Liaodai chengguo yingjian zhidu chutan" [Preliminary discussion on building formulas and systems in city construction of the Liao dynasty], in *Liao Jin shi lunji*, vol. 3, p. 57.

82. Compare Li Yiyou, "Liao Zhongjing yizhi" [The remains of the Liao Central Capital], in *Zhongguo dabaike quanshu: kaoguxue* 1986.1, p. 279.

83. *Liaoshi*, juan 32, p. 373.

84. Compare Li Yiyou, "Liao Zhongjing yizhi" [The remains of the Liao Central Capital], in *Zhongguo dabaike quanshu: kaoguxue* 1986.1, p. 279.

85. "Faku Yemaotai Liao mu jilue" [Excavation of the Liao tomb at Yemaotai, Faku], *Wenwu* 1975.12, col. pls. 1, 2; Yang Renkai did not refer to the hanging scroll (painted on silk tabby) as "Landscape with architecture" but as "Assembling in the deep mountains for a game of chess"; see Yang Renkai, *Yemaotai di qi hao Liao mu chutu guhua kao* [Investigation of the old paintings excavated from the Liao Tomb Number 7 of Yemaotai], p. 5. Yang Xiaoneng, *Chinese Archaeology*, p. 467; see also Wen C. Fong, "Images of the Mind," in Wen C. Fong, Alfreda Murck, Shou-chien Shih et al., *Images of the Mind*, p. 25.

86. Torii, *Sculptured Stone Tombs of the Liao Dynasty*, pp. 23–26, 27–28; Dieter Kuhn, *A Place for the Dead*, p. 357, fig. 8.9; Kuhn, *Die Kunst des Grabbaus*, pp. 89–90.

87. Yang Xiaoneng, *Chinese Archaeology*, pp. 456–57.

88. Huang Nengfu and Chen Juanjuan, *Zhongguo sichou keji yishu qiqiannian* [Seven thousand years of Chinese silk technology and craftsmanship], pp. 132–44.

89. Qi Xiaoguang et al., "Neimenggu Chifeng Baoshan," pp. 73–95, col. pls. 1–6; Yang Xiaoneng, *Chinese Archaeology*, p. 451.

90. Li Yufeng and Yuan Haibo, "Liaoning Fuxin Liao Xiao Jin mu" [The Liao tomb of Xiao Jin in Fuxin County, Liaoning Province], *Beifang wenwu* 1988.2, pp. 33–36.

91. Chen Shu (ed.), *Quan Liaowen* [*Complete Liao writings*], pp. 125–28; Zheng Shaozong, "Qidan Qin Jin guo dachanggongzhu muzhiming" [The epitaph of the Qidan princess supreme of Qin and Jin], *Kaogu* 1962.8, pp. 429–35.

92. *Quan Liaowen*, pp. 249–51; Wen Lihe, "Liaoning Fakuxian Yemaotai Liao Xiao Yi mu" [The Liao tomb of Xiao Yi near Yemaotai Village in Faku County, Liaoning Province], *Kaogu* 1989.4, pp. 324–30.

The Architectural Landscape
of the Liao and Underground Resonances

Nancy Shatzman Steinhardt

Liao architecture rises across several thousand kilometers of the Mongolian plain between the modern cities of Hohhot (Huhehaote) and Tongliao and southward into Liaoning Province. It stands, too, in northern Shanxi Province, Beijing, and north and eastward in Hebei Province. During the millennium that has passed since the Liao ruled these lands, natural evolution and human history have only slightly altered portions of the architectural landscape of Mongolia, Liaoning, and the sixteen northern Chinese prefectures ceded to the Liao in 938. Today, as then, octagonal brick and wooden pagodas tower above flat grazing lands or towns of humble, low dwellings (figs. 13, 14, 15i).

All three pagodas pictured in the figures were once part of temple complexes and thus were beacons of sedentarism in territory ruled by seminomadic lords. The construction, by this dynasty of nomadic origins, of not just monumental architecture but buildings of structural complexity and grandeur that challenged the limits of the Chinese building system is one of the most extraordinary legacies of the centuries of Liao rule.

Following a successful pattern of non-Chinese appropriation of Chinese territory and the subsequent erection of Chinese architecture to proclaim imperial aspirations, the Khitan established capitals and other urban centers.[1] The biography of the dynastic founder, Abaoji (Taizu, 872–926), records city after city built by him or his relatives in the first two decades of the tenth century.[2] Chief among them were Zuzhou, a walled ancestral prefecture, and Huangdu, literally, "emperor's walled city," enclosed in 918. Palace building did not commence until the year of Abaoji's death. The name by which the first Khitan city with a palace is usually known, Shangjing (Supreme Capital), was assigned in 938. Another nine years would pass before Liao succession was uncontested.

Shangjing was divided into two parts: Huangcheng and Hancheng. The palace area was roughly in the center of Huangcheng, or "imperial city."[3] Adjacent to Huangcheng's south was Hancheng, a smaller walled area for the Chinese, or Han,

fig. 13

fig. 14

population. Although much of Huangcheng was destroyed in 1120 by armies of the non-Chinese Jurchen, who had formed the Jin dynasty (1115–1234) in today's Heilongjiang Province and neighboring regions, segments of walls, north (fig. 13) and south pagodas, and Buddhist statuary dating from the Liao dynasty can be found in the area today. In 919, Abaoji designated a second capital, in the east, in territory that would officially be in the hands of the non-Chinese Bohai (Parhae) until the collapse of their empire in 926. The Eastern Capital also consisted of two separate walled areas; the northern area was known as Bencheng, or "native city," and the southern, again designated for its Chinese population, as Hancheng. The Eastern Capital region, which is today Liaoyang, had been a Han (206 BC–AD 220) military outpost, and after the fall of the Liao became the Eastern Capital of the Jin dynasty. It was a focus of construction by the Manchu Qing dynasty (1644–1911), whose capital from 1625 to 1644 was at Shenyang, seventy kilometers to the north.

The last year of the reign of the second Liao emperor, Deguang (Taizong, r. 927–47), coincided with the establishment of the Southern Capital, today Beijing. There, too, a masonry pagoda remains from the Liao dynasty; the city from then on would have a continuous history as a capital of both Chinese and non-Chinese dynasties.[4] The locations of nine districts, or wards (*lifang*), in the Southern Capital have been identified, and wall segments and artifacts can be seen today in the City Wall Museum in Beijing. The designation of a Central Capital (Zhongjing), in what is today Ningcheng County, near Inner Mongolia's border with Liaoning, occurred in 1007, during the reign of the sixth Liao emperor, Shengzong (r. 982–1031). Its mammoth white pagoda, repaired in Jin and Manchu times, is the tallest extant Liao structure, standing eighty meters from base to roof (fig. 14). The last Liao capital, the Western Capital, at what is today Datong, was established in 1044, during the reign of the eighth Liao ruler, Daozong (r. 1055–1101). Its most famous architecture—three Buddhist halls and a pavilion—is wooden.[5]

The monumentality evident in figures 13 and 14 was only one achievement of Liao builders; another was the intricate manipulation of wood. Small-scale wood carpentry, or *xiaomuzuo*, manifests itself in complex ceilings, cabinetry, bracket sets, and other miniature wooden designs, as well as in brick or plaster imitations of wooden

fig. 15a

fig. 15b

fig. 15c

fig. 15d

fig. 15e

fig. 15f

fig. 15g

fig. 15h

fig. 15i

fig. 15j

fig. 15k

fig. 15l

fig. 15m

fig. 15n

fig. 15o

fig. 16

fig. 17

decorative features. The contrast between the overwhelmingly detailed interiors and the understated exteriors of the buildings that house them is as strong as the contrast between the powerful verticality of pagodas and the grasslands above which they tower, or between the lifestyle of the Khitan and the Chinese they conquered.

Ten Liao wooden buildings stand today; each has had at least minor restoration, and one has been rebuilt. Another five survived until the 1930s or 1940s (fig. 15). A few employ construction techniques prevalent in the tenth century, while others exhibit features believed to be exclusively Liao.

Liao buildings that maintain architectural features prevalent in China in the tenth century are represented by the earliest and latest wooden halls: Wenshu (Mañjushrī) Hall of Geyuan Monastery in Laishui, Hebei Province, dated 966, and the three halls of Kaiyuan Monastery in Yi County, Hebei Province, built in the first quarter of the twelfth century and now destroyed (figs. 15a, 15m, 15n, and 15o).[6] Each building is supported by four (or in one case six) exterior pillars in front and back, plus one or two additional columns on the sides. Three are devoid of interior columns. Humble structural forms such as these had been common in China in the decades between the collapse of the Tang dynasty (618–907) in 907 and establishment of the Song in 960, and shortly thereafter. This period of political chaos, when five contending dynasties and ten kingdoms vied for power in China and the Khitan and others formed a power base in the north, hardly allowed time or money for grand, large-scale construction projects. The timber frame of the hall at Geyuan Monastery (fig. 15a) is almost indistinguishable from the frame of a hall built in 963 in Shanxi by the Northern Han (951–79) and of one in Fujian erected in 964 by the Wu-Yue (907–78), just as each of these dynasties was on the verge of collapse to the Song.[7] The late Liao structures were also constructed in years of dynastic decline, when Jin troops had already sacked the Liao Central Capital. They, however, possessed a feature that had become characteristic of Liao architecture but was not present in the tenth-century halls: the unadorned exteriors of the Kaiyuan Monastery buildings (figs. 15m, 15n, 15o) offered no hint of their dramatic interiors, especially their elaborately carved ceilings (fig. 16). A similar contrast between the exterior and unanticipated interior is present in the Sutra Library of Huayan Monastery in the Western Capital (fig. 15g), constructed in 1038; its recessed sutra cabinets are the most outstanding example of Liao carpentry known (fig. 17).[8]

Three Liao wooden buildings are as dramatic on the outside as they are on the inside. They exemplify the Liao's most exclusive construction features. The Guanyin (Avalokiteshvara) Pavilion of Dule Monastery, built in 984 in Ji County, Hebei

Fig. 16. The ceiling of Pilu Hall, Kaiyuan Monastery; ca. early twelfth century (destroyed)

Fig. 17. Sutra cabinets in the Sutra Library, Huayan Monastery, Datong, Shanxi Province, 1038

Fig. 18. Interior of Guanyin Pavilion, Dule Monastery, Ji County, Hebei Province, 984

Fig. 19. Sectional drawing of the Timber Pagoda, Fogong Monastery, Ying County, Shanxi Province, 1056

fig. 18

fig. 19

Province, is a massive structure with twenty-four varieties of enormous bracket sets (fig. 15b), but the two-story exterior with its clusters of wooden components—the third level is visible only from the inside—is no preparation for the open interior that houses a 16-meter-high statue of the bodhisattva Guanyin (fig. 18). Nor would one anticipate that when the upper-story central lattice doors are open, the eyes of the deity are focused, in protectorate fashion, on a white reliquary pagoda 380 meters to the south.[9]

Bold, massive structure, ingenuity of design, and layer upon layer of symbolism are interwoven in two other awe-inspiring Liao wooden buildings. The earlier, the main hall of Fengguo Monastery in Yi County, Liaoning Province, built in 1019 and measuring 55.8 meters by 25.91 meters, contains seven oversize Buddhas, which are perhaps the seven historical Buddhas, perhaps representatives of the six Liao rulers up to that time plus the father of the dynastic founder, or perhaps symbols of both groups (fig. 15d).[10]

Neither the Guanyin Pavilion nor the Fengguo Monastery hall is preparation for the greatest achievement in Liao wooden construction, the Timber Pagoda built in Ying County in 1056 (fig. 15j). The Timber Pagoda may be the most perfected example of a Chinese timber-frame structure ever conceived (fig. 19).[11] It had five stories, four mezzanine levels, six tiers of roof eaves, and fifty-four types of bracket sets. There were individual iconographic schema on each level, and no doubt a composite one throughout the building. Associations with the recently deceased ruler and his father's primary wife (but not the ruler's birth mother) were likely, as were associations with predictions of impending *mofa* (termination of the *dharma*, or Buddhist law). A treasure trove of scriptures and other relics were buried underneath or encapsulated in its images.

Even if they were not unique, the Guanyin Pavilion, the Great Buddha Hall of Fengguo Monastery, and the Timber Pagoda (figs. 15c, 15d, 15i, 19) were probably recognized as spectacular in their day. Certainly each dominated the monastery in which it stood, for Liao temple complexes were fairly compact. All three were in keeping with one of the standard features of Liao monastery layouts, which was to situate a tall building (a pavilion, pagoda, or other towering structure) behind the front gate so that it was on the main axis with the primary image hall and/or the hall for teaching Buddhist law. Sometimes a pair of pavilions was positioned on either side of the main axis, behind the tall building. Like earlier

fig. 20

fig. 21

Chinese monasteries, the Liao temple complexes were enclosed by covered arcades to which the front gate and side pavilions were joined. The monasteries in the Western Capital at Datong followed another type of Liao temple layout; instead of a dominant multistory structure, they had more than one single-story Buddhist hall on the main axis. These monasteries also had a pair of side halls, such as the pavilions at Shanhua Monastery (fig. 15j). Still, no monastery in the Western Capital had more than three significant image halls.[12] Neither physical nor textual evidence suggests that Liao monasteries were constructed on the scale of the greatest monasteries of the Tang dynasty, which were said to have had as many as three thousand or even four thousand rooms.[13]

The achievements of the Liao in constructing buildings of wood are echoed in their masonry architecture and their underground tombs. The shape of the footprints of Liao pagodas ranged from square to octagonal, with octagonal the most common. Extant pagodas dating from Tang China are primarily four-sided; however, the octagonal pagoda came into fashion throughout China during the tenth century and thus cannot be considered an innovation of Liao builders.[14] Both square and octagonal masonry pagodas built by the Liao are believed to follow the same forms and contain on its shafts the same kinds of iconography as those found in and on the wooden pagodas of the Supreme Capital and the Central Capital. It was common for a tall shaft that rose above a multilevel podium and had thirteen sets of roof eaves to be decorated with deities and pagodas (figs. 13, 14). An alternate style of Liao octagonal masonry pagoda had stories of diminishing size from base to roof. Examples of this type are the White Pagoda (figs. 59, 60) in Balin Right Banner, built in 1049, and the Thousand Buddhas Avatamsaka Sutra Pagoda in Hohhot, which has undergone numerous repairs since Liao times.[15] Whatever their shape, even Liao pagodas that today are unique or are considered of hybrid or heterodox form, such as the North Pagoda of Yunju Monastery in Fangshan, Hebei Province, had replication of architectural components, especially bracket sets, on their exteriors.[16] Bracket sets that radiate at thirty, sixty, and/or ninety degrees from the wall surface, a type often

Fig. 20. Detail of a relief sculpture on the southwest side of the White Pagoda in Balin Right Banner, Inner Mongolia, showing fan-shaped bracketing

Fig. 21. Detail of the north wall of the back chamber of the tomb of Zhang Kuangzheng, Xuanhua, Hebei Province, 1093

Fig. 22. Sarcophagus excavated from
Tomb Number 3 in Daiqintala Township,
Keyou Central Banner

fig. 22

known as fan-shaped, survive in wooden Liao architecture at Datong, in later Jin
architecture, in masonry pagodas (fig. 20), and on the walls of tombs.

Hundreds of Liao tombs have been opened, and presumably hundreds more
await excavation. A few structural features can be considered characteristic of Liao
funerary architecture. Liao tombs, into which one descends by ramps, have
between one and three main chambers, and as many as nine compartments when
side niches and antechambers are included in the count. Octagonal chambers are
common, no matter the size of the tomb or the number of rooms it contains. The
prevalence of octagonal chambers in the tombs is probably related to the prevalence of octagonal pagodas above ground. Round and hexagonal rooms are also
widespread in Liao tombs, whereas four-sided chambers, the norm in Tang and
pre-Tang tomb architecture, are rarer.[17] The tomb of the Princess of Chen and her
husband (see cat. 1–8) had a circular main chamber and two smaller, circular side
niches. Tombs of Han Chinese at the cemetery in Xuanhua, Hebei Province,
included hexagonal, round, and occasionally four-sided rooms.[18] The walls and
ceilings of Liao tombs, whether they were intended for the burial of Han Chinese
or Khitan, replicate, in paint and relief sculpture, elements of Liao wooden architecture. The north wall of the main chamber of Zhang Kuangzheng's tomb in the
Xuanhua cemetery is a good example (fig. 21). At his tomb, at royal Khitan burial sites in Qingzhou, at the tomb of Yelü Yuzhi in Aluke'erqin Banner, at a cemetery in Kulun Banner where members of one of the two rulings clans, the consort
family Xiao, were buried, and at numerous other tomb sites in Inner Mongolia,
architectural detail painted and sculpted onto the tomb walls confirms the Liao
penchant for complex interior woodwork similar to that seen in the ceilings of the
Kaiyuan Monastery halls, the Guanyin Pavilion, the Timber Pagoda, and the Sutra
Library cabinets (figs. 16–19).

In addition to wooden elements detailed in paint and relief sculpture on tomb
walls and entry facades, sarcophagi in the shape of buildings provide further information about Liao architecture. Four Liao wooden sarcophagi are especially

fig. 23

informative. One was uncovered in Tomb Number 3 at Daiqintala Township, Keyou Central Banner, Xing'an League (see cat. 80) (fig. 22).[19] It has four pillars across the front and the back, and two additional pillars on each side, which support a hip-gable roof. A second, similar, sarcophagus was found in 1988 in Beipiao, Liaoning Province.[20] The overall structure of both sarcophagi is similar to that of the Liao halls at Geyuan and Kaiyuan monasteries (fig. 15a, 15f), so that burial in a temple-coffin is a possible interpretation of both finds. If this is correct, then burial in Daiqintala Township and Beipiao follows a history of sarcophagi fashioned after temples; one of the most famous Tang examples is the pair of sarcophagi from the tomb of Li Jingxun in the collection of the Shaanxi Provincial Museum, and the temple of Nanchan Monastery on Mt. Wutai.[21] Much earlier examples of coffins that take the shape of temples or other aboveground architecture can be found among tombs of non-Chinese such as Kudi Huiluo, Ning Mao, Song Shaozong, and Yu Hong, all of whom were buried in China in the fifth and sixth centuries.[22] Although many examples of sarcophagi shaped as temples have been found in tombs of non-Chinese, there is no evidence that house- or temple-shaped sarcophagi are a non-Chinese phenomenon. Like the wooden temple, the sarcophagus modeled after architecture could have been adopted from China and then adapted to accommodate rituals or practices of the Khitan and other non-Chinese peoples.

A third Liao sarcophagus, found in a tomb in Balin Right Banner and today in the collection of the Museum of Balin Right Banner, provides evidence of how one aspect of Khitan burial was accommodated into the wooden coffins. The Balin Right Banner sarcophagus has the same number of base-to-roof wooden supports and the same hip-gable roof as the sarcophagus found in Tomb Number 3 at Daiqintala Township, Keyou Central Banner (fig. 22). In addition, both sarcophagi have parallel roof rafters that extend either from the main roof ridge or the gable ridges to the bottom of the eaves, although the Balin Right Banner coffin has more rafters. Both have owl's tail decorations (*chiwei*) on either end of the main roof ridge and an ornament at the center of the main roof ridge.[23] Both were also positioned on platforms on which there were coffin beds that were concealed by the wooden structure. Thus it was possible to retain the Khitan practice of placing the corpse on a flat platform in the total privacy afforded by a roof and four walls.

The Khitan showed themselves to be one among many successful non-Chinese dynasties that selected from the Chinese system some of its most potent symbolism—the timber-frame hall and burial in a coffin—while retaining their own nativist traditions.[24] Numerous Khitan corpses have been found, both on funerary beds and in sarcophagi, encased in metal suits of the kind in which the Princess of Chen and her husband were buried. This is a practice particularly associated with the Khitan and is traceable to one of the earliest dated Khitan burial sites, a tomb excavated in Baoshan, Chifeng County, Inner Mongolia, that is believed to be that of a young male of royal descent.[25] In addition, some Khitan followed burial practices traceable to North Asian peoples of the first millennium BC: soft tissue was removed from the corpse and replaced with less perishable materials, and face masks were used.[26] No matter how a body was prepared for the afterlife or whether it was placed on a coffin bed or inside a sarcophagus, all was kept within the ultimate privacy of a tomb that from the outside could be identified only by a mound.[27]

The fourth wooden sarcophagus is one of the best examples of the implementation of Chinese-style construction in a Liao burial site. It was found in Tomb Number 7 in Yemaotai, Faku County, Liaoning Province. A temple-shaped wooden coffin is supported by four pillars across the front and the back and one additional pillar on each side, similar in arrangement to the pillars found in the Daiqintala Township and Balin Right Banner sarcophagi. Its hip-gable roof has nine clearly defined roof ridges (fig. 23), whereas four of the roof ridges of the Daiqintala Township and Balin Right Banner sarcophagi continue as parallel roof rafters in front and back.[28] The Yemaotai burial consisted of an inner sarcophagus made of stone, which the wooden coffin fully enclosed (with a floor, walls, and roof); the wooden outer coffin even had a balustrade surrounding its four sides. In addition, two silk paintings hung, each on an interior side wall, as perhaps they would have been hung in a house or a temple.[29] At Yemaotai Tomb Number 7, in other words, the burial choices seem to point directly and exclusively to Chinese tradition.

It is unlikely that many more Liao wooden halls or monumental pagodas will be found. It is possible that a stele, text, or relic deposit might be discovered that would reveal additional information about Liao wooden structures and their builders or patrons. Still, it is unlikely that our understanding of Liao timber-frame architecture will be significantly altered or that a new form of Liao hall or pagoda will emerge. It is certain, however, that more sarcophagi that imitate wooden buildings will be uncovered, and it is possible that sarcophagi already uncovered will be reattributed to the Liao period. Thus, it is possible that new or refined understandings of Liao burial customs, and the spaces in which Liao burials occurred, will be gained in future decades. Based on what we now know, we still can assess the role of the Liao in the context of architecture in China and in the areas near its northern and western borders, and we can make suggestions about Liao architecture as a distinct entity from architecture of the non-Chinese Jin dynasty, which followed the Liao.

The Liao was one of three coexistent empires on the eastern half of the Asian continent that erected monumental architecture from the mid-tenth century through the first quarter of the twelfth century. The other two were the Northern Song dynasty (960–1127) and the Xi Xia, or Tangut, state (1038–1227). The landscape of Song China and the areas of Liao territory that had once been part of the Tang empire offered visual reminders of the Tang building system. In eastern China during the tenth and eleventh centuries, monastery architecture retained the curved beams of the Tang; the broadly sloping roof eaves that are associated with southern Chinese architecture also may have been influenced by the Tang.[30] Still, differences between the monastery halls of Song China and the Liao are apparent. Song architecture was usually built for cities and towns. Even though Song buildings were constructed in the countryside, they were not designed for grassland environments. Monastery halls in the Northern Song capital Bianliang (today Kaifeng), whose population exceeded one million, or in religious complexes under imperial Song patronage, such as Longxing Monastery in Hebei Province or the Jin shrines in Shanxi, had bracket sets that were smaller and had fewer varieties of design than those at the Guanyin Pavilion, Timber Pagoda, or Fengguo Monastery hall. Some Song pavilions have interiors that are largely open floor to ceiling, similar to the Guanyin Pavilion, to house a tall Buddhist image, but usually a few wooden columns or other supports have been employed to ensure the structure's stability. The Song often built octagonal masonry pagodas, and their surfaces contained a replication of architectural details; but so far, the iconographical complexity of the exterior images on a pagoda such as the White Pagoda in the Liao Central Capital or of the five levels of interior imagery on the Timber Pagoda has not been observed on either the outside or the inside of a Song pagoda.[31] While none of the timber pagodas constructed during the Song era have survived, perhaps the Liao Timber Pagoda's survival through more than ten earthquakes is due to the remarkable elasticity of its wooden frame and the ingenuity of its builders. The Xi Xia, who entered the imperial arena a full century after the Khitan, left no legacy of wooden architecture, but they constructed imperial necropolises as impressive as those of the Liao and the Song. Also, like the Song and the Liao, the Xi Xia built octagonal masonry pagodas and pagodas with circular footprints. Some Xi Xia pagodas have carvings of architecture in relief on their exteriors, but so far, no Buddhist images of the quality or complexity found on Liao pagodas have been found.[32]

Even if the Song and the Liao went their different ways in defining monumental building traditions, neither could have erected enduring architecture without having seen and understood the Tang building system. What accounts for their divergence, particularly the extraordinary ability of the Liao to manipulate pieces of wood to construct such buildings as the Timber Pagoda or Guanyin Pavilion? When the Khitan established a confederation in the ninth century, there were two building systems in their territory. One belonged to the Bohai, who ruled from five capitals in today's Liaoning, Jilin, and Heilongjiang provinces and northern Korea between 698 and 926. No wooden buildings survive from this kingdom, which straddled Tang China and Korea under United Silla (668–936). Extant Bohai stone pagodas follow a tradition that was inherited from both the United Silla kingdom in Korea and the Tang, and Bohai cities and some tombs also have been shown to follow patterns of the Tang and of the earlier Korean kingdoms.[33] Bohai buildings and tombs should have been known to the Khitan, but there is no reason to suggest that monuments scattered through former Bohai territory on the fringe of the Liao empire were a more tantalizing inspiration for Liao architecture than the Tang architecture from which the Bohai themselves, in all likelihood, learned to build enduring structures. The architecture of the Goguryeo kingdom (37 BC–AD 668), which was centered in today's Jilin Province and northern Korea before the rise of Bohai, and which was

| *Nancy Shatzman Steinhardt*

itself an influence on Bohai construction, is a second possible North Asian source of monumental architecture for the Liao. Particularly intriguing are the intricate ceilings found in a majority of the approximately one hundred painted tombs dating from the fourth to the seventh century that survive from the Goguryeo kingdom: they are the closest surviving examples in East Asia of possible precedents for the ceilings in the Guanyin Pavilion, the Timber Pagoda, and the no-longer-extant wooden buildings at Kaiyuan Monastery. But the possible relationship is visual and perhaps geographic: there is no record that a Khitan entered a Goguryeo tomb. Such ceilings may have existed in the wooden temples of Northeast Asia under Korean rule and the Khitan may have seen them, but the evidence to prove this has not yet been found. The most logical theory about the origins of Liao architecture is that, like the Song, Liao patrons observed Tang structures and employed builders who understood how they were constructed. Yet as patrons who aspired to grandeur, especially in locations not congested by urban life, the Liao sought monuments that soared to the heavens or impressed the viewer by the breathtaking intricacy of the woodwork in their interiors.

Easier to ascertain is the legacy of the Liao for later architecture, particularly in the region formerly known as Manchuria. The Liao Eastern, Western, Central, and Southern capitals were overrun by Jin conquerors in the second and third decades of the twelfth century. The major monasteries in all four capitals became Jin religious centers. The Jin were thus totally familiar with Liao buildings and structural forms. They took the open interior to greater extremes than their Liao predecessors, sometimes eliminating all but two or four interior pillars in large wooden halls. The Jin built smaller tombs than the Liao, often with only one main chamber and sometimes with one or more niches, but the painted and sculpted decoration in imitation of woodwork was more elaborate, sometimes covering every interior surface. Yet if the Jin built pavilions to house sixteen-meter statues or a wooden pagoda that towered over sixty meters high, they have not survived. Nor do sarcophagi that imitated wooden temples but concealed native burial practices. The Jin, at best, perpetuated an architectural system they inherited, but did not innovate.[34] Although renovated, restored, or refaced by the Jin and again by the Manchus, the White Pagoda and other buildings taken over by the Jin are justly considered Liao creations (fig. 14).

Liao architecture is ingenious, bold, powerful, decisive, and laden with symbols and potency. Above ground and beneath, in wood and in brick, of mammoth proportions and in miniature, even today Liao buildings are the only structures that break the continuity of the Mongolian grasslands or much of the North China plain. The tallest wooden building in China is Liao. So are scores of octagonal pagodas and more than ten times that number of octagonal burial chambers. Until the rise of the Manchus in the seventeenth century, the only premodern building system of permanent materials that successfully penetrated the Mongolian plain was that of the Liao.

1. The Tuoba-Wei is a famous earlier example of a non-Chinese dynasty that employed Chinese monumental architecture in the formation of its empire. The process began at the city of Shengle, which was used as a capital beginning about 258, and was followed by the establishment of the capital at Pingcheng, today Datong, in 398, followed by Luoyang in 493. The process of sinification of Buddhist cave architecture at Yungang and Longmen, located near the two later capitals, is well known. On the Northern Wei use of Chinese ritual architecture in empire formation, see Victor Cunrui Xiong, "Ritual Architecture under the Northern Wei," in Wu Hung (ed.), *Between Han and Tang: Visual and Material Culture in a Transformative Period*, pp. 31–95. Less studied but equally impressive was the construction of Chinese-style urban architecture by the initial rulers of each of the Sixteen Kingdoms (304–439); among them, Shi Le's building programs at Pingyang, Xiangguo, and Yecheng in the fourth century are the best known. The Liao use of monumental architecture in empire formation is a theme in Nancy S. Steinhardt, *Liao Architecture*.

2. *Liaoshi* [History of the Liao], juan 1:2–13, 215–24.

3. On the Liao Supreme Capital, see *Liao Shangjing yizhi jianjie* [Brief introduction to the remains of the Liao Supreme Capital], and for a more recent study, see Zhang Yu, "Liao Shangjing chengzhi kancha suoyi" [Notes on the excavation of remains of the city of Liao Shangjing], in Wei Jian, ed., *Neimenggu wenwu kaogu wenji*, vol. 2, pp. 525–30. For a general discussion of Liao capitals, see Nancy S. Steinhardt, *Chinese Imperial City Planning*, pp. 123–28, with additional bibliography in notes for those pages.

4. The pagoda is at Tianning Monastery. The most comprehensive study of Liao pagodas is still Sekino Tadashi and Takeshima Takuichi, *Ryō-Kin jidai no kenchiku to sono Butsuzō* [Liao-Jin architecture and its Buddhist sculpture], 2 vols (plates only); Takeshima's accompanying text was published under the same title by Ryū bun shokyoku in Tokyo in 1944.

5. I include the Sutra Library and Great Buddha Hall of Huayan Monastery and the Great Buddha Hall of Shanhua Monastery in the group of three, even though the Great Buddha Hall of Huayan Monastery is a Liao-Jin, or eleventh- to twelfth-century, structure.

6. On Mañjuśrī Hall, see Feng Bingqi and Jia Tian, "Xin faxian de Liaodai jianzhu—Laiyuan Geyuansi Wenshudian" [A newly discovered Liao building— Mañjuśrī Hall of Geyuan Monastery in Laiyuan], *Wenwu* 1960.8/9, pp. 66–67, and Mo Zongjiang, "Laiyuan Geyuansi Wenshudian" [Mañjuśrī Hall of Geyuan Monastery in Laiyuan], *Jianzhushi lunwen ji* 1979.2, pp. 51–71. On Kaiyuansi's architecture, see Liu Dunzhen, "Hebeisheng xibu gujianzhu diaocha jilüe" [Notes on the investigation of ancient architecture in western Hebei Province], *Zhongguo yingzao xueshe huikan* 5, no. 4 (1935), pp. 9–15.

7. On this subject, see Nancy S. Steinhardt, "Chinese Architecture, 963–66," *Orientations*, February 1995, pp. 46–52.

8. On the architecture of Huayan Monastery, see Liang Sicheng and Liu Dunzhen, "Datong gujianzhu diaocha baogao" [Report on the investigation of ancient architecture in Datong], *Zhongguo yingzao xueshe huikan* 4, nos. 3 and 4 (1934), pp. 7–76; Ding Mingyi, *Huayansi* [Huayan Monastery]; and Yuan Hairui and Tang Yunjun, "Huayansi" [Huayan Monastery], *Wenwu* 1982.9, pp. 78–91. Only the article by Liang and Liu includes discussion of Haihui Hall (fig. 15h), now destroyed.

9. On Dule Monastery, see Liang Sicheng, "Jixian Dulesi Guanyinge, Shanmen kao" [Research on Guanyin Pavilion and the gatehouse at Dule Monastery, Ji County], *Zhongguo yingzao xueshe huikan* 3, no. 2 (1932),

pp. 1–92, and Steinhardt, *Liao Architecture*, p. 410, n. 6. On the White Pagoda of Guanyin Monastery, see Liang Sicheng, "Jixian Guanyinsi Baita ji" [Notes on the White Pagoda of Guanyin Monastery, Ji County], *Zhongguo yingzao xueshe huikan* 3, no. 2 (1932), pp. 93–99, and Su Bai, "Dulesi Guanyinge yu Jizhou Yutian Hanjia [Guanyin Pavilion of Dule Monastery and the Han family of Yutian, Ji Prefecture], *Wenwu* 1985.7, pp. 32–48. Excavation beneath the White Pagoda in the aftermath of an earthquake revealed both its Liao structure and reliquaries inside. On this subject, see "Tianjin Jixian Dulesi ta" [The pagoda of Dule Monastery in Ji County, Tianjin], *Kaogu xuebao* 1989.1, pp. 83–119.

10. On Fengguo Monastery, see Sekino Tadashi, "Manshū Giken Hōkokuji Daiyūhōden" [Daxiongbao Hall of Fengguo Monastery in Yi County, Manchuria], *Bijutsu kenkyū* 1933.14, pp. 37–49; Du Xianzhou, "Yixian Fengguosi Daxiongdian diaocha baogao" [Report on the investigation of Daxiongbao Hall of Fengguo Monastery in Yi County], *Wenwu* 1961.2, pp. 5–13; and Shao Fuyu, "Fengguosi" [Fengguo Monastery], *Wenwu* 1980.12, pp. 86–87.

11. The major study of the Timber Pagoda is Chen Mingda, *Yingxian muta* [Ying County Timber Pagoda]. On aspects of architecture, symbolism, and history discussed here, see Steinhardt, *Liao Architecture*, pp. 102–21; and on the reliquaries of the pagoda, see Shanxi Cultural Relics Bureau and Chinese History Museum, *Yingxian Muta Liaodai mizang* [Liao esoteric relics in the Timber Pagoda].

12. On the architecture of the other Liao monasteries, Guangjisi and Kaishansi (figs. 15e, 15f), see Liang Sicheng, "Baodixian Guangjisi Sandashidian" [Hall of the Three Great Buddhas at Guangji Monastery, Baodi County], *Zhongguo yingzao xueshe huikan* 3, no. 4 (1932), pp. 1–50, and Qi Yingtao, "Hebeisheng Xinchengxian Kaishansi Dadian" [The main hall of Kaishan Monastery in Xincheng County, Hebei Province], *Wenwu cankao ziliao* 1957.1, pp. 23–29.

13. The largest Tang monasteries were in the capital cities, Chang'an and Luoyang. The monasteries of Chang'an are described by Song Minqiu in *Chang'an zhi* [Record of Chang'an], dated 1075.

14. Famous examples of tenth-century octagonal pagodas are the Jingzang Chan Master Pagoda at Huishan Monastery in Dengfeng, Henan Province; the pagoda at Tianning Monastery in Anyang, Henan Province; the Longhua Pagoda in Shanghai; the pagoda at Yunyan Monastery on Tiger Hill and the twin Luohan Pagodas, all three in Suzhou; and one of the twin pagodas at Guangjiao Monastery in Xuancheng, Anhui Province.

15. For illustrations of the White Pagoda in Balin Right Banner, see Sekino and Takeshima, *Ryū-Kin jidai*, vol. 2, pls. 8–21. The pagoda in Hohhot is not illustrated in Sekino and Takeshima's work. For illustrations, see Zhang Yuhuan and Luo Zhewen, *Zhongguo guta jingcui* [The cream of Chinese pagodas], p. 58.

16. For illustrations of the Yunju Monastery pagoda, see Sekino and Takeshima, *Ryū-Kin jidai*, vol. 2, pls. 105, 106.

17. Sometimes it is hard to determine if a chamber was intended to be circular or octagonal. For a study of plans of Liao tombs in Inner Mongolia, see Xiang Chunsong, "Zhaomeng diqu de Liaodai muzang" [Liao tombs in Zhaomeng], *Neimenggu wenwu kaogu* 1981.1, pp. 73–79; for tombs whose chambers may have been circular or octagonal, see fig. 2, nos. 22, 23. Among nine tombs excavated in the cemetery in Xuanhua County, Hebei Province, discussed below, one had four-sided rooms and the others had rooms of circular, octagonal, and hexagonal shape. For illustrations of those plans, see *Xuanhua Liaomu* [Liao tombs in Xuanhua], vol. 1, p. 5.

18. In spite of the lack of octagonal rooms in these two cemeteries, from which objects in the exhibition are taken, octagonal rooms dominate Liao burial sites. For a discussion of Liao tombs, with illustrations of octagonal burial chambers, see Li Yiyou, "Lielun Liaodai Qidan yu Hanren muzang de tezheng he fenxi" [Special features and analysis of Khitan versus Han Chinese tombs in the Liao dynasty], in *Zhongguo kaogu xuehui diliuci nianhui lunwen ji*, pp. 187–95; Li Yihou, "Liaodai Qidanren muzang zhidu gaishuo" [Introductory remarks on the burial system of the Khitan in the Liao period], in *Neimenggu Dongbuqu kaoguxue wenhua yanjiu wenji*, pp. 80–102; and Xiang Chunsong, "Zhaomeng diqu de Liaodai muzang," [Liao tombs in Zhaomeng], *Neimenggu wenwu kaogu* 1981.1, pp. 73–79.

19. On the sarcophagus excavated in Daiqintala Township, Keyou Central Banner, see Zhou Hanxin and Ha Si, "Keyouzhongqi chutu Liaodai muguoshi ji shichuang qianxi" [Brief analysis of the Liao wooden outer coffin and coffin-bed excavated at Keyou Central Banner], *Neimenggu wenwu kaogu wenji* 1997.2, pp. 567–79.

20. On the Beipiao tomb and sarcophagus, see Zhang Hongbo and Li Zhi, "Beipiao Quanjuyong Liaomufaxian jianbao" [Excavation of a Liao tomb in Quanjuyong, Beipiao], *Liaohai wenwu xuekan* 1990.2, pp. 24–28. For an illustration, also see Steinhardt, *Liao Architecture*, p. 331.

21. Elinor Pearlstein published the pair in "Pictorial Stones from Chinese Tombs," *Bulletin of the Cleveland Museum of Art* 71, no. 9 (1984), pp. 304–31, figs. 16, 20. The example from the tomb of Li Jingxun is one of many stone sarcophagi of Tang royalty fashioned like Chinese buildings that can be seen in the Shaanxi Provincial Museum.

22. Each of these coffins is discussed in an unpublished paper by Wu Hung, "House-shaped Sarcophagi," presented at the conference "Between Han and Tang: Visual and Material Culture in a Transformative Period," University of Chicago, October 2001.

23. For an illustration of the sarcophagus from Balin Right Banner, see *Qidan wangchao* [Qidan dynasty], p. 20.

24. The Mongols were masters of borrowing from the Chinese while maintaining their own traditions. Mongolian princes-of-the-blood slept in tents and hung animal skins on the interior walls of more permanent buildings, which had Chinese roofs; both the tents and the buildings were concealed behind the walls of a palace-city, which was further enclosed by the walls of the capital. On these practices, see Paul Ratchnevsky, "Über den mongolischen Kult am Hofe der Grosskhane in China" [On the Mongolian "ritual" at the court of the great khans in China] in Louis Ligeti (ed.), *Mongolian Studies*, pp. 417–43.

25. Baoshan Tomb Number 1 and Tomb Number 2 were excavated in 1994. A painting in Tomb Number 1 has the date 923. Not only were pieces of metal wire suits found, one tomb contained a sarcophagus in the shape of a building. For the report, see Ji Shaoguang et al., "Nei Menggu Chifeng Baoshan Liaomu bihuamu fajue jianbao" [Excavation report on Liao tombs with murals in Baoshan, Chifeng, Inner Mongolia], *Wenwu* 1998.1, pp. 73–95.

26. This practice of the Scythians was so well known that it was described by Herodotus. On its use by both peoples of the North Asian steppe and the Khitan, see Nancy S. Steinhardt, "Liao Archaeology: New Frontiers on China's Frontier," *Asian Perspectives* 37, no. 2 (1998), pp. 224–44.

27. The most famous examples of burial in metal wire suits are the corpses of the Princess of Chen and her husband, Xiao Shaoju, many of whose tomb treas-

ures are in the exhibition. The second Liao ruler, Deguang, and an unidentified female buried in Tomb Number 6 at Haoqianying, Chayouqianqi, Inner Mongolia, also were interred this way.

28. On the structure of the sarcophagus, see Cao Xun, "Yemaotai Liaomuzhong de guanchuang xiaozhang" [The small-scale "container" and coffin-bed in a Liao tomb at Yemaotai], *Wenwu* 1975.12, pp. 49–62. The study convincingly argues that the sarcophagus follows stipulations for a small-scale structure with nine roof ridges described in the twelfth-century Song architectural manual *Yingzao fashi*.

29. The two silk paintings from the tomb are among the most certifiably dated tenth-to-eleventh century Chinese paintings known. For illustrations, see the color plates in *Wenwu* 1975.12.

30. Of the four extant Tang wooden buildings, the beams of the East Hall of Foguang Monastery, dated 847, curve most sharply and the roof eaves slope most broadly. Both features appear in extant buildings of the 960s—in the Ten Thousand Buddhas Hall of Zhenguo Monastery in Haodong, Shanxi Province, dated 963, and in the Buddha Hall of Hualin Monastery in Fuzhou, Fujian Province, dated 964. The curved beams and broadly sloping roof eaves remained a feature of architecture in South China in the following century, under Northern Song rule. Buildings with such beams and eaves include the main halls of Xuanmiao Daoist Monastery in Putian, Fujian Province, dated 1013, and of Baoguo Monastery in Yuyao, Zhejiang Province, dated 1016.

31. Besides the White Pagodas of the Supreme Capital and the Central Capital (figs. 13, 14) and the Ten Thousand Buddhas Avatamsaka Sutra Pagoda in Hohhot, other examples of Liao octagonal masonry pagodas with Buddhist images on the faces of their shafts survive in Jinzhou and Chaoyang, Liaoning Province. None of the Five Dynasties or Song pagodas listed in note 14 has this kind of imagery.

32. For a major study of Xi Xia pagodas, see Lei Runze and Yu Cunhai, *Xi Xia Fota* [*Xi Xia Buddhist pagodas*]. For newer research, see *Baisigou Xi Xia fangta* [*The square Xi Xia pagoda in Baisigou*].

33. The Three Kingdoms of Korea were Silla, Baekje, and Goguryeo. They and other areas of what is Korea today were conquered and united under Silla rule in 668. On Bohai material culture, including architecture, see Johannes Reckel, *Bohai: Geschichte und Kultur eines mandschurisch-koreanischen Königreiches der Tang-Zeit* [*Bohai: History and culture of a Manchu-Korean dynasty of the Tang period*].

34. On Jin architecture, see Steinhardt, "A Jin Hall at Jingtusi: Architecture in Search of Identity," *Ars Orientalis* 33 (2003), pp. 76–119.

Archaeological Excavations of the Site
of the Liao City of Shangjing, 2001 to 2002

Ta La

The Liao city of Shangjing (Supreme Capital) was the very first capital to be established on the North China plain after the Khitan kingdom was founded. This important and special city was the political, economic, military, and cultural center of the Liao period.

Shangjing was located in the southern part of Lindong Town in Balin Left Banner, Chifeng City. It was in a basin encircled by mountains, with a river stretching to the southeast. To the northwest, the topography was higher than the city, while to the southeast it was lower (fig. 24). The city was founded in 918; it took more than twenty years to complete. The plan of the city was in the form of a 日 (the Chinese character for "sun"). Huangcheng, or "imperial city," was located in the north; it was shaped like an irregular hexagon and was 6,398.63 meters in circumference. Hancheng (Han, or Chinese, city) was in the south; it shared a city wall with Huangcheng and was square in shape and more than 5,800 meters in circumference (fig. 25). In 1120, when the Jin dynasty defeated the Liao, Shangjing's two centuries as a Liao capital came to an end. In 1138, Shangjing city was renamed the Beijing circuit. In 1150, the Beijing circuit became the Linhuang prefectural circuit, which in 1153 became the Dading prefectural circuit. After the Linhuang prefectural circuit was established as a governmental transfer post, the city thrived for almost another century. In 1234, the Jin dynasty fell and what had been the old city of Shangjing became the fiefdom of King Lu of the Quanning circuit of the Yuan dynasty. Sometime later, the city was deserted.

In 1961, the State Council designated the site of the Liao city of Shangjing an important historical and cultural relic under state protection. In 1962, a cultural relics study group from Inner Mongolia that had been doing research in Shangjing published a report entitled "Survey and excavation of the site of the Liao city of Shangjing."[1] In order to carry out the policy of "protection and usage of relics," as set forth by the National Cultural Relics Bureau and local government, and in order to study the Liao capital's layout, scale, and architecture—which we did not know much about, other than through the 1962 study—the Inner Mongolia Archaeological and Cultural Relics Research Institute, of which I am the director, organized a new group to do research on the Shangjing site from 2001 to 2002. We did mapping and drilling and excavated different areas. In 2001, excavation was conducted mainly in the southern part of Huangcheng, in the streets to the north and south of the palace. An exploratory, east-west trench ten meters by four meters was dug (trench serial number 01SJT1). In 2002, three locations for excavation were chosen. The first location was in Hancheng, near the Bayanguole River and opposite the Dashun Gate of Huangcheng, where four exploratory trenches, each five meters by five meters square, were dug (trench serial numbers 02SJT101–T104). The second location was in the southeastern part of Huangcheng, where two exploratory trenches, each ten meters by ten meters, were dug (trench serial numbers 02SJT201–T202). The third location was the southern wall of Huangcheng, which had been eroded by the Bayanguole River (trench serial number 02SJT203). The purpose of the excavations was to learn about the strata of Hancheng, the distribution of yurt relics in the southeastern part of

fig. 24

fig. 25

Huangcheng, and the structure of the Huangcheng city wall. At the second location, in the southeastern part of Huangcheng, the excavation was suspended when we found a platform structure made of tamped earth. At the other locations, the excavations were stopped when we reached the raw soil. The results of our excavations are summarized below.

	Soil color	Soil quality	Thickness of soil layer	Relics
1	yellow	relatively soft	4 cm–15 cm	none
2	gray	relatively hard	7 cm–42 cm	none
3	taupe	relatively hard	30 cm–75 cm	pottery, ironware, copper, coins, animal bones
4	grayish black	relatively soft	20 cm–45 cm	a few pieces of pottery
5	dark brown	relatively hard	15 cm–35 cm	a few ceramic shards and animal bones
6	tawny	relatively hard, compact	14 cm–55 cm	mainly pottery, a few animal bones
7	grayish black	relatively soft	20 cm–50 cm	lots of animal bones, a few ceramic shards
8	taupe	relatively hard	15 cm–40 cm	pottery, a few ceramic shards, animal bones, ironware
9	tawny	relatively hard, compact	12 cm–30 cm	not many relics; mostly ceramic shards, some animal bones and ironware
10	taupe	relatively hard	27 cm–44 cm	not many relics; mostly ceramic shards, some animal bones and ironware
11	gray	relatively soft	15 cm–40 cm	ceramic shards
12	grayish green	relatively soft	20 cm–38 cm	not many relics, a few incomplete pieces of tile

Chart 2. Strata of the Hancheng (the Chinese city) excavation site of Shangjing (the Liao Supreme Capital)

Hancheng

Taking the exploratory trench number 02SJT101 at the second location as an example, the excavations can be divided into twelve strata (see chart 2). Because the excavation area was limited, the findings were confined to the road surfaces, of which there were ten layers. From the remnants, it was determined that the road had been more than ten meters wide. Traces of tracks remained on some of the road surfaces, indicating that the road had been in use for a long time. From the position of the layers, we could see that layers one through five did not totally overlap. They were mainly located under stratum three and above stratum six. Layers six through eight, which were from an earlier period, were located under stratum seven and above stratum nine. Layer ten, the earliest of all, was located under stratum twelve, just above raw soil. Small buildings, as well as kitchens, holes for pillars, and trash pits, were found on both sides of the road. These were not constructed with great care, indicating the buildings were possibly used as workshops.

There were many relics, but few were complete and free from damage. There were mainly tile, pottery, and porcelain fragments, as well as animal bones and some copper coins and ironware.

Most of the pottery was muddy gray, although some was muddy brown. Since it was fired at relatively high temperatures, it was quite hard. Many pieces were undecorated, but some had combed lines as decoration. Judging from the extant fragments, we could tell that the vessels had been basins, jars, vases, urns, plates, lids, piggy banks, and disks. There were also a small number of fragments of lead-glazed pots.

Chart 3. Strata of the Huangcheng (the imperial city) excavation site of Shangjing (the Liao Supreme Capital)

	Soil color	Soil quality	Thickness of soil layer	Relics
1	yellow	relatively soft	44 cm–106 cm	none
2	dark brown	relatively hard	80 cm–86 cm	a few ceramic shards
3	tawny	relatively soft	0.8 cm–85 cm	ceramic shards
4	dark tawny	relatively hard	13 cm–28 cm	ceramic shards, copper coins, ironwares
5	dark brown	relatively hard	16 cm–84 cm	a few relics
6	tawny and dark brown	relatively soft	60 cm–70 cm	a few relics
7	dark brown	relatively hard	58 cm–71 cm	a few ceramic shards and animal bones
8	dark tawny	relatively hard	28 cm–48 cm	a few ceramic shards and animal bones
9	taupe	relatively soft	4 cm–50 cm	a few comb-pattern ceramic shards

The high-fired ceramics were mainly white glazed wares. Many of these white wares have coarse bodies and a yellowish tone in the white glaze. There were also some black wares, white wares painted with black patterns, green wares, and brown wares. The types of these vessels found included bowls, plates, vases, jars, bottles, chess pieces, and toys.

It was clear that the hairpins, brush holders, and bone tubes found during the excavation were made from animal bones including the shank bones of cattle, horses, sheep, and camels.

Some of the copper coins found at the site bore the inscription *Kaiyuan tongbao* (currency of the Kaiyuan era), and some were from the Northern Song dynasty. The Northern Song-dynasty coins had inscriptions in standard script, grass script, running script, clerical script, and seal script.

Huangcheng

Taking the exploratory trench number 02SJT203 in the third location as an example, the excavation can be divided into nine strata (see chart 3). Because the exploratory trench was beside the city wall, no traces of construction were found.

At the second location—the two exploratory trenches 02SJT201 and T202, each ten meters by ten meters, in the southeastern part of Huangcheng—the excavation was suspended when we reached the platform structure made of tamped earth, so we found very few remains of buildings. We found only five small houses, which were roughly constructed of unbaked bricks, recycled bricks, pantile, and stones. Two square lime pits were found near the houses. The lime pits broke through the platform structure of tamped earth, which indicated that they were from a later era than the platform.

Below these remains, there was the platform structure made of tamped earth. Judging from the straight sides of the platform, it was originally square or rectangular in shape, its sides more than 20 meters in length. The platform was made of alternating layers of loess and dark-brown clay; its surface was tamped smooth. Floor tile—gray pottery pieces—remained on some parts of it. On the northern side of the platform, there were many tamp marks, some 230 marks per square meter, while on the southern side there were only 40 to 90 tamp marks per square meter. The diameter of each tamp mark was 2.7 centimeters to 5.7 centimeters, and the depth of each mark was 1 centimeter to 2 centimeters.

There were even fewer intact objects from the Huangcheng site than from the Hancheng site. The objects from Huangcheng included bricks, flat tile, pantile, tile decorated with animal faces, dripstone, and foundation rocks. Pottery was also found, some of which had raised ridges or combed patterns, including hard, gray pottery and a few pieces of brown pottery. Types of vessels included basins, jars, urns, and lids. There were lead-glazed pottery pieces, which have pink clay bodies covered with cream-yellow or green glaze. Ceramics fired at high temperature were mainly white wares, although there were also black, brown, black-painted, green, yellow, and marble wares. The quality of these ceramics varied from coarse to smooth. Utensils included bowls, plates, jars, bottles, vases, boxes, chess pieces, and toys. They came from the Ding, Ru, Cizhou, Jun, Longquan, Jingdezhen, Yaozhou, and Gangwa kilns. There were a few coins; some of them were Northern Song, and others bore the inscription *Kaiyuan tongbao* (currency of the Kaiyuan era). There were also a few pieces of ironware and some animal bones. Marks on the surfaces of these animal bones show that they were once processed by human hands.

City Wall

Judging from a cross section of the city wall (trench serial number 02SJT203), it was composed of three parts: the main body, the protective slopes, and the *mamian*, or horse-face (a defensive projection attached to the wall).

The main body of the city wall is trapezoidal in shape. The wall was built of layers of tamped earth. Each of the layers was 20 centimeters to 24 centimeters thick. The tamp marks were round but irregular in shape, ranging from 3 centimeters to 8 centimeters in diameter and from 0.7 centimeters to 2 centimeters deep. There were approximately 270 tamp marks per square meter. The wall was constructed of alternating layers of loess and dark-brown clay. Inside the main body of the wall were remnants of wooden sticks that were used to support the wall. The remaining holes for the sticks measure 7 centimeters to 14 centimeters in diameter. Wood fragments were found in some of the holes. Many of the wooden sticks were stuck into the wall at an angle of ninety degrees to the horizontal layers of tamped earth. In the layers of tamped earth, pieces of pottery with combed decorations were found.

Protective slopes were built on the northern and southern sides of the main body of the wall to reinforce it. The slopes were constructed in two different stages. The bottom part, which was triangular in shape, was built first. Then earth was tamped to the top of the city wall. Each layer was 9 centimeters to 50 centimeters thick.

The *mamian* was located on the southern side of the city wall, pressing against the main body of the wall and the protective slopes; it was made of tamped earth, with each tamped layer 10 centimeters to 20 centimeters thick. A mixture of hay and mud was plastered to the places where the *mamian* joined the protective slopes. The plaster was 3 centimeters to 5 centimeters thick. Since the wall had been eroded by the river, the incomplete *mamian* retrieved from the site was only 2.66 meters to 3.88 meters wide.

Conclusion

To sum up, through these excavations, we found many layers of road surfaces, which indicate that the road was heavily used as a major connection to and from Huangcheng, passing through Dashun Gate. They also show the traffic conditions of Shangjing during different periods. The cultural relics discovered near the road reflect the development of small handicraft industries in Shangjing during different periods. Through the excavations, we discovered some aboveground structures at the southeastern corner of Huangcheng, which were previously unknown to scholars. The excavation of the city wall also led to a better understanding of the structure and the process of construction of the southern wall of Huangcheng—that is, the core of the city wall was tamped layer by layer with a protective slope on either side. Some of the excavated layers had clear ramming holes.

This excavation has supplied strong scientific support for further study of Shangjing. We plan to continue excavating in the western part of Huangcheng and in the northern part of Hancheng to learn more about the layout and practical history of Shangjing.

1. "Liao Shangjing chengzhi kancha baogao" [Survey and excavation of the site of the Liao city of Shangjing], in Li Yiyou and Wei Jian (eds.), *Neimenggu wenwu kaogu wenji* [*Essays on the archaeology of cultural relics in Inner Mongolia*], vol. 1, pp. 510–36.

A Liao-dynasty Tomb on Tuerji Hill

Ta La and Zhang Yaqiang

In March 2003, a group searching for mineral deposits found a tomb on Tuerji (or Tuiki) Hill, Tongliao City, Kezuo Rear Banner, Inner Mongolia. The Inner Mongolia Culture Department asked the Inner Mongolia Institute of Cultural Relics and Archaeology to do a spot reconnaissance and to organize a team of archaeologists to excavate the tomb.[1]

The Location and Structure of the Tomb

The Liao-dynasty tomb is located fifty kilometers to the east of Tongliao City. It is on the southeast slope of Tuerji Hill, one kilometer to the south of the administration village of the Tuerji Hill Honglingjin Reservoir. The reservoir is to the southwest of the tomb, and the Zhelimu League ore mine is to the northwest (fig. 26). The tomb is a stone structure, composed of a ramp, a gate, a paved path (*yongdao*) or corridor, a main chamber, and two small side chambers.

The ramp is forty-eight meters long. The stone walls along either side of the ramp are ten meters high and were designed to be collapse-proof. Near the tomb gate, the walls are plastered. Along the north wall and on the top of the tomb gate, there are ink paintings of fierce animals (fig. 27). There are also murals on the south wall; however, the south wall is badly damaged and many of the stones have fallen off, onto the ramp.

A stone slab sealed the gate of the tomb. The gate consists of a pair of wooden doors. On each door there are three rows of gilded-bronze studs, six studs to a row, as well as a number of wedges. There was also a lock, which was rusted.

A paved path (*yongdao*) leads from the gate to the tomb's main chamber, in which the sarcophagus was located. The main chamber is nearly square (length, 3.92 meters; width, 3.70 meters; height, 3.36 meters) and has a domed ceiling. There were once murals on the walls, but only a few remain. The dome is 1.78 meters in diameter. On it are painted a sun (fig. 28) and a moon (fig. 29). An *osmanthus* (sweet olive) tree

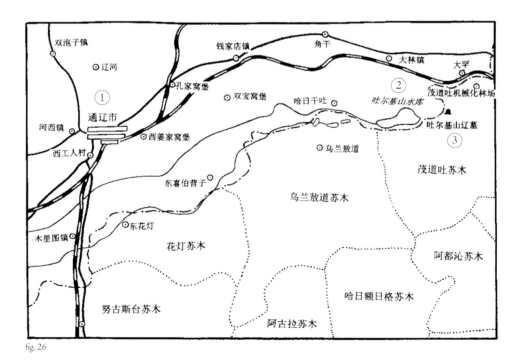

fig. 26

Fig. 26. Map of the area of the Tuerji Hill tomb site.
1. Tongliao City
2. Tuerji Hill Reservoir
3. Tuerji Hill Tomb

Fig. 27. Mural of the face of a fierce animal on one of the ramp walls of the Tuerji Hill tomb

Fig. 28. Sun on the dome of the main chamber of the Tuerji Hill tomb

Fig. 29. Moon on the dome of the main chamber of the Tuerji Hill tomb

Fig. 30. Painted wooden coffin and coffin-bed of the Tuerji Hill tomb

Fig. 31. Cranes painted on the wooden coffin of the Tuerji Hill tomb

Fig. 32. Phoenix painted on the wooden coffin of the Tuerji Hill tomb

fig. 27

fig. 30

fig. 28

fig. 29

fig. 31

fig. 32

and a rabbit are drawn in ink on the moon. A firebird is depicted in black inside the red sun. In the middle of dome is a round hole, in which there was once a bronze mirror. The mirror was found on the ground beneath the dome.

The small side-chambers, near the front of the main chamber, are rectangular in shape and have wooden doors. On each of the doors are three rows of gilded-bronze studs, three to a row.

The Sarcophagus

The sarcophagus includes a painted wooden outer coffin, an inner coffin, and a painted platform or coffin-bed.

The wooden outer coffin is 2.31 meters long, 1.3 meters wide, and 0.9 meters high. It is painted mainly in red and black and decorated with images of a crane, a phoenix, peonies, and auspicious clouds (figs. 30, 31, 32). Small gold bells are hung around the crane, the phoenix, and the leaves of the peonies. At the front of the coffin, there is a small door with a bronze lock, and a key in the lock. Two figures with *guduo* scepters in their hands stand facing each other on either side of the small door (fig. 33). They wear traditional Khitan costumes decorated with floral roundels and tied with silk belts. The floral roundels, the *guduo* scepters, and the boots the figures wear are decorated with gold. An arched bridge whose railing is decorated with flowers connects the small door in the front of the coffin to the floor of the chamber.

fig. 33

fig. 34

Fig. 33. Two figures with *guduo* scepters in their hands painted on the wooden coffin of the Tuerji Hill tomb

Fig. 34. Golden dragon roundel on the lid of the inner coffin of the Tuerji Hill tomb

On the lid of the inner coffin, there are three golden dragon roundels (fig. 34). On the sides of the lid, there are two pairs of flying phoenixes; one of them looks back at the other while in midflight (figs. 35, 36).

The painted platform or coffin-bed is wider at the top and the bottom and narrower in the middle. It is 2.56 meters long, 1.48 meters wide, and 1.07 meters high. The platform is made of eight layers. An openwork railing decorates the upper part of the platform, and six gilded-bronze lions are positioned on top of the railing, four in the front and two in the back. Below the railing are suspended two rows of bells decorated with pairs of painted phoenixes.

Fig. 35. Phoenix painted on the side of the lid of the inner coffin of the Tuerji Hill tomb

Fig. 36. Phoenix painted on the side of the lid of the inner coffin of the Tuerji Hill tomb

fig. 35

fig. 36

Funerary Goods

The work of sorting out the contents of the Tuerji Hill tomb is still in progress. So far, more than two hundred objects have been found there.

Objects made of bronze, silver, gold, lacquer (fig. 37), wood, glass (fig. 38), and silk, including equestrian gear, have been excavated from the main chamber. Inside the inner coffin, gilded-silver plaques with tassels, gold earrings, gold bracelets, gold finger rings, agate bracelets, round gilded-silver plates, gold ear scoops, agate necklaces, silk pouches, and bronze bells were among the items found.

The corpse was clothed in a thick hat, gloves, and eleven layers of garments. The outer layers of clothing were badly damaged, but the inner layers were in good

fig. 37

fig. 38

Fig. 37. Lacquer box with gold and silver inlay from the Tuerji Hill tomb

Fig. 38. Glass stemmed cup from the Tuerji Hill tomb

Fig. 39. Yellow silk skirt decorated with a pair of phoenixes, from the Tuerji Hill tomb

condition. Especially well preserved was the seventh layer, a beautiful yellow silk skirt in late-Tang-dynasty style, decorated with a pair of phoenixes (fig. 39).

Mercury was found in the corpse, in the bones and especially in the abdomen. The mercury was placed in glass containers and removed, and local archaeologists have begun testing it.

Bone Testing

Bone samples were sent to the Anthropology Research Center at the Jilin University Institute of Frontier Archaeology so that the physical traits and age of the deceased could be determined. The identification was done according to international conventions, and more than twenty measuring instruments were used, including a craniometer. The findings indicate that the corpse was that of a Mongolian female. She would have been from thirty to thirty-five years old at the time of her death, according to an examination of her pelvis, teeth, and vertebrae.

Conclusion

No epitaph was found in this tomb. The Khitan characters on one of the walls of the tomb were so damaged that they could not be deciphered; but the similarities between the gold and silver wares found in the tomb and those of the Tang dynasty suggest an early Liao date. For example, the shape of a gilded-silver lobed plate (fig. 40) found in the tomb is similar to that of one found in a Tang-dynasty hoard in Dingmaoqian, Jiangsu Province;[2] the only difference between the two is the ornamentation—a dragon-fish (*makara*) on the plate from the tomb and phoenixes on the Tang plate.

The square tomb chamber was prevalent during the Liao era. The tomb of the Prince of Wei, a son-in-law of the first Liao emperor, Abaoji—which is located in Dayingzi Village, in the Songshan District of Chifeng City, and is dated 959—is square.[3] Moreover, in the tomb at Tuerji Hill, there are murals depicting Khitan people in the main chamber and Khitan characters on one of the walls of the tomb ramp. It can therefore be concluded that this was the tomb of an aristocrat from the early Liao period.

A great quantity of precious cultural relics, including objects made of lacquer, wood, gold, silver, bronze, ceramics, glass, and silk were excavated from the Liao-period tomb on Tuerji Hill. Of special importance were the painted wooden coffin and coffin-bed, which are the first complete ones discovered in the Inner Mongolia Autonomous Region. Moreover, there were also many

fig. 39

Fig. 40. A gilded-silver lobed plate from the Tuerji Hill tomb

fig. 40

exquisitely patterned silk fabrics. The tomb is the most important find in Inner Mongolia since the discoveries of the tombs of the Princess of Chen and of Yelü Yuzhi and their spouses.

Postscript

For conservation reasons, archaeologists did not open the painted outer coffin in situ. Instead, the coffin was moved to the laboratory of the Inner Mongolia Institute of Cultural Relics and Archaeology for further study. That gave CCTV (China Central Television) an opportunity to produce a live broadcast of the opening of the coffin, which raised awareness of and interest in the excavation among the general public in China. Local television stations and other media have also done reports on the excavation. Thanks to the publicity, archaeology in Inner Mongolia has gained much attention and support from the general public. A complete report on the excavation is scheduled for publication in 2006.

1. "Neimenggu Tongliao shi Tuerji shan Liaodai muzang" [The Liao-period grave at Tuerji Hill, Tongliao City, Inner Mongolia], *Kaogu* 2004.7, pp. 50–53.

2. *Tangdai jinyin qi* [*Tang-dynasty gold and silver wares*], pl. 192.

3. "Chifengxian Dayingzi Liao mu fajue baogao" [Excavation report on the Liao-dynasty tomb at Dayingzi, Chifeng County], *Kaogu xuebao* 1956.3, pp. 1–26.

The Discovery of and Research on the Tomb of the Princess of Chen and Her Husband, Xiao Shaoju

Sun Jianhua

The tomb of the Princess of Chen and her husband, Xiao Shaoju, was one of the most important archaeological discoveries in China in the twentieth century. The tomb, which was found intact and contained an abundance of burial objects, was excavated by the Inner Mongolia Institute of Cultural Relics and Archaeology in 1986.

The Princess of Chen and Xiao Shaoju were buried together in a tomb that was located ten kilometers northeast of Qinglongshan Town, in Naiman Banner, Tongliao City, Inner Mongolia. The tomb was on the south side of a hill to the west of Sibugetu Village and was surrounded by hills. To the east of the tomb were the ruins of a Liao-dynasty building; bricks and tiles were strewn on the ground. Because there was a sacrificial site on the hill on which the tomb was located, people called it "Temple Hill." The slopes of Temple Hill embraced the east and west sides of the tomb and formed a natural, funnel-like barrier for the tomb. To the south of the tomb was a plain (fig. 41).

When a general investigation of cultural relics in Inner Mongolia was done in the early 1980s, several tombs dating from the Liao dynasty were found in the Qinglongshan area of Naiman Banner, and they were put under state protection. In 1985, the government of Qinglongshan Town planted fruit trees on the northwest slope of a hill near Sibugetu Village and constructed a reservoir at the foot of the hill. During the course of these activities, two additional Liao tombs were discovered, one of which was the tomb of the Princess of Chen and her husband. In 1986, the Inner Mongolia Institute of Cultural Relics and Archaeology began its excavation, which lasted from June to August. I was a member of the excavation team.

Due to the distribution of soil used in the construction of the reservoir, the area on top of the tomb had been flattened out, and bricks from the tomb had been uncovered. In order to find the tomb gallery, we built a small (1 meter by 3 meters) exploratory trench at the front of the tomb. Then, once we had found the gallery, we began to excavate, from the outside to the inside. Broken bricks and

fig. 41

Fig. 41. View of Temple Hill, the location of the tomb of the Princess of Chen and Xiao Shaoju, and the plain to the south

Fig. 42. Detail of a mural of grooms and horses facing the exit of the tomb of the Princess of Chen and Xiao Shaoju

Fig. 43. Detail of a mural of grooms and horses facing the exit of the tomb of the Princess of Chen and Xiao Shaoju

fig. 42

fig. 43

stones filled the gallery, and large stones filled the bottom of the tomb itself. The ramp (see fig. 46) was 6.7 meters long; it was on a slope, and there were sixteen steps from the top to the bottom. The walls on either side of the gallery were covered with plaster and painted with murals. Judging from the roughness of the surface of the plastered walls, the gallery was probably intentionally filled with broken bricks and stones soon after the murals were finished. On the east and west walls were murals of grooms and horses; they faced the exit, as if they were leaving the tomb (figs. 42, 43).

After we cleared the gallery, we found the tomb gate, which was plugged shut with narrow bricks (fig. 44). There was an oblong vertical air shaft in front of the gate. There were three layers of brick walls that were sealed with plaster; the walls were the same height as the tomb gate. The tomb gate was 4.42 meters high and was built to imitate wooden eaves. The face of the eaves was made of sculpted brick.

Fig. 44. Gate of the tomb of the Princess of Chen and Xiao Shaoju, plugged shut by narrow bricks, prior to excavation

Fig. 45. Painted peonies in the area above the gate of the tomb of the Princess of Chen and Xiao Shaoju

Fig. 46. Cross section showing the multichamber structure of the tomb of the Princess of Chen and Xiao Shaoju

Fig. 47. The interior of the tomb of the Princess of Chen and Xiao Shaoju. The structure includes a front chamber, a rear chamber, and, to the right and left, small side chambers

fig. 44

fig. 45

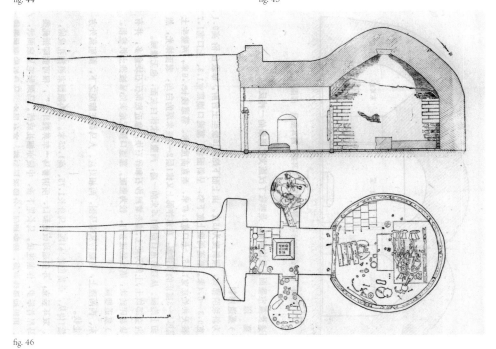

fig. 46

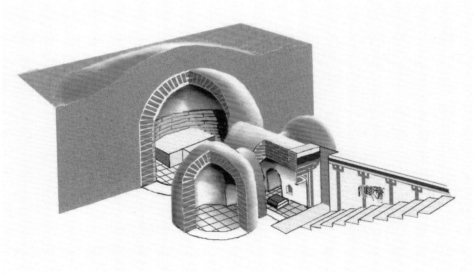

fig. 47

Fig. 48. Servants and flying cranes depicted on the mural on the east wall in the front chamber of the tomb of the Princess of Chen and Xiao Shaoju

Fig. 49. Flying cranes and guardians holding *guduo* staffs depicted on the mural on the west wall in the front chamber of the tomb of the Princess of Chen and Xiao Shaoju

fig. 48

fig. 49

The area above the gate was decorated with paintings of peonies (fig. 45). Although we took protective measures, the bricks sealing the gate were so firmly in place that when we opened the gate, the mural above it fell off. Inside the gate, there was a wooden door, which was already ruined.

Because the tomb door had been tightly sealed, there was no silt or debris inside. The tomb itself was a brick structure with many chambers, including a front chamber, a rear chamber, and, to the right and left, small side chambers (figs. 46, 47). The front chamber was oblong (length, 3.38 meters; width, 1.93 meters; height, 2.65 meters) and had a brick roof. On the east and west walls and the ceiling, there were murals: those on the east wall depicted servants; those on the west wall, guardians holding *guduo* staffs, both with flying cranes (figs. 48, 49); and those on the ceiling, the sun, the moon, and stars. The rear chamber, which was round and had a domed ceiling, was also decorated with paintings. It was where the coffin-bed

fig. 50

fig. 51

fig. 52

fig. 53

and table for offerings were placed. The round vaulted rear chamber reflected the shape of the yurts the Khitan lived in, while the decoration on top of the tomb gate reflected the architectural style of the Han Chinese. The structure of the tomb, therefore, reflected the cultural communication and integration between the Khitan and Han peoples. A large number of burial articles found in the tomb were made of extremely rare, valuable materials.

A stone tablet on which the tomb epitaph is engraved lay in the center of the front chamber (fig. 50). According to the epitaph and to the *Liaoshi* (History of the Liao), we know that the tomb was built in 1018, in the thirtieth year of the reign of the Liao emperor Shengzong (r. 982–1031). The Princess of Chen was the granddaughter of the Liao emperor Jingzong (r. 969–82) and the niece of the emperor Shengzong. Her father was Emperor Shengzong's younger brother Yelü Longqing. Her husband, Xiao Shaoju, was the elder brother of Shengzong's wife. When the princess died, she was only seventeen years old. Her husband died before her, but his age was not recorded. From his teeth, we estimate that he was around thirty years old when he died.

The small side chambers were domed, and the walls were covered with plaster. Each was 1.6 meters in diameter and 2.4 meters high. In the east chamber, there were

fig. 54

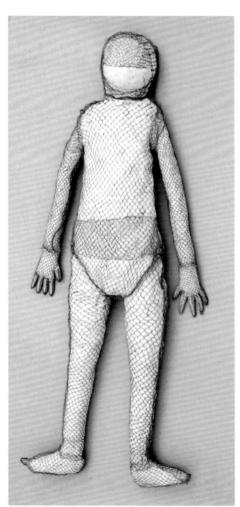

fig. 55

objects for daily life, including items made of silver, white porcelain, rock crystal, and agate (fig. 51). In the west chamber, there were two sets of equestrian gear made of silver with jade decoration, including stirrups, saddles, and halters (see cat. 12–16). These sets of equestrian gear were made for burial, although they were the same as actual gear for horseback riding (fig. 52). On the east wall of the tomb gallery, there was a mural of a yellow stallion outfitted with a whole set of such riding gear, which shows clearly how the equipment was used (fig. 53).

The rear chamber was 4.38 meters in diameter and 3.97 meters high. The brick walls were lined with cypress logs to the top of the tomb. The ceiling was badly damaged, and the wooden planks that once covered it had fallen. After we cleared away the fallen wood, we found burial articles, as well as two corpses lying side by side on the brick bed at the north end of the chamber. The corpses had rotted away, but the clothing and ornaments the deceased wore were still intact. The princess and her husband lay on a gold and silver pillow with floral decoration, dressed in silver-mesh burial suits (cat. 1), silver boots decorated with gilded phoenixes (cat. 4), gold face masks (cat. 2), and amber bead necklaces and plaques (cat. 37, 77). They also wore jewelry made of gold, silver, jade, pearl, and agate. From the burial suits, masks, and pendants they wore, we could determine which corpse was that of the princess and which that of her husband, Xiao Shaoju (figs. 54, 55).

The original structure of Xiao Shaoju's burial suit could not be determined because it had so seriously deteriorated. The princess's burial suit had only slightly deteriorated—its whole structure and the method of weaving were very clear—so it could be repaired (fig. 56). Why were the two burial suits in such different condition? We X-rayed both of them and used X-ray fluorescence spectrometry for quantitative analysis. We found a slight quantitative difference in the composition of the two suits. The princess's silver-mesh burial suit was 91.77 percent silver and 2.48 percent copper, whereas the prince's was 96.18 percent silver and 0.58 percent copper. The prince died first, in midlife. The princess died at a younger age; she was very thin and weak. Both the degree of corrosion of the corpse and the ratio of silver to copper affected the degree of deterioration of the silver mesh. The amber necklaces (cat. 37), the silver knife (cat. 43), and all kinds of jade decorations (cat. 38, 78) worn by the princess and her husband were strung on gold and silver wire. Although some of the

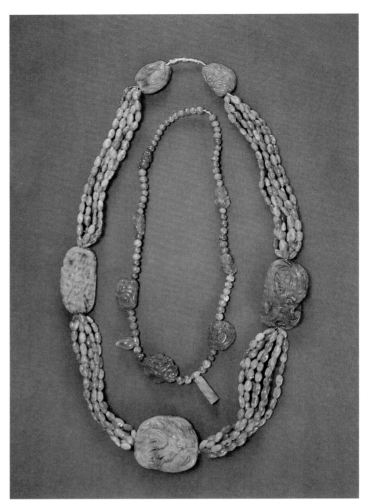

fig. 56

fig. 57

wire had ruptured, the original arrangement of the ornaments had not been disturbed. In order to restore these objects and preserve the silver-mesh burial suits, after we had finished drawing and photographing them, we used paper to cushion the bed on which the corpses rested and potassium-3 to seal and transport it back to the laboratory for further study.

Body netting was used for the burial suits of Khitan nobles, but silver-mesh body netting was used only for members of the imperial family. This kind of burial suit was made to fit the deceased, taking into account the person's height and figure; separate parts were made to fit the head, chest, belly, arms, hands, legs, and feet. After all the parts had been completed, the pieces were joined by silver string. The burial suits were worn over underwear; over the burial suit there were usually an overcoat, a belt, a mask, silver boots, and ornaments. Among the most attractive of the ornaments for the princess and her husband were the two amber necklaces each of them wore. These two sets of necklaces each consisted of a large, multistrand necklace and a smaller, single strand of amber beads. Although the silver wire connecting the amber beads had been broken, we were able to reconstruct the necklaces and arrange the beads in their original order (fig. 57, cat. 37).

Few Liao Khitan imperial tombs or tombs of nobles have been found intact. In addition to the tomb of the Princess of Chen and her husband, there are five others: the tomb of the Prince of Wei in Dayingzi, Chifeng City, excavated by Zheng Shaozong, of what was then the Jehol Museum, in 1953;[1] an early Liao tomb excavated at Faku Yemaotai, Liaoning Province, by the Provincial Museum of Liaoning in 1974;[2] Haoqianying Tomb Number 6 in Chayou Front Banner, excavated by the

Fig. 56. Silver-mesh body netting created for the Princess of Chen

Fig. 57. The Princess of Chen's amber necklace with the beads placed in their original order

Inner Mongolia Institute of Cultural Relics and Archaeology in 1981;[3] the tomb of Yelü Yuzhi and his wife, Chonggun, at Hansumu Township, Aluke'erqin Banner, excavated by the Inner Mongolia Institute of Cultural Relics and Archaeology in 1992;[4] and a Liao tomb excavated at Tuerji Hill, Kezuo Rear Banner, Tongliao City, by the Inner Mongolia Institute of Cultural Relics and Archaeology in 2003.[5]

After excavating the tomb of the Princess of Chen and her husband, we made facsimiles of the murals. The tomb was then sealed up for protection. All the relics found in the tomb were taken to the Inner Mongolia Institute of Cultural Relics and Archaeology. After that, we invited experts from the Chinese Academy of Social Sciences Archeological Research Institute to help us repair the silver-mesh netting, gilded-silver crown (cat. 3), gilded-silver boots, silver belt (cat. 21), equestrian gear, glass wares, and bronze wares. Some silver and jade items were sent to the structure analysis laboratory of the Chinese University of Science and Technology for testing and study. The Chinese Building Research Institute and the Inner Mongolia Forestry University researched and analyzed, respectively, the glass and wooden objects. We tried to protect the amber jewelry from the tomb by sealing it with various chemical compounds but were unsuccessful since amber is a resin. Protection of the amber is a subject for future study, which we plan to pursue.

1. Qian Rehe sheng bowuguan choubeichu, "Chifengxian Dayingzi Liao mu fajue baogao" [The excavation report on the Liao-dynasty tombs at Dayingzi, Chifeng County], *Kaogu Xuebao* 1956.3, pp. 126.

2. Liaoningsheng bowuguan, "Faku Yemaotai Liao mu jilue" [Brief report on the Liao tomb at Yemaotai, Faku], *Wenwu* 1975.12, pp. 26–36.

3. Wumeng wenwu gongzuo zhan and Neimenggu wenwu gongzuo dui, *Qidan nushi* [*The remains of Khitan females*], Hohhot: Neimenggu renmin chubanshe, 1985, pp. 10–31.

4. Neimenggu zizhiqu wenwu kaogu yanjiusuo, "Liao Yelü Yuzhi mu fajue jiainbao" [Brief report on the excavation of the Liao tomb of Yelü Yuzhi], *Wenwu* 1996.1, pp. 4–32.

5. Neimenggu zizhiqu wenwu kaogu yanjiusuo, "Neimenggu Tongliao shi Tuerji shan Liao dai muzang" [The Liao-period grave at Tuerji Hill, Tongliao City, Inner Mongolia], *Kaogu* 2004.7, pp. 50–53.

The Discovery and Protection of the Liao-dynasty Cultural Relics from the White Pagoda in Balin Right Banner

Sun Jianhua

Since the Liao-dynasty Shijiafo Sheli Pagoda (Shakyamuni Buddha Relic Pagoda) in Balin Right Banner is white, it is often referred to as the White Pagoda. It is located in the northwestern corner of the old town of Qingzhou, in Suoburiga Township, Balin Right Banner (fig. 58). The pagoda, which was built in 1047, during the reign of the Liao emperor Xingzong (r. 1031–55), is now a historical and cultural relic under state protection. The pagoda is 71.43 meters high and has seven stories (fig. 59). It is octagonal and of half-timber construction. According to the pagoda's epigraph, it was built by the empress dowager Zhangsheng, the mother of emperor Xingzong, to house sutras and Buddhist relics.

The foundation of the tower is square, and the inside is a single room with a domed ceiling. The seven floors are each sealed off, with no connection between them. There are, all together, twenty-eight doorways on the seven levels, although the doors do not actually lead anywhere. On either side of each doorway, there are bas-reliefs of gods. From the second to the seventh story, there are white marble pillars on which Buddhist *dhāraṇīs* (incantations) are engraved. There are also bas-reliefs of flowers, clouds, canopies, dragons, *jialingpinjia* (creatures with a human head and the body of a phoenix), *qilin* (Chinese unicorns), lions, elephants, Tatars presenting treasures, *apsaras*, and dancers with musical accompanists. The bas-reliefs are rich in content and unmatched in the technical skill of their rendering (fig. 60). Confucianism, Buddhism, and Daoism are all represented in the bas-reliefs; the combination of the three is a characteristic of Buddhist art and architecture of the Liao dynasty. There are 856 bronze mirrors embedded on the exterior of the pagoda (see cat. 73a–c). The mirrors on the first, third, fifth, and seventh floors are diamond shaped, and those on the second, fourth, and sixth floors are round. On the surface of some of the mirrors, there are images of the Buddha and inscriptions (fig. 61).

fig. 58

fig. 59

fig. 60

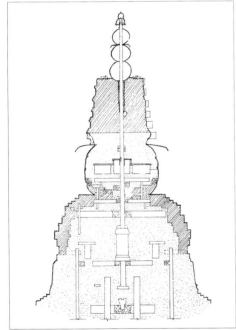
fig. 62

fig. 61

Fig. 58. Aerial photo of Qingzhou, Balin Right Banner

Fig. 59. The White Pagoda at Qingzhou, Balin Right Banner

Fig. 60. Relief carving on the exterior of the White Pagoda

Fig. 61. A bronze mirror incised with a Buddha image and an inscription

Fig. 62. Cross section of the *cha* of the White Pagoda

The White Pagoda is nearly one thousand years old, and because of exposure to the elements, it has badly deteriorated. It was renovated during the Qing dynasty (1644–1911). In 1988, the State Bureau of Cultural Relics and Archaeology was sanctioned to maintain the pagoda. While the bureau has maintained it, its main priority has been to reinforce the pagoda.

In 1989, maintenance engineering began. Although the White Pagoda had been repaired during the Qing dynasty, the *cha* (a steeple shaped like a small pagoda, at the top of the pagoda) was tilting and unstable, appearing as though it might separate from its base. So the first job was to take apart and remove the *cha*, which had been added during the Qing dynasty, and then restore the *cha* to the way it had been during the Liao dynasty. Taking apart and removing the *cha* was done according to strict excavation procedures and maintenance-engineering operating rules, from the upper floor to the lower floor (fig. 62). First, the treasury bottle, jewelry, canopy, and *chattra* para-

fig. 63

fig. 64

fig. 65

fig. 66

Fig. 63. A statue of Shakyamuni Buddha, showing his entry into nirvana

Fig. 64. The five deposit rooms inside the *cha* of the White Pagoda

Fig. 65. The stele on which a *fokan* (niche for the Buddha) is engraved

Fig. 66. Scripture container in the form of a miniature pagoda; cypress

sols (*xianglun*) added during the Qing dynasty were removed. When the fourth *chattra* parasol was removed, a small broken stele dating from the Qing dynasty was found. When the arched area (called the *fubo*, or inverted bowl) between the *chattra* parasols and the base of the *cha* was dismantled, a simple cave chamber dating from the Liao dynasty was found in the middle of the northern edge of the base of the *cha*. In the cave chamber, there was a statue of Shakyamuni made of brick covered with gold leaf (fig. 63). When the floor of the fifth level was removed, a trough covered with an iron plank was discovered on one side of the center pole. On the iron plank, the following inscription was engraved: "This pole was placed here on the twentieth day of the seventh month, the eighteenth year of Chongxin by . . . [name]." In the trough, there was a gold sheet and a silver sheet on which *dhāraṇīs* were inscribed (see cat. 62, 63). On the gold sheet, the characters for *Xiangluntang zhong tuoluoni zhou*, the Chinese title of the *Dhāraṇī inside the Cavity of Chattra Parasols*, are engraved, as well as the text of the sutra in Sanskrit. On the silver sheet, there is an inscription explaining the efficacy of the *dhāraṇī*. Five connected rooms covered by cypress boards were found under the trough, in and around the center pole. Many objects had been placed in these five rooms (fig. 64). When two layers of bricks under the five rooms were removed, some scattered sutras were found near the base of the bronze *fubo*, below the parasols. Because of leaks, some of the sutras were damaged. Near the base of the *fubo*, there was a wooden miniature pagoda that had been placed there during the Qing-dynasty restoration.

When taking apart the *cha*, we found traces of the original Liao-dynasty construction, as well as of the Qing-dynasty restoration. Most of the surface layer dated

Fig. 67. Reliquary in the form of a lotus bud; amber

Fig. 68. A scripture container decorated with the image of the bodhisattva Avalokiteshvara

Fig. 69. A statue of Shakyamuni Buddha; gold leaf on wood

from the Qing-dynasty restoration, but most of the interior had been built during the Liao dynasty. To the north and south of the center pole, there were two brick steles dating from the Liao dynasty. One of the steles was 111.5 centimeters high and was composed of three parts: a top, a body, and a pedestal. A *fokan* (a niche for the Buddha) was engraved on the top part of the stele. Inside the *fokan,* images of Shakyamuni, seated on a lotus throne, and his disciples Kashyapa and Ānanda, standing on either side of him, were engraved. Flanking the *fokan* are two entwined *chi* dragons. The inscription records the names of officials and members of Buddhist religious orders who had sponsored the construction of the relic deposit or who had placed Buddhist relics there (fig. 65). The other stele, which is rounded on top, records the names of the craftsmen involved in the construction of the pagoda, as well as construction procedures—important material for studying the White Pagoda. At the four corners of the base of the *cha*, there were four separate pits, each containing a miniature pagoda on which the Buddhas of the Ten Directions were carved. Under the base of the center pole, there was a wood carving of a lotus lamp with a bronze base. In the *cha* were 490 coins, of thirty different types. The oldest was a *banliang* (half a tael) coin from the Han dynasty (206 BC–AD 220), and the most recent was a coin used during the Northern Song dynasty (960–1127). But there were no coins from the Liao dynasty.

The objects found in the deposit are numerous and of many different types (see chart 4). In the five-chamber deposit alone, there were more than six hundred items, including a gilded-silver miniature pagoda (cat. 66) and 108 wooden miniature pagodas (cat. 61a–b, 64, 65a, 71a–c). In these pagodas were hidden Buddhist scriptures wrapped in white silk; long narrow silk flags were tied to the tops of the pagodas. In one plain, unpainted wooden miniature pagoda, there was hidden a lotus bud-shaped bottle that contained relic grains (figs. 66, 67). One tubular sutra container is decorated with a 7-centimeter-high amber statue of Avalokiteshvara on the top; the tube itself decorated with a dragon carved in relief (fig. 68). Among the many other treasures found were a 25-centimeter-high statue of Shakyamuni Buddha made of wood with gold leaf (fig. 69) and two miniature volumes of Buddhist scriptures. One of the miniature volumes contains a transcription of the *Diamond Sutra* (Sanskrit: *Vajracchedika-prajñāpāramitā-sūtra*; Chinese: *Jin'gang banruo boluomi jing*) (fig. 70); it is 5.5 centimeters

Type of Object	Excavation Location	Quantity
Large miniature wooden pagoda (with Buddhist scriptures inside), decorated with seven gilded carved Buddhas	middle room	1
Iron hairpin, decorated with woven-silk thread	middle room	1
Miniature gilded-silver pagoda (with a *dhāraṇī* incantation incised on a sheet of silver inside), its finial in the shape of a phoenix with a string of pearls in its mouth	middle room	1
Long-necked silver bottle with Buddhist relic grains inside	middle room	1
Agalloch eaglewood (medicinal material)	middle and south rooms	2 pieces
Silver spoon with the inscription "*qiannian wanzai*" (a thousand years and myriad annual cycles)	middle room	1
Woven-silk, butterfly-shaped hairpin (incomplete)	middle room	1
Sandalwood (medicinal material)	middle room	4 pieces
Frankincense (medicinal material)	middle room	several p.
Miniature pagodas (with Buddhist scriptures inside), decorated with seven gilded carved Buddhas	south, east, and west rooms	5
Gilded miniature pagodas (with Buddhist scriptures inside)	east and west rooms	2
Miniature pagodas (with a sutra inside), decorated with seven painted Buddhas	north, south, east, west and rooms	97
Miniature book of the *Diamond Sutra*	east room	1
Twenty-one-lobed white foliate dishes (on which lilac flowers were found)	north and east rooms	2
Six-lobed white foliate dishes (on which lilac flowers, frankincense, and nutmeg were found)	north, south, and east rooms	5
Five-lobed white foliate dish (on which betel nuts were found)	east room	1
Six-lobed silver foliate plates (on which nutmeg, lilac flowers, betel nuts, and frankincense were found)	south, east, and west rooms	5
Eighteen-lobed white foliate dish (on which lilac flowers were found)	east room	1
Woodcarving of a seated Shakyamuni Buddha, covered with gold leaf	south room	1
Tubular container decorated with an amber-carving of Avalokiteshvara on the top	south room	1
Fourteen-lobed white foliate dish (on which lilac flowers were found)	north room	1
Dark-green glass bottle (with Buddhist relic grains inside)	north room	1
Plain miniature pagoda (with a lotus bud-shaped bottle carved of amber inside)	south room	1
Miniature pagodas (with Buddhist scriptures inside), decorated with seven gilded carved Buddhas	north room	2
Four-lobed white foliate dishes (on which lilac flowers and cinnamon were found)	south room	2

Type of Object	Excavation Location	Quantity
Silver bowls (in which betel nuts and lilac flowers were found)	south room	2
Lacquer plates (on which lilac flowers and nutmeg were found)	south room	1
Miniature book of the *Great Marīci Sutra*	south room	1
Rock-crystal cup (with frankincense inside)	south room	1
Small pot carved out of a fruit kernel (with frankincense inside)	south room	1
Small carved-wood tripod (with frankincense and lilac flowers inside)	south room	1
Shells	north and suth rooms	2
Gold sheet incised with the *Dhāraṇī inside the Cavity of Chattra Parasols*	middle room	1
Silver sheet incised with a passage from the *Great Dhāraṇī Sutra of Stainless Pure Light*	middle room	1
Iron plank with an inscription dated to the eighteenth year of the Chongxi era (1049)	middle room	1
Woodblock-printed Buddhist scriptures	*fubo*	6 scrolls
Hand-copied Buddhist scriptures	*fubo*	24 scrolls
Statue of Shakyamuni made of brick covered with gold leaf	*fubo*	1
Stele decorated with a *chi* serpent on the top	square pit below the deposit within the *cha*	1
Stele with rounded top	inside the *cha* structure	1
Miniature pagodas, each decorated with the Buddhas of the Ten Directions, painted carved wood (with a scroll of the *Lotus Sutra* inside)	square pit below the deposit within the *cha*	4
Lotus lamp with bronze base	inside the *cha* structure	1
Coins	beneath the pits, close to the bottom of the *cha*	490
Blue silk gauze handkerchiefs with plum, bamboo, bee, and butterfly pattern	north, south, east, and west rooms	4
Orange silk gauze handkerchief with an embroidered pattern of joined pearls and dragons in clouds	south room	1
Red silk gauze sutra wrapper embroidered with a figure riding a horse, within a pearl roundel	chavity inside the *chattra* parasols	1
Various types of silk textiles, including handkerchiefs, book covers, and pagoda streamers	north, south, east, west and middle rooms	270

fig. 70

fig. 71

Chart 4. Objects excavated from the White Pagoda in Balin Right Banner

Fig. 70. Miniature book of the *Diamond Sutra*

Fig. 71. Miniature book of the *Great Marīci Sutra* (*Foshuo molizhitian jing*)

long, 4 centimeters wide, and 0.5 centimeters thick. The other contains a transcription of the *Great Marīci Sutra* [*Foshuo molizhitian jing*]; it is 5.2 centimeters long, 3 centimeters wide, and 1.5 centimeters thick (fig. 71). In addition, there were offering vessels made of silver, porcelain, lacquer, rock crystal, amber, and glass. Seven types of Chinese herbs were found in the vessels: lilac, clove, agalloch eaglewood, frankincense, sandalwood, betel nut, and nutmeg. There were silk sutra covers, as well as silk covers or mats for vessels used in offerings. Thirty volumes of Buddhist scriptures, some handwritten and some printed, were scattered inside the *fobo*. Because they had been in the relic deposit, they were well preserved. After excavation, these relics were immediately sterilized, disinfected, and cleaned. The silk was authenticated by the Chinese Silk Museum in Hangzhou. Some damaged Buddhist scriptures were restored.

The relic deposit in the White Pagoda is an important archaeological discovery. It provides precious materials for studying the Buddhist culture of the Liao period and the construction of the White Pagoda in Balin Right Banner. Construction of the pagoda began at the height of Buddhism in the Liao era, during the reign of the emperor Xingzong. Xingzong's mother—the empress dowager Zhangsheng, a wife of the late emperor Shengzong (r. 982–1031)—wanted to control the Liao empire after Shengzong's death. She initiated a conspiracy to get rid of empress dowager Rende, another of Shengzong's wives, and succeeded in doing so. In 1034, she attempted to enthrone Xingzong's younger brother Chongyuan, but failed and was charged with a crime. Her imperial seal was taken away from her, and she was assigned to live in the funerary city adjacent to the imperial mausoleums in Qingzhou.[1] Several years later, emperor Xingzong regretted forcing his mother away and permitted her to return to court. It is likely that the construction of the White Pagoda in Balin Right Banner is related to the empress dowager Zhangsheng's residence near the Qing Mausoleums.

All of the objects excavated from the White Pagoda are now in the collection of the Museum of Balin Right Banner. Because of exposure to and changes in the natural environment, there have been small changes in the relics excavated from the pagoda. At present, the State Administration of Cultural Relics has asked the China National Institute of Cultural Property to draw up and execute a plan for protecting and repairing the relics.

---

1. *Liaoshi* [*History of the Liao*], *juan* 18, pp. 216, 221.

復如是以稱
定智惠力得諸國土王於三界帀說

王不肯順伏如来賢聖與之共戰其有功者

心亦歡喜於四衆中為說諸經令其心悦賜以禪

定解脱无漏根力諸法之財又復賜與涅槃之城

言得滅度引道其心令皆歡喜而不為說真法華

經文殊師利如轉輪王見諸兵衆有大功者心甚

歡喜以此難信之珠火在髻中不妄與人為今與

之如来亦復如是於三界中為大法王以法教化一

切衆生見賢聖軍與五陰魔煩惱魔死魔共戰有

Hsueh-man Shen

Praying for Eternity:

Use of Buddhist Texts in Liao Buddhist and Funerary Practices

In China, as elsewhere, art created for funerary use and for religious use often over-lap. This is especially obvious in Buddhist relic deposits and in secular tombs created for cremated remains, for both pagodas where the Buddha's relics were enshrined and tombs that sheltered the remains of the deceased dealt with the notion of *body* and the notion of *death*. While Buddhist relic deposits could be perceived as representing the burial of the deity, burials for cremated remains could be seen as secular expressions of the sacred transcendence of death. Yet in Buddhism, nirvana refers to the extinction of all return to reincarnation with its associated suffering, and to entry into bliss. Nirvana may be enjoyed in the present life as an attainable state, hence it is not necessarily associated with death. Nirvana cannot be equated with human death; therefore, the burial of one who has entered into nirvana (including the Buddha) is inappropriate. Besides, Buddhists cremate the dead so that they can become detached from the world of material things.[1] Building an underground tomb for the dead in their afterlife is at odds with Buddhist concepts. In other words, both relic deposits and burials for cremated remains seem to be out of line with Buddhist teachings.

However, through the use of Buddhist texts—the Buddha's *dharma* relic—Liao Buddhists worked out a way to enshrine the Buddha's relics while at the same time celebrating his eternal being; the deposit of scriptures inside the White Pagoda (referred to as Shijiafo Sheli Pagoda, or Shakyamuni Buddha Relic Pagoda, during the Liao dynasty) in Balin Right Banner, Inner Mongolia, is one example. The practice of depositing scriptures inside a pagoda was later combined with the worship of the Buddha in his human form, as in the scripture deposit inside the statue of Shakyamuni in the Timber Pagoda at the Liao Western Capital, in what is today Datong, Shanxi Province. In an explicit way, the relics lent life to Buddhist statues. Buddhist texts were also used by the Liao in secular tombs to enable the deceased to transcend to a better place, where they would no longer suffer. Examples come from a number of burials of cremated remains, among them the Zhang family tombs in Xuanhua, Hebei Province, are the most well known.

Texts Manifesting the Buddha's Eternal Presence:
The Relic Deposit in the White Pagoda, Balin Right Banner, Inner Mongolia

No texts record when Buddhism was introduced to the Liao state. However, scattered entries in historical sources show that Buddhist monasteries were constructed as early as the reign of the first Liao emperor, Abaoji (Taizu, r. 907–25). In 949, a *sarīra* relic was buried underneath a pagoda that was built under the sponsorship of the third Liao emperor, Shizong (r. 947–51). *Sarīra* (Chinese: *sheli*) is a Sanskrit word that refers to "corpus" but does not necessarily refer to the entire body. The first *sarīra* was that of Shakyamuni Buddha. After solemn funeral rites, the Buddha was cremated and the *sarīra* emerged. Stupas were erected to enshrine *sarīras*. Regarding *sarīras* as manifestations of the Buddha himself, Buddhists came to worship the *sarīras* at the stupas and to meditate on the Buddha's teachings. Subsequently, the practice of venerating stupas in which *sarīras* were housed arose. As sutra texts embodied the heritage of the Buddha's teachings, Buddhists worshipped them as they did the physical remains of the Buddha. Therefore, stupas were also erected to enshrine scriptures.[2]

There was a noticeable increase of interest in Buddhism during the reign of Emperor Shengzong (r. 982–1031), and attention to Buddhist activities continued under his successors, particularly emperors Xingzong (r. 1031–55) and Daozong (r. 1056–1101). Many members of the imperial clan built temples, made offerings to the monastic communities, participated in Buddhist ceremonies, and sponsored study and duplication of Buddhist texts. Among these activities, the duplication and preservation of Buddhist texts seem most important. For example, a wooden hall was built under the auspices of the Emperor Xingzong in 1038 on the premises of Huayan Monastery in the Western Capital to store 579 portfolios of Buddhist sutras.[3] Moreover, the emperor granted an annual budget to restart the project of carving the complete Buddhist canon in stone at Yunju Monastery (Cloud Dwelling Monastery) in the mountains of Fangshan County, about seventy kilometers southwest of Beijing; the project had been initiated by the monk Jingwan (d. 639) during the Sui period (581–618), but had been discontinued for centuries.[4]

There are two major reasons why Liao Buddhists were keen on duplicating and preserving Buddhist texts. The first was that they wanted to preserve Buddhist law for the coming of *mofa* (final *dharma* or final law), the dark age of Buddhism, during which, it was believed, scriptures would be in danger of extinction.[5] The second was that they considered Buddhist texts as manifestations of the Buddha's spiritual body; hence the texts were highly esteemed and widely venerated in pagodas. Inscriptions from a relic deposit on top of the pinnacle of the North Pagoda (referred to as Yanchang Pagoda during the Liao period) in present-day Chaoyang, Liaoning Province, show that the Liao people built the deposit in preparation for the coming of *mofa*. One example reads: "On Great Khitan Chongxi the twelfth year, the fourth month, the eighth day at noon (1043), [the relic was] reburied. In eight years, the *xiangfa* will become *mofa*, so [we] place this record" (fig. 72).[6] In anticipation of the coming of *mofa*, a further deposit of Buddhist relics in the form of texts was built into the pinnacle of the White Pagoda in present-day Balin Right Banner, Inner Mongolia, in 1049, three years before the supposed coming of *mofa*.

Abundant written materials from the deposit in the White Pagoda show that Buddhist scriptures were categorized as *sarīra* relics, or, more precisely, spiritual *sarīra* relics of the Buddha, and were therefore enshrined in the deposit. According to the excavation report, the deposit comprises five chambers inside the pinnacle of the pagoda (fig. 73). Among the many objects found in the deposit were 109 pagoda-

fig. 72

Fig. 77. The position of the large statue on the first floor and four other groups of sculptures in the Timber Pagoda at Fogong Monastery in Yingxian, Shanxi Province

Fig. 78. Statue of Vairocana on the first level of the Timber Pagoda at Fogong Monastery in Ying County, Shanxi Province

Fig. 79. Detail of Vairocana's throne of lotus petals, on the first level of the Timber Pagoda at Fogong Monastery in Ying County, Shanxi Province

fig. 78

fig. 79

Transcending Death through the Use of Texts: The Zhang Family Tombs in Xuanhua, Hebei Province

Pictorial images or actual texts of Buddhist scriptures have been unearthed in a number of Liao tombs. The most well-known and probably the most representative examples come from a group of tombs that belonged to the Zhang family in present-day Xuanhua in northern Hebei Province. Sandwiched between the Western Capital and the Southern Capital (modern Datong and Beijing) of the Liao state and situated at the Song-Liao frontier, Xuanhua was annexed by the Liao in 938 as Xiongwu Prefecture. According to the epitaphs unearthed from these tombs, the Zhang family members were involved in various kinds of Buddhist activities, including reciting and duplicating Buddhist scriptures, sponsoring the building of Buddhist monasteries, and making regular offerings at temples. Many of their children had names with Buddhist connotations, and a number of the Zhang women became Buddhist nuns.[28] In the case of Zhang Shiqing (d. 1116), his epitaph explicitly states that his remains were cremated in accordance with Indian Buddhist customs.[29]

Although the tombs were for the burials of three generations of the Zhang family, they were built during a relatively short time, from 1093 to 1117, and followed a rather standard layout. Most of them consist of an antechamber, which is connected to a rear chamber by a short arched hallway. While the walls of the antechamber are often painted with scenes of tea or wine preparation, the walls of the rear chamber are painted with scenes of the serving of tea or wine. In addition, equipment used for writing—such as brushes, ink and inkstone, and paper—were depicted on the walls of the rear chamber. At the back of the rear chamber, which is the main chamber, there is a platform made of bricks on which a wooden coffin sits (fig. 80). Buddhist texts, a majority of them *dhāraṇīs*, were written in ink on the exterior of these wooden coffins. Most of them have a Chinese heading, written from top to bottom, followed by a Sanskrit text (fig. 81).

The selections on these coffins appear to have been limited to eighteen particular *dhāraṇīs*, a majority of which share a common function—to help the deceased eliminate sins and achieve rebirth in the Pure Land. For example, the *Dhāraṇī of Buddha Jñānolkā to Break Hell* (Sanskrit: *Jñānolkā -dhāraṇī*; Chinese: *Zhiju rulai xin po diyu*

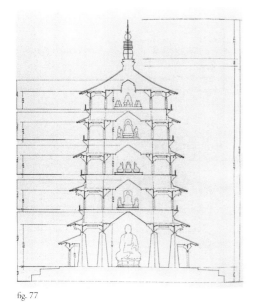

fig. 77

fig. 80

Fig. 80. Offerings on the altar table in front of the wooden coffin in the rear chamber of Tomb IM7 in Xuanhua, Hebei Province

Fig. 81. Wooden coffin from Tomb IM7 in Xuanhua, Hebei Province

tuoluoni) says that those who wish to save a person from hell may make offerings of incense or flowers and recite this *dhāranī* every seven days for three weeks immediately after the death of that person. Hell will thus be broken, and people in hell will all be saved.[30] Bodhisattva Avalokiteshvara, an attendant of Buddha Amitābha, vows to empty hell; those who call the name of Amitābha and recite the *Dhāranī of the Bodhisattva with a Thousand Hands and Eyes Who Regards the World's Sounds with Great Compassion* (Sanskrit: *Nīlakantha-dhāranī*; Chinese: *Qianshou qianyan guanshiyin pusa dabeixin tuoluoni*)—a *dhāranī* devoted to Avalokiteshvara, will be awarded merits, including elimination of all sins and a rebirth in any Buddha land of their wish.[31]

While some *dhāranī*s are related to the cult of Avalokiteshvara, some other texts, including the *Mantra of Taking the Percepts of Bodhi-citta* (*Shou putixin jie zhenyan*) and the *Heart Sutra* (Sanskrit: *Prajñāpāramitā-hrdaya*; Chinese: *Banruo boluomiduo xin jing*), are associated with the Buddhist notion of nirvana or enlightenment.[32] The *Verse concerning the Sarīra of the Dharma-body* (Sanskrit: *Dharma-kāya Gāthā*; Chinese: *Fasheli zhenyan*) expounds the nature of *dharma* law: the transcendence of causality is the cessation of affiliations (that is, nirvana). It summarizes the principal idea of Buddhism that all phenomena rise from causation and that the extinction of causations is the way to achieve nirvana.[33]

An inscription that appears repeatedly on the covers of the wooden coffins concludes the function of these texts. It refers to the *Dhāranī of the Jubilant Corona* and reads:

> The *dhāranī* coffins are efficacious in protecting what comes under their shadow. It is hoped that they will transcend the substance of the returning *hun* soul, exempt it from hell, and further award it with an eternal heavenly body. We trust that the good causes of dust [on the *dhāranī* coffins] and ink [used to duplicate the *dhāranī*] are as indestructible as [the universe, which is sustained by] the energy of *qian* and *kun*. Thus recorded with respect.[34]

fig. 81

fig. 82

fig. 83

Fig. 82. East wall of the rear chamber of Tomb IM1 in Xuanhua, Hebei Province

Fig. 83. East wall of the rear chamber of Tomb IM7 in Xuanhua, Hebei Province

The *Dhāraṇī of the Jubilant Corona* was well known for its efficacy in saving people from hell and rewarding them with rebirth in heaven. Those who lay in the shadow of the pillars on which the *dhāraṇī* was inscribed were promised elimination of all sins. The same blessing was awarded to those who touched the dust blown from the pillars on which the *dhāraṇī* was inscribed. Salvation was also given to those who had fallen into hell, provided that their descendants sprinkled earth consecrated by this particular *dhāraṇī* over their tombs. Writing the *dhāraṇī* on the lid of a coffin may have been a variant of the same practice and may have been a way to save whoever was buried in the coffin.[35]

Apart from the *dhāraṇī* inscribed on coffins, a variety of Buddhist texts were deliberately mentioned in epitaphs in order to impress the intended audience for the epitaphs—invisible spirits or deities.[36] For example, Zhang Shiqing's epitaph (dated 1116) gives many details of all sorts of activities that he had engaged in to fulfill his duties as a faithful Buddhist during his lifetime, including sponsoring construction of temples and pagodas, providing feasts for the poor and for monastic communities, and reciting and copying sutras. Among the scriptures that were mentioned are the *Lotus Sutra*, which he had recited a hundred thousand times, and the *Golden Light Sutra* (Sanskrit: *Suvarna-prabhāsottama-sūtra*; Chinese: *Jinguangming zuishengwang jing*), which he had recited two thousand times.[37] He also commissioned the printing and distribution of several scriptures, including the *Diamond Sutra* (Sanskrit: *Vajracchedika-prajñāpāramitā-sūtra*; Chinese: *Jin'gang banruo boluomi jing*),[38] the *Dhāraṇī of the Jubilant Corona*, the *Guanshiyin Sutra Promoted by King Gao* (*Foshuo gaowang guanshiyinjing*),[39] and a variety of other *dhāraṇīs*.

Some of these scriptures are even depicted on the tomb walls as part of the scene known as "preparation of sutras." For example, on the east wall of the rear chamber of the tomb of Zhang Shiqing, the *Diamond Sutra* is depicted as a book placed on a table beside a rectangular bookcase (fig. 82). To the right of the table, as one faces it, is a half-open door through which a servant can be seen bringing an additional bookcase. The scriptures were prepared for duplication, as is evidenced by the actual writing tools found in the Zhang family tombs and those depicted on the murals of the tombs' walls (fig. 83). It seems that scriptures and other necessities were provided to the deceased so that they could live on and continue earning merits.

Parallel renderings of the same Buddhist scriptures in pictorial images on tomb walls and in words on coffins or epitaphs show a correlation in which words and images functioned together to serve a similar purpose—that is, to assist tomb occupants in transcending death when their physical remains were deposited in mannequin-like figures inside the coffins. Made of wood or straw, these funerary figures are life-size; they have movable joints and lifelike faces rendered in detail with individuality. They were fully dressed and laid in the *dhāraṇī* coffins mentioned above. Two mannequins made of straw and filled with the cremated remains of two people were found in the wooden coffin at the back of the tomb of Zhang Wenzao and his wife (Tomb Number IM7, dated 1093). Two human skulls and many bone fragments were wrapped into the straw bodies (fig. 84). The mannequins were originally dressed in multiple layers of silk clothing; leather shoes and caps as well as fragments of the clothing have survived (compare cat. 52). Like the statue of Shakyamuni Buddha at the Timber Pagoda, who was "brought to life" through the relic deposit made inside his body, the bodies of the deceased were retrieved by means of the installation of their cremated remains (i.e., their "essence of life"). In front of the coffin was a wooden table on which offerings of food such as jujube dates were placed in vessels made of fine ceramics (see fig. 80). Apparently, the mannequins received a burial that was no different from one an actual corpse would have received. In other words, the mannequins filled with the ashes of the deceased were regarded as the tomb's occupants, and thus as the ultimate recipients of the merits promised by the texts.

Conclusion

The use of Buddhist texts in the two different contexts shows the ways in which Liao Buddhists perceived death and the body. In building *sarīra* pagodas, Liao Buddhists chose to enshrine Buddhist texts in order to make tangible the eternal *dharma*-body of the Buddha. This approach successfully captured the true meaning of the Buddha's body; it is very different from the approach used for relic deposits made in adjacent Song China, where several devices, such as guardian figures and coffin-shaped reliquaries, found in secular tombs were used to accommodate the bodily remains of the "deceased" Buddha.[40]

Belief in the efficacy of Buddhist texts is evident in Liao tombs. Scriptures presented in pictorial images on the walls or in inscriptions on coffins were believed to have had the power to rescue the dead and allow them to transcend to a better place. In the use of Buddhist texts, funerary and religious practices intersected, as the preference for certain texts in both contexts demonstrates. For example, the *Verse concerning the Sarīra of the Dharma-body* explains the fundamental concept of Buddhism—that extinction of causality is the way to nirvana—and manifests the Buddha's *dharma*-body. This verse played an important role in Liao relic pagodas.[41] It was incised, together with the *Great Dhāraṇī Sutra of Stainless Pure Light*, on the long gilded-silver sheet enshrined at the very center of the deposit built on top of the White Pagoda. The same verse was also one of the eighteen scriptures selected and transcribed on the *dhāraṇī*-coffins at the Zhang family tombs in Xuanhua. In addition, the *Heart Sutra* was inscribed on most of the Xuanhua coffins. At the relic deposit built on top of the North Pagoda in Chaoyang (deposit date 1043), the *Heart Sutra* was lavishly engraved on a 362-centimeter-long sheet of silver that was enshrined in a pagoda-shaped container, which was, in turn, placed at the center of the deposit. Another copy of the sutra was carved on a stone sutra-pillar that was enshrined in a separate relic deposit underneath the foundation of the same pagoda (deposit dated 1044). Yet another copy of the *Heart Sutra* was carved on the lid of a large stone reliquary in the underground deposit (fig. 85).[42]

Fig. 84. Two mannequins in the coffin in Tomb IM7 in Xuanhua, Hebei Province

Fig. 85. Rubbing of the *Heart Sutra* carved on the lid of the stone reliquary discovered in the relic deposit underneath the North Pagoda in Chaoyang, Liaoning Province; deposit dated 1044

fig. 84

fig. 85

However, it seems it was far more difficult for Liao Buddhists to incorporate the Buddhist idea of body into secular tombs. The Zhang family tombs in Xuanhua represent a distinctive hybrid of Chinese tomb traditions and Buddhist ideas, which are somewhat contradictory in nature. Although the deceased were cremated and buried in accordance with Indian methods, many elements in their tombs were not Buddhist but rather followed Chinese burial traditions. For instance, building an underground structure with living spaces for the deceased is typical of Chinese tombs. The Chinese believed that in constructing a tomb they were creating a universe in which the deceased continued to live after death.[43] Similar notions led to the idea of providing nourishment for the deceased. In addition, according to Chinese tradition, it was important to preserve the bodies of the deceased because they would need their bodies in the afterlife. In the Zhang tombs, the mannequins filled with the remains of the deceased reflect an intention to retrieve bodies that were lost as a result of cremation.[44] This practice was obviously at variance with the Buddhist notion of nirvana, or transcendence from the world of phenomena. Tombs where Buddhist texts and offerings were provided became places where the dead collaborated with the living to initiate the power of texts, so that the tombs' occupants could transcend to a better place. Therefore, unlike the texts in Liao pagodas that materially represent the Buddha's eternal body, texts in tombs functioned more as talismans to save people from sufferings, or even as "visas" that opened up the door to a better place.[45] Buddhist texts in Liao pagodas transcended the boundary between life and death and represented the eternal presence of the Buddhist wisdom; whereas in tombs they became a pass one used to cross the borderline between life and death.

1. The Buddhist practice of cremation is modeled after that of Shakyamuni Buddha. In his discussion of the symbolism of Buddhist cremation, John Strong argues that cremation may be seen as a rite that accelerates the process of passage, and the relics as a sign of attaining that new state. See John Strong, *Relics of the Buddha*, pp. 115–16.

2. For types of Buddha relics and their relationship with the burial practices in India and beyond, see Strong, *Relics of the Buddha*, pp. 8–18.

3. The Liao scriptures are no longer extant. But according to a stone stele that is dated to 1162 and recorded the history of the scripture depository, the deposit was built in 1038; see *Huayansi* [Huayan Monastery] pp. 2–7.

4. For information about the Fangshan stone carvings made prior to the Liao dynasty, see Lothar Ledderose, "Massenproduktion angesichts der Katastrophe" [Mass production in view of catastrophe], *Asiatische Studien/Études Asiatiques* 44.2 (1990), pp. 217–33; Lothar Ledderose, "Changing the Audience: A Pivotal Period in the Great Sutra Carving Project at the Cloud Dwelling Monastery near Beijing," in John Lagerwey (ed.), *Religion and Chinese Society*, pp. 385–409. For support of the project from the Liao rulers, see Tanii Toshihito, "Kittan bukkyō seijishi ron" [A study on the Buddo-political history of the Khitan], in Kegasawa Yasunori (ed.), *Chūgoku Bukkyō sekkei no kenkyū: Bōzan Unkyoji sekkei wo chūshin ni* [*Essays on Chinese Buddhist stone sutras: Principally the stone sutras at Cloud-Dwelling Monastery in Fangshan*], pp. 133–91.

5. The Buddhist concept of *mofa* refers to the third of a three-part system that it was thought the history of the Buddhist religion would go through over time. Building on concepts from Indian sources, East Asian Buddhists formulated a system of three periods in the history of the Buddhist religion that were expected to occur in the following sequence: (1) the period of the true *dharma* (*zhengfa*), immediately following the death of the Buddha, during which it is possible to attain enlightenment by practicing the Buddha's teachings; (2) the period of the semblance *dharma* (*xiangfa*), during which a few may still be able to reach the goal of enlightenment, but most Buddhists simply carry out the external forms of the religion; and (3) the period of the final *dharma* (*mofa*), during which traditional religious practice loses its effectiveness and the spiritual capacity of human beings reaches an all-time low. For a detailed discussion of the tripartite system in East Asia, see Jan Nattier, *Once Upon a Future Time: Studies in a Buddhist Prophecy of Decline*, pp. 95–118.

6. A metal pagoda-shaped sutra container from the same deposit was engraved with a similar inscription. See *Wenwu* 1992.7, p. 6; p.9, fig. 13.

7. See *Wenwu* 1994.12, pp. 4–33.

8. The three-body theory refers to the Buddha's *dharma*-body, reward-body, and transformation-body. The reward-body is an ideal body, possessed by those who have awakened to the true principle based on meritorious practice. It is the living form of the true principle and possesses individuality. The transformation-body is considered to be the Buddha's manifest body, which has the power to assume any shape in order to propagate the truth or to save sentient beings.

9. See *Taishō Tripitaka* (hereafter T) 262, 9:31b.

10. The idea was explored in further detail in a commentary on the sutra, the *Foding zunsheng tuoluoni jing shu* (Commentary on the Dhāraṇī of the Jubilant Corona) by Monk Fachong (ca. 763–764). In this text, an analogy was drawn between the *dhāraṇī* and the *Lotus Sutra*. See T 1803, 39:1037a.

11. This text was found in 106 of the 109 miniature pagodas from the deposit. It has not been recorded

in the *Taishō Tripitaka* and might have been a Liao compilation. According to the short preface to the text, it was compiled by a monk who was attached to Minzhong Monastery in Yanjing (modern Beijing). See *Wenwu* 1994.12, p. 16, fig. 35.

12. The sutra was translated into Chinese by Amoghavajra (705–74). Two versions exist. See T 1022A, 19:710a–712b; and T 1022B, 19:712b–715a. Archaeological evidence shows that this sutra was popular in both the Liao area and the southeastern coast of China during the Song period. Yet little consideration from scholars has been made. For a discussion on the links between the two regions in their practice of relic deposits, see Hsueh-man Shen, "Liao yu Beisong shelita nei cang jing zhi yanjiu" [Scriptures deposits of the Liao and Northern Song], *Taida Journal of Art History*, 2002.12, pp. 169–212.

13. The sutra was translated into Chinese in 704. See T 1024, 19:717c–721b. For the mentioned passage, see T 1024, 19:719a.

14. See T 1024, 19:718b–719c.

15. See *Wenwu* 1994.12, p. 15, fig. 33; pp. 18–23, 29–32.

16. Enshrining Buddhist scriptures inside images of the Buddha is actually a practice inherited from India. In *Nanhai jigui neifa zhuan* (Record of the Dharma Sent Back from the Southern Seas), the monk Yijing (635–713) recorded the practice of depositing the "*Gāthā* of the Chain of Causation" inside statues of the Buddha and stupas in early-seventh-century India. See T2125, 54.226c. The monk Xuanzang (died 664) also recorded such Indian practice in *juan* 9 of his *Da Tang Xiyu ji* (Record of the Western Regions during the Great Tang Dynasty). See T2087, 51.920a.

17. For the excavation report, see *Wenwu* 1982.6, pp. 1–8. For a complete catalogue of excavated objects, see *Yingxian Muta Liaodai micang* [*Liao hidden relics in the Ying County Timber Pagoda*]. Neither the construction of the sculpture nor the construction of the deposit was recorded in historical texts. But evidence of carbon 14 tests and the latest dated scripture, which has a date of the Tianhui reign mark (1123–37), indicate that the contents were sealed up during the last years of the Liao period, about 1110–25. See *Wenwu* 1982.6, p. 8. Archaeologists have suggested that the three printed illustrations and box containing a *sarira* tooth relic found underneath the Buddha image on the third story could have been moved out of the deposit on the fourth story during the Cultural Revolution, and thus could be counted as part of the relic deposit inside the Buddha image on the fourth story. See *Wenwu* 1982.6, p. 2.

18. Vairocana is generally recognized as the spiritual or essential body of Buddha-truth, and as being like light pervading everywhere.

19. These four buddhas are Aksobhya, Ratnasambhava, Amitābha, and Amoghasiddhi of the Diamond World. They are identified by their mudras.

20. The five buddhas of Diamond World (*vajradhātu*) in Esoteric Buddhism, as represented in the *vajradhātu-mandala*, include four buddhas occupying the four directions and Vairocana in the center.

21. See Marilyn Leidig Gridley, *Chinese Buddhist Sculpture under the Liao*, p. 64; Nancy S. Steinhardt, *Liao Architecture*, pp. 120–21; Marilyn Gridley, "Images from Shanxi of Tejaprabha's Paradise," *Archives of Asian Art* 51 (1998–99), pp. 10–11.

22. See T 1484, 24:997c. The scheme also refers to the *Flower Ornament Scripture*, in which Vairocana is the ultimate truth. Therefore, this image of Vairocana in the Lotus Petal Treasure World may well represent a Huanyan representation of Vairocana, as opposed to the esoteric representation of Vairocana on the fifth level of the same pagoda. In fact, Kamio Kazuharu has

pointed out that the esoteric and the Huayan schools of Buddhism were the most dominant in Liao Buddhist culture. During the reigns of Liao emperors Xingzong and Daozong, many efforts were made to combine the two schools. See Kamio Kazuharu, *Kittan bukkyō bunka shi kō* [*Historical researches on the history of Khitan Buddhism*], pp. 103–106.

23. They were recognized because of the systematic numbering given to each of them. The "thousand character script" was used to number the Liao Buddhist canon. It also appeared on the Liao sutra carvings on stone slabs at Yunju Monastery in Fangshan. In fact, this numbering system had been used by the Song to number a triptych in 971 before being adopted by the Liao.

24. For example: the "Da cheng ba guan zhai jie yi" (The manner of conducting the eight precepts of the Mahayana), dated 1112; the "Shi jie" (The ten precepts); the "Yuquansi pusa jie tan suo die" (License to the practice of Bodhisattva precepts in Yuquan Monastery), carved from 1101 to 1110; and the "Pusa jie tan suo die" (License to the practice of Bodhisattva precepts), carved from 1111 to 1120, are all related to the *vinaya*. See *Wenwu* 1982.6, p. 5, table 2.

25. They include philosophical treaties, punctuations and interpretations, personal reading notes, miscellaneous notes on lectures, and songs. See *Wenwu* 1982.6, p. 5, table 2.

26. See T 262, 9:42c. Moreover, the *Anguttaranikāya* expounds the idea that Shakyamuni Buddha lives forever and says that Shakyamuni Buddha lives forever in his *dharma*-body. "The Buddha told Ānanda: 'After I enter nirvana, the *dharma* will live for ever. . . . I, Shakyamuni Buddha, have extremely long life. The reason why it is so is that when my flesh body takes the way of nirvana, my *dharma*-body remains present.'" See T 125, 2:787b. A similar idea is expounded in the *Mahāparinibbana-suttanta*, see T 7, 1:192c–196b.

27. The "Fo xingxiang zhong anzhi fasheli ji" (Instructions in enshrining *dharma-sarira* inside Buddha images), which was excavated from the deposit and was not included in the existing *Tripitaka*, is likely to be a Liao compilation and may provide important information on the practice of depositing the Buddha's spiritual relics in his images during the Liao period. Unfortunately, the content of this text still awaits publication.

28. See *Xuanhua Liao mu* [*Liao tombs in Xuanhua*], vol. 1, pp. 65–68, 123–25, 158–61, 236–38, 265–67, 286–87.

29. See *Xuanhua Liao mu*, vol. 1, pp. 236–38.

30. See T 1397, 21:913c–914b for a Chinese transliteration of the *dhārani*. In addition, the "Zhunti tuoluoni" (Cundī-*dhārani*), which was also inscribed on some of the coffins, grants all sorts of merits, including elimination of sins and rebirth in Buddhist lands, to those who recite the *dhārani*. See T 1076, 20:178c–185a, especially 178c–179a, 183c for the Sanskrit (with a Chinese transliteration).

31. See T 1064, 20:115b–119c. *Dhāranis* such as the *Dhārani of Six Characters* and the *Dhārani of Great Mercy* refer to the power of Avalokiteshvara and reflect the belief in his power of salvation. See T 1060, 20:105c–111c for the Chinese transliteration of the *dhārani*, and see T 1061, 20:112a–113c for the Sanskrit. For a comprehensive study of Avalokiteshvara, see Chün-fang Yü, *Kuan-yin: The Chinese Transformation of Avalokiteshvara*.

32. See T 915, 18:941a for a Chinese transliteration of the *Mantra of Taking the Precepts of Bodhi-citta*. One who takes the precepts of *bodhi-citta* (meaning the will to attain Buddhahood) takes the vow to maintain his *bodhicitta* will until he attains Buddhahood.

The *Heart Sutra* expounds the idea of formlessness and emptiness in Buddhism. See T 251, 8:848c. The mantra at the end of the exoteric sutra, which seems to say "understood, understood, understood what is beyond, completely understood what is beyond, enlightenment, svāhā," connotes progression toward a goal, and hence has the qualities of blessing and protection. See Donald S. Lopez, Jr., *Elaborations on Emptiness: Uses of the Heart Sutra*, pp. 165–86.

33. The *gāthā* appears in the *Fo shuo zao ta gongde jing* (Scripture on the Merits of Building Stupas) and reads: "All *dharmas* come into being through primary and then conditional causes, and I offer his teaching of those primary and conditional causes. When the primary and conditional causes come to an end, and the *dharmas* become extinct, I then perform that kind of explanation." See T 699, 16:801b. In the *Fo shuo zao ta gongde jing*, the Buddha expounds the importance of this *gāthā* and the reason why the *gāthā* was named the *Dharma-kāya Gāthā*. "Such a verse is named 'the Buddha's *dharma-body*.' You must transcribe, duplicate, and enshrine it in stupas. Why? Because the *dharma*-nature of all causations and those things that are derived from causations is emptiness . . . If there are multitudes who understand this meaning of causation, you must know, they see the Buddha.'" See T 699, 16:801b.

34. For a drawing of such coffin lid, see *Xuanhua Liaomu* [Liao tombs in Xuanhua], vol. 1, p. 134, fig. 108. Tansen Sen has provided a translation of the paragraph that is slightly different from the author's translation. See Tansen Sen, "Astronomical Tomb Paintings from Xuanhua: Mandalas?" *Ars Orientalis* 29 (1999), pp. 29–54.

35. See T 967, 19:967.349b–352c, especially 351b–351c. See also Liu Shufen, "*Foding zunsheng tuolu-*

oni jing yu Tangdai Zunsheng jingchuang de jianli—jingchuang yanjiu zhi yi" [The *Dhāraṇī of the Jubilant Corona* and the Tang-dynasty Zunsheng sutra-pillar: Series of the study on sutra-pillars, part 1], *Zhongyang yanjiuyuan lishi yuyan yanjiusuo jikan* 67.1 (1996), pp. 145–93.

36. It has been pointed out that tomb inscriptions or land contracts found in tombs are meant to be read by invisible spirits or deities rather than by the descendants of the deceased. Archaeology has revealed rich materials, much discussed, on the communications with the bureaucracy of the afterlife. For a few examples of the scholarship, see Anna Seidel, "Traces of Han Religions: In Funeral Texts Found in Tombs," in Akitsuki Kan'ei (ed.), *Dōkyō to shūkyōbunka* [Daoism and religious cultures], pp. 678–714. See also Terry Kleeman, "Land Contracts and Related Documents" in *Chūgoku no shūkyō shisō kagaku* [Chinese religious thoughts], pp. 1–34.

37. T 665, 10 *juan*. The sutra expounds the idea of the Buddha's three bodies and has the power to remove all obstacles in order to save people from sufferings.

38. The sutra expounds the Buddhist wisdom. T 235, 1 *juan*.

39. T 2898, 85:1425b–1426a. It is expounded in this sutra, which is a Chinese indigenous scripture, that by reciting the *dhāraṇī* of Bodhisattva Avalokiteshvara, one's sins are eliminated, and one will be resurrected.

40. Archaeological evidence from the Yellow River area shows that people there were convinced that the historical Buddha was dead, and a relic deposit was dedicated to him, which was just like a tomb for their deceased ancestors. For a detailed discussion of the

Northern Song relic deposits made in the Yellow River area, see chapter 3 of Hsueh-man Shen, *Buddhist Relic Deposits from Tang (618–907) to Northern Song (960–1127) and Liao (907–1125)*, particularly section 2, "Where did the Buddha go."

41. The verse was enshrined at a number of Liao pagodas, including Beizheng Village Pagoda in Fangshan, the North Pagoda at the Cloud Dwelling Monastery, and Dule Pagoda (dated 1058) in Ji County, Hebei Province. For a discussion of the verse and its relation to the Liao relic pagodas, see Hsueh-man Shen, "Realizing the Buddha's *Dharma* Body during the *Mofa* Period: A Study of Liao Buddhist Relic Deposits," *Artibus Asiae* 61.2 (2001), pp. 263–303, esp. pp. 269–71.

42. See *Wenwu* 1992.7, p. 19, fig. 45; p. 22, fig. 51.

43. See Jessica Rawson, "Creating Universes: Cultural Exchange as Seen in Tombs in Northern China between the Han and Tang Periods," in Wu Hung (ed.), *Between Han and Tang: Cultural and Artistic Interaction in a Transformative Period*, pp. 113–49.

44. The burial practice represented in Xuanhua is a complex mixture of Buddhist cremation and Chinese tomb traditions, which are fundamentally incompatible. However, driven by the wish for Buddhist rebirth and Daoist resurrection, the two were brought together and thus generated a unique burial pattern. For a full discussion of the topic, see Hsueh-man Shen, "Body Matters: Manikin Burials in the Liao Tombs of Xuanhua, Hebei Province," *Artibus Asiae* 65.1 (2005), pp. 99–141.

45. Here I borrow Anna Seidel's idea of using a land deed as a passport to the afterlife. See Seidel, "Traces of Han Religions."

Catalogue

The Nomadic Heritage

The Han Chinese Burial Tradition

Religious Life

Luxuries and Necessities

The Nomadic Heritage

Prior to the 1950s, much of our knowledge about the Liao dynasty was based on historical texts that portray the people and their culture and customs in words rather than in images. In the early twentieth century, a few finds of Liao archaeological sites provided limited visual images of the Khitan people and their way of living. Over the past several decades, as archaeology flourished in China, sites of Liao temples and tombs have revealed vivid images of the Khitan people and their life, in both pictorial and sculptural form. A pair of stone sculptures in this exhibition (cat. 9) depicts a male and a female servant in distinctive Khitan costumes. An earthenware funerary urn (cat. 10) is in the form of a miniature yurt, like the yurts that would have been used by Khitan nomads. Hunting and archery on horseback, which were skills common to Khitan nomads, are represented by hunting tools such as awls (cat. 18a–b), sheathed knives (cat. 43a–b), bow cases (cat. 19), and arrows excavated from Liao sites. Falconry was an integral part of Khitan culture, too, and is represented by the arm protector (cat. 8) included in this exhibition. Plaques carved into the form of bears (cat. 78), fish (cat. 35, 38, 79a), and swans (cat. 36) show the significance of these animals to the life of the Khitan. Images of flying geese and flowers are often seen on textiles; the patchwork (cat. 120a–b) found in Tomb Number 3 at Daiqintala in Keyou Central Banner is one example. Three wooden panels (cat. 49) from a tomb at Zhanpu, Linxi County, depict in ink and colors a garden scene and a boy herding cattle in a mountain valley, reflecting the semisedentary lifestyle of the Liao.

The horse was the most valued animal in Liao society, for it provided not only mobility but also food. The importance of the horse to the Khitan nomads is reflected by the fact that equestrian gear is frequently found in Khitan tombs. Harnesses made of precious materials were found in the tombs of people of high status; the most splendid sets of harnesses are from the tomb (dated 959) of the Prince of Wei and his wife (cat. 17) and from the tomb (dated 1018) of the Princess of Chen and her husband, Xiao Shaoju. In the multichambered tomb of the Princess of Chen and her husband, two sets of harnesses (each comprising nine components) were deposited in one of the side chambers; five out of the eighteen pieces—ranging from saddle flaps to a bridle to stirrups—are shown in the exhibition (cat. 12–16). That they were made of hammered silver sheets and further adorned with gilding or jade carvings reflects the high status of their owners.

The link between the Khitan and the steppe tradition is also evident in the Khitan's distinctive mortuary practices. These included careful preparation of the corpse by wrapping the limbs in silk and clothing the body in metal burial attire, consisting of a face mask and body netting. The elaborate burial attire of the Princess of Chen, which includes a silver mesh burial suit (cat. 1), a gold face mask (cat. 2), and gilded-silver boots (cat. 4), is by far the most splendid. In addition to being clothed in metal burial attire, the corpses of the princess and her husband were crowned (cat. 3) and adorned with heavy jewelry (cat. 27, 31, 33, 37, 45), belts, and pendants (cat. 21–24, 35–36, 77, 38, 44). They were then laid flat on a wooden death-bed toward the back of the tomb, with lavishly decorated silver headrests (cat. 5) underneath their heads.

While adhering to their nomadic tradition, the Khitan were quick to adopt aspects of the sedentary culture of China. Walled cities, timber structures, and brick buildings were built throughout the countryside, although they were concentrated near the Liao capitals. The production of high-fired ceramics was also taken up. Such ceramics production requires not only mastery of shaping, glazing, and firing but also strict control of resources (clay, fuel, and laborers) and the actual building of kilns. The production of high-fired ceramics had a long history in central and southern China but remained unknown in the northeast until the Liao subsumed the sixteen northern prefectures of the Song in 938 and several kilns were built in the areas around the Liao capitals. Some Liao ceramics were particularly designed to serve the Khitan nomadic lifestyle, as exemplified by the ox-leg bottle (cat. 42) that was used for fermenting milk and storing wine. In addition, the shape of the distinctive bag-shaped flask (cat. 39–41) was based on leather or wood prototypes—materials that were particularly suitable for the mobile lifestyle of the nomads. That such a practical leather bag was transformed into a freestanding porcelain flask signifies the amalgamation of the nomadic and sedentary ways of living.

HMS

1. Burial suit

Liao dynasty, 1018 or earlier
From the tomb of the Princess of Chen
and Xiao Shaoju at Qinglongshan Town
in Naiman Banner
Silver wire
Height of suit: 168 cm;
diameter of wire: 0.05 cm
Research Institute of Cultural Relics
and Archaeology of Inner Mongolia

This suit, worn by the Princess of Chen, was part of an elaborate set of burial attire, which also included a gold face mask (cat. 2) and gilded-silver boots (cat. 4). The mesh netting, made by twisting silver wire into interlocking hexagonal cells, was fashioned into seven separate pieces—for the head, arms, hands, front and back torso, legs, and feet—and then pieced together to form a complete suit. Wire made of silver rather than bronze was used in accordance with the princess's royal status as the granddaughter of the Liao emperor Jingzong (r. 969–982).[1]

It is not entirely clear why the Khitan elite clothed the deceased in burial attire. One theory suggests that the custom may have been related to their belief in shamanism or Buddhism.[2] A more convincing hypothesis is that burial attire was believed to help preserve the body and protect it from decay. Chinese texts document the Liao custom of embalming the dead, a practice that must have been perceived as highly unusual by the Han Chinese. A twelfth-century *jinshi*[3] scholar, Wen Weijian, describes the corpse of a high-ranking Khitan being cut open, cleansed, and filled with aromatic herbs, salt, and alum before being sewed up with five-colored silk thread; after the skin was pierced with a pointed reed to drain off the fat and blood, the face was covered with a metal mask, and the hands and feet with bronze netting.[4] In two excavated Liao tombs, traces of arsenic and mercury have been discovered in the stomachs of the deceased, indicating a possible attempt at embalming.[5] The idea of preserving the body after death is an ancient one and can be found in many cultures. Embalming was practiced in the fifth century AD by nomads in the Altai Mountains, South Siberia, where the limbs of the deceased were sometimes buried entwined with grass.[6] The Liao use of burial attire may well be related to this Altaic custom.

HK

1. A complete body suit made of bronze wire was found in a joint tomb at Chenggou Village, Fuxin, Liaoning Province (*Beifang wenwu* 1998.2, pp. 25–28), and another in the tomb of a female at Haoqianying, Chayouqian Banner, Inner Mongolia (*Wenwu* 1983.9, pp. 1–8). The deceased did not have epitaphs, and thus could not be identified, but judging from the contents of their tombs, it is unlikely that they were of royal status.

2. Mu Yi has summarized these different theories in "Liao mu chutu de jinshu mianju, wangluo ji xiang-guan wenti" [Metal facemasks and netting excavated from Liao tombs and other questions], *Beifang wenwu* 1993.1, pp. 28–34.

3. The highest degree awarded in the imperial civil service examinations.

4. *Luting shishi* [*Veritable facts from the caitiffs' court*], in Tao Zongyi (ed.), *Shuofu* [*Florilegium of (unofficial) literature*], *juan* 8:49a. This passage is also translated by Karl A. Wittfogel and Fêng Chia-shêng, *History of Chinese Society: Liao, 907–1125*, p. 280, n. 215, and Herbert Franke and Hok-lam Chan, *Studies on the Jurchens and the Chin Dynasty*, pp. 178–86.

5. Both were female corpses; one was found with bronze netting (see note 1, above) (*Wenwu* 1983.9, pp. 1–8), and the other was clothed in layers of silk (Ta La, "Jiekai muzhu shenfen zhi mi" [Unveiling the identity of the tomb occupant], *Zhongguo guojia dili*, 2004.9, pp. 133, 142).

6. In Pazyryk, South Siberia, the corpses of nomads were found to have been embalmed (Sergei Rudenko, *Frozen Tombs of Siberia: The Pazyryk Burials of Iron Age Horsemen*, p. 70), and in Oglakty, Minusinsk, South Siberia, the limbs of mummified and trepanned (i.e., with a hole cut into the skull) corpses dating from between 100 BC to AD 100 were wrapped with twists of fine grass (A.M. Tallgren, "The South Siberian Cemetery of Oglakty from the Han Period," *Eurasia Septentrionalis Antiqua* 9 [1937], pp. 69–90).

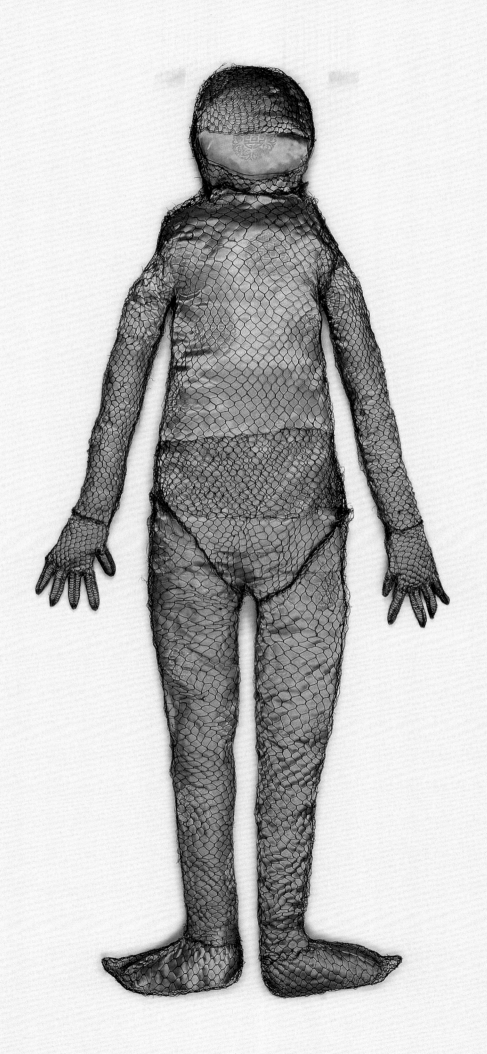

2. Burial mask

Liao dynasty, 1018 or earlier
From the tomb of the Princess of Chen
and Xiao Shaoju at Qinglongshan Town
in Naiman Banner
Gold
Length: 20.5 cm; width: 17.2 cm;
thickness: 0.05 cm
Research Institute of Cultural Relics
and Archaeology of Inner Mongolia

Placing a metal mask on the face of the deceased is, within the realm of China, a burial custom unique to the Liao. Masks, fashioned in a variety of shapes and sizes, were highly personalized. There was a distinct hierarchy as to what metal was used, depending on the status of the wearer. The simplest were made of thinly hammered bronze sheet; some were made more precious by the addition of gilding.

This mask, belonging to the Princess of Chen and fashioned from pliable gold sheet, fit for only a member of the imperial clan, is an example of the finest quality. The facial features of the seventeen-year-old princess have been carefully incised on the surface. The mask is deeper than most others, which tend to be more two-dimensional, and the addition of ears is an unusual feature. Covering the entire face and the ears would appear to have been related to the high status of the princess. Small holes pierced around the edge of the mask once served to attach it to silver body netting (cat. 1).

Covering the face of the deceased is closely linked with ideas of life after death. The Egyptians, the Greeks, and many other peoples have, in the past, covered the faces of the dead with face masks. The Chinese in the Eastern Zhou period (770–256 BC) also covered the faces of deceased members of the elite with jade masks. After the Han dynasty (206 BC–AD 220), however, the tradition of covering the faces of the deceased seems to have disappeared in China proper, and it did not reappear until the Liao era (907–1125). Archaeological evidence has shown that between the second and the eighth centuries, burial masks were in use in areas west of China, namely in Xinjiang and South Siberia.[1] This suggests that face masks are likely to have been a tribal tradition that the Khitan retained when they ruled northern China, and not a Han Chinese custom.

HK

---

1. For a discussion of historical evidence of burial attire and its links with the steppes, see Hiromi Kinoshita, "Hybridity and Conquest: Patterns of Liao (AD 907–1125) Khitan Tomb Burial," *Toronto Studies in Central and Inner Asia*, no. 6 (2004), pp. 135–43.

3. Crown

Liao dynasty, 1018 or earlier
From the tomb of the Princess of Chen
and Xiao Shaoju at Qinglongshan Town
in Naiman Banner
Gilded silver
Height: 30 cm; diameter: 19.5 cm
Research Institute of Cultural Relics
and Archaeology of Inner Mongolia

Tall and elegant, this regal headdress, which belonged to the Princess of Chen, is made from thinly hammered silver sheets with a design of phoenix-type birds among scrolling foliage cut out in openwork. Adding to the imposing silhouette are two elongated side flaps, one on either side, with long-tailed phoenixes set against scrolling tendrils. Embellishing the top of the crown is a Daoist figure, who can be identified by his long robes and pointed beard. He is depicted seated cross-legged on a lotus-petal base; behind him is a mandorla composed of *ruyi*-shaped cloud motifs. All the details are finely chased, and the overall design is parcel-gilded, creating a dazzling effect. The back of the crown is plain, suggesting that this crown was made for burial.

The finial on the crown is distinctive.[1] The Daoist image is a synthesis of Buddhist and Daoist iconography and can be identified as the deified Laozi, who, beginning in the early Tang dynasty (618–907), is sometimes depicted seated on a lotus throne.[2] The Khitan rulers were staunch supporters of not only their own tribal religion but also the Three Doctrines—Confucianism, Daoism, and Buddhism—and temples of all three belief systems were constructed beginning at the time of Abaoji's reign (907–26).[3]

Texts show that the metal used in crowns was an indicator of status and that gold was worn only by the high-ranking ruling elite.[4] This specific form of headdress appears to have been worn only by high-ranking females.[5] The prototype and associations for the phoenix-type bird design that decorates the princess's headdress, as well as her boots

(cat. 4) and headrest (cat. 5), are found in late imperial Tang China. There are two recorded instances when the Khitan were able to appropriate Chinese imperial motifs from the Later Jin (936–46): the first was in 938, with Chinese carriages and robes, and the second in 947, when members of various government departments, artisans, maps, books, armor, weapons, and other paraphernalia were transported to the Supreme Capital.[6] By using the Chinese imperial system and its associated motifs, such as the dragon and the phoenix, which were highly visible and immediately recognizable not only to Han Chinese but also to other tribes, the Khitan could well support the legitimacy of their rule.

HK

1. Phoenix-bird finials appear to be more common; for examples, see *Wenwu* 1993.3, p. 60, figs. 8.7, 8.8; *Chengjisi han: Zhongguo gudai beifang caoyuan youmu wenhua* [*Chinggbis Khan: The ancient nomadic culture of northern China*], p. 196.
2. Stephen Little and Shawn Eichman, *Taoism and the Arts of China*, pp. 182–84.
3. *Liaoshi* [*History of the Liao*], p. 13.
4. Crowns were worn at the birth of an imperial son (*Liaoshi*, p. 872), and to officiate at ritual ceremonies, such as the ceremony to appease the Muye Mountain god; see Karl A. Wittfogel and Fêng Chia-shêng, *History of Chinese Society: Liao, 907–1125*, pp. 272–73 for an entire description of this ceremony.
5. A gilded-bronze example of similar form, but with a scrolling floral design, was worn by the female in a joint burial excavated at Wenduo'er, Aluke'erqin Banner, Inner Mongolia (*Wenwu* 1993.3, p. 59, fig. 7, pl. 6.1). A silk headdress found in the tomb of a female at Yemaotai, Faku, Liaoning Province, is of the same elongated shape, with vertical side flaps on either side (*Wenwu* 1975.12, p. 36, figs. 16, 17).
6. *Liaoshi*, pp. 59–60, 901; see also Wittfogel and Fêng, *History of Chinese Society*, pp. 152, 256.

4. Pair of boots

Liao dynasty, 1018 or earlier
From the tomb of the Princess of Chen
and Xiao Shaoju at Qinglongshan Town
in Naiman Banner
Gilded silver
Length: 29.2 cm; height: 37.5 cm
Research Institute of Cultural Relics
and Archaeology of Inner Mongolia

This pair of boots is part of a set of burial attire, which includes a face mask (cat. 2) and burial suit (cat. 1), found adorning the body of the Princess of Chen. Constructed in much the same way as it would have been if it were made of a pliable material such as felt or leather, each boot consists of a leg, a shoe, and a sole which were crimped, soldered, and then stitched together with silver wire. Phoenix-type birds, with long-plumed tails and wings outstretched, are depicted soaring amid wispy cloud motifs; the pattern was chased into the surface of the metal, then parcel gilded for dazzling effect. These are clearly imperial boots made for use in the afterlife. Boots were practical and necessary footwear for the seminomadic Khitan. They provided warmth and protected their wearers not only from the elements but also from chafing when riding. A mural in a tomb excavated in Aohan Banner, Inner Mongolia, shows a group of five attendants preparing for a hunt, one carrying a pair of boots in his arms.[1] The high value the Khitan accorded to boots is recorded in Chinese texts when, in the eleventh century, the Song and Liao emperors exchanged leather boots and other luxurious goods as birthday gifts.[2]

The attention paid to the feet in burial is, not surprisingly, common in other ancient nomadic cultures, where people's livelihood depended on their mobility. Silver shoe soles with elaborate interlocking scrolling designs were found in a fourth- to third-century BC Ordos tomb in Southwest Inner Mongolia,[3] and in Jilin Province, in Northeast China; studded shoe soles made of iron and bronze, which archaeologists postulate may have also been used in real life, were found in Goguryeo tombs.[4]

HK

1. *Qidan wangchao* [*Khitan dynasty*], p.113. For the excavation report, see *Neimenggu wenwu kaogu* 1999.1, pp. 90–97.
2. Karl A. Wittfogel and Fêng Chia-shêng, *History of Chinese Society: Liao, 907–1125*, pp. 147–48.
3. *Neimenggu wenwu kaogu* 1992.1/2, pp. 91–96, illustrated on p. 93, fig. 2.3.
4. *Liaohai wenwu xuekan* 1993.2, pp. 108–9.

5. Headrest

Liao dynasty, 1018 or earlier
From the tomb of the Princess of Chen
and Xiao Shaoju at Qinglongshan Town
in Naiman Banner
Gilded silver
Length: 30 cm; width: 40.8 cm;
height: 13.2 cm
Research Institute of Cultural Relics
and Archaeology of Inner Mongolia

Made from a sheet of hammered silver, this cloud-shaped headrest with a crimped-on rim is supported at a slight angle by a stand that is soldered onto the headrest. A chased design depicting a pair of majestic phoenix-type birds hovering above *ruyi*-shaped clouds decorates the slightly concave surface. The birds flank an intertwined *ruyi*-cloud motif in the center of the pillow, the tips of their long tail feathers meeting to frame a large flaming pearl. The entire design is highlighted by mercury amalgam gilding. The same phoenix-type birds decorate the princess's crown (cat. 3) and boots (cat. 4), giving a sense of continuity to her burial attire.

Headrests are not commonly found in Liao burials. This phenomenon may be due to the friability of the material from which they were made. In Tang and Song China, ceramic pillows were often buried with the deceased, but none have been found in Liao tombs. Instead, different materials appear to have been used by the Liao, depending on the status of the tomb's occupant. Pillows made of fabric and stuffed with buckwheat husks may have been the most common.[1] In the burials of richer individuals, wood appears to have been the material of choice[2] and stone appears to have outranked wood; two headrests lobed in form, like this example, but made from gray and green sandstone were excavated from the tomb of Geng Yanyi and his wife.[3] Geng Yanyi was a highly decorated Chinese official who served the Liao government, and his wife, Madame Han, was posthumously awarded the imperial name of Yelü.[4] Unlike the Princess of Chen and her husband, however, they did not belong to the imperial family. The princess and her husband's pillows are the only silver examples to have been excavated thus far.

HK

1. Buckwheat husks, along with fragments of fabric that archaeologists postulate may have once been a pillow, were found underneath the head and shoulder area of the deceased in the tomb of a male at Bayankuren, Chenba'erhu Banner, Inner Mongolia (*Kaoguxue jikan*, 2004.14, p. 269).

2. A solid wood pillow described in the archaeological report as being lobed in form was excavated from a joint tomb dated to the second half of the eleventh century in Jiefangyingzi, Wengniute Banner, Inner Mongolia (*Kaogu* 1979.4, p. 331). Two wooden pillow tops of similar silhouette to that of the Princess of Chen's pillow and a lobed rectangular pillow base were excavated from a joint tomb in Xiaonurimu Village, Kezuo Central Banner, Inner Mongolia (*Beifang wenwu* 2000.3, p. 35; color pl. 1.4). In both cases, the tombs also contained wood furniture.

3. The tomb, located in Guyingzi, Chaoyang, Liaoning Province, is dated 1019, one year later than the Princess of Chen's tomb. One headrest is plain, while the stand of the other is decorated with scrolling chrysanthemums amid leaves (*Kaoguxue jikan* 1983.3, p. 188, figs. 24.1, 24.2).

4. Madame Han was herself from a distinguished Chinese family, and a number of male family members held important posts in the government (*Kaoguxue jikan* 1983.3, p. 194).

6. Burial mask with head netting

Liao dynasty, 1018 or earlier
From the tomb of the Princess of Chen
and Xiao Shaoju at Qinglongshan Town
in Naiman Banner
Mask: gold; netting: silver
Length: 21.7 cm; width: 18.8 cm
Research Institute of Cultural Relics
and Archaeology of Inner Mongolia

This face mask, which belonged to Xiao Shaoju, the husband of the Princess of Chen, is similar to his wife's burial mask (cat. 2) in that it, too, is made of hammered gold sheet, and it clearly defines the facial features of the prince. The ears, however, were made separately and attached by three rivets to either side of the mask. Remains of silver netting still attached to the mask confirm that Xiao Shaoju was also dressed in body netting.

The burial masks of the princess and Xiao Shaoju are the only ones thus far excavated that are made of gold. Masks have been found in other Khitan tombs, but they are made of bronze, gilded bronze, and sometimes silver.[1] Both the quality of the metal used and the size of the mask (and how much of the face it covers) appear to be directly related to the status of the deceased. The amount of body attire also depended on social ranking; thus masks have sometimes been found alone and sometimes in conjunction with body netting and shoe soles.

Although some silver was mined in Liao territory[2] and silver and gold were worked in Liaoning, Jehol (today's Northeast Hebei and Southwest Liaoning provinces), and Hebei,[3] limited supplies meant that both gold and silver were considered precious materials during the Liao dynasty. The amount of gold and silver given as tribute to the Liao by the territories they conquered shows that the emperor, his court, and the Liao elite desired these precious metals. The Later Tang (923–36) and Later Jin (936–46) sent gold to the Liao on three occasions,[4] and the Northern Song (960–1127) was the largest contributor of silver, giving up to a hundred thousand taels annually between 1005 and 1042 under the terms of the Treaty of Shanyuan.[5]

HK

1. For bronze examples, see *Kaogu* 1978.2, pp. 119–21 and *Wenwu* 1961.9, pp. 44–49. Gilded-bronze examples are illustrated in *Kaogu* 1960.2, pp. 21–24, *Neimenggu wenwu kaogu* 1981.4, pp. 77–79, and *Wenwu* 1993.3, pp. 57–67, and a silver example is illustrated in *Liaohai wenwu xuekan* 1986.1, pp. 32–51.

2. Mines were located north of Pingquan County in the Central Capital area (Karl A. Wittfogel and Fêng Chia-shêng, *History of Chinese Society: Liao, 907–1125*, p. 77).

3. Wittfogel and Fêng, *History of Chinese Society*, p. 143.

4. In 939 (*Liaoshi* [*History of the Liao*], p. 46); 941 (*Liaoshi*, p. 49); and 943 (*Liaoshi*, p. 53).

5. Wittfogel and Fêng, *History of Chinese Society*, p. 326.

7a–b. Pair of handheld amulets

Liao dynasty, 1018 or earlier
From the tomb of the Princess of Chen
and Xiao Shaoju at Qinglongshan Town
in Naiman Banner
Amber, gold
a. Amulet adorned with two phoenixes
confronting one another: length: 6.2 cm;
width: 4.3 cm
b. Amulet adorned with a crouching dragon:
length: 6.7 cm; width: 4 cm
Research Institute of Cultural Relics
and Archaeology of Inner Mongolia

The carved amber amulet adorned on one side with an image of two phoenixes confronting one another was placed in the hand of the Princess of Chen when she was buried in 1018.[1] The phoenixes have prominent hooked beaks, a characteristic of Khitan imagery that reflects their passion for falconry. A similar amulet, carved in the round to depict a crouching horned dragon with its head turned backward, was found in her other hand.[2] The amulets (*woshou*) are each drilled through horizontally to accommodate the attachment of a gold loop-in-loop chain to hold the amulet in place. The tomb of the Princess of Chen and her husband, Xiao Shaoju, is the only undisturbed Liao royal tomb that has been discovered so far, allowing scholars to learn firsthand how many tomb artifacts were used.

Xiao Shaoju was also buried with handheld amulets, but they are significantly different in design from those of the princess. The dragon that forms one of his amulets is a dynamic creature, full of vitality and motion in comparison to the princess's static recumbent dragon.[3] Two long-tailed birds resting on a lotus flower enhance his other amulet;[4] they are rather tame in comparison to the two phoenixes with rapacious beaks that adorn the princess's amulet, suggesting that these personal ornaments may have been gender specific as well as indicative of status.

Placing a precious object in the hands of the dead has Chinese roots, traceable to at least the Han dynasty (206 BC–AD 220).[5] The addition of gold chains to handheld burial amulets appears to be a specific Khitan contribution and is not seen on handheld amulets found in Han burial sites.

Amber appears to have been highly regarded by the Khitan, and innumerable artifacts were fashioned from this supposedly magical substance. Amber is fairly soft to carve, like wood, but it is extremely brittle; it can chip, but it is easily smoothed. Recent research indicates that much of the amber used by the Khitan was from the Baltic Sea region, far to the west, and was acquired through long-distance trade and tribute with Uighur and Persian emissaries, as well as with Buddhist missionaries from Central Asia.[6]

ECB

1. *Qidan wangchao* [*Khitan dynasty*], p. 47.
2. *Liao Chenguo gongzhu mu* [*Liao tomb of the princess of the state of Chen*], p. 102, fig. 65.2.
3. *Liao Chenguo gongzhu mu*, p. 102, fig. 65.3.
4. *Liao Chenguo gongzhu mu*, p. 102, fig. 65.4.
5. For example, jade pigs were frequently placed in the hands of the deceased during the Han period in ancient China (Jessica Rawson, *Chinese Jade from the Neolithic to the Qing*, pp. 319–20).
6. For an extensive discussion of amber, its sources, and its prominence in Khitan art of the Liao dynasty, see Emma C. Bunker, Julia M. White, and Jenny F. So, *Adornment for the Body and Soul: Ancient Chinese Ornaments from the Mengdiexuan Collection*, pp. 153–60; Jenny F. So (ed.) *Noble Riders from Pines and Deserts: The Artistic Legacy of the Qidan*, pp. 35–37.

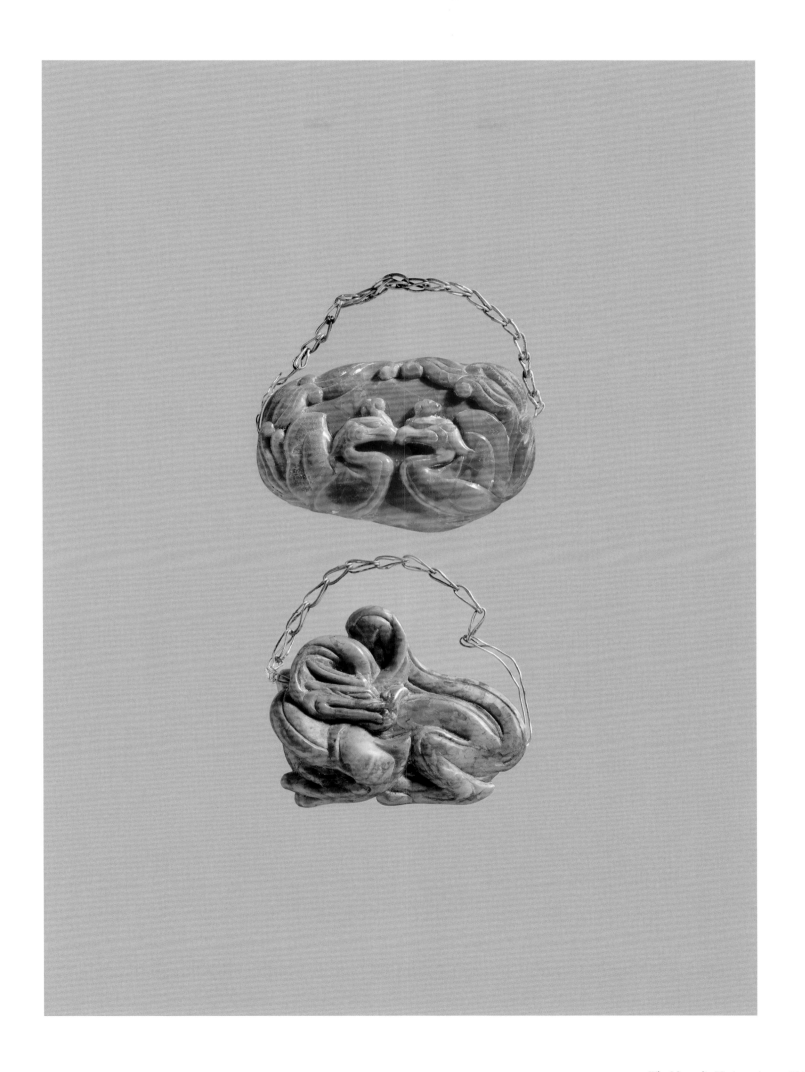

8. Arm protector

Liao dynasty, 1018 or earlier
From the tomb of the Princess of Chen
and Xiao Shaoju at Qinglongshan Town
in Naiman Banner
White jade
Length: 9 cm; width: 3.4 cm;
thickness: 0.35 cm
Research Institute of Cultural Relics
and Archaeology of Inner Mongolia

This elongated, slightly convex arm protector is fashioned from white jade, which may have been burned or treated in some way, resulting in its chalky gray-white appearance. The two long sides were each pierced with an aperture to which a gold loop-in-loop chain[1] was attached, enabling the piece to be fastened to the left arm of the Princess of Chen.

Arm protectors (*gou*) were necessary pieces of equipment in falconry, to protect the forearm of the handler from the birds' sharp talons. This example may not have been used in real life, however, as jade is not a material upon which a bird can secure a firm grip, especially a piece such as this, with a polished surface. Jade is not commonly found in Liao tombs. The tomb of the Princess of Chen and Xiao Shaoju, however, is an exception; an unprecedented number of jade pendants were found there, no doubt because of the princess's imperial status.[2]

Falconry was an integral part of Khitan culture. Mural paintings decorating the walls of Khitan tombs, especially those excavated in Aohan Banner, Inner Mongolia, illustrate birds of prey in different settings: sitting on their perches,[3] resting on the arms of attendants,[4] or as part of a hunting party.[5] At the imperial level, hunting with birds of prey was part of an annual ritual ceremony held every spring, during the first ten days of the first month. At this time, the emperor and his entourage would travel to a temporary residence located in today's Ningjiang region in Jilin Province. There, the emperor would hunt swan and wild geese, using falcons. The first swan caught would be offered as a sacrifice at the ancestral temple.[6] Texts show that the Liao emperor acquired birds of prey used for hunting swan, wild geese, and hare as regular tribute gifts.[7]

HK

---

1. The loop-in-loop technique, whereby loops of metal were linked together in various ways to form a chain, was introduced into China during the late Warring States period (475–221 BC) (see Julia M. White and Emma C. Bunker, *Adornment for Eternity: Status and Rank in Chinese Ornament*, p. 47). That there is visible evidence that loop-in-loop chains were in use in Sumeria and Egypt in the third millennium BC, and later in the fourth to third century BC by the Greeks in their metalworking, shows how this technique moved from West to East.

2. A *gou* excavated from a rich but nonimperial Khitan burial site and made of gilded silver is illustrated in *Liaoning kaogu wenji* [*Collected works on Liaoning archaeology*], color pl. 13.2, with a description on pp. 89–90.

3. From Tomb Number 2, with a hexagonal tomb plan painted on the northwest wall (*Neimenggu wenwu kaogu* 1999.1, p. 58, fig. 17.3, and color. pl. lower right of inside back cover).

4. Painted on the doors of a coffin made of cypress wood panels, now in the Museum of Aohan Banner (*Neimenggu wenwu kaogu*, 1999.1, p. 85).

5. From a tomb excavated at Lamagou, Aohan Banner, Inner Mongolia (*Neimenggu wenwu kaogu*, 1999.1, p. 90 and front cover; also illustrated in *Qidan wangchao* [*Khitan dynasty*], p. 113.

6. Karl A. Wittfogel and Fêng Chia-shêng, *History of Chinese Society: Liao, 907–1125*, p. 132.

7. Eagles and falcons were given to the Liao emperor by the Tieli tribe (located in today's Jilin Province) in 952, and the Xi Xia paid to the Liao, among other things, five falcons for catching hares (Wittfogel and Fêng, *History of Chinese Society*, p 332; p. 354, n. 42).

9a–b. Two figures

Liao dynasty, 993 or earlier
From the tomb of Han Kuangsi and Xiao
at Baiyinwula Township, Balin Left Banner
Sandstone
a. Height: 62 cm; b. Height: 63.5 cm
Research Institute of Cultural Relics
and Archaeology of Inner Mongolia

In 2000, the Research Institute of Cultural Relics and Archaeology of Inner Mongolia launched a survey of some forty ancient tombs situated in the Baiyinhan Mountain area in Balin Left Banner. Among the three Liao tombs that were excavated thereafter, Tomb Number 3 is identified as belonging to Han Kuangsi, who died in 983 and was buried in 985, and his wife, Xiao, who died and was buried in 993. The large brick tomb is composed of a long ramp (22.65 meters), a reception courtyard (5.9 meters by 2.7 meters), a short ramp behind the entrance door (5.5 meters), a square front chamber (5.05 meters by 5.44 meters), a round rear chamber (6.54 meters in diameter), and two side chambers (each 1.6 meters by 1.17 meters). The two stone statues exhibited here were unearthed high above the reception courtyard, side by side facing the long ramp.[1] The fact that the statues were found above the entrance to the tomb indicates that they might have been added after the tomb was sealed, to provide additional protection for the tomb occupants.

The two statues, each carved from a large piece of sandstone, represent a Khitan male and a Khitan female. The male figure is clothed in a typical nomadic robe—its outer panel is fastened on the left side of the chest, and the underlying, inner panel is fastened on the right. A pair of earrings adorns his pierced ears. Suspended from his belt is a knife that resembles the knives found on the corpse of Xiao Shaoju, the husband of the Princess of Chen (cat. 43a–b). His head is shaved except for the hair around the forehead and near the neck; this is a typical Khitan hairstyle. This male figure stands with both eyes looking downward, his hands held together toward his belly, as if he were waiting for instructions to act. The female figure has a similarly solemn expression and wears similar earrings. Her braided hair is tied with a knot on her forehead. She wears a tight-fitting, narrow-sleeved robe that overlaps to the left, and holds a piece of cloth in her hands.

Archaeological evidence shows that in their tombs the Liao replaced the pottery figures often found in Tang-dynasty tombs, to guarantee perpetual offerings to the deceased, with pictorial images of servants and attendants on wall murals. However, stone statues fashioned in a style similar to that of the Tang dynasty figures have been recovered from a small number of early Liao tombs.[2] The meaning of large stone sculptures in early Liao tombs remains unclear and awaits further research.[3]

HMS

---

1. For the excavation report, see "Baiyinhan shan Liaodai Han shi jiazu mudi fajue baogao" [Excavation report of the Liao-dynasty Han family cemetery in Baiyinhan Mountain], *Neimenggu wenwu kaogu* 2002.2, pp. 19–42.

2. Such statues include six in the tomb at Sunjiawan in Chaoyang, Liaoning Province, and the male figure in the tomb (dated 986) of Yelü Yanning. See *Wenwu* 1992.6, pl. 3; 1980.7, pl. 5.1. A headless statue and a sculpture of a dog—both life-size—in the collection of the Museum of Balin Left Banner, are said to have come from the mausoleum of Abaoji (d. 926), founder of the Liao empire.

3. In a late Liao tomb at Changping, Beijing, a notable pair of pottery figures (one male and one female, each measuring about 50.5 centimeters high) was placed on either side of the niche where the ashes of the tomb's occupant were placed, toward the back of the tomb. See *Wenwu* 1993.3, pp. 74–75, figs. 24–28.

10. Funerary urn in the form of a yurt

Liao dynasty, tenth century
Excavated from a tomb at Hadatu Village,
Hadayingge Rural Area, Balin Left Banner
Earthenware
Overall height: 24 cm;
diameter of base: 31 cm
Museum of Balin Left Banner

This gray pottery urn in the form of a yurt (*qionglu*) has a conical top resembling the round, arched roof of a yurt and three openings that form two windows and a door. At the pointed tip of the urn is a round lid, which imitates the dome cap that covers the roof window of a traditional yurt. Incised images of ten deer decorate the exterior of the urn.

The Khitan were originally nomads who lived in yurts. Even when they gradually adopted a sedentary lifestyle and began building cities, they maintained their steppe traditions. In several sites, such as the Supreme Capital and Zuzhou in Balin Left Banner, there were areas within the walled cities where no buildings were erected, so that the Khitan could set up their yurts.

Deer, an important prey of Khitan hunts, were depicted in various mediums ranging from pottery to painting.[1] Hunting was an integral part of the nomadic lifestyle of the Khitan, for it provided not only a supply of meat but also military training. Textual records on imperial seasonal hunting show that deer, tigers, bear, and foxes were particularly worthy of an emperor's effort. Hadayingge Rural Area, where this urn was unearthed, is near Qingzhou, which was known as the autumn deer hunting grounds of the Liao emperors.[2]

Like the round or octagonal Liao tombs and tomb chambers, which are also based on the yurt, the yurt-shaped burial urn reflects the nomadic tradition of Liao culture (see cat. 46). While the tombs have a hole on top of their conical ceilings, which is then covered by a stone slab, the yurt-shaped urn's dome hole is capped with a round lid.[3] The house-shaped coffin along with the wooden furniture found in a tomb at Jiefangyingzi, Wengniute Banner (cat. 46a–d) were originally encased in a wooden structure resembling a yurt.

HMS

---

1. A well-published example from an archaeological context is the mural painting in the Dongling Mausoleum of the Liao emperor Shengzong (r. 982–1031) or Xingzong (r. 1031–1055), one of a group of imperial mausoleums in Qingzhou referred to as the Qing Mausoleums. See Tamura Jitsuzō, *Keiryō no hekiga: kaiga, chōsoku, tōji* [*Murals in the Qing Mausoleums: paintings, carvings, ceramics*], pp. 49–53, 95–114.

2. See Fu Lehuan, "Liao dai sishi nabo kao wu pian" [Five essays on the Liao emperor's seasonal residences], *Liao shi cong kao*, pp. 36–172, especially pp. 54–63.

3. Xiang Chunsong, "Neimenggu Jiefangyingzi Liao mu fajue jianbao" [Excavation report of a Liao tomb in Jiefangyingzi, Inner Mongolia], *Kaogu* 1979.4, pp. 330–34. Xiang Chunsong, "Neimenggu Wengniuteqi Liaodai Guangdegong mu" [The Liao tomb at Guangdegong, Wengniute Banner, Inner Mongolia], *Beifang wenwu* 1989.4, pp. 41–44.

11. Black burnished bottle

Liao dynasty, 942 or earlier
From the tomb of Yelü Yuzhi and Chonggun
at Hansumu Township, Aluke'erqin Banner
Earthenware
Height: 31.3 cm; diameter of mouth: 13.7 cm;
diameter of base: 10.7 cm
Research Institute of Cultural Relics
and Archaeology of Inner Mongolia

This bottle from the tomb of Yelü Yuzhi
(890–941) and his wife, Chonggun (d.
942), has an ovoid body that is divided into
eight lobes by seven evenly spaced vertical
indentations. The bottle is made of gray
earthenware that is burnished to a bright
black color, except on the base and the lower
quarter of the body. Encircling its shoulder
is a raised line that separates the body from
the tapering neck and bowl-shaped mouth.
Dense, vertical combed lines decorate the
unburnished lower part of the body. A similar bottle, with a slightly flaring foot, covered
with a glossy russet glaze, was discovered in
the same tomb (fig. 86).

Such burnished earthenware with combed
lines on the lower body is distinctively from
the Liao period and has been found in a
number of early Liao tombs.[1]

HMS

Fig. 86. Brown-glazed bottle; from the tomb
of Yelü Yuzhi and Chonggun at Hansumu
Township, Aluke'erqin Banner, Inner Mongolia

1. For example, see Li Yiyou and Wei Jian, eds.,
Neimenggu wenwu kaogu wenji [*Essays on the archaeology of cultural relics in Inner Mongolia*], vol. 1, p. 456, fig. 3.1; *Kaogu*
1984.2, p. 154, figs. 2.1, 2.6, 2.11; *Kaogu* 1987.10, p.
891, fig. 4.3; p. 901, fig. 17.1; *Liaohai wenwu xuekan*
1991.1, p. 108, fig. 3.5.

12a–d. Saddle ornaments

Liao dynasty, 1018 or earlier
From the tomb of the Princess of Chen
and Xiao Shaoju at Qinglongshan Town
in Naiman Banner
Gilded silver
a. Pommel: height: 24.5 cm
b. Cantle: height: 38 cm
c,d. Side pieces: length: 16.5 cm
Research Institute of Cultural Relics
and Archaeology of Inner Mongolia

Originally attached to a wooden saddle frame (fig. 87), these four ornaments, which once decorated the saddle of Xiao Shaoju, are fashioned from hammered silver sheets gilded, decorated in repoussé, and embellished with chased detailing. The high-arching pommel ornament is decorated in repoussé with forty small birds with wings outstretched, depicted flitting among scrolling tendrils against a punched ground. The cantle ornament has similar decoration, but with fifty birds, while the two side pieces have seven birds each.

That the horse was considered important to the Khitan is confirmed by the prevalence of equestrian gear in most Khitan tombs. Saddle ornaments similar to these, however, are found only in the tombs of the more well-to-do.[1]

Burying riding equipment and weapons with the deceased was a tradition common among nomadic horse-riding peoples in North China. During the Han dynasty (206 BC–AD 220), Xiongnu warriors were laid to rest along with their bows, arrows, and swords, and often their steeds.[2] In the Northeast, in the fourth and fifth centuries, high-status Murong Xianbei were buried with gilded-iron stirrups and gilded-bronze openwork pommel and cantle ornaments similar in form to Liao examples.[3]

Although burying equestrian gear may have been a nomadic practice, this set of saddle ornaments belonging to Xiao Shaoju was probably made by Han Chinese. Since the establishment of their dynasty, the Khitan took Chinese prisoners of war, especially skilled craftsmen, and relocated them to Liao territory. The decoration of this set of saddle ornaments is closely related to late Tang gold and silver work.

HK

1. Saddle ornaments made from silver sheet have been excavated from the side chamber in the tomb of the Prince of Wei (d. 959) in Chifeng City, Inner Mongolia (*Kaogu xuebao* 1956.3, color pl. 5.1–5.4), and from an unidentified but richly furnished tomb at Daiqintala Township, Keyou Central Banner, Xing'an League, Inner Mongolia, where a wooden rack for holding a saddle was also found (*Neimenggu wenwu kaogu wenji*, 1997.2, pp. 651–67).
2. Zhao Fangzhi (ed.), *Caoyuan wenhua* [*Grassland culture*], pp. 108–14.
3. The tombs of the Murong Xianbei are found around Chaoyang in Liaoning Province (*Wenwu* 1997.11, pp. 19–32). They ruled the former Yan kindgoms in the Northeast during the Six Dynasties period (220–589). The Khitan are thought to have been a branch of the Xianbei clan.

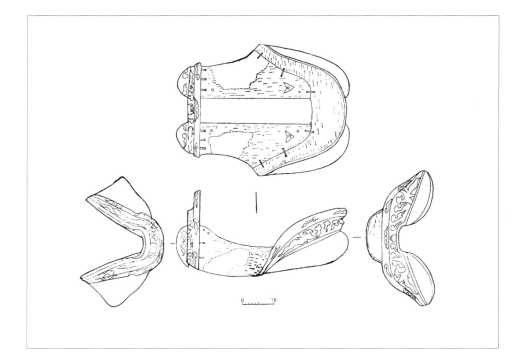

Fig. 87. Wood saddle decorated with gilded-silver ornaments, found in the west side chamber of the tomb of the Princess of Chen (d. 1018) and her husband, Xiao Shaoju, in Naiman Banner, Inner Mongolia

13. Bridle with animal-shaped ornaments

Liao dynasty, 1018 or earlier
From the tomb of the Princess of Chen
and Xiao Shaoju at Qinglongshan Town
in Naiman Banner
Silver, jade
Length: 50 cm; width: 30 cm
Research Institute of Cultural Relics
and Archaeology of Inner Mongolia

The horse was the most prized animal in Liao society. Surviving on grass and water, the hardy steppe animal was easy to keep, while providing not only mobility—enabling the Khitan to herd, hunt, and fight—but also a source of food, in the form of koumiss (fermented mare's milk). So important were horses that they were often buried or burned along with clothing and other personal objects at the funeral of the departed.[1] In an attempt to stop such a wasteful and costly funeral custom, however, in the late tenth century the government forbade the killing of horses.[2] Thereafter, equestrian gear made of metal was placed in tombs instead.

The quality of the material used, the workmanship, and the amount of horse tack (saddles, bridles, and harness ornaments) buried in a tomb depended on the status of the deceased. This bridle along with the breastplate (cat. 14) and crupper (cat. 15) are the only excavated examples made from silver and jade. Hammered silver strips replace what normally would have been leather straps to make up the halter, which is decorated all over with recumbent jade animals and circular bosses attached by silver pins. Judging by the materials, they were made specifically for the tomb.

Adorning a horse with ornate decorations not only signals the importance and high regard accorded the animal but also is an ancient custom common to the horse-riding cultures of the Eurasian steppes. Archaeological evidence shows that as early as the fifth century BC, elite nomads of the Altai Mountains in Pazyryk, South Siberia, were buried with elaborately decorated horse tack made of leather embellished with intricate wood carvings.[3]

HK

1. A horse skeleton was found in the passageway of a fairly simple tomb belonging to a fifty-year-old female in Aohan Banner, Inner Mongolia (*Neimenggu wenwu kaogu* 1984.3, pp. 75–9), and the jaw bone of a horse was found in Tomb Number 1 at Kulun Banner, Zhelimu, Inner Mongolia (*Wenwu* 1973.8, p. 5).

2. *Liaoshi* [*History of the Liao*], p. 142; Karl A. Wittfogel and Fêng Chia-shêng, *History of Chinese Society: Liao, 907–1125*, p. 261.

3. Horses, horse tack, and wagons were buried with the deceased. A leather bridle was excavated from the burial mound of a rich nomad; its straps were decorated with wooden plaques carved with griffin and eagle motifs and originally covered with gold or tin (Liudmila Barkova, "The Nomadic Culture of the Altai and the Animal Style," in Joan Aruz, Andrei Alekseev, Elena Korolkova [eds.], *The Golden Deer of Eurasia: Scythian and Sarmatian Treasures from the Russian Steppes*, p. 244, no. 190).

14a–b. Breastplate and stirrups

Liao dynasty, 1018 or earlier
From the tomb of the Princess of Chen
and Xiao Shaoju at Qinglongshan Town
in Naiman Banner
a. Breastplate: silver, jade; length: 170 cm
b. Stirrups: gilded iron; length: 19.5 cm
Research Institute of Cultural Relics
and Archaeology of Inner Mongolia

Archaeological evidence shows that the use of breastplates and cruppers with *diexie* belts (cat. 15) on horses was popular among the Tang elite.[1] That this tradition continued into the Liao dynasty is confirmed by the number of tomb murals depicting caparisoned steeds with similar gear.[2]

This breastplate, designed to encircle the lower neck of the horse and attach to the front of the saddle by two short straps, would have been used to keep the saddle in its correct position and prevent it from slipping backward. Made of hammered silver sheet, it is decorated all around with recumbent equines and felines carved from jade and attached by silver pins. Silver stirrup straps, each with a buckle allowing the strap to be lengthened or shortened, hang from the ends of the short straps that are attached to the top of the breastplate. Most stirrups found in Liao tombs are made of iron; these stirrups were made more precious by gilding.

The stirrup was introduced into China by horse-riding peoples from the steppes.[3] The earliest archaeological evidence of the use of stirrups in China proper appears in fourth-century Jin tombs, from which pottery figures of horses modeled with a single stirrup as well as with two stirrups have been excavated.[4] Using metal or metal sheets around a wood core to fashion stirrups is a tradition that developed in Northeast China among the Murong Xianbei in the third or fourth century and then spread to Korea and Japan.[5] Both single stirrups and pairs have been excavated—the latter in greater quantity, presumably as the advantages of riding with two stirrups became apparent.[6]

HK

1. For example, murals depicting a hunting expedition in the Tang tomb of Prince Zhang Huai illustrate horses with cruppers and breastplates (*Zhongguo meishu quanji, Huihua bian* [Complete treasury of Chinese fine arts, Painting Series], vol. 12, *Mu shi bihua* [Tomb mural paintings], no. 114). Two stone relief panels in the collection of the University of Pennsylvania Museum that were excavated from the Tang emperor Taizong's tomb (r. 626–49) depict his favourite steeds, Autumn Dew and Saffron Yellow Battlecharger. Both are shown wearing a breastplate and crupper with *diexie* belt (Robert E. Harrist, Jr., *Power and Virtue: The Horse in Chinese Art*, pp. 18–19, figs. 1a, 1b).

2. Feng Enxue, "Liaodai Qidan maju tansuo" [Exploring Liao Khitan horse gear], *Kaoguxue jikan* 2004.14, p. 451, fig. 11.

3. A.D.H. Bivar, "The Stirrup and its Origins," *Oriental Art*, Summer 1955, p. 62.

4. A pottery figure of a horse, its rider seated on a saddle with a single stirrup, was excavated from a Western Jin (265–316) tomb in Changsha dated to 302: see Sun Ji, "Tangdai de maju yu mashi" [Tang-dynasty horse gear and ornaments], *Wenwu* 1981.10, p. 82, fig. 1.1. A pottery caparisoned horse with a saddle fitted with two stirrups was found in an Eastern Jin (317–420) tomb, dated circa 322, in Nanjing (*Wenwu* 1972.11, p. 40).

5. For a discussion of the development of horse ornaments in Northeast China from the Sixteen Kingdoms to Goguryeo, Korea, and Japan, see Dong Gao, "Gongyuan san zhi liu shiji Murong Xianbei, Gaogoli, Chaoxian, Riben maju zhi bijiao yanjiu," *Wenwu* 1995.10, pp. 34–42.

6. The earliest stirrup made of metal excavated in China was found in a fourth-century Jin tomb near Anyang, Henan Province, thought to belong to a non-Han Chinese. The similarity of the tomb and its contents, including the saddle ornaments and stirrup, to Murong Xianbei tombs has prompted speculation that the ornaments and stirrup were made in Liaoxi, the territory ruled by the Murong Xianbei (Tian Likun and Li Zhi, "Chaoyang faxian de San Yan wenhua yiwu ji xiangguan wenti" [Three Yan cultural relics excavated from Chaoyang and related questions], *Wenwu* 1994.11, p. 30).

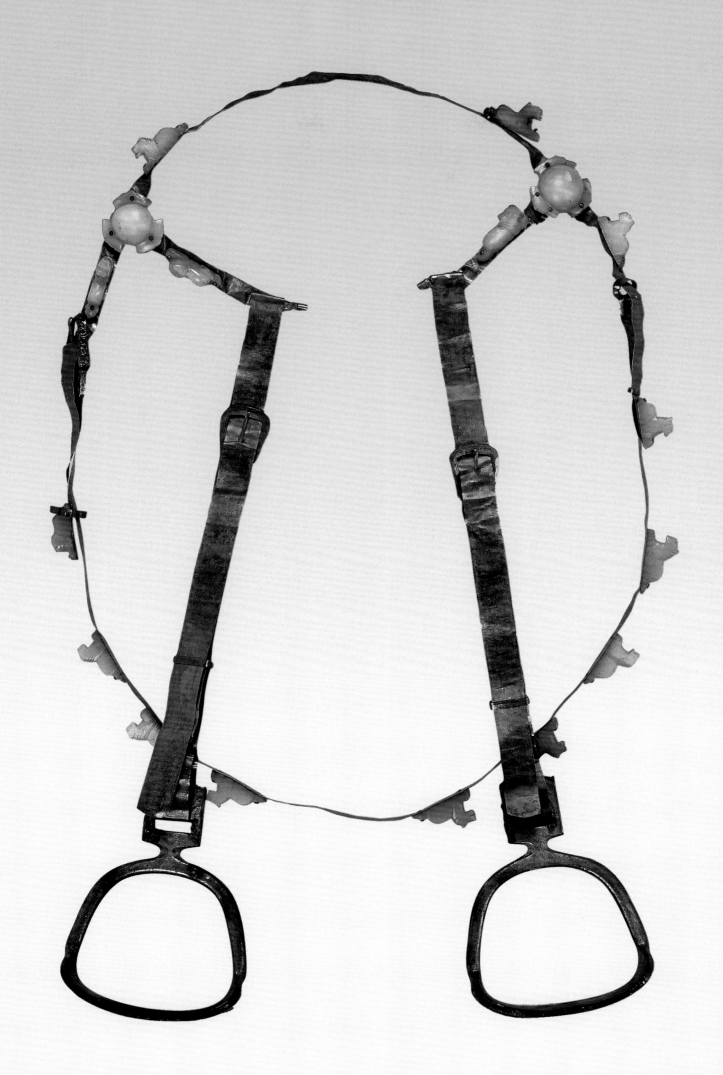

15. Crupper with *diexie* belts

Liao dynasty, 1018 or earlier
From the tomb of the Princess of Chen
and Xiao Shaoju at Qinglongshan Town
in Naiman Banner
Silver, jade
Length: 320 cm
Research Institute of Cultural Relics
and Archaeology of Inner Mongolia

Attached to the back of a saddle and passing under the horse's tail, a crupper would have prevented the saddle from slipping forward. This crupper is still attached to two triangular-shaped ornaments that would have decorated the back part of the saddle on either side of the cantle. Each ornament has four pendant straps, known as *diexie*, which would have hung across the horse's flanks. The entire assemblage is made from silver sheet, and the straps are decorated with sixty-four recumbent white-jade horses.[1] Murals of ornately caparisoned horses in the tombs of wealthy Liao illustrate how this type of horse gear was worn.[2]

The combination of a crupper and *diexie* attached to the rear of the saddle is likely to have originated in the Western Regions.[3] In a shrine at Dandān-oilik in Xinjiang, near Khotan, the British archaeologist Sir Marc Aurel Stein discovered, in 1900–1901, a sixth-century painting on a wooden panel of a figure riding a horse with a crupper and *diexie* belts.[4] An even earlier depiction of *diexie* belts can be found in a Northern Wei (386–534) mural depicting the *jataka* story of the nine-colored deer, in Mogao Cave 257 at Dunhuang, Xinjiang.[5] By the Tang dynasty (618–907), many horses are depicted with this type of horse gear,[6] and it is most certainly through the Tang that the Liao adopted this particular equine decoration.

Horse ornaments of the elite have been found embellished with agate and rock crystal.[7] This is the only set thus far excavated that is decorated with jade carvings. Jade was considered a precious material during the Liao era, and jade carvings have only been found in tombs of the wealthy or in pagoda relic deposits.[8]

HK

1. *Liao Chenguo gongzhu mu* [*Liao tomb of the princess of the state of Chen*], p. 109.

2. Tomb M1 in Kulunqi, Naiman Banner; Zhang Shiqing's tomb in Hebei Province; Qingling mausoleum (where the Liao emperors Shengzong, Xingzong, and Daozong are buried); and the Princess of Chen's tomb. Also, Baoshan Tomb Number 1 at Chifeng, Inner Mongolia (*Wenwu* 1998.1, color pl. 4.1; p. 84, fig. 27).

3. Feng Enxue, "Liaodai Qidan maju tansuo" [Exploring Liao Khitan horse gear], *Kaoguxue jikan* 2004.14, p. 452. Emma Bunker also suggests that this may have originated from a Turkic tradition (Emma C. Bunker, Julia M. White, and Jenny F. So, *Adornment for the Body and Soul: Ancient Chinese Ornaments from the Mengdiexuan Collection*, pp. 243–44).

4. Roderick Whitfield and Anne Farrer, *Caves of the Thousand Buddhas: Chinese Art from the Silk Route*, cat. no. 133.

5. In the second scene of the story, the king, identified by his crown, is depicted searching for the nine-colored deer. He sits astride a caparisoned horse with *diexie* belts, clearly depicted in white, hanging from the back of the saddle (*Zhongguo meishu quanji, Huihua bian* [*Complete treasury of Chinese fine arts, Painting series*], vol. 14, *Dunhuang bihua* [*shang*] [*Dunhuang murals (first part)*], p. 25, no. 24, with a detail on p. 27, fig. 26).

6. See cat. 14 in this catalogue, footnote 1.

7. A set of agate horse ornaments was excavated from the tomb of the Prince of Wei (*Kaogu xuebao* 1956.3, p. 13), and a bridle inlaid with rock crystal was found in the tomb of a rich female in Yemaotai, Faku, Liaoning Province (*Wenwu* 1975.12, p. 27).

8. For a list of jade artifacts excavated from Liao sites, see the appendix to Xu Xiaodong's, *Liaodai Yuqi Yanjiu* [*Research on Liao jades*], pp. 188–94.

16a–b. Saddle flaps

Liao dynasty, 1018 or earlier
From the tomb of the Princess of Chen
and Xiao Shaoju at Qinglongshan Town
in Naiman Banner
Silver with painted decoration
Length: 59 cm; width: 66 cm
Research Institute of Cultural Relics
and Archaeology of Inner Mongolia

Once colored in red, the top part of these two saddle flaps fashioned from hammered silver sheet delineates the area where the saddle would have been placed. Two apertures remain where the flaps were attached to either side of the wooden saddle frame. Three peacock-type birds with dense plumage and long tail feathers, each facing a flaming pearl, decorate the surface: the one in the center stands majestically, with wings held high and one leg raised; it is flanked by the two others, their wings outstretched in midflight amid scrolling clouds.[1]

In the Northern and Southern Dynasties period (c. 386–589), saddle flaps were larger in size, extending below the horse's belly, and were made from stiff material such as bamboo or birch bark so that they would not flap when the horse was on the move; by the Tang and Liao eras, however, flaps had become reduced in size, and softer materials, such as embroidered cloth, were used.[2] These hard, brittle silver saddle flaps could hardly have been intended for practical use and, like the rest of the Princess of Chen's silver horse tack, were made specifically for burial.

Liao saddles were quality objects. In 1005, to celebrate the birthday of the Northern Song emperor Zhenzong (r. 997–1022), the Liao emperor Shengzong (r. 982–1031) sent gifts made in Liao territory. Among the presents were saddles decorated with gold and silver dragons and phoenixes, as well as saddlecloths made of embroidered red silk, felt, and swordfish skin.[3] Other gifts included furs, leather boots, a whip, a bow, and arrows—items that were highly valued by the horse-riding Khitan.

HK

---

1. Two types of bird decorations, phoenix-type and peacock-type, are often found on Liao objects. The latter are distinguishable from the former by their hooked beaks and wispy, flowing plumage.
2. Feng Enxue, "Liaodai Qidan ma ju tansuo" [Exploring Liao Khitan horse gear], *Kaoguxue jikan* 2004.14, p. 453. Embroidered cloth saddle flaps were excavated from the tomb of a rich female in Yemaotai, Faku, Liaoning Province (*Wenwu* 1975.12, p. 27).
3. Karl A. Wittfogel and Fêng Chia-shêng, *History of Chinese Society: Liao, 907–1125*, p. 147.

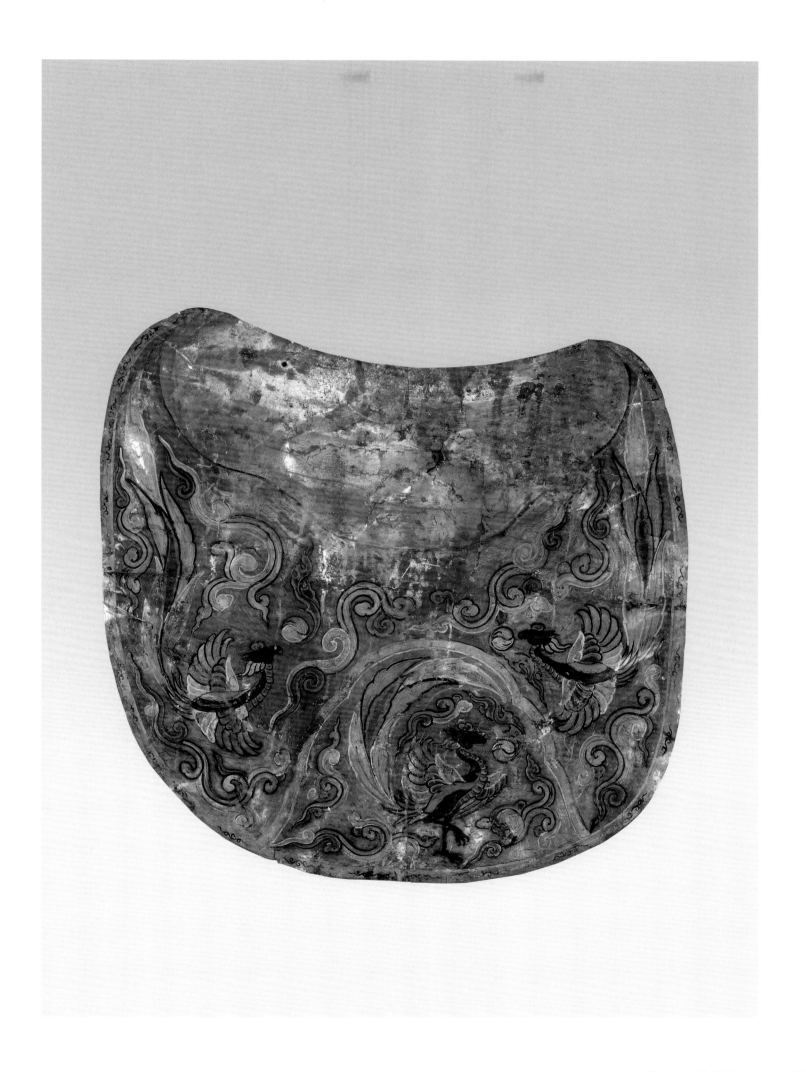

17. Harness ornaments

Liao dynasty, 959 or earlier
From the tomb of the Prince of Wei
(posthumous title of Fuma Xiao Shagu)
and Zhigu at Dayingzi, Linxi County,
Chifeng City
Gilded silver
T-shaped fittings: length: 9.2 cm;
width: 5.9 cm; height: 1.6 cm
Rectangular pieces: length: 4.5 cm;
width: 2.6 cm
Museum of the Inner Mongolia
Autonomous Region

Equestrian gear has been found in many Khitan tombs; however, what distinguishes this set of gilded-silver harness ornaments is the quality of the workmanship. Excavated from the joint tomb of Xiao Shagu, the Prince of Wei, and his wife, Zhigu, the daughter of Abaoji, the first Liao emperor,[1] this set was found along with seven other harness sets made of gilded silver, gilded bronze, and agate.[2] Writhing dragons dominate the design: four, cast in profile, surround a swirling pearl on each of the scalloped-edged T-shaped fittings, while a single dragon fills each of the twelve rectangular pieces. Pins on the reverse of each ornament indicate that they were probably once attached to fabric or leather straps.

The dragon motif, which was strictly controlled by sumptuary law during the Liao dynasty (see cat. 22a–h), had imperial associations: the *Liaoshi* (History of the Liao) describes the emperor and empress sitting on cushions with dragon designs during the all-important ceremony of making sacrifices to Muye Mountain.[3] Not surprisingly, dragon designs are most often found on precious materials such as gold, silver (cat. 93, 96), embroidery, and other textiles[4] in the tombs of members of the Liao elite.

It is no coincidence that the dragons on these harness ornaments resemble dragons from the Tang and Five Dynasties periods. Soon after the establishment of their empire, the Liao consciously appropriated Chinese imperial paraphernalia: in 947, after the conquest of the Later Jin dynasty (one of the short-lived Five Dynasties and a puppet regime of the Liao), a large quantity of Chinese products, including armor and weapons, musical instruments, astronomical charts, and other imperial paraphernalia, was seized and transferred to the Supreme Capital.[5] Skilled Chinese artisans were also captured and brought to the northern part of the territory. Although these harness ornaments may have been produced by Han Chinese artisans, richly ornamenting the horse is very much a steppe tradition.

HK

1. Xiao Shagu's epitaph is reproduced and explained in Gai Zhiyong, *Neimenggu Liaodai shikewen yanjiu* [*Research on Liao stone inscriptions in Inner Mongolia*], pp. 33–41. Xiao Shagu was the son of the elder brother of Empress Yingtian, the wife of Abaoji (*Qidan wangchao* [*Khitan dynasty*], p. 102).
2. Despite having been robbed, the tomb contained an extraordinary amount of finely worked equestrian gear; the side chamber where the eight sets of harnesses were found also contained saddle ornaments, bits, and stirrups (*Kaogu xuebao* 1956.3, pp. 10–15).
3. *Liaoshi*, p. 834.
4. Examples are illustrated in Zhao Feng, *Liao Textiles and Costumes*, p. 135.
5. Karl A. Wittfogel and Fêng Chia-shêng, *History of Chinese Society: Liao, 907–1125*, p. 256.

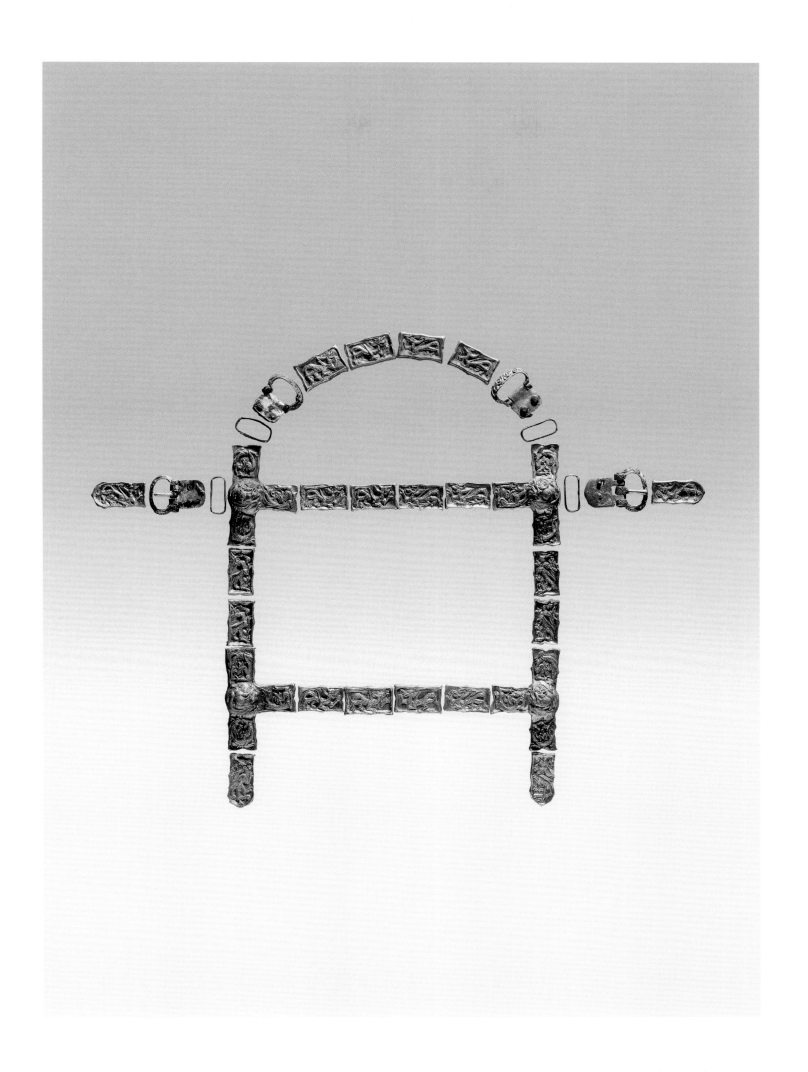

18a–b. Awl and sheath

Liao dynasty, 1018 or earlier
From the tomb of the Princess of Chen
and Xiao Shaoju at Qinglongshan Town
in Naiman Banner
a. Awl: silver with jade handle;
length: 17.8 cm
b. Sheath: gilded silver; length: 14.8 cm
Research Institute of Cultural Relics
and Archaeology of Inner Mongolia

While the Princess of Chen was found with
small boxes and pendants of gold and jade
suspended from her belt, her consort, Xiao
Shaoju, had various tools suspended from his
belt. This awl was excavated along with two
other sheathed knives (see cat. 43a–b) near the
waist of the prince. The handle, of circular
shape, is made of polished white jade, while the
sharp pointed awl is cast from silver. The
sheath is made of gilded silver and has a silver
loop-in-loop chain that would have fastened
the implement to the prince's *diexie* belt (cat.
21).[1] Knives and other tools excavated from
most Khitan tombs are usually made of iron.[2]
This awl, made of silver and jade, could have
only belonged to someone of high status.

An awl is listed as part of the kit of a Liao
cavalryman and was a necessary tool for
hunting.[3] Hunting was an integral part of
Khitan culture and played a central role in
politics and society. It was not only enjoyed
as a sport but also seen as a means of honing
warfare skills and practicing military maneu-
vers, since hunting required discipline, organization, and excellent riding and shooting
skills.[4] On the state level, swan hunting, in
particular, was an important annual ritual
carried out by the emperor. The *Liaoshi*
(History of the Liao) describes a royal hunting expedition to Duck River every spring
during which the emperor released specially
trained falcons to catch wild swans.[5] As the
fallen birds lay on the ground, attendants
would use their awls to remove the swans'
brains to feed the exhausted falcons. The
emperor would then offer the largest swan to
the ancestral temple.[6]

HK

1. *Liao Chenguo gongzhu mu* [*Liao tomb of the princess of the state of Chen*], p. 45.
2. The intact tomb of a female contained an iron knife and other tools (*Beifang wenwu* 1992.3, p. 40, figs. 5.2, 7–9.)
3. Karl A. Wittfogel and Fêng Chia-shêng, *History of Chinese Society: Liao, 907–1125*, p. 523.
4. Wittfogel and Fêng, *History of Chinese Society*, p. 526.
5. This special breed of birds is referred to in the *Liaoshi* as *haidongqing*.
6. *Liaoshi*, p. 132. Falcons are not domesticated, as such, but are trained to hunt down their food when released; so a piece of the prey must be given to them after each successful kill. For a discussion of awls, see Sun Ji, "Yi zhi Liaodai ci'e zhui" [A Liao-dynasty swan-piercing awl], *Wenwu* 1987.11, pp. 36–37.

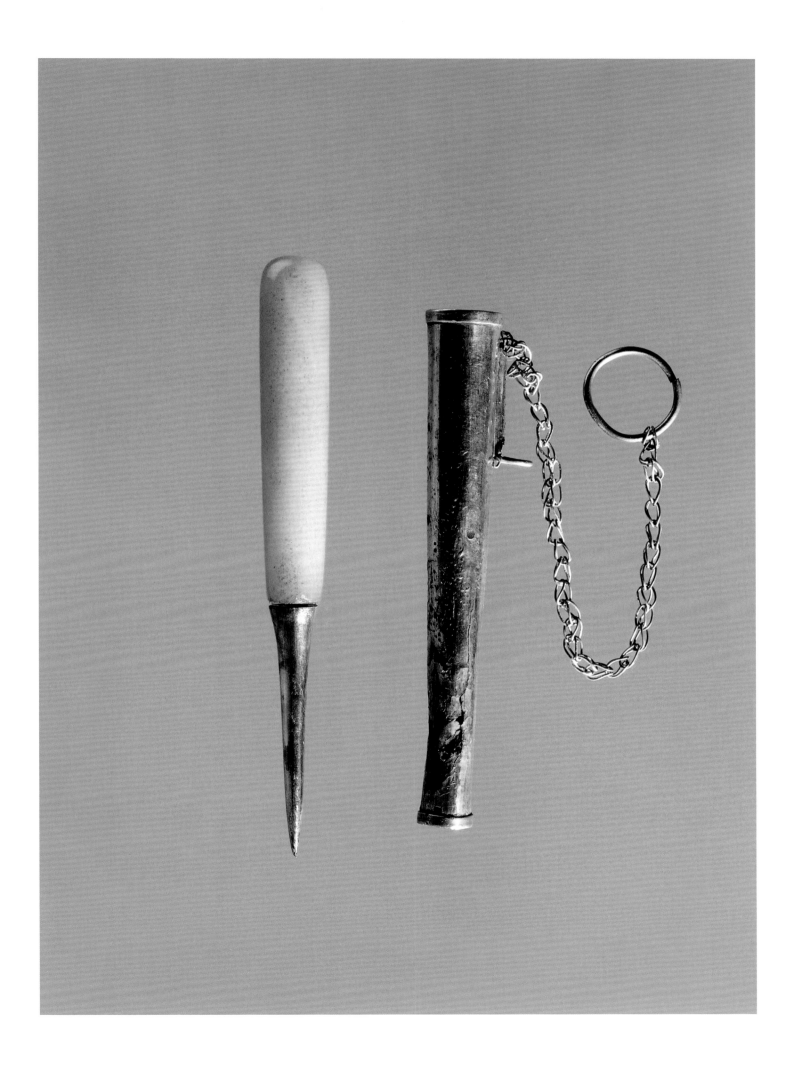

19. Painted wood bow case

Liao dynasty, 1018 or earlier
From the tomb of the Princess of Chen
and Xiao Shaoju at Qinglongshan Town
in Naiman Banner
Cypress
Length: 74.5 cm; width: 10 cm to 25 cm
Research Institute of Cultural Relics
and Archaeology of Inner Mongolia

Archery, especially on horseback, was a skill of many ancient horse-riding peoples and an integral part of Khitan culture and identity. Bows and arrows were not only effective weapons[1] but also important hunting equipment.[2] Archaeological evidence shows that the Khitan used at least seven types of iron arrowheads for different purposes. The types are similar to those found in third- to fourth-century Xianbei graves, suggesting that archery technology changed relatively little from then up to the Liao era.[3]

This bow case is made from two pieces of cypress wood; each side is hollowed out in the interior to fit the lower half of a bow.[4] The remains of a wooden bow were discovered nearby, and a strand of bronze wire found inside the case is thought to have been the bowstring. The exterior surface, which has been polished, is reddish brown in color. Traces of colored pigment depicting a cloud design remain near the top of the case, a large circle dominates the middle, and a long-tailed bird amid clouds decorates the narrowest part. Three silver hinges spaced evenly along the straight edge join the two halves of the case, and another hinge, on the opposite side, acts as a fastener. An aperture in the top corner allowed the case to be suspended from a *diexie* belt (see cat. 21).

Most bow containers were made from light and flexible material such as cloth or leather,[5] not wood; articles fashioned from wood found in Liao tombs tend to be furniture or architectural pieces, such as coffins, platforms, and miniature housing, or the figurines sometimes found in the tombs of people of high status. This bow case and the remains of a bow were found on the east side of the tomb's rear chamber, where the bodies of the Princess of Chen and her husband were laid to rest. Their positioning in the most important part of the tomb suggests that they were considered to be among the deceased's more valued possessions. Indeed, literary records show that on the state level, bows and arrows were given as gifts or exchanged as a sign of friendly relations.[6]

HK

---

1. A mural in the north passage of the antechamber of the Eastern Mausoleum belonging to the Liao emperor Shengzong (r. 982–1031) depicts a male Khitan attendant standing guard at the entrance holding a *guduo* scepter; a bow in its case is suspended from his belt in much the same way a knife or sword would be (Tamura Jitsuzō and Kobayashi Yukio, *Tombs and Mural Paintings of Ch'ing-ling: Liao Imperial Mausoleums of 11th Century A.D. in Eastern Mongolia*, vol. 2, pl. 21).

2. In Aohan Banner, a mural excavated from the tomb of an elite Khitan depicts a group of attendants preparing for a hunt, with one attendant carrying a bow (see *Qidan wangchao* [Khitan dynasty], p. 113, and *Neimenggu wenwu kaogu* 1999.1, front cover and the excavation report on pp. 90–97).

3. Liu Bing, "Qian tan Liaodai gongjian" [Brief discussion on Liao bows and arrows], *Neimenggu kaogu wenji* 1997.2, p. 558.

4. *Liao Chenguo gongzhu mu* [Liao tomb of the princess of the state of Chen], p. 62.

5. A leather bow case was excavated from the tomb of a male in Chenba'erhu Banner, Northeast Inner Mongolia. A circular patch of leather sewn onto the middle of the case closely resembles the circular design on the wood case. It is difficult to say whether it was part of the design or simply a repair, as noted by the archaeologists (*Kaoguxue jikan* 2004.14, p. 277, fig. 10.1).

6. In 938, the Liao emperor Shengzong exchanged bows, arrows, saddles, and horses with Yelü Xiezhen in front of Empress Dowager Chengtian and agreed to be friends (*Liaoshi* [*History of the Liao*], p. 111), and a leather-covered birch bow was included among a list of gifts given by Shengzong to the Song emperor on his birthday (Karl A. Wittfogel and Fêng Chia-shêng, *History of Chinese Society: Liao, 907–1125*, p. 147).

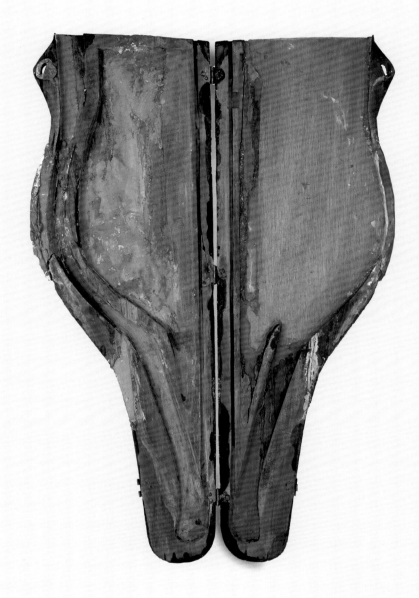

20. *Guduo* scepter

Liao dynasty
Excavated in Shuiquan Village,
Salibaxiang, Aohan Banner
Jade with bronze fitting
and remains of wood shaft
Length: 8.4 cm; width: 8.4 cm;
height: 8.8 cm
Museum of Aohan Banner

This almost spherical piece of semitranslucent jade was once mounted atop a wooden handle, traces of which still remain in its hollow interior. A bronze cap, now corroded to a malachite shade of green, covered the uppermost tip of the wooden shaft.

Visual records of what *guduo* scepters looked like and how they were used have been preserved in tombs of the Khitan elite. Mural paintings usually depict male Khitan attendants with different length scepters guarding doorways or participating in processions. The scepters have either long, staff-length shafts[1] or shorter handles that allow them to be held upright at waist level.[2]

Guduo appear to have been used both as weapons and as items of regalia. The army section of the *Liaoshi* (History of the Liao) lists *guduo* along with bows, arrows, axes, and armor as part of a soldier's kit.[3] Although there is no textual evidence describing what *guduo* looked like, that the characters for the word have a metal radical indicates that they were made of some type of metal. Iron as well as bronze examples[4] have been found grouped with swords and arrowheads in some Khitan tombs, and one of a pair of painted ferocious door guardians excavated from a tomb at Bayanerdeng, Balin Right Banner, Inner Mongolia, wields a *guduo* weapon made of metal.[5] Bronze mace heads with spiked projections found in the Ordos region, west of China, are the earliest actual metal examples to have been found, prompting speculation that *guduo* may have originated in the nomadic steppe cultures.[6]

This rare example made of jade, with its finely polished faceted surface, is most likely to have been used as an item of regalia rather than as a weapon. By the Song dynasty (960–1279), *guduo* scepters were fairly common symbols of authority.[7]

HK

---

1. Two Khitan male attendants holding long *guduo* scepters, leading a group with a horse and female attendants, are depicted along the north wall of the passageway of Tomb Number 2 at Kulun Banner (Wang Jianqun and Chen Xiangwei, *Kulun Liaodai bihua mu* [*Liao mural tombs at Kulun*], p. 41, fig. 30; p. 42, fig. 31, color pl. 6).

2. Two male guards are painted by the door to the side chamber containing the Princess of Chen's armory, each holding a *guduo* in his right hand (*Liao Chenguo gongzhu mu* [*Liao tomb of the princess of the state of Chen*], color pl. 2.2).

3. Karl A. Wittfogel and Fêng Chia-shêng, *History of Chinese Society: Liao, 907–1125*, p. 523.

4. *Wenwu* 1985.3, p. 59, fig. 6. A ceramic *guduo* has also been excavated from a tomb in Fuxin, Liaoning Province (*Fuxin Liao Jin shi yanjiu* 1995.2, p.125).

5. The other guardian holds a sword. The pair of guardians was painted on the outside of the doors, while a pair of generals graced the inside (Adam T. Kessler, *Empires Beyond the Great Wall: The Heritage of Genghis Khan*, p. 114, fig. 74; *Qidan wangchao* [*Khitan dynasty*], pp. 64–67).

6. *Liaohai wenwu xuekan* 1989.1, p. 255; *Kaogu yu wenwu* 1982.5, pp. 98–101.

7. *Liaohai wenwu xuekan* 1989.1, p. 257; Su Bai, *Baisha Song mu* [*Song tomb at Baisha*], pp. 21, 32.

21. *Diexie* belt

Liao dynasty, 1018 or earlier
From the tomb of the Princess of Chen
and Xiao Shaoju at Qinglongshan Town
in Naiman Banner
Jade, gilded bronze, bronze, silk
Length: 156 cm; width: 2 cm;
thickness: 0.1 cm
Research Institute of Cultural Relics
and Archaeology of Inner Mongolia

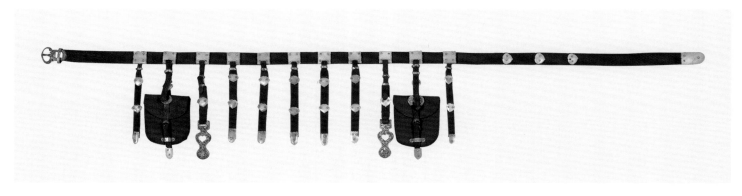

Belts with pendant straps (*diexie*) were worn by mounted horsemen both as symbols of rank and for practical use. This belt set, which belonged to Xiao Shaoju, comprises sixty jade, gilded-bronze and bronze ornaments that were once sewn onto a silk sash similar to this modern replacement.[1] The main part of the belt is decorated with jade ornaments: eleven square plaques, three peach-shaped plaques, and an end piece. Each square plaque has a slit from which to suspend a strap to which decorative pendants, pouches, or implements such as a knife (cat. 43a–b) or an awl (cat. 18a–b) could be hung. An hour-glass-shaped, gilded-bronze filigree end piece decorates the ends of two pendant straps.

The earliest evidence of *diexie* belts comes from Pazyryk, in the Altai region of South Siberia, where a belt decorated with cast-silver plaques and pendant straps was excavated from a fifth-century BC burial mound.[2] Liao *diexie* belts are most closely related to Turkic prototypes and are constructed in a very similar manner; a *diexie* belt fashioned from leather and decorated with cast-gold plaques was excavated in Sunite Right Banner, Xilinguole League, Inner Mongolia. Two

knives and two pouches once hung from the belt. The tomb is thought to have belonged to a high-status Turk (Tujue) and dates to the early Tang dynasty (seventh century).[3] Depictions of Turkic warriors on eighth-century stone grave monuments in Tuva, Central Asia, and of a Uighur prince discovered in Xinjiang dating to the ninth century,[4] all wearing *diexie* belts, are further evidence that such belts originated from the Western Regions via the Turks.

During the Liao era, belts were decorated with plaques made of different materials depending on the status and rank of those who wore them.[5] The belts worn by the emperor on ceremonial occasions were decorated with gold, jade, and rhinoceros horn.[6]

HK

1. The belt set was found in the northeast part of the tomb's rear chamber, in which the Princess of Chen and her husband were laid to rest (*Liao Chenguo gongzhu mu* [*Liao tomb of the princess of the state of Chen*], pp. 74–77, fig. 47).

2. Sergei Ivanovich Rudenko, *Frozen Tombs of Siberia: The Pazyryk Burials of Iron Age Horsemen*, p. 99, pl. 67a, b, d,

e. Belts without *diexie* straps, suspended with weapons and ornaments, were worn by members of nomadic cultures at least three centuries earlier: the occupant of an eighth-to-seventh-century BC nomadic grave, excavated from Zhoujiadi, Aohan Banner, Southeast Inner Mongolia, was found wearing two leather belts decorated with bronze plaques. Found suspended from the narrower of the two belts were a bronze knife, a bronze awl, and a bronze needle (*Kaogu* 1984.5, pp. 424–25, col. pl. 6).

3. Zhao Fangzhi (ed.), *Caoyuan wenhua* [*Grassland culture*], pp. 144–145, nos. 163–166; *Chengjisi han: Zhongguo gudai beifang caoyuan youmu wenhua* [*Chingghis Khan: The ancient nomadic culture of northern China*], pp. 156–57.

4. See Emma C. Bunker, Julia M. White, and Jenny F. So, *Adornment for the Body and Soul: Ancient Chinese Ornaments from the Mengdiexuan Collection*, p. 30.

5. Compare the Liao *diexie* belt decorated with gilded-copper peony-motif ornaments and hung with two leather pouches and a knife that was excavated from Chifeng, Inner Mongolia (*Chengjisi han*, pp. 188–89). Also illustrated is another belt set decorated with peony motifs, but cast in gold, which was excavated from Nailingao, Naiman Banner, Tongliao City, Inner Mongolia. Originally, the belt had ten short straps and two pouches

6. *Liaoshi* [*History of the Liao*], p. 906.

22a–h. Belt set with dragon design

Liao dynasty, 1018 or earlier
From the tomb of the Princess of Chen
and Xiao Shaoju at Qinglongshan Town
in Naiman Banner
Gold
Each plaque: length: 10.6 cm to 12.4 cm;
width: 6.2 cm
Research Institute of Cultural Relics
and Archaeology of Inner Mongolia

The Liao adopted Chinese clothing from the Tang, and, with it, sumptuary laws and dress regulations associated with defining status and rank.[1] During the Tang era (618–907), the number of plaques on a belt indicated the rank of the wearer—the larger the number of plaques, the higher the rank. So did the material they were made of—jade and gold signifying the highest rank, followed by rhinoceros horn, silver, brass, bronze, and, lastly, iron.[2]

Three different types of belts were found in the tomb of the Princess of Chen and Xiao Shaoju: so-called foreign-style *diexie* belts (see cat. 21); Chinese-style (or Tang-style) belts, without pendant straps; and this eight-plaque gold belt set found around the waist of the princess. Each rectangular plaque is the same width and is solidly cast in high relief with a three-clawed dragon depicted in three-quarter view, its heads raised or lowered, twisting and writhing above a ground of crested waves, craggy rocks, and scattered magical *ruyi* fungi—symbols of longevity.[3]

The arrangement of the eight plaques in graduated sizes, with the shortest on the outside and the tallest in the center, is unusual. To date, no other belt set like this has been discovered in a Liao tomb.

The use of the dragon motif, reserved for high-status members of Liao society, was strictly regulated. An entry in the *Liaoshi* (History of the Liao) states that in 1078, an imperial edict forbade common people "to wear brocade and variegated silk with decorations of the sun, moon, mountains, or dragons."[4]

HK

clothes, as did his brother, Yelü Longqing (Karl A. Wittfogel and Fêng Chia-shêng, *History of Chinese Society: Liao, 907–1125*, pp. 227–28, fn 16).

2. *Xin Tangshu* [*New history of the Tang*], p. 529.

3. A rare piece of *kesi* silk tapestry with this design but without the *ruyi* was discovered in a tomb in Yemaotai, Faku, Liaoning Province, covering a deceased female (Xu Bingkun and Sun Shoudao, *Dongbei wenhua* [*Northeast culture*], p. 179, nos. 221–22). The woman has not been identified, but the large quantity of textiles and other items found in her tomb indicate that she was of high status. For the excavation report, see *Wenwu* 1975.12, pp. 26–36.

4. *Liaoshi*, p. 281.

---

1. The *Liaoshi* notes that from 938 to 947 the officials of the Northern Region wore Khitan-style clothing, whereas the emperor and the officials of the Southern Region wore Chinese-style clothing. After 1055, all officials in the Northern Region wore Chinese clothes at important ceremonies, although at regular court audiences they would wear Khitan clothing. In 1008, a Song envoy to the Liao court noted that the Liao emperor Shengzong (r. 982–1031) wore Chinese

23. Sachet with openwork decoration

Liao dynasty, 1018 or earlier
From the tomb of the Princess of Chen
and Xiao Shaoju at Qinglongshan Town
in Naiman Banner
Gold alloy
Length: 13.4 cm; width: 7.8 cm
Research Institute of Cultural Relics
and Archaeology of Inner Mongolia

Found in the tomb (dated 1018) of the Princess of Chen and Xiao Shaoju, this pouch was discovered near the waist of the corpse of the princess and was attached to a belt by a loop-in-loop chain, as were several other objects in the exhibition—the jade pendants (cat. 38, 44), the rock crystal cups (cat. 101a–c), and the gold cylindrical container (cat. 24).

The sachet is made of two identical heart-shaped metal sheets connected by gold threads, which pass through ten pairs of holes along the edges. The hammered-metal sheets are decorated with tendril scrolls, with the background etched out. A cover flap in a similar, but smaller, heart shape is hinged to the pouch. A small loop and a hook made of metal wire are placed at the tip of the flap and on the pouch to secure the cover. According to the archaeological report, the metal sheets were made of an alloy of 90.65 percent gold and 8.24 percent silver.[1] Fragments discovered inside the pouch indicate that originally it had a silk lining.[2]

HMS

1. Wang Changwui and Jia Yunpo, "Chen guo gongzhu yu fuma hezang mu bufen jinyinqi de fenxi" [Scientific analysis of some of the gold and silver wares from the joint burial of the Princess of Chen and her husband], *Liao Chenguo gongzhu mu* [*Liao tomb of the princess of the state of Chen*], pp. 166–170.
2. *Liao Chenguo gongzhu mu*, p. 28.

24. Cylindrical container

Liao dynasty, 1018 or earlier
From the tomb of the Princess of Chen
and Xiao Shaoju at Qinglongshan Town
in Naiman Banner
Gold
Length: 11.7 cm; diameter: 1.2 cm
Research Institute of Cultural Relics
and Archaeology of Inner Mongolia

This container is one of several accoutrements made of precious materials—including the amber and jade containers (cat nos. 35, 36, 38a), gold sachet with openwork decoration (cat. 23), rock crystal cups (cat. 101a–c), and jade pendant (cat. 44)—that once hung from the belt of the Princess of Chen. It is made of hammered gold sheet and decorated with a chased design of scrolling tendrils against a finely punched ground. The long edges are joined to form a thin cylinder with a circular base sealing the bottom, and a gold loop-in-loop chain attaches to either side of the opening at the top to allow the container to be suspended from a belt. The domed cover, with radiating leaf decoration in repoussé, is also attached to the chain.

It is not certain what was stored in this container, although its elongated cylindrical form seems suited to holding something long and thin.[1] The Chinese archaeologists who excavated the tomb of the Princess of Chen and Xiao Shaoju describe this piece as a needle container (zhentong).[2] One piece of textual evidence mentions a needle container: in the Han Chinese dress (Han fu) section of the Liaoshi (History of the Liao), a needle container was one of seven implements, including a knife, a grinding stone, and a flint, that military officials of the fifth rank and above could wear on their diexie belts.[3] The Liao ruling class followed strict dress codes that helped to define status and rank.[4] It is interesting to note that belt implements were not only rank specific but also job specific, as civil and military officials wore different ornaments on their belts. It is not known whether needle containers were exclusive to male officials, but it does seem unusual that

the princess would be wearing an accoutrement normally reserved for a male military official. Because this gold cylindrical container was empty when it was found, it is difficult to ascertain whether it was, indeed, used as a needle case.

HK

1. Hairpins, usually made from bone, have been excavated from Liao tombs, but they are generally too long to fit into this container. One found in the tomb of a female measures 16.5 cm (Liaohai wenwu xuekan 1991.1, pp. 112–13, fig. 9.1), while another measures 12 cm (Neimenggu wenwu kaogu wenji, 1997.2, p. 646).
2. Liao Chenguo gongzhu mu [Liao tomb of the princess of the state of Chen], p. 28; however, there is no archaeological evidence to support this claim.
3. Liaoshi, p. 910. There were two types of dress during the Liao: national (Khitan) dress and Han Chinese-style dress. During the Huitong period (938–47), the officials of the Northern Region dressed in national style, while the emperor and the officials of the Southern Region dressed in Han Chinese style. By 1055, all officials dressed in Chinese-style clothing at important ceremonies, but at regular court ceremonies, the Huitong-period system was still followed (Liaoshi, p. 908). See also Karl A. Wittfogel and Fêng Chia-shêng, History of Chinese Society: Liao, 907–1125, pp. 227–28, where a full commentary about clothing is given.
4. The Jiu Tangshu (Old History of the Tang Dynasty) records the same seven implements allowed to be worn on the diexie belts of military officials of the fifth rank and above (Jiu Tangshu, p. 1953).

25 and 26a–b. Earrings in form of dragon-fish

Liao dynasty, 942 or earlier
From the tomb of Yelü Yuzhi and
Chonggun at Hansumu Township,
Aluke'erqin Banner
25: Gold and turquoise; height: 4.4 cm;
width: 3.5 cm; thickness: 1.6 cm
26a–b: Gold; height: 4.4–4.5 cm;
width: 3.5–4.4 cm; thickness: 1.6 cm
Research Institute of Cultural Relics
and Archaeology of Inner Mongolia

These three earrings, which were excavated from the tomb of Yelü Yuzhi (890–941) and his wife, Chonggun (d. 942), in Hansumu Township, Aluke'erqin Banner, take the shape of a dragon-fish, or *makara*, curled into a U-shape. The *makara*, a mythical creature of Indian origin, has two horns (although there are no horns on two of these earrings), winglike fins, a prominent snout, and a noticeable tail.

The earrings were formed by soldering together two halves, each made of hammered gold. Details such as whiskers and scales were chased or engraved onto the creature's face and body. Projecting pins below the jaws of the *makaras* suggest that there might have been additional components attached.[1] The single earring, which is larger in size than the pair, is further decorated with turquoise inlays, adding to its luxurious quality.

U-shaped earrings were a signature body ornament of the Khitan. Similar earrings have been excavated from a number of Khitan tombs.[2] Their unusual shape may be linked to ancient Etruscan and late Byzantine prototypes. Their popularity among the Khitan reflects the long-distance ties of the Liao empire with West Asia.[3]

HMS

---

1. Comparable examples have been found in a number of Liao tombs. See *Beifang wenwu* 2000.3, pl. 1.3; *Kaogu* 1996.6, p. 46, fig. 8.
2. Similar dragon-fish earrings have been found in Nailin'gao, Zhelimu League, Inner Mongolia, and in Jianping, Liaoning Province. A pair of dragon-fish earrings was worn by a Khitan woman who was buried at Daiqintala Township in Keyou Central Banner, Inner Mongolia. See Wei Jian, ed., *Neimenggu wenwu kaogu wenji* [*Essays on the archaeology of cultural relics in Inner Mongolia*], vol. 2, color pl. 4.3. The recent discovery at Tuerji Hill of the tomb of a Khitan woman yielded a pair of dragon-fish earrings, too. See Liu Laixue, ed., *Neimenggu kaogu wushi nian* [*Fifty years of archaeology in Inner Mongolia*], p. 98.
3. Xu Xiaodong, "East-West Connections and Amber under the Qidans," in Jenny F. So (ed.), *Noble Riders from Pine and Deserts: The Artistic Legacy of the Qidan*, pp. 34–37.

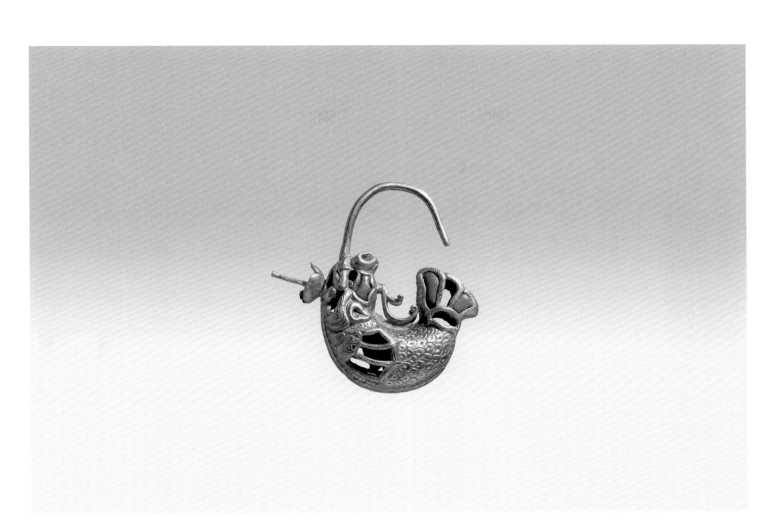

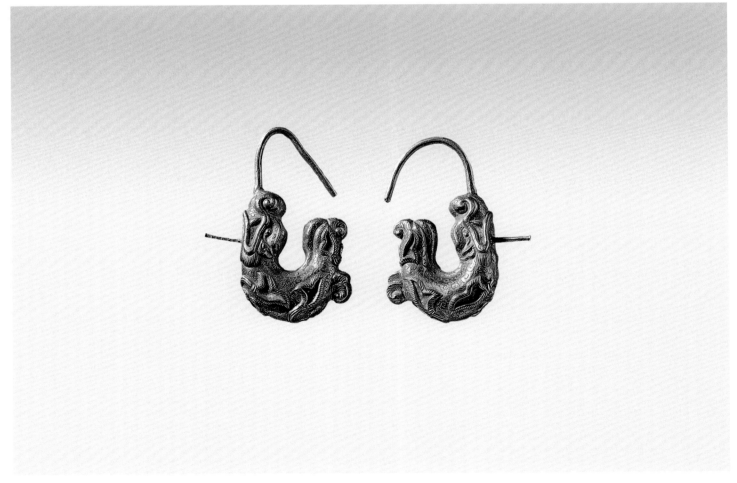

27. Double-dragon headdress

Liao dynasty, 1018 or earlier
From the tomb of the Princess of Chen
and Xiao Shaoju at Qinglongshan Town
in Naiman Banner
Amber, pearls, gold
Length: 30 cm
Research Institute of Cultural Relics
and Archaeology of Inner Mongolia

This unusual headdress adorned the head of
the Princess of Chen when she was buried in
1018.[1] It is formed by three strands of pearls
that go over the head, with two pendant
openwork amber plaques, each in the shape
of a crouching dragon in the round, hanging
down on either side, near the ears. Three
hammered-gold-sheet pendants with dangles
are suspended by twisted wire from each of
the dragon plaques and would have caught
the light when they moved. The large cutouts
have an inverted lotus-leaf shape and the
smaller dangles are petal shaped.

The dragons are typical sinuous Khitan dragons with crests, powerful legs, clawed paws,
and slightly open jaws that reveal sharp teeth.
Lingzhi-shaped (magic fungus) forms depicted
beneath the dragons' paws suggest clouds, an
appropriate setting for dragons, which are
said to inhabit clouds and bring rain.

The pearls that embellish the headdress must
have come via trade routes from the south;
they were probably harvested from beds off
the coast of Southwest Guangdong or the
seas of Southeast Asia.[2] Pearls are beautiful
gems and need no cutting, but they tend to
decay, as they have done on this headdress.
Pearls have always had an aura of wonder for
the Chinese, who frequently associated them
with the treasure hoard of a dragon. After
the introduction of Buddhism, pearls were
also considered a symbol of the Buddha and
his laws.

ECB

1. *Qidan wangchao* [*Khitan dynasty*], p. 134.
2. See Julia M. White and Emma C. Bunker,
Adornment for Eternity: Status and Rank in Chinese Ornament,
p. 37, for a brief discussion of the use of pearls by the
Chinese.

28. Gold ornament in the shape of a five-petal flower

Liao dynasty, 923 or earlier
From Tomb Number 1 at Baoshan
in Aluke'erqin Banner
Gold
Width: 3.5 cm
Museum of Aluke'erqin Banner

This gold ornament made of twisted wire is in the shape of a five-petal flower. It was excavated in 1994 from Tomb Number 1 at Baoshan in Aluke'erqin Banner, which belonged to Qinde, a fourteen-year-old boy whose father was a well-known Khitan noble-man around the time of the founding of the Khitan state.[1] Located near the Liao dynasty's Supreme Capital (Shangjing), this is the earliest Liao tomb excavated so far.[2]

An examination of the ornament suggests that the gold wire used to form it was drawn rather than strip-twisted, since the spiral lines that mark strip-twisted wire are absent.[3] Drawn wire was known as early as the sixth century AD in Korea, so knowledge of the technique by the Khitan in the tenth century is not surprising.[4] The ornament represents an early phase of Khitan art, and perhaps dates to the period before the Khitan had come into close contact with the more sophisticated metallurgical techniques of Song China.

ECB

1. *Qidan wangchao* [*Khitan dynasty*], p. 135.
2. Xiaoneng Yang, "Unearthing Liao Elite Art and Culture: An Empire in Northern China from the 10th to the 12th Century," *Orientations*, October 2004, p. 70.
3. For the difference between strip-twisted and drawn wire, see Emma C. Bunker, "Gold Wire in Ancient China," *Orientations*, March 1997, pp. 94–95.
4. Jack Ogden, "Connections between Islam, Europe, and the Far East in the Medieval Period," in Paul Jett, Janet G. Douglas, Blythe McCarthy, and John Winter, *Scientific Research in the Field of Asian Art: Proceedings of the First Forbes Symposium at the Freer Gallery of Art*, pp. 2–7.

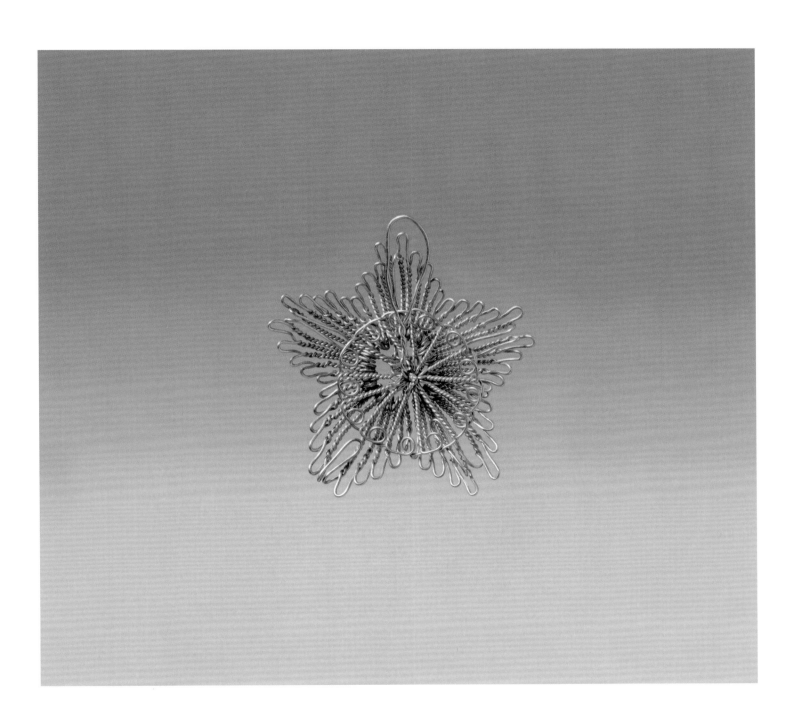

29. Gilded-silver hairpin in the shape of a phoenix

Liao dynasty
Acquired in the Chifeng District
Gilded silver
Length: 16 cm
Cultural Relics Store of Chifeng City

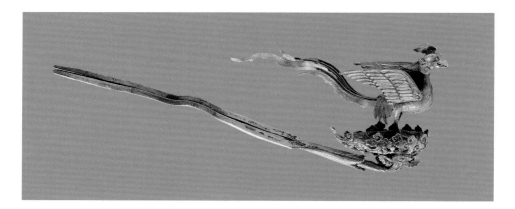

A crested phoenix with outspread wings and a flowing tail stands amid scattered *lingzhi*-shaped (magic fungus) clouds on this handsome gilded-silver hairpin from the Chifeng District.[1] In both Chinese and Khitan iconography, the phoenix was considered a feminine symbol, suggesting that this gloriously flamboyant hairpin may once have adorned the hair of an elite Khitan woman. The phoenix on the hairpin has an unfriendly-looking hooked beak, a characteristic of Liao-dynasty phoenix images that reflects the Khitan's hunting heritage and their passion for falconry.[2] For the Khitan, falconry was practiced in one of the four seasonal ritual hunts; this ritual hunt was known as *chunshui* (spring water) and was conducted in early spring, when falcons were used to hunt swans and wild geese along the many streams and rivers that ran through Liao territory.

The body of the phoenix is hollow; it is made from two halves of repoussé silver, with the details reinforced by chasing. The various parts of the bird were attached by crimping and soldering to create a three-dimensional image. Each of the wings appears to have been attached by a rivet, and the *lingzhi* base

assembled from several pieces. The phoenix and double-pronged hairpin were then mercury amalgam gilded and fitted together.

This hairpin is very similar in concept and workmanship to contemporary Song Chinese hairpins, except for the rapacious beak, which was a specifically Khitan motif.[3] The metalworking techniques used had already been perfected by Song-dynasty (960–1279) artisans, suggesting that Song artisans employed by the Khitan could well have made this hairpin and added the beak to the phoenix image to appeal to Khitan taste.[4]

ECB

1. *Qidan wangchao* [*Khitan dynasty*], pp. 136–37.
2. For the importance of falconry in Khitan culture, see Emma C. Bunker, Julia M. White, and Jenny F. So, *Adornment for the Body and Soul: Ancient Chinese Ornaments from the Mengdiexuan Collection*, pp. 19–22.
3. For comparison, see the straight pointed beaks on the phoenixes that adorn two Song-dynasty Chinese hairpins, Bunker et al., *Adornment for the Body and Soul*, p. 278.
4. For typical Song metalworking techniques, see Bunker et al., *Adornment for the Body and Soul*, pp. 274, 278.

30a–c. Three shield-shaped finger rings

Liao dynasty, 942 or earlier
From the tomb of Yelü Yuzhi
and Chonggun at Hansumu Township
in Aluke'erqin Banner
Gold
Length: 3.2 cm; width: 1.9 cm
Research Institute of Cultural Relics
and Archaeology of Inner Mongolia

These three gold rings were excavated from the tomb of Yelü Yuzhi (890–941) and his wife, Chonggun (d. 942), at Hansumu Township in Aluke'erqin Banner.[1] They are each penannular in shape, which would allow them to be fitted over the metal-mesh gloves that encased the fingers of the deceased. Various repoussé floral decorations adorn the shield of each ring. Linear floral scrolls with finely chased surface details and a three-dimensional ball soldered in the center of the shield distinguish two of the rings. The third ring displays on its shield a raised flower in full bloom within a leaf-motif frame.

Ornate rings, ranging from simple shield-shaped examples to more elaborate versions surmounted by three-dimensional animal images in the round appear to have been very popular personal ornaments among the Khitan.

ECB

---

1. *Qidan wangchao* [*Khitan dynasty*], p. 138.

31a–b. Pair of bracelets

Liao dynasty, 1018 or earlier
From the tomb of the Princess of Chen
and Xiao Shaoju at Qinglongshan Town
in Naiman Banner
Gold
Diameter: 5.5 cm
Research Institute of Cultural Relics
and Archaeology of Inner Mongolia

These two gold C-shaped bracelets adorned
the arms of the Princess of Chen when she
was buried at Qinglongshan Town, Naiman
Banner, in Southeast Inner Mongolia in
1018.[1] The bracelets were lost-wax cast, and
each is distinguished by dragon-headed terminates that are connected by a scaly body
enhanced with punched and chased textural
and anatomical details. According to the
archaeological evidence, such bracelets were
worn only by women during the Liao
dynasty, and always in pairs—sometimes a
pair on each wrist or sometimes one bracelet
on each wrist.

C-shaped bracelets with animal terminates were
first produced in the ancient Near East during
the first millennium BC; they later spread across
Eurasia, all the way to the Far East.[2] The sub-
stitution of dragons for the usual West Asian
animals was a Khitan innovation. The Khitan
also decorated C-shaped bracelets with phoenix
heads and floral motifs.[3]

ECB

1. *Qidan wangchao* [*Khitan dynasty*], pp. 140–41.
2. Edith Porada, *The Art of Ancient Iran: Pre-Islamic
Cultures*, pp. 172–73.
3. Jenny F. So (ed.), *Noble Riders from Pines and Deserts:
The Artistic Legacy of the Qidan*, pp. 168–75.

32. Agate and Rock-crystal beaded necklace with two gold amulets

Liao dynasty, 942 or earlier
From the tomb of Yelü Yuzhi
and Chonggun at Hansumu Township
in Aluke'erqin Banner
Agate, rock crystal, gold
Length: 78 cm
Research Institute of Cultural Relics
and Archaeology of Inner Mongolia

This lovely necklace was found in the tomb of Yelü Yuzhi (890–941), a first cousin of the founding ruler of the Liao dynasty, and his wife, Chonggun (d. 942), at Hansumu Township, Aluke'erqin Banner, in Southeast Inner Mongolia.[1] The necklace is formed by alternating tubular agate and round crystal beads, along with two curious gold amulets decorated with floral motifs. The two amulets are quintessentially Khitan in form; one is slightly heart-shaped, and the other is in the shape of a faceted, elongated T.

Khitan amulets of this specific type always occur in matched pairs, either loose or on necklaces associated with the elite—the heart-shaped one on the wearer's right and the T-shaped one on the wearer's left.[2] They first appeared in northern China with the arrival of the Khitan and disappeared with their demise. They were made in a wide range of materials, including agate, amber, bronze, crystal, gilded copper, gold, jade, and turquoise.[3] To date, their ancestry and meaning remain elusive, and their significance is not yet understood.[4] The horizontal attachment loop on top of each amulet is basically a Western device, and it is possible that the amulets were popular among the Uighurs, who then introduced them into the Khitan world; there is, however, little confirmed evidence for this theory.[5]

Agate was regarded as a valuable material by the Khitan and was used extensively for making jewelry and small vessels during the Liao period. Agate comes in a wide range of colors and was often used in ancient China during the Han period (206 BC–AD 220) to adorn belt hooks; it became extremely popular during the

Liao era.[6] Rock crystal was highly valued by the Khitan but is almost nonexistent in Song Chinese contexts.[7] Rock crystal is extremely hard and not as easily carved as agate or amber.

ECB

1. *Qidan wangchao* [*Khitan dynasty*], pp. 44–45.
2. Emma C. Bunker, Julia M. White, and Jenny F. So, *Adornment for the Body and Soul: Ancient Chinese Ornaments from the Mengdiexuan Collection*, p. 32; Jenny F. So (ed.), *Noble Riders from Pines and Deserts: The Artistic Legacy of the Qidan*, p. 35.
3. For other examples made of amber, agate, bronze, crystal, gold, turquoise, gilded copper, and jade, see So (ed.), *Noble Riders*, pp. 144–47.
4. Although excavated scientifically, the elements that form this necklace were scattered when they were first discovered. The present form is a careful, recent reconstruction.
5. For the possibility of a Western ancestry for these two amulets, see So (ed.), *Noble Riders*, p. 35.
6. Bunker et al., *Adornment for the Body and Soul*, p. 37.
7. So (ed.), *Noble Riders*, p. 190.

33. Rock-crystal beads

Liao dynasty, 1018 or earlier
From the tomb of the Princess of Chen
and Xiao Shaoju at Qinglongshan Town
in Naiman Banner
Rock crystal
Length: 152 cm
Research Institute of Cultural Relics
and Archaeology of Inner Mongolia

This simple necklace made of irregular-shaped rock-crystal beads was buried in 1018 with the Princess of Chen and Xiao Shaoju at Qinglongshan Town, Naiman Banner, in Southeast Inner Mongolia.[1] Geologically, rock crystal is transparent, colorless quartz. It was much favored by Khitan artists, and not at all popular with the Song Chinese.

Archaeological evidence confirms that rock crystal was used in China as early as the Shang dynasty at a circa 1300–1030 BC site in Henan Province.[2] Rock crystal is described as *shuiyu* (water jade) in the *Shanhaijing* (Classic of Mountains and Seas), a late Warring States (475–221 BC) period text that was a major source for fantastic geographic and zoomorphic peculiarities when it was written.[3]

Rock crystal is extremely hard and difficult to carve. The irregular beads on this necklace were probably formed from polished alluvial pebbles; it would have been extremely time-consuming to create beads that were perfectly spherical from such a hard stone.

ECB

---

1. *Liao Chenguo gongzhu mu* [*Liao tomb of the princess of the state of Chen*], pl. XXIV.2.
2. Zhao Songling and Chen Kangde, *Zhongguo bao yu* [*Precious jades of China*], p. 119.
3. *Qingdai fushi zhanlan tulu* [*Catalogue of the exhibition of Qing-dynasty costume accessories*], pp. 39–41.

34a–d. Four silkworm chrysalis-shaped pendants

Liao dynasty, 1018 or earlier
From the tomb of the Princess of Chen
and Xiao Shaoju at Qinglongshan Town
in Naiman Banner
Amber
Length: 4.5 cm; width: 1.5 cm to 1.9 cm
Research Institute of Cultural Relics
and Archaeology of Inner Mongolia

These four carved-amber, silkworm chrysalis-shaped amulets belong to a set of eight that may have been suspended from the Princess of Chen's belt when she was buried.[1] In excavation photographs, the eight amulets are seen lying on her right thigh, where they may have fallen when her body disintegrated.

Each chrysalis is realistically rendered in the round, with its two wing portions folded tight against the body. The bodies are each marked by circular ridges and taper to a rounded point. Each head has a horizontal perforation with remaining bits of metal wire that must have formed loops for attaching the amulets to the belt.

For the Chinese, the evolution of the silkworm from its suspended cocoon stage to its ultimate emergence as a winged moth was a symbol of the metamorphosis of the human soul from death to rebirth, and so the chrysalis was an appropriate amulet for the dead.

ECB

---

1. *Liao Chenguo gongzhu mu* [*Liao tomb of the princess of the state of Chen*], pl. 23:2.

35. Fish-shaped container

Liao dynasty, 1018 or earlier
From the tomb of the Princess of Chen
and Xiao Shaoju at Qinglongshan Town
in Naiman Banner
Amber, gold
Length: 7.8 cm; width: 4.7 cm
Research Institute of Cultural Relics
and Archaeology of Inner Mongolia

This amber fish-shaped container was buried with the Princess of Chen in 1018; it was found lying on her lower body when her tomb was opened in 1986 and probably hung from her belt.[1] It is similar to the fish-shaped container made of white jade also buried with the princess (cat. 38); but, the amber container has a simple gold loop-in-loop attachment chain and ring whereas the white jade container has a fancy gold-wire chain decorated with beads and a toggle. Both containers have the same loop-and-pin plate closure.

These tiny portable containers illustrate the Khitan's extraordinary creativity and the dexterity of their artisans.[2] The size and shape of each container made of jade or amber is dictated by the size and shape of the raw material available; thus, no two examples are identical. Instead, the containers are an amazing blend of natural materials and human ingenuity. The plethora of jade, gold, and amber objects hanging from the princess's belt must have been a gloriously colorful addition to her dress and appearance. Although amber was also quite popular during the Qing period (1644–1911), the amber artifacts produced for the Khitan elite during the Liao dynasty represented a high-water mark of amber carving that has never been equaled since in the arts of China.

ECB

1. *Qidan wangchao* [*Khitan dynasty*], pp. 160–61.
2. For an in-depth discussion of these tiny Khitan containers, see Jenny F. So, "Tiny Bottles: What a Well-dressed Qidan Lady Wears on her Belt," *Orientations*, October 2004, pp. 75–79.

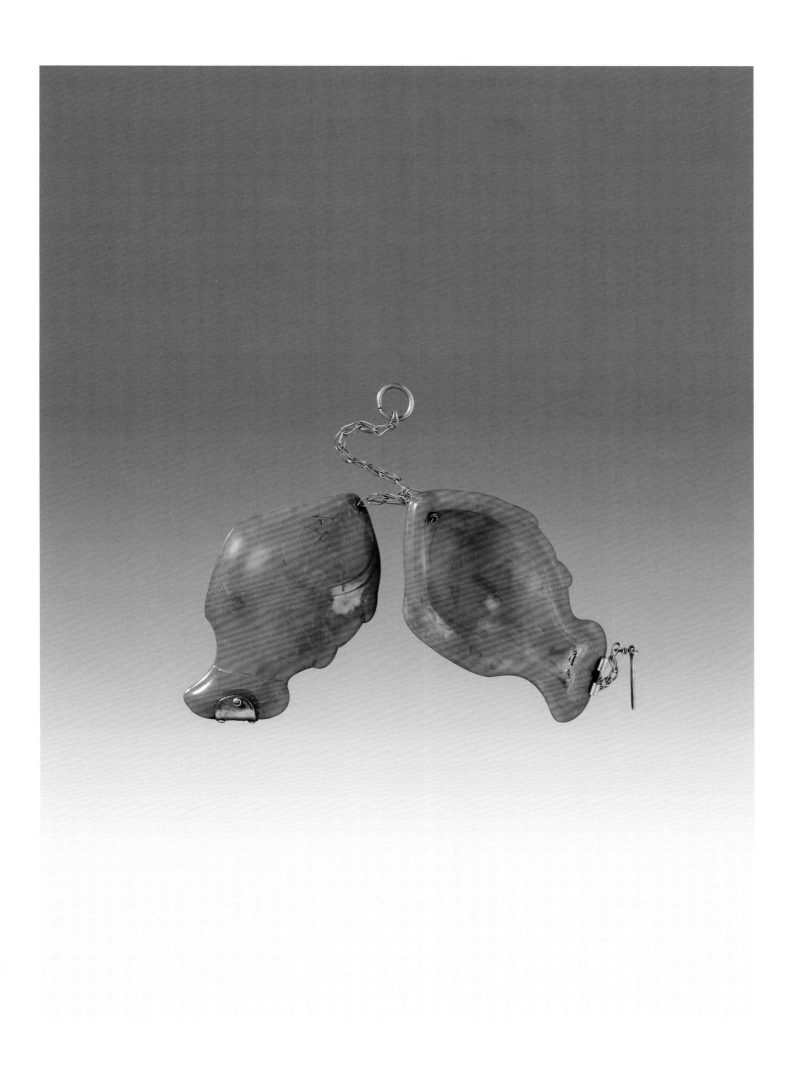

36. Swan-shaped container

Liao dynasty, 1018 or earlier
From the tomb of the Princess of Chen
and Xiao Shaoju at Qinglongshan Town
in Naiman Banner
Amber, gold
Length: 5.3 cm; height: 4 cm
Research Institute of Cultural Relics
and Archaeology of Inner Mongolia

This graceful swan-shaped amber container was among the many portable possessions that were hung from the belt of the Princess of Chen when she was buried in 1018 at Qinglongshan Town in Naiman Banner, Southeast Inner Mongolia.[1] Such containers were treasured Khitan possessions, primarily worn by elite Khitan women.[2] The portability and practicality of such small containers were attuned to the Khitan's mobile lifestyle.

Swans were plentiful in Northeast China, and the Khitan hunted them with falcons each spring, in great ceremonial hunts often attended by the Liao ruler.[3] This swan is shown naturalistically in a recumbent pose, with its head turned backward against its body and with its beautifully rendered feet underneath the body. The artist obviously understood the essential characteristics of a swan, particularly the distinctive long, flat beak with two parallel lines marking the featherless area in front of the eyes. This container is similar to a jade version in the Xiwenguo Zhai Collection, Hong Kong, but displays more accurate and finer anatomical details than the jade version.[4] Such differences suggest that the amber container was carved locally by a Khitan craftsman, while the jade container may have been carved by a Song craftsman who would not have been familiar with amber or with the anatomy of a swan.

The container is cleverly designed with a closing device that could function under mobile conditions. A tiny cavity has been drilled into the back of the swan and covered with a tight-fitting gold cap, which is attached by a loop-in-loop chain to a ring around the swan's neck.

ECB

1. *Qidan wangchao* [*Khitan dynasty*], p. 162.
2. For the best study of portable containers created by the Khitan during the Liao dynasty, see Jenny F. So, "Tiny Bottles: What a Well-dressed Qidan Lady Wears on her Belt," *Orientations*, October 2004, pp. 75–79.
3. Karl A. Wittfogel and Fêng Chia-shêng, *History of Chinese Society: Liao, 907–1125*, p. 236. For a discussion of Khitan falconry, see Emma C. Bunker, Julia M. White, and Jenny F. So, *Adornment for the Body and Soul: Ancient Chinese Ornaments from the Mengdiexuan Collection*, pp. 19–22.
4. So, "Tiny Bottles," p. 76, fig. 5.

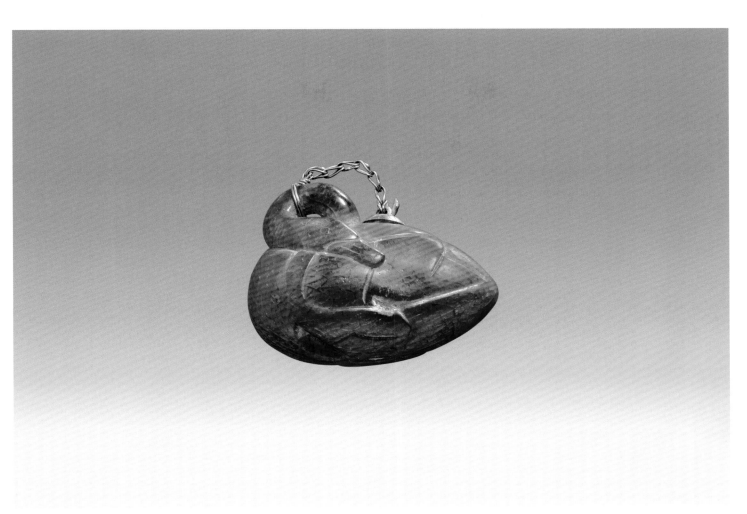

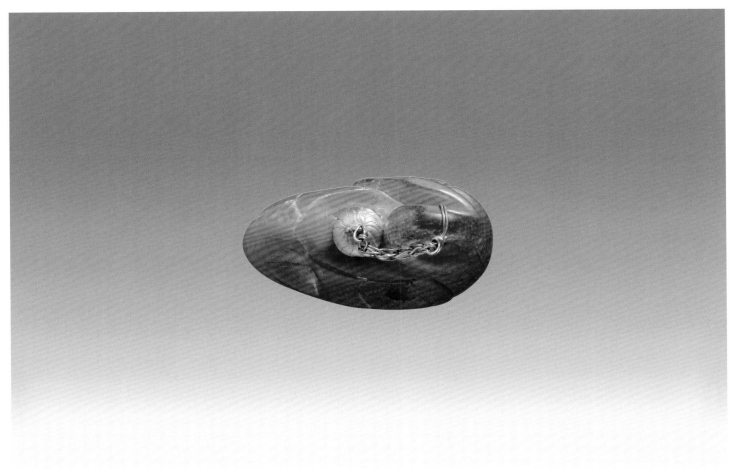

37a–b. Two amber bead necklaces

Liao dynasty, 1018 or earlier
From the tomb of the Princess of Chen
and Xiao Shaoju at Qinglongshan Town
in Naiman Banner
Amber
a. Larger necklace: length: 159 cm
b. Single-strand necklace: length: 113 cm
Research Institute of Cultural Relics
and Archaeology of Inner Mongolia

This lavish amber necklace (*yingluo*) and smaller accompanying amber necklace were found around the neck of the Princess of Chen when her tomb was first opened in 1986.[1] The larger necklace is formed by five strands of irregular-shaped amber beads strung together and bound by five amber zoomorphic-decorated plaques that serve as spacers. The accompanying smaller necklace is a single strand of beads interspersed with smaller zoomorphic-decorated spacers and the two characteristic Khitan amulets.[2] The princess's husband also wore a *yingluo* (length 173 cm) and a single-strand necklace with two amulets (length 107 cm), but his *yingluo* was longer than hers and was formed by six strands and three spacers, perhaps reflecting a different status within the royal hierarchy.[3]

The spacers are all beautifully carved in the shape of birds, fish, animals, and flowers. These auspicious designs each symbolize a wish for good luck and happiness and serve as charms against evil. The majority of the symbols can be traced to China, suggesting that the artisans may have been captive or itinerant Chinese artisans well skilled in jade and stone carving. The symbols may have originally been Chinese, but their selection was specifically Khitan.

Bead necklaces strung with spacers are Indian in origin and can be seen on certain Buddhist images in India, Six Dynasties China, Tang China, and occasionally in paintings at sites in Xinjiang along the Silk Road.[4]

ECB

1. *Liao Chenguo gongzhu mu* [*Liao tomb of the princess of the state of Chen*], color pl. III, XXV.1; *Qidan wangchao* [*Khitan dynasty*], pp. 164–65.
2. For a discussion of these two amulets, see cat. 32 in this publication.
3. *Liao Chenguo gongzhu mu*, color pl. XXV.2.
4. For India, see Douglas Barrett and Basil Gray, *Painting of India*, p. 29; for examples from Six Dynasties China, see Rajeshwari Ghose (ed.), *In the Footsteps of the Buddha: An Iconic Journey from India to China*, nos. 101, 104, pp. 313–14, 318–20; for the Silk Road, see Sun Dawei, *The Art in the Caves of Xinjiang*, especially the Kumutula cave Xin 2, late Six Dynasties, illustrated in pl. 72.

38. Fish-shaped container

Liao dynasty, 1018 or earlier
From the tomb of the Princess of Chen
and Xiao Shaoju at Qinglongshan Town
in Naiman Banner
Jade, gold, pearls, turquoise, amber, crystal
Length: 23.5 cm
Research Institute of Cultural Relics
and Archaeology of Inner Mongolia

This fascinating container in the shape of a fish is carved from the prized white jade of ancient Khotan (Yutian) and is quintessentially Khitan in its functional portability and in its multicolor combination of gold, jade, and rough-hewn precious stones. It was found suspended from the belt of the Princess of Chen in her tomb at Qinglongshan Town in Naiman Banner, Southeast Inner Mongolia.[1] Fish-shaped pendants hung from belts as indicators of status can be traced to the Tang court, where high-ranking officials carried such ornaments suspended from their belts.[2]

This tiny container formed by two halves of the fish is ingeniously closed with a pin inserted through the two loops attached to gold plates, one on each side of the fish's tail. The two halves are held together at the mouth by gold wire that is strung with pearls, irregular-shaped turquoise, amber and crystal beads, and a white jade toggle.[3] Only six such beads now exist, although when the container was first published there were seven beads.[4]

Such containers visually define the aesthetics of the Khitan and their mobile lifestyle.

> Hung from the waist and carried wherever the owners went, they performed designated functions and added glamour to an otherwise drab and harsh existence. As status symbols, they are beautiful markers of social and political rank . . . As artistic creations, their seemingly limitless variety mirrors the adaptability necessary for a very mobile life under harsh natural conditions and unpredictable acts of violence.[5]

ECB

1. *Qidan wangchao* [*Khitan dynasty*], pp. 155, 168.
2. Jenny F. So (ed.), *Noble Riders from Pines and Deserts: The Artistic Legacy of the Qidan*, p. 258, n. 1.
3. Description here based on Jenny F. So, "Tiny Bottles: What a Well-dressed Qidan Lady Wears on her Belt," *Orientations*, October 2004, p. 76.
4. For a drawing of the pendant with all seven beads, see *Liao Chenguo gongzhu mu* [*Liao tomb of the princess of the state of Chen*], p. 83, fig. 50.1.
5. The definition of such containers by Jenny So cannot be improved upon, and so is quoted here verbatim, see So, "Tiny Bottles," p. 79.

39. Flask with handle

Liao dynasty, 941 or earlier
From the tomb of Yelü Yuzhi
and Chonggun at Hansumu Township,
Aluke'erqin Banner
Stoneware with transparent glaze
Height: 30.4 cm
Research Institute of Cultural Relics
and Archaeology of Inner Mongolia

40. Flask with horizontal lugs and figures

Liao dynasty, tenth century
From a tomb in Guangde Rural Area,
Wengniute Banner
Lead-glazed earthenware
Height: 24 cm; width: 16 cm
Museum of Wengniute Banner

41. Wood flask

Liao dynasty, 1018 or earlier
From the tomb of the Princess of Chen
and Xiao Shaoju at Qinglongshan Town,
Naiman Banner
Painted wood
Height: 29.2 cm
Research Institute of Cultural Relics
and Archaeology of Inner Mongoli

A signature form in Liao ceramics, such flasks have conventionally been called "cockscomb flasks" because of the resemblance of some of their lug handles to cockscombs. Yet recent scholarship has questioned the name and origin of this type of flask and proposed various alternatives, including "bag-shaped flask."[1]

The examples in the exhibition represent two of the many variations of this type of flask. The stoneware flask (cat. 39) from the tomb of Yelü Yuzhi and Chonggun has a globular lower body, a short tubular spout, and a loop-handle, all of which refer to a soft leather prototype. A raised ridge encircling the contour of the flask resembles a seam on sewn leather. The compact white body of the flask is coated with transparent glaze, which is smooth and glossy. A similar flask, made of silver with a flaring foot and a lid, from the mid-eighth-century hoard found in Hejia Village near Xi'an, is a luxurious version of the same type of flask.

The earthenware flask (cat. 40) has a relatively long and flat body, which is decorated with incised tendril scrolls. Behind the lidded spout are two perforated slab-handles, each with a figure hugging it from behind. Raised lines running along the sides of the flask serve as reminders of the leather prototype of such flasks. Its reddish clay body is covered with dark-green glaze. Large areas of the body are covered with silvery specks, due to the extended time it was buried underground. Flasks similar in shape have been found in a number of Liao tombs in Inner Mongolia, Liaoning Province, and Hebei Province. A similar green-glazed flask was found in a Liao tomb (dated to the early Liao dynasty) at Haiwang Village, Beijing.[2] Moreover, the appliquéd motif on the upper part of the flask in the exhibition resembles the motif on the green-glazed bottle excavated from the tomb (dated 942) of Yelü Yuzhi and his wife, and hence suggests it dates from the tenth century (see cat. 76).

The simple wood flask (cat. 41) discovered in the tomb of the Princess of Chen and Xiao Shaoju is the only surviving example of a Liao wood flask. The flask, shaped like a saddle in profile, is made from two pieces of prickly cypress, each hollowed out in the interior. The two pieces were glued together, leaving a square opening at the top. This flask was placed in a large bronze basin (see cat. 117) in the rear chamber of the tomb, where the bodies of the princess and her husband were laid. The flask might have been part of a set of archery equipment, because a wooden bow case and the remains of a wooden bow were also found in the same chamber (see cat. 19).

HMS

1. See Zhang Songbai, "Guanyu jiguan hu yanjiu zhong de jige wenti" [Several issues concerning the research of cockscomb flasks], in Wei Jian ed., *Neimenggu wenwu kaogu wenji* [*Essays on the archaeology of cultural relics in Inner Mongolia*], vol. 2, pp. 584–91. For an analysis of the major types of Liao bag-shaped flasks, see Harold Mok Kar Leung, "Ceramic Flasks of the Liao Dynasty," *Oriental Art*, Autumn 1989, pp. 150–62. For a study of the provenance and chronology of Liao bag-shaped flasks, see Xie Mingliang, "Ji pinang shi hu" [Research notes on bag-shaped flasks], *Gugong wenwu yuekan* 18.1 (2000), pp. 46–63.

2. See *Kaogu* 1972.3, p. 37, fig. 3. A nearly identical flask can be found in the collection of the Museum of Fine Arts, Boston.

42. Bottle with inscriptions on the shoulder

Liao dynasty, early twelfth century
Excavated in Biliutai, Balin Left Banner
Stoneware with tea-dust glaze
Height: 69 cm; diameter of mouth: 6 cm;
diameter of base: 13 cm
Museum of Balin Left Banner

This bottle is made of hard gray stoneware covered with thick olive-green glaze. It has an extremely long ovoid body that tapers to a flat, unglazed base. The upper part of the bottle curves in at the shoulder to a short neck and a small, inverted mouth. Conventionally called "chicken-leg" or "ox-leg," elongated ovoid bottles were a signature Liao type; they were used for fermenting milk and storing wine. Many of the bottles are horizontally fluted from shoulder to base, although this one is not.

Four characters are incised on the shoulder near the mouth of the bottle. It is unclear whether they are Chinese or Khitan characters. Similar bottles from Inner Mongolia and Liaoning Province bear inscriptions at the shoulder that refer to dates such as the second, third, and fifth year (1102, 1103, and 1105) of the Qiantong era during the reign of Emperor Tianzuo (r. 1101–25), hence suggesting that this bottle dates from around the same time.[1]

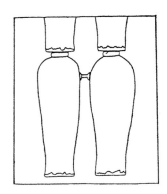

Shards of Liao ox-leg bottles have been unearthed from several kiln sites, including Baiyinguole in Balin Left Banner, where a particular type of heatproof stick was used to hold these elongated bottles and prevent them from tipping during firing (fig. 88). In addition, instead of being placed in saggers, bottles were piled one on top of another to save space in the kiln. Glaze was wiped off the rim of the mouth and the foot-ring to prevent the bottles from sticking to each other. The unglazed rim of the mouth and foot as well as the large spur marks on the shoulder of the bottle in the exhibition confirm its provenance from the Baiyinguole kilns.[2]

HMS

1. See Tamura Jitsuzō, *Keiryō no hekiga: kaiga, chō soku, tō ji* [Murals in the Qing Mausoleums: Paintings, carvings, ceramics], pp. 240–42, 300–301; pl. 41. Hasegawa Michitaka, "Ryō, Kin, Gendai no nagatsubo" [Slender bottles of the Liao, Jin, and Yuan dynasties], *Tōyōtōji*, 17 (1987–1989), pp. 39–57.
2. See *Kaogu xuebao* 1958.2, pp. 97–107.

Fig. 88. Drawing showing the use of heatproof sticks in firing ox-leg bottles

43a–b. Knife and sheath

Liao dynasty, 1018 or earlier
From the tomb of the Princess of Chen
and Xiao Shaoju at Qinglongshan Town
in Naiman Banner
a. Knife: silver, amber; length: 30.4 cm
b. Sheath: gilded-silver; length: 32 cm
Research Institute of Cultural Relics
and Archaeology of Inner Mongolia

The luxury materials from which this knife is made signal the elite status of its owner, Xiao Shaoju.[1] The sharp single-edged blade tapering to a point is forged from silver, while the short rounded handle is fashioned from a piece of polished amber. The sheath is made from hammered silver sheet that has been bent to form an oval container and gilded; it has a loop-in-loop chain. This knife was found on the right side of the prince's *diexie* belt (cat. 21)[2] along with a jade-handled silver awl (cat. 18a–b) and jade-handled knife—all necessary tools for hunting and daily use. Along with an awl, a knife was an integral part of a Khitan soldier's gear.[3]

What is unusual about this knife is its amber hilt. An unprecedented amount of amber was found in the tomb of the Princess of Chen and Xiao Shaoju, mainly in the form of carved pendants, handheld amulets, and necklace beads (for example, cat. nos. 7, 35, 36, 37a–b, 77). That this reddish-brown, semitranslucent resin has been excavated from pagoda reliquary deposits[4] and from tombs of high-ranking Khitan[5] indicates that amber was considered by the Khitan to be a highly valued material. Natural deposits of amber have been found in China;[6] however, tests on excavated Liao amber have revealed that it originates from the Baltic region. Liao amber is likely to have come from the Baltic by way of trade and barter through the Uighurs in Central Asia.[7] The consort clan of the imperial family, the Xiao, are thought to have had Uighur Turkic connections, which may explain the relative abundance of the material in the Liao era.

HK

1. Most knives were made from iron. Compare the iron knife with a green jade handle and a sheath covered in what is possibly silver, found in the tomb of a male in Bayankuren, Chenba'erhu Banner, Northeast Inner Mongolia; other hunting gear, such as a birch bow and arrows, leather bow case and quiver, was found nearby (*Kaoguxue jikan* 2004.14, p. 276, fig. 9.6).
2. *Liao Chenguo gongzhu mu* [*Liao tomb of the princess of the state of Chen*], p. 44.
3. See Karl A. Wittfogel and Fêng Chia-shêng. *History of Chinese Society: Liao, 907–1125*, p. 523.
4. A group of amber carvings were enshrined in the stupa of Dule Monastery in Jixian, Tianjin (*Kaogu xuebao* 1989.1, p. 106, fig. 28), and an amber carving was found in the Northern Pagoda (Beita) in Chaoyang, Liaoning (*Wenwu* 1992.7, pp. 1–28).
5. For example, in the tomb of a rich female at Yemaotai, Faku, Liaoning Province (*Wenwu* 1975.12, pp. 26–36); in the Geng family tombs in Chaoyang, Liaoning Province (*Kaoguxue jikan* 1983.3, pp. 168–195); and in a tomb in Maiwanggou, Ningcheng, Inner Mongolia (*Neimenggu wenwu kaogu wenji*, 1997.2, pp. 609–630).
6. In Fushun, Liaoning; Nanyang, Henan; Enshi, Hubei; Tengchong, Yunnan; and Pingnan and Guixian in Guangxi (*Qingdai fushi zhanlan tulu* [*Catalogue of the exhibition of Qing-dynasty costume accessories*], pp. 20, 38).
7. Berthold Laufer, "Historical Jottings of Amber in Asia," in *Memoirs of the American Anthropological Association*, vol. 1, pp. 239–41. For a discussion of Liao amber, see Emma C. Bunker, Julia M. White, and Jenny F. So, *Adornment for the Body and Soul: Ancient Chinese Ornaments from the Mengdiexuan Collection*, pp. 153–60.

44. Pendant set with decorations of the five poisonous animals

Song or Liao dynasty, 1018 or earlier
From the tomb of the Princess of Chen
and Xiao Shaoju at Qinglongshan Town,
Naiman Banner
Jade, silver
Length: 15 cm
Research Institute of Cultural Relics and
Archaeology of Inner Mongolia

This set of pendants excavated from the tomb of the Princess of Chen and Xiao Shaoju consists of a jade disk and gilded-silver chains with five jade animals. The finely polished disk and animals are all made of white jade, which might have come from Khotan in the present-day Xinjiang area of China.[1] Incised counterclockwise on the front of the disk, which is bordered with cloud designs, are the twelve animals of the Chinese zodiac. The animal pendants dangling below the disk are in the shape of a snake, a monkey, a scorpion, a toad, and a lizard. Like several other pendants in the exhibition, this set was laid on the princess's belly.

In China, jade has long been associated with immortality, and jade *bi* disks (wide disks with proportionately small central holes) with protecting the body of the deceased. Pendant sets composed of plaques and beads strung together perpetuate an ancient tradition indigenous to China. To wear images of potentially life-threatening creatures, such as a snake, a scorpion, or a lizard, as a way of warding off evil spirits is also a common Chinese practice. This jade pendant set, therefore, shows the Liao's knowledge of traditional Chinese belief systems.

Two others sets of jade pendants similar in structure—several smaller pendants strung with gilded-silver chains to a large plaque—were found near the corpse of the princess. One set has an openwork design resembling ribbon on the top, which is connected to five pendants with auspicious motifs—a dragon-fish, a double fish, double phoenixes, double dragons, and a single fish—at the bottom (fig. 89). The other has an openwork plaque of lotus-flower design and seven (originally there were eight; one is missing) suspended tools, including a spoon, a drill, and a pair of scissors (fig. 90).

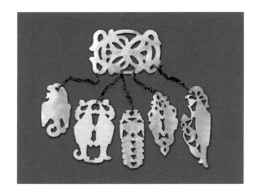

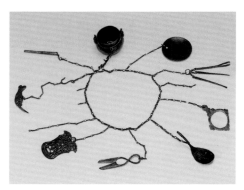

Necklaces and bracelets with pendants shaped like weapons and shields originated in India. A gold chain with pendants in the shape of weapons and shields was found at a site in central Inner Mongolia dating from the third to the fourth century, proving the transmission of fashion between India and northern China early on.[2] It is noteworthy that a gilded-bronze chain with pendants shaped like tools similar to those on the jade pendant with suspended tools (fig. 90) was found in the front chamber of the multichamber relic deposit (dated 874) underneath the foundation of Famen Pagoda in Shaanxi Province. These tools were thought to have been necessities for the everyday life of Buddhist monks (fig. 91).

HMS

1. For Khotan's use of jade as tributes to neighbors including the Song, see *Songshi* [*History of the Song*], *juan* 490, pp. 14106–14108.
2. See James C.Y. Watt et al. *China: Dawn of a Golden Age, 200–750 AD*, p. 133.

Fig. 89. Pendant set with five auspicious motifs, excavated from the tomb of the Princess of Chen and Xiao Shaoju at Qinglongshan Town, Naiman Banner; jade; overall length 14.8 cm

Fig. 90. Pendant set with suspended tools, excavated from the tomb of the Princess of Chen and Xiao Shaoju at Qinglongshan Town, Naiman Banner; jade; overall length 18.2 cm

Fig. 91. Chain with pendants in the shape of tools, excavated from the front chamber of the relic deposit underneath the foundation of Famen Pagoda in Fufeng, Shaanxi Province; gilded bronze; collection of the Museum of Famen Temple

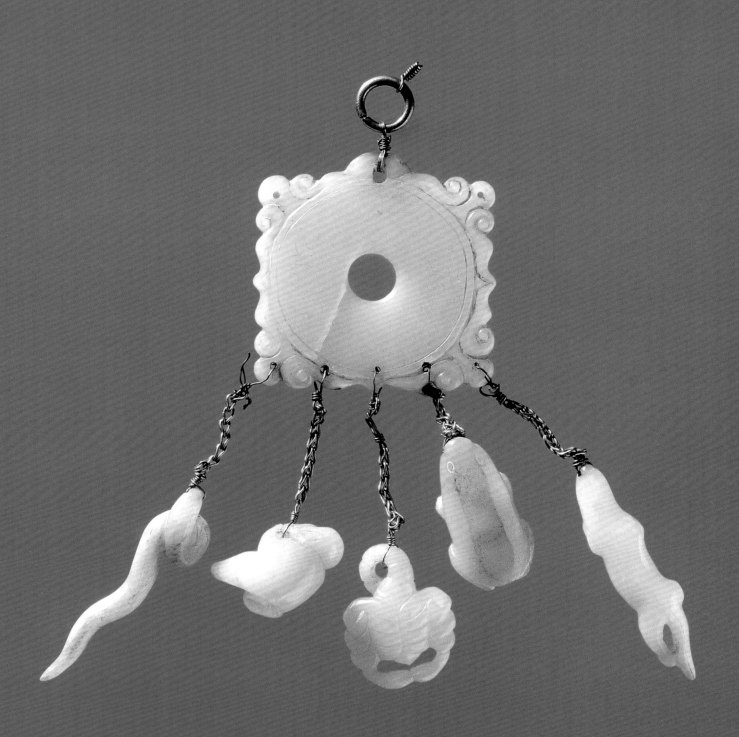

45a–b. Pair of earrings

Liao dynasty, 1018 or earlier
From the tomb of the Princess of Chen
and Xiao Shaoju at Qinglongshan Town,
Naiman Banner
Amber, pearl
Length: 13 cm
Research Institute of Cultural Relics
and Archaeology of Inner Mongolia

Four amber carvings and a string of pearls
constitute each earring. Each of the four
amber carvings illustrates an interesting boat-
ing or fishing scene: two people with paddles
in their hands row a boat in the shape of a
dragon-fish (*makara*). The boat has a roofed
area, providing shelter to the rowers. There
are masts at the bows of two of the boats.
None of the boats are exactly the same.
Carved with such creativity, the earrings represent the highest level of the craftsmanship
for amber artifacts known in the Liao era.

In no other period in Chinese history was
amber made use of as enthusiastically as it
was in the Liao era. A large number of finely
carved amber artifacts have been recovered
from the tombs of high-ranking individuals
and from pagodas, signifying the status of
such objects in Liao material culture. Although
there are no textual records of the sources of
Liao amber, scientific analysis suggests a
close connection between the amber used by
the Liao and Baltic amber, testifying to the
Liao empire's long-distance trade contacts.[1]

HMS

1. For a discussion of Liao amber artifacts, see
Emma C. Bunker, Julia M. White, and Jenny F. So,
*Adornment for the Body and Soul: Ancient Chinese Ornaments
from the Mengdiexuan Collection*, pp. 153–66.

The Han Chinese Burial Tradition

In China, the structure and interior decorations of a tomb, along with the burial objects placed within it, were consciously constructed and arranged to create a "personal universe" for the deceased. The way in which tombs were constructed was closely related to Chinese beliefs in and ideas about the afterlife. Since the Han dynasty (206 BC–AD 220), the Chinese had built tombs that resembled underground shelters for the living. Food and services were provided to sustain the deceased's life in the netherworld. While the basic contents of the Liao tomb and the covering of the body with metal burial attire closely followed steppe burial customs, Liao tombs borrowed elements from traditional Chinese tombs, as evidenced by the similarities in tomb structure, provisions to sustain the deceased in a life after death, and writings to communicate with the spirits. The Khitan tomb thus is a hybrid, an amalgamation of different burial practices, integrating aspects of Siberian steppe burial traditions with Chinese tomb traditions.

The Chinese tomb tradition is discernible in the tomb (dated 1018) of the Liao Princess of Chen and her husband, Xiao Shaoju; many burial objects from their tomb are presented in this exhibition. Their underground, multichambered tomb consisted of a ramp 6.7 meters long and four domed chambers. Each of the chambers contained a distinctive group of funerary objects, namely, vessels for eating and drinking in the east side-chamber; equestrian gear in the west side-chamber; a stone tablet on which the tomb's epitaph is engraved, in the very center of the front chamber; and more goods, which served as offerings, and body ornaments in the rear chamber, where the corpses were placed. Similarities in structure and provisions can be found in other tombs of eminent Khitan, such as the tomb of Yelü Yuzhi (890–941) and his wife, Chonggun (d. 942).

Unlike the tombs of the Tang dynasty (618–907), Liao-dynasty tombs contain few three-dimensional figures. Instead, pictorial images were used to the fullest, to provide the deceased with all sorts of necessities for a comfortable life after death. The painted interior of a Liao-dynasty tomb, like the tombs of the Han Chinese, is often decorated with images of attendants. The most outstanding examples are the murals from tombs in Aohan Banner, Inner Mongolia, as well as the Zhang family tombs in Xuanhua, Hebei Province. Musicians and attendants were regularly painted in bright colors on the walls of the Xuanhua tombs. The images depicted in the murals, together with the real vessels and food presented to the deceased on the altar table in front of the coffin, guaranteed perpetual offerings to the deceased. In rare cases, images of attendants were translated into relief carvings, such as the images of a musical performance and wine serving on the two stone panels (cat. 50a–b) included in this exhibition. In one example of sculpture in the round included in the exhibition, a pair of large stone statues, one of a male and one of a female servant (cat. 9a–b), was buried above the entrance to the large brick tomb (dated 993) of a Liao high official, Han Kuangsi, and his wife, Xiao.

At Tomb Number 3 in Daiqintala, Keyou Central Banner, two corpses were laid on a flat platform inside a wooden house-like sarcophagus resembling the one on display in this exhibition (cat. 46a). In front of the deathbed, inside the wooden house, were six parcels of silk garments (cat. 80, 120a–b, 121) that were presented to the deceased. An early Liao-dynasty tomb (Tomb Number 7) at Yemaotai in Faku, Liaoning Province, also had an elaborate wooden house-like sarcophagus (fig. 10), but it was a step closer to Chinese tomb tradition, since it contained a lidded, rectangular sarcophagus made of stone (fig. 11), in which the corpse was placed. The stone sarcophagus was decorated with the symbolic animals of the four directions (the green dragon, the white tiger, the vermillion bird, and the tortoise with a snake; compare cat. 48a–d, 57) and the twelve animals of the Chinese zodiac, all of which are rooted in traditional Chinese culture.

Other Chinese imagery incorporated by the Liao into their tomb decorations include the Daoist Eight Hexagrams and tomb guardians. The latter are associated with the traditional Chinese belief in the need to protect the deceased from attacks by evil spirits. A pair of painted wooden doors (cat. 51a–b) and two bronze plaques (cat. 58a–b), both decorated with guardian warriors, are evidence of Liao adoption of this belief. Interestingly, the wooden doors depict demon-like guardians on one side and warrior-like guardians on the other. While images of demon-like guardians are associated with the world of demons in hell, warrior-like guardians are derived from images of the Buddhist Heavenly Kings, who guard the Buddhist realm. As potent representations of cosmological ideas, mirrors were employed in the center of the ceilings of many Song tombs, and they were used in the same way in a number of Liao tombs (cat. 55).

As Buddhism gained popularity among the Liao people, the Buddhist practice of cremation became prevalent. Wooden boxes were used to house the ashes of Buddhist monks who had been cremated. The yurt-shaped funerary urn in this exhibition (cat. 10) represents a marriage of the Khitan nomadic heritage with the adopted foreign practice. In contrast with metal mesh suits and masks typical of nomadic burial customs (cat. 1, 2, 6), life-size wooden mannequins—such as the example in the exhibition (cat. 52), which is made of seventeen sections, joined together by sockets that allow free movement—functioned as containers for the cremated remains of the deceased. The ashes were inserted into an opening in the mannequin's chest, demonstrating a desire to replace the body that was lost in cremation. Within a traditional Chinese context, the deceased needed their bodies for the afterlife. Inserting cremated human remains into a wooden mannequin is a Liao invention that fuses the dictates of Buddhist cremation with the traditional Chinese idea of an afterlife. In the case of Tomb Number IIM1 in Xuanhua, Hebei Province, both metal burial attire and a wooden mannequin were employed in a single tomb for two different persons, showing that, to the Liao, the two types of burials were considered compatible.

HMS

46a–d. House for coffin-bed, bed, table, and chair

Liao dynasty, eleventh or early twelfth century
From Wengniute Banner
Ink and color on wood
a. House rooftop: length: 240 cm;
width: 200 cm; height: 100 cm
b. Bed: length: 237 cm;
width: 112 cm; overall height: 72 cm
c. Table: length: 63 cm;
width: 46 cm; height: 59 cm
d. Chair: length: 53 cm; width: 46 cm;
height of chair: 59 cm
Museum of the Inner Mongolia
Autonomous Region

The context in which this set, consisting of a wooden house and furniture, was discovered is unclear. However, a very similar set was excavated from a Liao tomb at Jiefangyingzi in Wengniute Banner, and it sheds light on the ways in which the set on view in the exhibition might have been used in a tomb. The large wooden house from the tomb at Jiefangyingzi is a sarcophagus that contained the remains of a male and a female, both of whom were found lying on a wooden bed toward the rear of the house when the tomb was opened in 1970. The tomb's occupants, positioned with their heads toward the east, had bronze masks on their faces. In addition, they were originally clothed, and some of their clothing has survived in fragments. A small wooden chair and a low table in front of the bed were intended for use in making funerary offerings; several vessels for food and drink, made of silver, were found on the table. The domed tomb chamber, built in an octagonal shape with cypress logs, is in imitation of a traditional yurt.

While placing a metal mask on the face of the deceased is a burial custom unique to the Khitan people (see cat. 2), building an underground structure with living spaces is typical of Chinese burial traditions. The Chinese believed that a tomb was a universe in which the deceased continued to live after death.[1] From such notions derived the idea of providing nourishment to the deceased. In its use of burial masks in an underground tomb that has chambers and is furnished with offering goods, the burial site in Wengniute Banner represents a distinctive hybrid of Khitan and Chinese burial traditions.

A similar but more elaborate set of wooden house and furniture was found in a Liao tomb (datable to early in the Liao dynasty) at Daiqintala Township in Keyou Central Banner, where a large number of fine textiles was also found (see cat. 120, 121).[2] A wooden house-shaped sarcophagus containing a stone coffin and equipped with a stone altar table, in addition to a wooden table and a wooden chair, was found in an early-Liao tomb at Yemaotai in Faku, Liaoning Province.[3]

HMS

1. See Jessica Rawson, "Creating Universes: Cultural Exchange as Seen in Tombs in Northern China between the Han and Tang Periods," in Wu Hung (ed.), *Between Han and Tang: Cultural and Artistic Interaction in a Transformative Period*, pp. 113–49; Jessica Rawson, "The Power of Images: The Model Universe of the First Emperor and Its Legacy," *Historical Research* 75, no. 188 (2002), pp. 123–154.

2. See Wei Jian ed., *Neimenggu wenwu kaogu wenji* [*Essays on the archaeology of cultural relics in Inner Mongolia*], vol. 2, p. 567, fig. 1.

3. See *Wenwu* 1975.12, p. 28, fig. 4, and Cao Xun, "Yemaotai Liao muzhong de guanchuang xiaozhang" [The small-scale "container" and coffin-bed in a Liao tomb at Yemaotai], *Wenwu* 1975.12, pp. 49–62. Two more wooden houses are in the collection of the Museum of Balin Right Banner; one of them has been published in *Neimenggu wenwu kaogu* 1996.11, pp. 82–86.

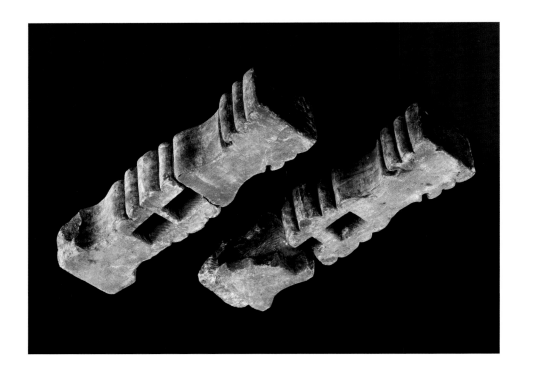

47. Table top and two legs

Liao dynasty, tenth century
From Tomb Number 4 at
Sumuchuangjingou in Balin Right Banner
Painted sandstone
Table top: length: 76.5 cm;
width: 57 cm; thickness: 7 cm
Legs: length: 37.5; width: 7 cm;
thickness: 10 cm
Research Institute of Cultural Relics
and Archaeology of Inner Mongolia

The top of this stone table was elaborately decorated with relief carvings painted in bright colors. At the center of the table is a pair of flying phoenixes, one of which has a peony branch in its mouth. Four additional peony sprays fill the lozenge-shaped space within which the phoenixes are portrayed. Four triangles are joined to the four corners of the lozenge-shaped space, thus forming a design called "lozenge-within-rectangle." Each of these triangles contains a peony spray painted on a vivid red background. Inside the four trapezoids at the rim of the table top are floral scrolls.

The table top was supported by four detachable legs, which were painted white and red (two of them are on display in the exhibition). The double sockets on one side of each of the legs suggest that the legs were originally connected by two horizontal bars, which have been lost. A very similar but considerably smaller wooden table, dating from the eleventh century, was found in an anonymous tomb in Chaoyang, Liaoning Province. It is decorated with a comparable lozenge-within-rectangle design filled with floral sprays.[1]

As is evidenced by the wooden tables and the food items found inside the main chamber of Tomb Number 7 (dated 1093) in Xuanhua, Hebei Province, funerary tables were used for the presentation of offerings to the tomb's occupants (see fig. 80). They were often paired with chairs and were placed in front of the coffin (compare cat. 46). Altar tables made of stone comparable to the one in the exhibition were found in the tomb (dated 942) of Yelü Yuzhi and his wife, Chonggun, and in Tomb Number 7 (second half of the tenth century) at Yemaotai in Faku: the occupants of both tombs were of high social status.[2]

HMS

1. See *Liaobai wenwu xuekan* 1997.1, p. 36, fig. 8.1.
2. See *Wenwu* 1996.1, p. 8; *Wenwu* 1975.12, p. 26.

48a–d. Wood carvings of the four directional animals

Liao dynasty, eleventh century
Excavated in Baomotugacha in
Chaogewendu Township, Wengniute Banner
Ink and color on wood
Length: 30–50 cm
Museum of Wengniute Banner

The animal symbols of the four directions (known in Chinese as *Sisheng* or *Siling*, the Four Divinities)—namely, the Azure Dragon of the East, the White Tiger of the West, the Vermillion Bird of the South, and the Dark Warrior of the North, consisting of an entwined turtle and snake—are depicted on this group of four carved wood panels. While the Azure Dragon and the White Tiger are shown in profile, the Vermillion Bird and the Dark Warrior are portrayed in frontal view. The top half of the Dark Warrior was missing when the panels were unearthed. These panels are rare examples of Liao wood carvings. Pigments on the carvings show that they were originally painted in colors that correspond to the names of the animals, that is, green on the dragon, white on the tiger, red on the bird, and black on the warrior. There are fragments of iron nails on each of the panels, indicating that they were initially attached to the four sides of a wooden coffin (compare with cat. 57).[1]

The animal symbolism of the four cardinal directions, which originated in central China, was established by the Han dynasty (206 BC–AD 220). Images of the four directional animals are abundant in tombs of the Han and subsequent dynasties. They were frequently represented—together with other cosmological features, such as constellations and the twelve animals of the Chinese zodiac (corresponding to the twelve divisions of the celestial equator)—on the backs of bronze mirrors or on the stone slabs on which tomb epitaphs were inscribed (fig. 92).[2] It was believed that, in a funerary context, depictions of images that illustrate the directional or temporal order in the structure of the uni-

verse embody talismanic powers and would therefore expel evil spirits.[3] Inclusion of the imagery of the four directional animals in Liao tombs is evidence of Liao culture's adoption of Han Chinese tomb traditions.

HMS

Fig. 92. Ink rubbing of the cover slab for the epitaph from an anonymous tomb in Baomotugacha, Chaogewendu Township, Wengniute Banner; Liao dynasty

1. A number of Liao coffins decorated with images of the four directional animals have been found in Liaoning Province. See *Wenwu* 1975.12, p. 28, fig. 5 (Tomb Number 7 at Yemaotai in Faku); *Wenwu* 1983.9, pp. 35–36, figs. 21–24 (tomb, dated 1039, of Zhao Weigan in Chaoyang); *Wenwu* 2000.7, pp. 61–62, figs. 32.4–6 (anonymous tomb at Xishngtai in Chaoyang); *Wenwu* 1980.7, p. 19, fig. 4 (tomb, dated 986, of Yelü Yanning in Chaoyang); *Liaohai wenwu xuekan* 1997.1, p. 32, figs. 3.2–5 (anonymous tomb at Goumenzi in Chaoyang).

2. An epitaph is usually inscribed on a square stone slab, on top of which is a matching square stone slab with four sloping sides. The name and title of the tomb's occupant(s), surrounded by images such as the four directional animals or the twelve animals of the Chinese zodiac, are inscribed on the cover slab.

3. For an extensive discussion of ancient Chinese mirrors and their legacies in the medieval periods, see Caroline Schulten, "Ancient Chinese Mirrors and Their Legacies in the Tang (AD 618–906), Liao (AD 907–1125) and Song (AD 960–1279) Periods."

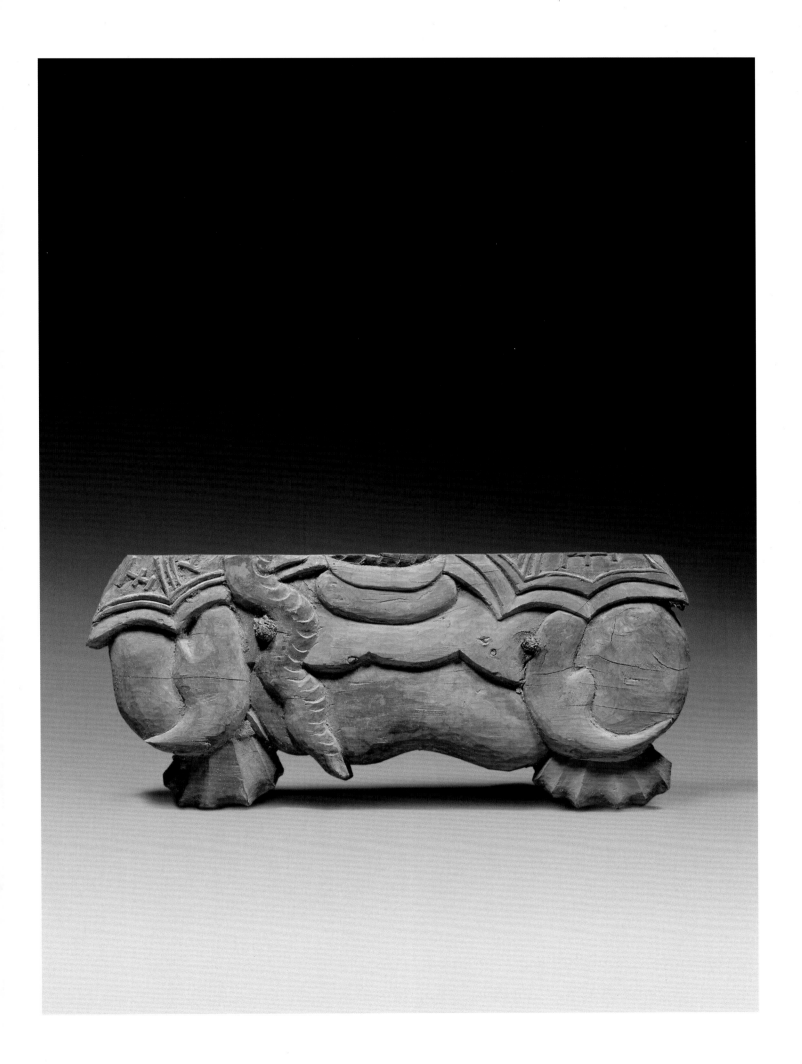

49a–c. Three painted panels

Liao dynasty, eleventh or early twelfth century
From a tomb at Zhanpu, Linxi County
Ink and color on wood
Height: 115.5–116 cm;
width: 59.5–62.5 cm; thickness: 4.5 cm
Museum of Linxi County

Each of the three wooden panels painted in ink and colors is made of three long wooden strips connected by *shun* sockets. On the first panel a T-shaped rock is depicted, with plantain and peonies in the background. Two butterflies fly above the plants; in front of the rock are railings, suggesting a garden scene.

The same railing appears in the foreground of the second panel, giving a structural continuity to the two panels. Two birds stand beside a thriving tall tree at the center; in the middle ground are hills stretching toward the background, implying imagined space beyond. Two Khitan characters are written in ink in the upper right-hand corner of the panel. A similar image of a tree in the middle of a valley appears in the third panel, in which a Khitan boy is depicted herding a group of cattle, reflecting the semisedentary lifestyle of the Liao. Three magpies fly above the top of the tree.

The original position of these panels in the tomb is unclear. However, the railings depicted on two of the panels echo those found on Liao burial platforms (compare cat. 46b), hence suggesting that the panels were possibly positioned surrounding the burial platform of the tomb. This theory is confirmed by an ink-painted panel found inside a wooden house in an early Liao tomb, Tomb Number 7 at Yemaotai in Faku, Liaoning Province.[1]

Images of figures beneath trees appeared on screen panels enclosing coffins in China no later than the sixth century and remained a favored subject well into the ninth century. In the late Tang dynasty, flowers and rocks entered the subject matter of tomb decora-tion, and an arrangement of motifs along a central axis became fashionable. The rapid acceptance of bird-and-flower paintings during the Liao dynasty is seen in tomb murals. The most well known examples come from the Zhang family tombs (dated 1093–1123) in Xuanhua, Hebei Province.[2] These three wooden panels seem to have followed tradition in their symmetrical images of rocks, flowers, and figures along a central axis, while additional Khitan elements (such as the boy with his herd of cattle) were introduced.

HMS

---

1. See *Wenwu* 1975.12, p. 35, fig. 12.
2. For a detailed discussion of the use of bird-and-flower motifs in Chinese tombs, see Ellen Johnston Laing, "Auspicious Motifs in Ninth- to Thirteenth-Century Chinese tombs," *Ars Orientalis* 33 (2003), pp. 33–75.

earlier
e Xiao
Woli,
n Left Banner

: 74 cm;

Banner

tomb was discovered at
Left Banner. The tomb
ly bone fragments of a
o stone panels in the
and a stone on which
l, all retrieved from the
ed to have come from
shows that the tomb
who died in 1009, and

erformance (cat. 50a)
0b) are carved in relief
the twelve musicians
nd-collared robe and a
n the lower-right-hand
ed head and does not
variety of wind, string,
nents in their hands.
ated figures are repre-
all of the other musi-
three-quarter view,
toward their left.
e figures is represented
ne. Some figures hold
posture, as if waiting
ir master, while others
ious utensils, such as a
cups. The third figure
op row clutches a fan
e center of the panel is
s an ewer in his right
mall table with his left
o put the ewer into the
r at the far end of the
warm.

and wine or tea serv-
represented in Liao
gs or in murals. Very

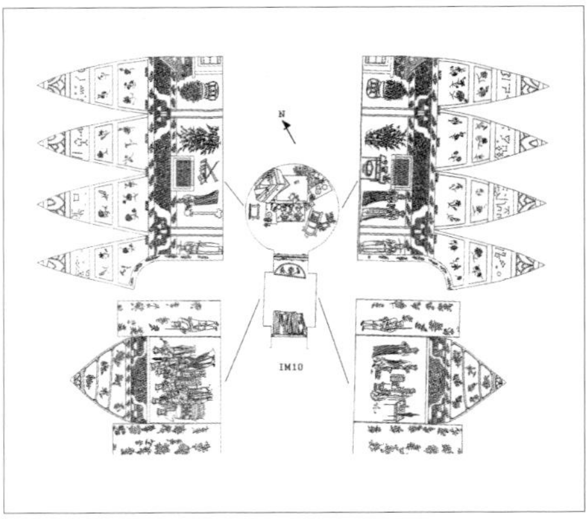

often the two themes appeared together near
the entrance to the main chamber of the
tomb, where the corpse was found. The
most well known examples are the murals in
the Zhang family tombs at Xiabali Village in
Xuanhua, Hebei Province. In the Zhang
family tombs, nearly all of the murals
depicting musical performances and wine or
tea serving were on the side walls of the
front chamber that leads to the main chamber where the corpse was found (fig. 93).[1]
The hinges on the long sides of the stone
panels in the exhibition indicate that the
panels were probably a pair of doors at the
entrance to what was a single-chamber
tomb, which is consistent with the fact that
such imagery is usually situated at the
threshold to the main chamber.

Providing food, drink, and entertainment to
the deceased has a long history in China. In
ancient times, the Chinese believed that the
spirits of the deceased could affect the fate
of their descendents. The living, therefore,
had to treat their ancestors well, by making
offerings to them and paying regular visits to

their shrines or tor
(ca. 1600–ca. 105(
1050–256 BC) dy
were placed in tomb
dynasty (206 BC–A
tures of dancers, to
and entertainment f
Pictorial images of v
performance in the L
and her husband a
time-honored practi

HMS

1. For example, see
tombs], vol. 1, pp. 31–32,
10, dated 1093); pp.
Number 7, dated 1093);
6); pp. 188–89, figs. 15
162–63 (Tomb Number

Fig. 93. Plan of Tomb
Xuanhua, Hebei Provin

51a–b. Pair of painted wooden doors

Liao dynasty, eleventh century
Excavated from a tomb at Bayan'erdeng
Township, Balin Right Banner
Ink and color on wood
Height: 121 cm; width: 53 cm;
thickness: 1.5 cm
Cultural Relics Management Institute
of Linxi County

Monstrous figures with terrifying expressions are painted on the front of this pair of wooden doors; on the back are two generals with solemn looks on their faces. The two brutish, muscular demonlike figures, facing each other, have flaming hair and bulging eyes; in their hands one holds a sword and the other a *guduo* scepter (a scepter with spiked projections; see cat. 20). The two generals, also facing each other, are clad in armor, pleated skirts, and pointed shoes; behind their heads are halos with short white beams. Each of the generals holds a spear and stands on a rocky platform. They are distinguished from one another by the different interpretations of the heads: one has a bushy beard and wears a tight-fitting helmet with a plume on top and flaps covering the ears; the other's hair is swept up into a knot and adorned with jewels.

Although different in appearance, both pairs of figures represent Buddhist guardians who protect the main deities and temples, as well as the Buddhist law. Half-naked, muscular athletes with grotesque faces, like the demonic figures on the front of the doors, are associated with the Buddhist guardians of gates or temples (*dvāra-pālas*), whereas generals clad in armor and brandishing weapons refer to the Buddhist heavenly kings (*lokapālas*). The identity of the *lokapālas* is further confirmed by their halos and fluttering scarves and tunics, while the jutting teeth and speckled patterns covering the legs of the *dvāra-pālas* link them with the human-faced tomb-guardian creatures that were often placed in Tang-dynasty tombs to ward off evil spirits.

Archaeological evidence shows that heavenly king figures appeared in Chinese tombs as tomb guardians no later than the third quarter of the seventh century. They replaced the tomb-guardian warriors and functioned, as did the warriors, to protect the tomb's occupants. The heavenly king tomb figures usually appeared in pairs and were placed with a pair of tomb-guardian creatures at either side of the entrance to the main chamber of the tomb, where the corpse was laid to rest.[1] They are considerably larger in size than other figurines found in tombs, indicating their significance and prominent status. This example, in which the monstrous creatures are painted on the front and the generals on the back of the doors, appears to be a Liao reminiscence of Tang tomb traditions, with some distinctive Liao features, such as the *guduo* scepter, a signature weapon of the Liao, in the hand of one of the monstrous guardians.

HMS

---

1. For example, see *Yanshi Xingyuan Tang mu* [*Tang tombs at Xingyuan in Yanshi*], p. 17, fig. 10; color pl. 1.1; pls. 4.1, 4.2, 4.5, 5.4–5.6 (tomb of Li Siben, dated 709). See also Wang Renbo, "Xi'an diqu Beizhou Sui Tang muzang taoyong de zuhe yu fenqi" [Chronology and typology of pottery tomb figurines in Northern Zhou, Sui, and Tang tombs in the Xi'an area], in Zhongguo kaoguxue yanjiu lunji bianweihui (ed.), *Zhongguo kaoguxue yanjiu lunji: Jinian Xia Nai xiansheng kaogu wushi zhounian* [*A collection of the research articles on archaeology in China: In memory of Xia Nai on his fiftieth anniversary in archaeology*], pp. 428–56. Mary Fong, "Tomb-Guardian Figures: Their Evolution and Iconography" in George Kuwayama (ed.), *Ancient Mortuary Traditions of China: Papers on Chinese Funerary Sculptures*, pp. 84–105.

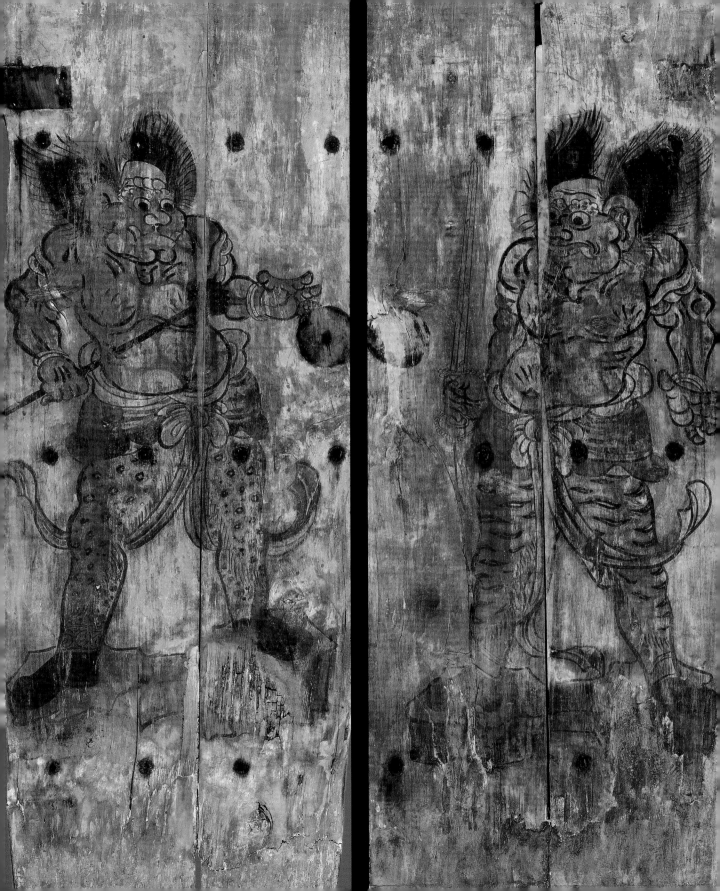

52. Mannequin

Liao dynasty, eleventh or early twelfth century
From a tomb at Yihenuoer Township, Balin
Right Banner
Wood
Height: 180 cm
Museum of Balin Right Banner

Composed of seventeen different wooden parts, this mannequin is modeled to represent a male figure. Its parts are connected by joints and sockets, which allow free movement of the limbs, so that the figure can be posed like a doll or moved like a puppet. Fragments of pigments show that the figure's head, neck, and the lower part of its arms were originally painted. Details such as raised eyebrows and prominent earlobes give the face its individuality.[1] That the paint did not continue onto the rest of the body indicates that the figure was originally clothed, possibly in textiles that decayed over time. The figure's chest is hollowed out so that it could contain the cremated remains of the deceased.

Such mannequins have been discovered in a number of tombs near the Supreme Capital (in modern Balin Left Banner) and the Southern Capital (modern Beijing) of the Liao. Three features, in particular, of these mannequins make them extraordinary: first, they all have joints that allow their bodies to move freely; second, they each contain the cremated remains of a deceased person; and, third, each has distinctive physical features that correlate to the specific identities of the deceased described in the tomb inscriptions. The mannequins were dressed and then either placed in a large, rectangular wooden coffin or laid on a coffin-bed in the tomb. Apparently the mannequins received a burial that was no different from the burial a real corpse would have received, and it seems that the mannequins were believed to represent the deceased whose ashes they contained.

A distinctive synthesis of Buddhist funerary practices and Chinese tomb traditions can be observed in such burial practices. On the one hand, many of the tombs where such mannequins were found were associated with Buddhist monks or devout laypersons, hence suggesting a connection with the Buddhist practice of cremation, which is intended to break human attachment to the body. On the other hand, driven by the wish for immortality, and in accordance with the indigenous tomb traditions in China, devices, including mural paintings and actual objects, were provided to help the deceased sustain a life after death and cultivate his body in the tomb. Provided with these necessities for cultivating the body, the tomb's occupants—embodied in the mannequins with movable joints—could live on in their tombs until they were able to leave the tomb for heaven.[2]

HMS

---

1. No excavation report of the find has been published yet. However, Yang Xiaolei, director of the Museum of Balin Right Banner, revealed to the author that a mannequin in the form of a female figure was found in the same tomb. Like the male figure, this female figure contains cremated human remains.

2. For a full discussion of Liao mannequin burials, see Hsueh-man Shen, "Body Matters: Manikin Burials in the Liao Tombs of Xuanhua, Hebei Province," *Artibus Asiae* 65.1 (2005), pp. 99–141.

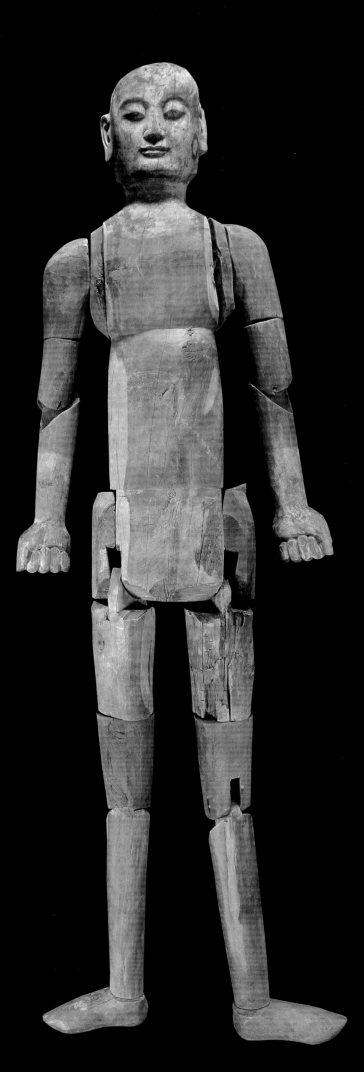

53a–d. Writing utensils

Liao dynasty, eleventh or early twelfth century
From Tomb Number 7 in Yingfenggou,
Xindi Township, Aohan Banner
Silver
a. Brush handle: length: 25 cm
b. Ink-tray: length: 21.1 cm; height: 2.1 cm
c. Cup-shaped brush washer: height: 3.8 cm;
diameter: 9.6 cm
d. Tray: length: 24 cm; width: 12.9 cm;
height: 2.8 cm
Museum of Aohan Banner

This unusual set of writing implements came to light when archaeologists of the Museum of Aohan Banner excavated a cemetery containing eight Liao and Jin tombs.[1] It was discovered in a large, multi-chamber structure, labeled Tomb Number 7, where it had originally been placed on an offering table in front of the coffin of a married couple. The identity of the deceased remains unknown, but their Khitan ethnicity is suggested by the tomb's contents, some of which had inscriptions in Khitan characters, including the silver tray (cat. 53d) and cup-shaped brush washer (cat. 53c). Eight Khitan and two Chinese characters (*tianguan*, Heaven's Office) are engraved on the bottom of the tray; nine Khitan characters are on the foot-ring of the brush washer, and a tenth on its bottom. The meaning of the characters is unclear, but some of them are identical on both the tray and the cup. Not all of the characters were written at the same time or by the same person.

The cup and the tray are not typically considered calligraphy implements, and these examples may indeed have served as drinking utensils at some point early in their life. At the time of the burial, however, they were indeed part of a writing set; the cup still contains remnants of dried ink, and a ring-shaped water stain on the tray shows where the cup once stood. A silver ink-tray (cat. 53b) was used instead of the traditional inkstone. It is shaped like a dustpan with a handle, a form not common in central and southern China.[2] It appears to have been designed specifically to be carried, for a small hole at the back of the ink receptacle may, according to Shao Guotian of the Museum of Aohan

Banner, have allowed the ink to flow into the handle when the tool was tilted.[3] Most unusual is the double-tube brush handle (cat. 53a). While traces of ink remain on one end of the handle, no hairs have survived from which the original tip—or tips—of this rather large brush could be reconstructed. But a comparable example discovered in 1992 provides some clues, for it still contained remnants of bamboo in one of the tubes, suggesting that various brush tips could be inserted on the handle as needed.[4] It is not known whether this type of double-tube handle was ever used with two tips simultaneously. Writing tools are frequently present in Liao tombs, both as actual objects and depicted in murals; they were often placed there to ensure that the deceased could copy holy Buddhist texts, even after death, and thus continue to gain merit and improve their fate.[5]

FL

1. The writing set is discussed in detail in Shao Guotian, "Aohanqi Yingfenggou 7 hao Liao mu chutu yinzhi wenju kao" [The writing utensils excavated in Liao Tomb Number 7 at Yingfenggou, Aohan Banner], *Neimenggu wenwu kaogu* 2003.2, pp. 71–77.

2. Shao Guotian, "Aohanqi Yingfenggou 7 hao," p. 74.

3. Shao Guotian, "Aohanqi Yingfenggou 7 hao," p. 74.

4. It was discovered in the tomb of Xiao Beiteben (d. 1080) and his wife, Yelü Ruolan, in Ningcheng County. That tomb also included a gilded-bronze inkstone with a handle. "Ningcheng xian Liwanggou Liaodai mudi fajue jianbao" [Brief report on the discovery of a Liao tomb at Liwanggou, Ningcheng County], in *Neimenggu wenwu kaogu wenji* 1997.2, p. 627, pl. 17.

5. Hsueh-man Shen, "Body Matters: Manikin Burials in the Liao Tombs of Xuanhua, Hebei Province," *Artibus Asiae* 65.1 (2005), pp. 99–141.

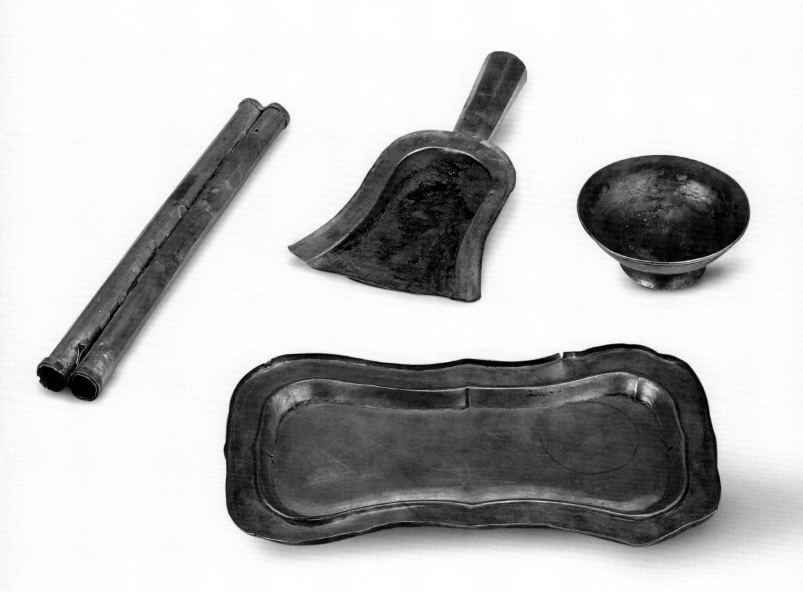

54a–c. A lobed bowl and two inkstones

Tenth or early eleventh century,
1018 or earlier
From the tomb of the Princess of Chen
and Xiao Shaoju at Qinglongshan Town,
Naiman Banner
Jade
a. Bowl: height: 2.3 cm; diameter of mouth:
5.6–6.9 cm; diameter of base: 3.7–4.4 cm
b. Inkstone: height: 4.1 cm; length: 12 cm;
width: 7.1 cm
c. Inkstone: height: 2.1 cm; length: 8.5 cm;
width: 5.2 cm
Research Institute of Cultural Relics
and Archaeology of Inner Mongolia

Among the many treasures excavated from the tomb of the Princess of Chen and Xiao Shaoju, only three were vessels carved of jade—a shallow lobed bowl and two inkstones—testifying to the rarity of jade in Liao tomb objects. Each of the inkstones is shaped like a dustpan. There are two short legs under the open end of the inkstone, creating a slope toward the bottom, where the ground ink can collect.

Many of the inkstones recovered from Liao tombs are dustpan shaped; they have a border along the top and sides and are open at the end. This shape originated in the Tang dynasty but continued to be popular in the Song and Liao periods.[1] It is recorded in the *Songshi* (History of the Song) that jade inkstones, cups, and dishes were looted from the residence of Yang Xingmi (who reigned in Southeast China as King of Wu from 902 to 905) in present-day Shandong Province during warfare in 956.[2]

Very few jade vessels have been found in the tombs of the Liao dynasty or the parallel Northern Song dynasty, reflecting the rarity of the material and the difficulty involved in carving it.[3] The source of the translucent green jade with brown flawed areas used by the Liao is unclear. It has been suggested that this jade came from northwestern China or from Central Asia.[4] Yet, given the Khitan's origins in northeastern China, where, since the Neolithic period (Hongshan Culture, ca. 4000–ca. 2500 BC), there had been a history of using local material for jade carving, it is also possible that this jade came from southern Inner Mongolia or western Liaoning Province.

HMS

1. Ji Ruoxin, "Shuo 'Liao yan'" [Liao inkstones], *Gugong wenwu yuekan* 2000.6, pp. 37–49.

2. See *Songshi, juan* 261, p. 9045.

3. Among the few jade vessels unearthed from Liao tombs are two cups from Shangdu, Inner Mongolia (early eleventh century). See *Beifeng wenwu* 1990.2, p. 50, figs. 2.8, 2.9. Several jade vessels came from Liao pagodas, such as Dule Temple Pagoda in Tianjin (deposit dated 1058). See *Kaogu xuebao* 1989.1, p. 103, fig. 24.

4. See Xu Xiaodong, *Liaodai yuqi yanjiu* [*Research on Liao jades*], pp. 113–14.

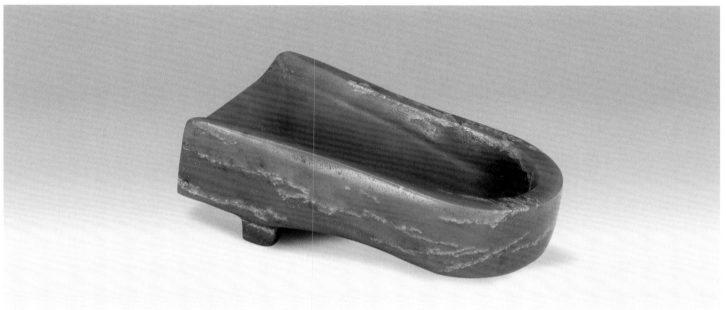

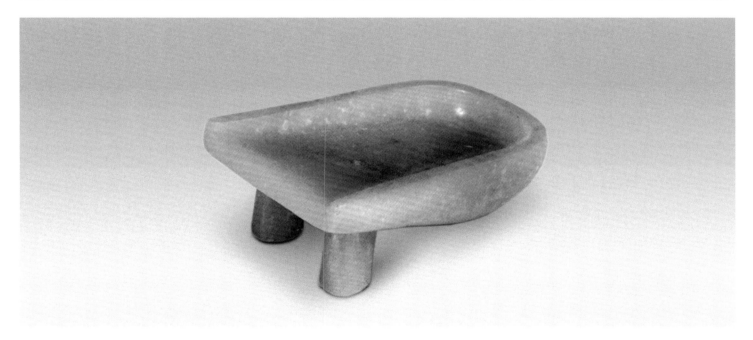

55. Mirror decorated with a coiled dragon

Liao dynasty, 942 or earlier
From the tomb of Yelü Yuzhi
and Chonggun at Hansumu Township,
Aluke'erqin Banner
Gilded bronze
Diameter: 28 cm; thickness: 1 cm
Research Institute of Cultural Relics
and Archaeology of Inner Mongolia

The back of this large mirror is decorated with a single scaly dragon in relief. To fit into the circular area of the mirror, the long creature's body is twisted and his legs, which end in four claws, are turned up into the air. His long, thin tail entwines around one of his hind legs before curling upward. His head looks back over his body, and his mouth is wide open, as if he were going to swallow the knob, or pearl, inside it. In comparison with his muscular and dynamic body, his neck is strangely thin.

Mirrors such as this one were cast in piece-moulds. The design on the back was carved into the moulds; after the mirrors were cast, the reflecting surface was finished by grinding and polishing. The unusually shiny and silvery quality of this mirror suggests the use of an alloy with high tin content, although the exact components await scientific analysis. Traces of gold indicate that the back of the mirror was originally gilded. Mirrors decorated with similar-style coiled dragons have been found in a number of Liao tombs, yet none of them rivals this one in terms of quality. The gilding and the fine craftsmanship of this mirror are indicative of the high status of its owner, Yelü Yuzhi, the Grand Mentor of the Eastern Capital, who died in 941.

The dragon, more than any other animal, is identified with China. However, the image of this mythical creature went through several changes over time before it came to be rendered with a long wriggling body, scales, a large head, a pair of horns, and powerful legs with claws. Scaly dragons carved in stone found at several of the Northern Song imperial mausoleums in Gongyi, Henan

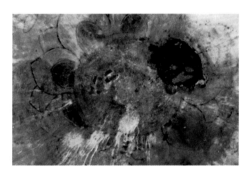

Province, are depicted in a style closely resembling that of this mirror, indicating the exchange of ideas and art forms between the Liao and the Song.[1]

The original position of this mirror in the tomb is not known because the tomb was disturbed before excavation. However, a mural in the center of the ceiling of the tomb (dated 993) of Han Kuangsi depicting a similar coiled dragon suggests that this mirror might have occupied a similar position (fig. 94).[2] Excavation reports show that during the Liao dynasty, it became common to place mirrors on the ceiling of a tomb rather than inside or near the coffin. The positioning of mirrors on the ceilings of Liao tombs is best known from the Zhang family tombs in Xuanhua, Hebei Province. In at least four of the tombs, a mirror was placed in the center of a cosmological painting adorning the ceiling above the coffin. But this position is also documented for a number of Liao tombs, including the early Liao tomb (dated 959) of Xiao Qulie at Dayingzi in Chifeng City, Inner Mongolia.[3]

It is noteworthy that bronze mirrors were also discovered in similar positions on the ceilings

of at least three Five Dynasties tombs in Zhejiang and Hebei provinces,[4] hence indicating links the Liao had with the Song Chinese either at the frontier or in the Southeast via the sea route.[5]

HMS

1. See *Bei Song haungling* [*Imperial mausoleums of the Northern Song*], p. 66, fig. 45.1; p. 158, fig. 137; p. 231, fig. 210; p. 250, fig. 227; p. 276, fig. 253. A Yue celadon bowl unearthed from the tomb (dated 1000) of Empress Li, of the Song dynasty, is incised with a similar dragon in the middle. See *Bei Song haungling*, p. 322, fig. 286.

2. See *Neimenggu wenwu kaogu* 2002.2, color pl., back cover.

3. See *Kaogu xuebao* 1956.3, pp. 1–26.

4. Three tombs in Lin'an, near Hangzhou in Zhejiang Province, belonged to the ruling clan of the Wuyue kingdom: Shui Qiu (died in 901), wife of Qian Kuan, the first ruler of Wuyue; Qian Yuanguan (tomb dated 942) and his concubine Wu Hanyu (tomb dated 952); and another member of the same ruling clan. See *Zhejiang sheng wenwu kaogusuo xuekan* 1981.1, pp. 94–104; *Kaogu* 1975.3, pp. 186–94; *Wenwu* 1975.8, pp. 66–72. Similar to the mirror found in the tomb of Shui Qiu, the mirror found in the tomb (dated 924) of Wang Chuzhi, in Quyang, Hebei Province, was set in the center of a large map of constellations painted on the ceiling. See *Wudai Wang Chuzhi mu* [*The Five Dynasties tomb of Wang Chuzhi*], pp. 18, 20.

5. For a detailed study of Liao mirrors, see Caroline Schulten, "Ancient Chinese Mirrors and Their Legacies in the Tang (AD 618–906), Liao (AD 907–1125) and Song (AD 960–1279) Periods," chapter 4, "Bronze Mirrors of the Liao (AD 907–1125) and Song (AD 960–1279) Period."

Fig. 94. Mural in the center of the ceiling of the front chamber of the tomb (dated 993) of Han Kuangsi

56a–b. Two spoons

Liao dynasty, 1018 or earlier
From the tomb of the Princess of Chen
and Xiao Shaoju at Qinglongshan Town,
Naiman Banner
Gilded silver
Length: 28 cm
Research Institute of Cultural Relics
and Archaeology of Inner Mongolia

These two spoons, excavated from the tomb of the Princess of Chen and Xiao Shaoju, are identical in form and design. They were made of hammered silver sheets and were gilded all over. Their long and curving handles are chased in fine lines at intervals to resemble bamboo stalks and at the tip to represent double fish.

Comparable silver spoons and chopsticks have been found in Liao tombs, such as the gilded-silver spoon (length 30.5 cm) from the tomb of Yelü Yuzhi (buried 942) and his wife.[1] Other metal spoons and chopsticks have also been found in pagodas, such as the silver chopsticks and spoon (length 16.2 cm) from the relic deposit (date 1058) inside the pagoda at Dule Monastery in Tianjin.[2] Although they may have been placed in tombs or pagodas to guarantee perpetual offerings of food, they were probably related, in particular, to the ceremonial function of tea drinking in both Buddhist and funerary practices.[3] However, a smaller silver spoon (length 9 cm) found in the White Pagoda (completed in 1049) in Balin Right Banner seems, according to the archaeological report, to have been used to scoop relic grains contained in a silver bottle found in the immediate vicinity of the spoon.[4]

HMS

a silver spoon (length 26.7 cm) and a pair of silver chopsticks were also found. See *Kaogu* 1960.2, pp. 17, 20, pl. 1.10. For more examples from tombs, see *Kaogu xuebao* 1956.3, pl. 7.7; *Liaohai wenwu xuekan* 1997.1, p. 35, figs. 7.13, 7.14; *Kaogu* 1987.3, p. 243, fig. 5; *Liaohai wenwu xuekan* 1986.1, p. 37, fig. 5.1.

2. *Kaogu xuebao* 1989.1, pp. 104–5, figs. 26.7, 26.8.

3. The most well known example is an elaborate set of vessels for tea drinking, including silver spoons and chopsticks, that was given as a gift to the Buddhist relic and was eventually buried with the relic underneath the foundation of Famen Pagoda (deposit dated 874). See Niigata kenritsu kindai bijutsukan, *Tō kōtei kara no okurimono* [*Gifts of the Tang emperors: Hidden treasures from Famen Temple*], pp. 83–94. For a discussion of the bronze spoons found in tombs and pagodas datable from the Northern and Southern Dynasties, Sui, and Tang dynasties, see Han Zhao, "Nanbeichao Sui Tang shidai tong ping 'tong chi' yongtu bianxi: jiantan yu riben zuopoli qi zhi guanxi" [Analytical study on the usage of bronze bottles and spoons of the Northern and Southern Dynasties, Sui, and Tang: Also on their relations with the Japanese *Sapoli* bronzes], *Yuan wang ji: Shaanxi sheng kaogu yanjiusuo huadan sishi zhounian jinian wenji* [*Looking forward: Anthology in honor of the fortieth anniversary of the Research Institute of Archaeology of Shaanxi Province*], pp. 768–81.

4. See *Wenwu* 1994.12, p. 13, fig. 21.2; p. 14.

---

1. See *Wenwu* 1996.1, p. 11; p. 14, fig. 27.2. Other examples from tombs include a silver spoon (length 27 cm) found in a Liao tomb at Shuluke in Jianping, Liaoning Province. It bears an inscription in Khitan characters on the back. According to the archaeological report, the inscription is identical to that incised on the two silver dishes found in nearby Zhangjiayingzi, where

57. Plaque in the form of a bird

Liao dynasty, 942 or earlier
From the tomb of Yelü Yuzhi
and Chonggun at Hansumu Township,
Aluke'erqin Banner
Gilded bronze
Height: 24.3 cm; width: 30.5 cm;
thickness: 0.03 cm
Research Institute of Cultural Relics
and Archaeology of Inner Mongolia

This plaque is made from a bronze sheet, gilded on the side where details of a large falcon with a sharp beak and claws are engraved. The bird has long, pointed, powerful wings, a bushy tail that stretches upward, and two powerful legs. It is depicted in a curious frontal view, with its wings spread out and its tail curving above its head, as if it were flying through the air, ready to halt for hunting, or were about to take off.

The bird has been described by archaeologists as a *haidongqing* (specially trained falcon) at the moment of seizing its prey. Yet its cloud-shaped comb, pointed ears, and spotted legs indicate that it is more likely to have been a mythical, hybrid creature, a combination of beast and bird. The similarity between this bird and the Vermillion Bird of the South (cat. 48c) suggests an analogous identity. The similar posture of the vermillion birds carved on the stone coffins excavated from the Liao tombs at Yemaotai in Faku (second half of the tenth century) and at Qianchuanghu Village in Chaoyang (late tenth or early eleventh century), both in Liaoning Province, confirms the theory.[1]

Because the tomb of Yelü Yuzhi (890–941) and Chonggun (died 942) was looted before excavation, it is unclear where this plaque was originally positioned. However, small holes around the edge of the plaque indicate that it might have been attached to the wooden coffin-bed, which had decayed.

HMS

1. See *Wenwu* 1975.12, p. 35, fig. 13; 1980.12, p. 19, fig. 4.

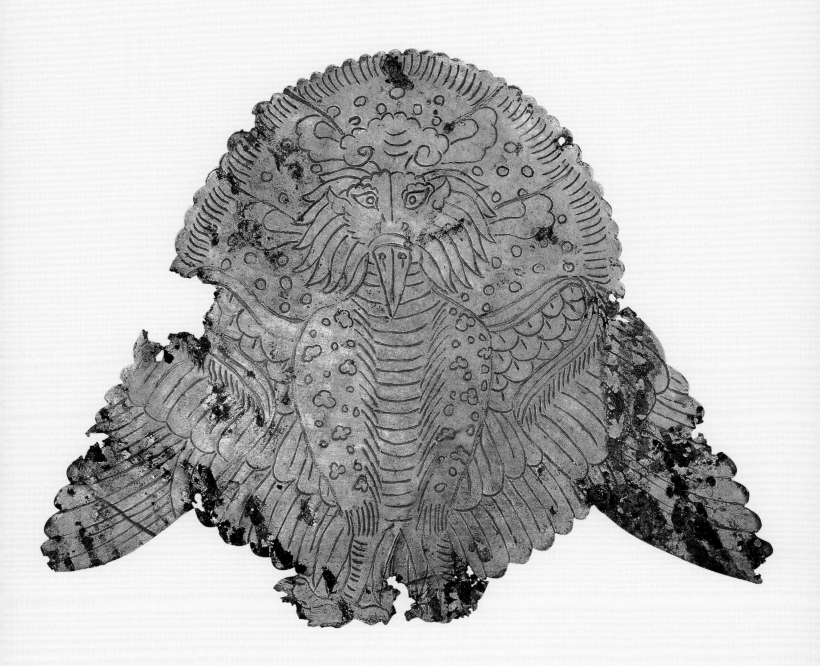

58a–b. Two plaques
of guardian-warriors

Liao dynasty, 942 or earlier
From the tomb of Yelü Yuzhi and
Chonggun at Hansumu Township,
Aluke'erqin Banner
Gilded bronze
a. Height: 38 cm; b. Height: 35 cm
Research Institute of Cultural Relics
and Archaeology of Inner Mongolia

These two plaques were made from gilded-bronze sheets engraved with a large figure standing on a rocky ledge. The figures on both of the plaques are similarly garbed in armor and a long, pleated skirt, and each wears a helmet in the form of a tiger's head. Each has one hand clenched in a fist and the other holding a weapon—a sword in the hand of the figure on the left (58a) and an axe in the hand of the figure on the right (58b). A similar but larger plaque (height 40.8 cm) was reported to have been found in the same tomb.[1]

Guardian figures assuming a threatening pose and towering over dwarflike creatures are associated with the Buddhist Heavenly Kings (*lopakālas*), protectors of the Buddhist realm. By the third quarter of the sixth century, armored guardians standing atop monstrous animals or demons appeared in Chinese tombs. A pair of such guardian figures was depicted in life size on the heavy stone gate that led to the main chamber of the tomb of Yelü Yuzhi (890–941) and his wife, Chonggun (died 924). However, these two plaques seem to have followed a separate tradition. Recent scholarship has shown that among all figurines found in Tang-dynasty tombs, guardians who wore a tiger's head helmet formed a separate group, for they did not tread on dwarflike creatures, and they appeared only in a very limited area, namely present-day Hebei, Henan and Shanxi provinces. It has been suggested that the iconography might have been borrowed from that of *gandharva*, one of the eight kinds of spiritual beings that protect the Buddhist laws at the conclusion of Mahāyāna scriptures.[2]

Since the tomb was looted before excavation, it is impossible to reconstruct the original position of these two plaques. However, small holes along the edges of the plaques indicate that they might have been used as attachments.

HMS

---

1. See *Wenwu* 1996.1, p. 17, fig. 34.2.
2. See Xie Mingliang, "Xila meishu de dongjian?" [Transmission of Greek art to the East?], *Gugong wenwu yuekan* 15.7 (October 1997), pp. 32–53.

From early in the Liao dynasty, the Liao imperial household supported the construction of Buddhist temples and pagodas, the printing of the Buddhist canon, and the carving of texts from that canon in stone. The Liao Buddhists believed that in 1052 the Buddhist religion would come to the phase of *mofa* (final *dharma* or final law), when the three treasures of Buddhism—namely, the Buddha, the *dharma* law, and the monastic community—would become extinct. As part of the imperial endeavour to prepare for the coming of the final *dharma*, scripture deposits were built at the North Pagoda in Chaoyang, Liaoning Province, and at the White Pagoda in present-day Balin Right Banner, Inner Mongolia.

Completed in 1049, three years before the anticipated coming of the final *dharma*, the deposit inside the White Pagoda in Balin Right Banner comprises five rooms inside the pinnacle of the pagoda. Among the many objects excavated from this deposit, the most important, and the most numerous, were the 109 pagoda-shaped containers (cat. 61a–b, 64–66, 71), each of which contained sutra scriptures. While most of the scriptures inside the pagoda-shaped containers were woodblock prints (bearing dates ranging from 1007 to 1021; see cat. 65c), some were hand-copied scrolls (cat. 72, 74).

The Liao scripture deposits were connected with relic veneration, as Buddhist scriptures were believed to be a manifestation of the Buddha's *dharma*-body or the Buddhist *dharma* law. The *Great Dhāraṇī Sutra of Stainless Pure Light* (Sanskrit: *Rashmivimalavishuddhaprabhā-dhāraṇī*; Chinese: *Wugou jingguang da tuoluoni jing*) (cat. 62–63), which articulates this concept, was commonly enshrined in Liao relic deposits. It promises numerous merits to those who venerate Buddhist scriptures, which manifest all Buddhas. These spiritual relics of the Buddha were thus carefully wrapped in fine silk (cat. 59) and enshrined in miniature pagodas, which were, in turn, enshrined on top of the White Pagoda. Offerings such as coins, herbal medicines, textiles (cat. 81), silver wares, and fine ceramics were made to the Buddha, and then were sealed, along with the relics, inside the pagoda.

At Cloud-Dwelling Monastery, in the vicinity of the Southern Capital (in what is today Beijing), there was a project to carve scriptures on stone in order to preserve the Buddhist law. This was a continuation of a project that was initiated during the Sui dynasty (581–618). From the 1020s to 1095, with the aid of the Liao court, more than four thousand stone tablets were engraved with the text of the Khitan edition of the Buddhist canon. In 1118, to prevent them from destruction, 4,260 of these stone tablets were buried underneath a stone pillar at the monastery. There was also a project in the Southern Capital, from the 1030s to 1068, to make woodblock prints of the entire Khitan canon; this is one of the greatest achievements in the history of printing in East Asia. It comprises 579 bundles, and an entire set was stored in the Sutra Library—built in 1038 at the command of Emperor Xingzong (r. 1031–55)—on the premises of Huayan Monastery in the Western Capital (present-day Datong, Shanxi Province). During the reign of Emperor Daozong (r. 1055–1101), a copy of the Buddhist canon was presented as a gift to Korea. Unfortunately, the Khitan canon does not survive in its entirety today. Only stray remnants from sites such as the White Pagoda in Balin Right Banner and the Timber Pagoda in Yingxian, Shanxi Province, provide clues to this extensive Liao publication (cat. 65c, 72, 74).

The worship of texts, together with a preference for the *Great Dhāraṇī Sutra of Stainless Pure Light,* is a distinctive feature of Liao relic deposits and is not found in the Yellow River area inhabited by the Song. It was, however, linked with Korea, where there was a similar tradition of text veneration, especially veneration of the *Great Dhāraṇī Sutra of Stainless Pure Light.* It was also connected with Japan, where people also believed that the final *dharma* would come in 1052.

In addition to scriptures, freestanding sculptures of Buddhist images were erected and venerated during the Liao era. The most impressive extant examples of Liao Buddhist sculptures are the twenty-nine clay figures (fig. 95) enshrined in the Sutra Library at Huayan Monastery. Archaeology has revealed various types of Liao Buddhist sculptures made of different materials, ranging from votive stone sculptures of Shakyamuni Buddha (cat. 67, 75) to bodhisattvas made of sculpted earthenware (cat. 70) to high-fired sculptures of Shakyamuni's disciples made of porcelaneous stoneware covered with white glaze (cat. 68) or with colorful lead glazes. A number of gilded-bronze sculptures are in public collections outside of China, including the Nelson-Atkins Museum of Art in Kansas City, the Avery

Fig. 95. Central group of statues in the Sutra Library at Huayan Monastery

Brundage Collection at the Asian Art Museum of San Francisco, and the Royal Ontario Museum in Toronto.

Characteristic of Liao Buddhist sculptures, of both standing and seated figures, are their elongated torsos and very straight posture. In addition to Shakyamuni Buddha and his attendants, the esoteric Four Buddhas of the Diamond World (namely, Ratnasambhava, Akshobhya, Amitābha, and Amoghasiddhi), as well as Vairocana Buddha (manifestation of Buddha nature), were commonly portrayed in sculptural form, as evidenced by the colossal Buddhist statues distributed over the five floors of the Timber Pagoda, or carved in relief on the exterior of Liao brick pagodas, of which the North Pagoda in Chaoyang is most representative.

Both textual materials and visual images show that the Buddhism practiced by the Liao people was a mixture of the Three Teachings—Buddhism, Daoism, and Confucianism. The Buddhist anthology *Collection of Essentials to Becoming a Buddha through the Perfect Penetration of the Exoteric and Esoteric* (*Xian mi yuantong chengfo xin yao ji*), compiled by the monk Daoyin in the late eleventh century, shows that by the end of the Liao dynasty Daoist concepts such as immortality were incorporated into Liao Buddhism in order to help explain the difficult notion of Buddhahood. The Daoist idea of *liberation from the corpse* was fused with the Buddhist ideas of rebirth and nirvana, thus resulting in the mannequin burials at the Zhang family tombs (late Liao dynasty) in Xuanhua, Hebei Province. The mannequins found in the Zhang family tombs are similar to the mannequin included in the exhibition (cat. 52).

HMS

59. Red sutra wrapper embroidered with a rider in a pearl roundel

Liao dynasty, 1049 or earlier
Excavated from the White Pagoda
in Balin Right Banner
Silk, gauze, tabby, embroidery
with silk threads
Length: 27.7 cm; width: 27 cm
Museum of Balin Right Banner

This embroidered textile was, like the blue gauze (cat. 81), among the many textiles that were discovered from 1988 to 1992 in the deposit inside the *cha* (the finial or steeple shaped like a pagoda) at the top of the White Pagoda in Balin Right Banner.[1] The ribbons in the lower right-hand corner on the backside of the cloth indicate that it was most likely used as a sutra wrapper.

The embroidery shows a rider sitting on a horse, which is at full gallop, within a pearl roundel. The rider is depicted with his upper body facing the viewer. Both his arms are raised, and a falcon rests on each hand. From numerous references in the *Liaoshi* (History of the Liao) and on other Liao artifacts,[2] it appears that falconry was a popular form of hunting for the Khitan.[3] The Liao emperor and empress often participated in ceremonial hunts in which falconry was used.[4] Several Liao tomb murals show attendants carrying falcons on their arms.[5] According to the *Liaoshi*, regulations allowed common people and officials of lower ranks to keep falcons, but the taming of the highly esteemed gyrfalcons imported from the northeast was a privilege for the upper class.[6]

The rider is dressed in a colorful robe, fastened by a broad sash, and is wearing brown boots. The flaps of his cap are folded back above his ears, and the ribbons with which they are fastened are fluttering in the air.[7] During the colder seasons, the flaps can be let down for extra protection.[8] Various emblems are scattered around the horse and rider: pearls, interlocked coins, a rhinoceros horn, a piece of silver bullion, and a rock-shaped ornament. These objects are also rep-

resented on a Liao mural in Xuanhua, Hebei Province.[9] The rock-shaped ornament, in particular, is nearly identical to the rock depicted on a wooden panel from Zhanpu, Linxi County (cat. 49a). The emblems could represent what are traditionally referred to as the eight treasures of Confucianism, which might have been adopted as auspicious insignia by the Khitan.[10]

Pearl roundels appear often in the Sassanid art of Persia;[11] they consist of a central figure or group of humans and/or animals, framed by a band of pearls. The motif was transmitted via the Silk Route to China during the Tang dynasty (618–907).[12] The embroidered sutra wrapper shows that the pearl roundel motif was assimilated by the Khitan and modified to suit their imagery.

SLG

1. See "Neimenggu Balinyouqi Qingzhou baita faxian Liaodai fojiao wenwu" [Buddhist relics from the White Pagoda in Qingzhou, Balin Right Banner, Inner Mongolia], *Wenwu* 1994.12, pp. 4–33.
2. For an example of an embroidery with a falcon chasing a deer, from Yelü Yuzhi's tomb at Hansumu Township in Aluke'erqin Banner, see Gai Zhiyong, *Tanxun shiqu de wangchao: Liao Yelü Yuzhi de mu* [*Exploring a lost dynasty: The tomb of Yelü Yuzhi*], p. 108.
3. Emma C. Bunker, Julia M. White, and Jenny F. So, *Adornment for the Body and Soul: Ancient Chinese Ornaments from the Mengdiexuan Collection*, p. 19.
4. Karl A. Wittfogel and Fêng Chia-Shêng, *History of Chinese Society: Liao, 907–1125*, p. 236.
5. For examples of tomb murals with depictions of falcons in Jiefangyingzi, Wengniute Banner, Inner Mongolia, see Xiang Chunsong, *Liaodai bihua xuan* [*A selection of Liao-dynasty mural paintings*], fig., 42, and in Lamagou, Kelidai District, Aohan Banner, see *Qidan wangchao: Neimenggu Liaodai wenwu jinghua* [*Khitan dynasty: Liao archaeological treasures from Inner Mongolia*], pp. 113–15.

6. Wittfogel and Fêng, *History of Chinese Society*, p. 236.
7. Similar caps can be seen in murals in Tomb Number 1 (dated ca. 1080), Kulun Banner, Jilin Province, see *Wenwu* 1973.8, p. 31; pl. 2.
8. Zhao Feng, *Liao Textiles and Costumes*, p. 220.
9. See emblems placed in a wooden container in a mural on the northwest wall of the rear chamber in Tomb Number 4, of Han Shixun (d. 1110), in *Xuanhua Liaomu bihua* [*Liao-dynasty murals in tombs in Xuanhua*], pl. 96.
10. The eight treasures of Confucianism are the pearl, the musical stone, the coin, the rhombus, the book, the painting, the rhinoceros horn, and the artemisia leaf. Wolftram Eberhard, *Times Dictionary of Chinese Symbols: An Essential Guide to the Hidden Symbols in Chinese Art, Customs and Beliefs*, p. 91.
11. Pearl roundels originally represented the victory given by the goddess Anahita to the Sassanid king Khussrau II (590–628) on the occasion of his investiture. Patricia Eichenbaum Karetzky, "Engraved Designs on the Late Sixth Century Sarcopahgus of Li Ho," *Artibus Asiae* 47.2 (1986), p. 90, n. 28.
12. For a discussion of the transmission of the pearl roundel motif, see Roger Goepper, "Dressing the Temple: Textile Representations in the Frescoes at Alchi," in Jill Tilden (ed.) *Asian Art: The Second Hali Annual*, pp. 110–13, and Elisabeth M. Owen, "A Stitch in Time: The Pearl-bordered Medallion from Persia to Japan" (paper presented at the Third Silk Road Conference at Yale University, New Haven, Dec. 1998).

60a–b. Architectural components in the form of dragon heads

Earthenware
a. Liao dynasty, eleventh century
From Wanbu Huayanjing Pagoda,
Baita Village, near Hohhot, Inner Mongolia
Height: 56 cm; length: 55 cm
Museum of the Inner Mongolia
Autonomous Region
b. Liao dynasty, 1049 or earlier
From the White Pagoda in Balin
Right Banner
Approximate height: 35.6 cm;
width: 58.4 cm; depth: 33 cm
Museum of Balin Right Banner

In 1983, during repair work at Wanbu Huayanjing Pagoda, outside of present-day Hohhot, a number of architectural components were unearthed from below ground level; among them was a large gray pottery dragon head (cat. 60a). Similarly, when restoration work was undertaken at the White Pagoda in Balin Right Banner (pagoda completed in 1049) from 1988 to 1992, a number of finely sculpted dragon heads and phoenixes were found that had adorned the ends of the upper eaves and roof ridges of the pagoda (fig. 96); this example (cat. 60b) was one of them. Several types of dragon heads have been identified from the White Pagoda site, all of them have round bulging eyes, curly hair, sharp teeth, and notably large nostrils. The sockets that attached these architectural components to the eaves were cleverly built into the hollow bodies of the sculptures or added as an extension to the back (fig. 97).

Wanbu Huayanjing Pagoda and the White Pagoda share several architectural features; both are brick buildings with seven stories, are octagonal in shape, and have decorations carved in relief on their exteriors. The decorative motifs range from imitation doors and windows to pagodas to Buddhist figures such as bodhisattvas and guardians. While the octagonal pagoda is a legacy of the Liao, decorating the eaves and roof ridges of monumental buildings with pottery animal sculptures has a long history in China. Examples can be found on temples, such as the Yongning Temple of the Northern Wei period (386–534) in Luoyang, Henan Province; palace buildings, in sites like the Supreme Capital of the Bohai kingdom

(698–926) in Nong'an, Heilongjiang Province; and imperial mausoleums, such as the tomb of Empress Zhu (died 1103) of the Song dynasty.[1] Comparable dragon heads have been found at several other Liao sites,

including Wu'anzhou in Aohan Banner, Raozhou in Linxi County, Inner Mongolia, and Xiuyan in Liaoning Province.[2]

HMS

1. See *Beiwei Luoyang Yongningsi* [*The Northern Wei Yongning Monastery in Luoyang*], pls. 117, 118; Tsugio Mikami, ed., *Sekai tōji zenshū* [*Catalogue of the world's ceramics*], vol. 13, *Ryō, Kin, Gen* [*Liao, Jin, Yuan*], pp. 143–45; *Liudingshan yu Bohaizhen* [*Liudingshan and Bohai Town*], pls. 97, 98; *Bei Song huangling* [*Imperial mausoleums of the Northern Song*], color pl. 8.3.

2. See *Neimenggu wenwu kaogu* 1997.1, p. 47, fig. 8; Feng Yongqian, *Dongbei kaogu yanjiu*, [*Essays on the archaeology of northeast China*], vol. 1, p. 233, fig. 18; *Kaogu* 1999.6, p. 63, fig. 6.

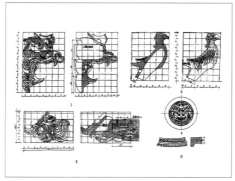

Fig. 96. A dragon head that adorned an upper eave of the White Pagoda in Balin Right Banner

Fig. 97. Dragon heads and phoenixes from the White Pagoda in Balin Right Banner

61a–b. Two miniature pagodas

Liao dynasty, 1049 or earlier
Excavated from the White Pagoda
in Balin Right Banner
a. Wood; height: 30 cm;
diameter of base: 8.4 cm
b. Gilded wood; height: 28.5 cm;
diameter of base: 8 cm
Museum of Balin Right Banner

During a major renovation of the White Pagoda in Balin Right Banner from 1988 to 1992, a deposit comprising five linked pits (totaling 1.53 square meters) was discovered inside the *cha*, or top structure, of the pagoda (see figs. 62, 64).[1] Approximately 800 objects, including 109 miniature pagodas and 276 pieces of textile, were excavated from the pits. In addition, two stone steles, four miniature pagodas, and 490 coins were found beneath the pits, close to the bottom of the *cha*. These two miniature pagodas and several other items in the exhibition (cat. 62–67, 71–73, 74) were among the many objects found in the pagoda.

The White Pagoda is situated in the northern half of the walled city of Qingzhou (fig. 58), some ten kilometers from the imperial mausoleums of the Liao emperors Shengzong (r. 982–1031), Xingzong (r. 1031–1055), and Daozong (r. 1055–1101).[2] According to a stone stele installed beneath the multichamber deposit, construction of the pagoda —referred to as *Shijiafo Sheli Pagoda* (Shakyamuni Buddha's Relic Pagoda) in the Liao text on the stele—began at the command of Empress Dowager Zhangsheng, the consort of Emperor Shengzong, in 1047 to enshrine Buddhist relics. Two years later, in 1049, *jin fa sheli* (spiritual relics made in metal), along with ninety-nine copies of *zhanggan tuoluoni* (*dhāraṇīs* on sticks), were enshrined inside the *cha* before the completion of the pagoda.

These miniature pagodas represent two of the seven types excavated from the site.[3] They are similar in shape; both have a stepped pedestal and a plain tubular body crowned with a series of parasols of diminishing size.

According to the excavation report, all of the miniature pagodas except for one were elaborately decorated with gilding or painting and were used as containers for Buddhist scriptures; the one exception (cat. 61a) is undecorated and encloses an amber container of relic grains (fig. 67).

HMS

---

1. The pagoda is a Chinese interpretation of the Indian stupa, which was a funerary mound erected in honor of a great ruler. Buddhists adopted the stupa as a receptacle for sacred relics, and the stupa in Buddhist terms came to symbolize entry into final nirvana. An ancient Indian stupa consists of a low dome, surrounded by a railing, and a top structure, comprising symbolic parasols (called *chattra* in Sanskrit), and a surrounding railing. The top structure of a pagoda is called *cha* in Chinese.

2. For the excavation report, see *Wenwu* 1994.12, pp. 4–33. See also Sun Jianhua, "The discovery and protection of the Liao-dynasty cultural relics from the White Pagoda in Balin Right Banner," in this catalogue.

3. Chinese archaeologists have categorized the miniature pagodas found in the multichamber deposit into five major types and seven subtypes; see *Wenwu* 1994.12, p. 29, table 2.

62. Metal sheet with incision of the *Dhāraṇī inside the Cavity of Chattra Parasols*

Liao dynasty, 1049 or earlier
Excavated from the White Pagoda
in Balin Right Banner
Gold
Length: 16.7 cm; width: 9.6 cm;
thickness: 0.03 cm
Museum of Balin Right Banner

63. Metal sheet with incision of a passage from the *Great Dhāraṇī Sutra of Stainless Pure Light*

Liao dynasty, 1049 or earlier
Excavated from the White Pagoda
in Balin Right Banner
Silver
Length: 21.2 cm; width: 11.6 cm;
thickness: 0.03 cm
Museum of Balin Right Banner

These two metal sheets were retrieved from the middle room of the multichamber deposit inside the top structure of the White Pagoda in Balin Right Banner.[1] According to the excavation report, they together form a single scroll, although it is unclear how they were connected. On the gold sheet is inscribed in Sanskrit the text of the *Dhāraṇī inside the Cavity of Chattra Parasols*, accompanied by its Chinese title (*Xiangluntang zhong tuoluoni zhou*) to the left. On the silver sheet is incised in Chinese an inscription instructing people to make 99 copies of the *Dhāraṇī inside the Cavity of Chattra Parasols* and to enshrine them inside the cavity of the parasols on top of the pagoda. It then states that if the instructions were followed, 99,000 *sarīra* relics would be enshrined and 99,000 relic pagodas built (the numbers 99 and 99,000 both serving as metaphors for countless). It thus shows that in venerating Buddhist scriptures that manifest all Buddhas, one is rewarded with numerous merits.

This inscription dictated the content of the relic deposit in the White Pagoda, where 106 copper sheets inscribed with the *Dhāraṇī inside the Cavity of Chattra Parasols* were found in the four rooms inside the cavity of the *chattra* parasols. The inscription is an excerpt from the *Great Dhāraṇī Sutra of Stainless Pure Light* (Sanskrit: *Rashmivimalavishuddhaprabhā-dhāraṇī*; Chinese: *Wugou jingguang da tuoluoni jing*), an esoteric scripture venerated by the Liao in various Buddhist contexts.[2] The preference for this particular sutra links the Liao more closely with the Korean tradition than with the form of Buddhism practiced in the Yellow River area. In Korea, there was a long tradition of venerating Buddhist texts in pagodas; among those texts, the *Great Dhāraṇī Sutra of Stainless Pure Light* was the most prominent. The Liao also shared with their neighbors in Japan and Korea a feature in the making of scripture deposits: the use of durable materials—such as metal—as surfaces on which to transcribe and preserve texts. In addition to the finds at the White Pagoda, there are examples from the North Pagoda in Chaoyang, Liaoning Province (two deposits dated, respectively, to 1043 and 1044).[3] The *Diamond Sutra* (Sanskrit: *Vajracchedika-prajñāpāramitā-sūtra*; Chinese: *Jin'gang banruo boluomi jing*) transcribed on copper plates that were deposited in the foundation of the wooden pagoda at the Chesoksa Temple site (ca. 600–640) is the earliest known example from Korea, whereas in Japan the earliest example is from the sutra burial at Kinpunsen, Nara (dated 1007).[4]

HMS

1. For the excavation report, see *Wenwu* 1994.12, pp. 4–33.
2. See T 1024, 19.717c–721b. For the mentioned passage, see T 1024, 19.719a. The particular passage describes the occasion on which the Buddha expounded the method of venerating the *Dhāraṇī inside the Cavity of Chattra Parasols* in the cavities of *chattra* parasols on the tops of pagodas. The *Great Dhāraṇī Sutra of Stainless Pure Light* introduces the Five Great *Dhāraṇīs*, including the *Dhāraṇī inside the Cavity of Chattra Parasols*, which could protect people from sufferings in this world and could save them from hell. The main purpose of the sutra is to encourage the construction of pagodas to enshrine these *dhāraṇīs*, which represent the *tahtāgata-garbha*, the possibility to achieve Buddhahood that is innate in every creature.
3. For the excavation report, see *Wenwu* 1992.7, pp. 1–28.
4. See Hsueh-man Shen, "Buddhist Relic Deposits from Tang (618–907) to Northern Song (960–1127) and Liao (907–1125)," vol. 1, pp. 175–89, for a discussion of the connections between the Liao and Korea and Japan in their practice of relic deposits.

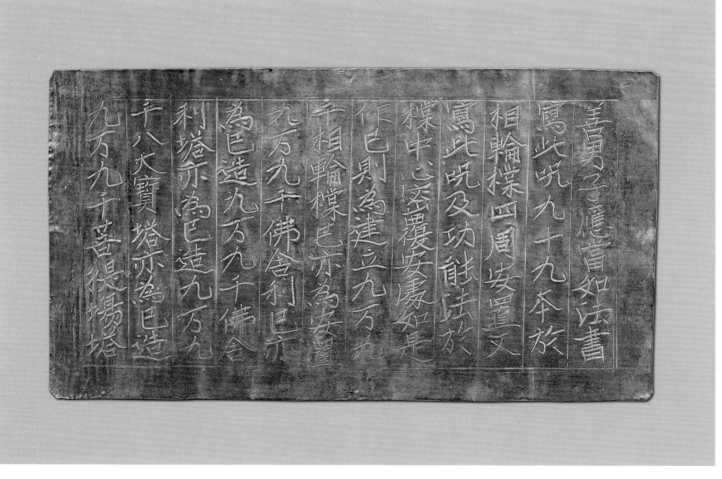

64. Miniature pagoda decorated with the Buddhas of the Ten Directions

Liao dynasty, 1049 or earlier
Excavated from the White Pagoda
in Balin Right Banner
Ink and color on wood
Height: 45.5 cm; diameter of base: 13 cm
Museum of Balin Right Banner

In addition to the 109 miniature pagodas found in the multichamber deposit inside the cavity of the *chattra* parasols, four additional miniature pagodas were discovered in a square pit below the deposit within the *cha*, or top structure, of the White Pagoda in Balin Right Banner. Through the very center of the pit is the *yasti* pole, the central axis of the whole structure of the pagoda. To the north and south of the pole are two stone steles on which the construction of the pagoda is recorded (see fig. 65). The four miniature pagodas were installed at the four corners of the pit, surrounding the *yasti* pole and the two stone steles.

These four miniature pagodas are larger than any of the others found in the pagoda; each is decorated with ten images of the Buddha that were carved in relief and arranged in two registers. A cartouche inscribed with *shi fang fo* (Buddhas of the Ten Directions) on the lower register identifies these images as the Buddhas of the Ten Directions. While the ten directions in Buddhism refer to the four cardinal directions, the four intermediate directions, the zenith and the nadir, the Buddhas of the Ten Directions refer to the Buddhas of all directions.

The prominent size and the careful positioning of these four large miniature pagodas are indicative of their status and significance. According to the excavation report, each of the four miniature pagodas contained a woodblock-printed scroll of the *Lotus Sutra* (Sanskrit: *Saddharmapundarīka-sūtra*; Chinese: *Miaofa lianhua jing*). The sutra was wrapped in a fine piece of white silk, which was inscribed in ink with thirteen characters reading *Fahua*

jing yibu quanshen sheli zai ci ta zhong (the whole of the *Lotus Sutra* as the entire-body *sarīra* [of the Buddha] is here in the pagoda).[1] The passage was likely an excerpt from the *Lotus Sutra*, in which Section Ten, "The Teacher of the Law," articulates this idea.[2] It explains well the motivation behind the construction of scripture deposits during the Liao era.

HMS

1. See *Wenwu* 1994.12, p. 27; p. 24, fig. 53.
2. See T 262, 9:31b. One additional scroll of the *Lotus Sutra* was enshrined inside a large carved wood miniature pagoda, which was deposited in the central room of the complex multichamber structure. See *Wenwu* 1994.12, pp. 22–23; p. 17, fig. 38.

65a–c. Miniature pagoda, layered streamer with attached fish, and a *Dhāraṇī* scroll

Liao dynasty, 1049 or earlier
Excavated from the White Pagoda
in Balin Right Banner
a. Miniature pagoda: painted cypress
wood with gold leaf; height: 23 cm;
diameter of base: 9.1 cm
b. Layered streamer with attached fish:
gauze, samite, amber; length (not including
cord): approximately 23 cm
c. *Dhāraṇī* scroll: ink on paper, gilded copper
Museum of Balin Right Banner

The body of this miniature pagoda is decorated with the images of the Seven Buddhas of the Past, which are carved in relief and covered with exquisite gold leaf so that those who saw them could visualize the golden body of the Buddha.[1] The seven Buddhas are represented in three-quarter view and are shown in a procession moving counterclockwise on a cloud. An elaborate streamer made of red gauze and samite and decorated with fish dangles accompanies the pagoda and adds to its grandeur.

The iconography is repeated on 104 other miniature pagodas discovered in the multichamber deposit inside the top structure of the White Pagoda, although only one of them is identical in size and has the same color scheme as this one. Each of these miniature pagodas contained a copper sheet carved with the *Dhāraṇī inside the Cavity of Chattra Parasols* (*Xiangluntang zhong tuoluoni zhou*), as well as two scrolls of miscellaneous *dhāraṇīs*—including the *Fundamental Dhāraṇī* (*Genben tuoluoni*)—printed on paper. The copper sheet was rolled up to make a *zhanggan* (core or stick) for the woodblock-printed paper sheets to be wrapped around. The copper and paper sheets together formed a *zhanggan tuoluoni* (*dhāraṇī* on a stick)—as they were described on a stone stele (dated 1049) found with them. The *zhanggan tuoluoni* was wrapped in a piece of white silk cloth. An inscription written in ink on each of the silk wrappings refers to these scriptures as *sheli* (*sarīra* relics). It shows that these scriptures were enshrined in the pagoda as relics of the Buddha. The Liao's use of texts as relics and their desire to enshrine the ultimate truth is a distinct feature of Liao Buddhist relic deposits, and is not found in the Yellow River region of the Song.

It is also noteworthy that both the *Dhāraṇī inside the Cavity of Chattra Parasols* and the *Fundamental Dhāraṇī* were extracted from the *Great Dhāraṇī Sutra of Stainless Pure Light* (Sanskrit: *Rashmivimalavishuddhaprabhā-dhāraṇī*; Chinese: *Wugou jingguang da tuoluoni jing*), which is the most favored sutra among all Liao relic deposits.

HMS

1. A golden body is one of the thirty-two physical traits of the Buddha.

66. Miniature pagoda decorated with a phoenix

Liao dynasty, 1049 or earlier
Excavated from the White Pagoda
in Balin Right Banner
Gilded silver, silver, and pearls
Height: 40 cm; diameter of base: 10.5 cm
Museum of Balin Right Banner

This sutra container, whose structure is very similar to that of an actual Liao pagoda, consists of a distinct pedestal, a hexagonal body, and a tall top structure.[1] It is made of sheets of silver that were hammered separately, incised with patterns, nailed, and then welded together. Five sides of the body of the pagoda are decorated with human figures in gestures of veneration, and the sixth with a closed door. An elaborate railing surrounds the lower part of the pagoda, which rests on a domed lotus pedestal. In the front of the base is a standing Buddha with a monk's staff and an alms bowl in his hands; his identity is confirmed by the *uṣṇīṣa* protuberance on his skull, one of the thirty-two traits of the Buddha. The pagoda is crowned by a large structure that is composed of a lotus pedestal, a dome, and three large balls alternating with lotus flower-shaped parasols along a long shaft. Tassels comprising chains and small bells adorn the parasols and connect the shaft with the six points of the eaves of the pagoda. A crested phoenix with spread wings and a long tail sits on the top of the shaft. In its hooked beak is a string of twenty-four pearls.

The miniature pagoda was discovered in the central room of the multichamber relic deposit (dated 1049) on top of the White Pagoda. A large wooden miniature pagoda carved and painted with the images of seven Buddhas on the exterior—the largest miniature pagoda in the deposit—and a silver relic-container in the form of a long-necked bottle were discovered in the same room. That the two miniature pagodas were isolated from the other 107 pagoda-shaped scripture containers in the deposit is an indication of their status and significance.

Unlike all of the other miniature pagodas found in the deposit, which contain printed scriptures on paper, this elaborately decorated pagoda contains a long scroll of silver sheet (length 112 cm, width 9 cm) on which Buddhist scriptures and votive inscriptions are engraved. The Buddhist scriptures include six *dhāraṇīs* extracted from the *Great Dhāraṇī Sutra of Stainless Pure Light* (Sanskrit: *Rashmivimalavishuddhaprabhā-dhāraṇī*; Chinese: *Wugou jingguang da tuoluoni jing*)—the most favored Buddhist scripture in the Liao era[2]— and the *Verse on the Dharma-body* (*Fa sheli zhenyan*)

and are followed by an inscription, dated 1049, dedicating the merits of the scriptures to the imperial family (fig. 98).[3]

Buddhist scriptures engraved on metal sheets were also found in the relic deposit (dated 1043) on top of the North Pagoda in Chaoyang, Liaoning Province. Like the deposit at the White Pagoda, this deposit was built under the sponsorship of the imperial house. Inside the deposit room and in front of the coffin-shaped reliquary is a miniature pagoda made of four layers of gold and silver sheets; it contains a silver scripture scroll that is 362.2 centimeters long and 11.3 centimeters wide.[4] The use of precious metals for the inscription of sutras, unusual in a Chinese context, seems to have its roots in the Korean peninsula rather than in central China (compare cat. 62, 63).

HMS

---

1. For a detailed discussion of various types of Liao pagodas, see Nancy Shatzman Steinhardt, "The Architectural Landscape of the Liao and Underground Resonances," in this catalogue.

2. Passages taken from T 1024, 19.718b–719a, 19.719c–720a, 19.720c–721a.

3. For a transcription of the inscription, see *Beifang wenwu* 2002.1, pp. 52–53.

4. For a report of the excavation, see *Wenwu* 1992.7, pp. 1–28.

Fig. 98. Long scroll of gilded silver sheet (section), from the silver pagoda miniature excavated from the deposit on top of the White Pagoda in Balin Right Banner

67. The recumbent Buddha (*parinirvana*)

Liao dynasty, mid-eleventh century
Excavated from the White Pagoda in Balin Right Banner
Marble with polychrome
Length: 60 cm; width 33 cm
Museum of Balin Right Banner

The sculpture is one of three *parinirvana* Buddhas found in the White Pagoda (fig. 99) in Balin Right Banner, at Qingzhou, the site of three Liao imperial tombs. In 1988, archaeologists found a small gilded one 13.6 cm long in a brick casket in the top portion (Sanskrit: *laksata*; Chinese: *cha*) of the pagoda (fig. 100).[1] The other two were found earlier elsewhere in the pagoda and taken out in the 1970s. They were then collected back from villagers by the Museum of Balin Right Banner.[2] These two are approximately the same size; they are more elaborately carved and considerably larger than the one found in the *cha*. One of the two is damaged; its feet are partially broken off, and the paint has largely fallen off (fig. 101). The one in the exhibition (cat. 67), however, is in excellent condition, retains much of its original green and red paint, and has finer articulation of the robe and features.

Shakyamuni, "sage of the Shakya clan," lies on his right side on an elongated *sumeru* pedestal, that is, one with a narrowed waist, symbolizing the Buddhist world mountain, Mount Meru, connecting the wider base and platform, which symbolize earth and heaven. Eight lions adorn this pedestal, making an impressive bier for Shakyamuni—who is also called Shakyasinha, "lion of the Shakya clan"—as he enters nirvana. Another symbol of Buddhism, a lotus flower, decorates the pillow on which his head rests. The Buddha's long left arm lies extended along the contour of his body and emphasizes the long torso and short legs that are characteristic of Liao style. Also characteristic of Liao style is the mannered treatment of the four elegant swirls at the ends of the folds of his robe, where they meet the pedestal.[3]

Because the smallest of the three sculptures was thoroughly integrated into the *cha*, one assumes it was placed there in 1049, when the *cha* was finished under the direction of Empress Dowager Zhangsheng (d. 1058). She must have commissioned the sculpture that is included in the exhibition when her son, the emperor Xingzong, died in 1055. Xingzong; his father, Emperor Shengzong (d. 1031); and successor, Emperor Daozong (d. 1101), are buried in the three tombs.[4] Presumably, the third sculpture was commissioned on the death and interment of Daozong.

As the Far Eastern equivalent of Indian burial mounds or stupas, pagodas symbolize the death or *parinirvana* of the historical Buddha, Shakyamuni. The sculptures were perfectly suited to augment that symbolism and serve the purposes of the site of the royal necropolis.[5]

MG

1. For analysis of the development of this motif, see Marilyn Leidig Gridley, *Chinese Buddhist Sculpture under the Liao (Free Standing Works in Situ and Selected Examples from Public Collections)*, p. 61.
2. For the sculpture from the *cha*, see *Wenwu*, 1994.12, color plate inside front cover and pp. 25–26.
3. Tian Caixia, "Liao Qingzhou Baitazang shijiafo niepan shi xiang" [The stone sculpture of the parinirvana of Shakyamuni from the depository of the Liao White Pagoda in Qingzhou], *Wenwu* 2002.11, p. 93 and color plate on back cover. Additional information was sent to the author by Sun Jianhua in an e-mail attachment, May 19, 2005.
4. Nancy S. Steinhardt, *Liao Architecture*, pp. 260–63.

Fig. 99. The White Pagoda in Balin Right Banner

Fig. 100. *Parinirvana* from the *cha* of the White Pagoda in Balin Right Banner

Fig. 101. *Parinirvana* sculpture on display in the Museum of Balin Right Banner in August, 1993

68a–b. Kashyapa and Ānanda

Liao dynasty, eleventh century
From Qianwulibuge Village, Nailingao
Township, Kulun Banner
Porcelaneous stoneware
a. Kashyapa: height: 26.5 cm
b. Ānanda: height: 27 cm
Museum of Tongliao City

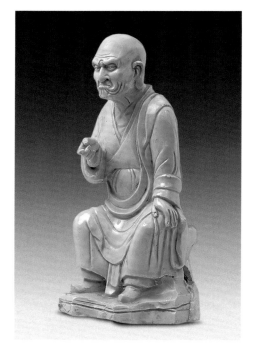

Shakyamuni's old and young disciples, Kashyapa (cat. 68a) and Ānanda (cat. 68b), sit Western style, with legs pendant, on a rocky outcropping representing the wilderness setting ascetics prefer for meditation. As is typical of Liao images, their legs are short in proportion to their torsos.

The pair make a delightful vignette of an exchange one might expect between an older disciple and his younger counterpart, who is well known for having nearly fallen from grace on many occasions. Kashyapa's expression suggests fierce disapproval. He leans forward slightly, holds his right hand at chest level, and extends his index finger a bit, as though making a point in the discussion. Ānanda's mouth is set in a rather grim half-smile. He clutches a rosary in his right hand and leans back as if reacting to the force of Kashyapa's scolding demeanor.

This pair is a dramatic rendering of youth and old age. Ānanda's face is smooth; Kashyapa's is bony, and his skin deeply creased. The tendons in his neck stand out sharply in contrast to the ring of flesh that curves softly around the base of Ānanda's neck. Their robes also emphasize their differences: Ānanda's is voluminous and flowing; Kashyapa's is tightly wrapped, its folds sharp edged.

Herdsmen found these two images together with a headless Shakyamuni in August 1980 at Qianwulibuge Village after a flood of the Xinkai River. On the east bank of that river in the Liao period was the Shun'an county seat, Yizhou, private city of Zhang Gongzhu, a devout Buddhist and eldest daughter of Emperor Shengzong (r. 982–1031).[1] Liao princesses were among those in the Liao imperial family who were allowed to build such cities and populate them with their personal bondsmen.[2]

The three small sculptures appear to have been a set, possibly for a family shrine.[3] It is unusual to have seated disciples attending Shakyamuni. They have a milk-white glaze like that of Liao white ware from kilns in Chifeng County, Inner Mongolia.[4] This Ānanda and Kashyapa are exceptionally important as rare Liao representations of disciples and also as rare examples of Liao fired-ceramic Buddhist sculptures.[5]

MG

1. Shao Qinglong, "Liaodai baici foxiang" [Liao-dynasty white ware Buddhist images], *Neimenggu wenwu kaogu* 1981.1, pp. 143–44; see p. 144 for a small image of the Shakyamuni sculpture. See also Karl A. Wittfogel and Fêng Chia-shêng. *History of Chinese Society: Liao, 907–1125*, p. 66.
2. For a detailed explanation of this system for settling and protecting Liao territory, see Wittfogel and Fêng, *History of Chinese Society*, pp 65–66.
3. Shao Qinglong, "Liaodai baici foxiang," p. 144.
4. See Yutaka Mino's analysis of wares from Gangwayaotun, Houtougou Rural Area, Chifeng, Inner Mongolia, in Yutaka Mino, *Ceramics in the Liao Dynasty North and South of the Great Wall*, p. 17.
5. Sculptures of the two disciples dating from 1038 attend Buddhas at the Preservation of the Sutras Hall at Lower Huayan Monastery in Datong, Shanxi. See Marilyn Leidig Gridley, *Chinese Buddhist Sculpture under the Liao (Free Standing Works in Situ and Selected Examples from Public Collections)*, pp. 68, 125. For other Liao ceramic Buddhist sculptures, see Marilyn Gridley. "Three Buddhist Sculptures from Longquanwu and the Luohans from Yi Xian." *Oriental Art*, Winter 1995/96, pp. 20–29.

69. Censer in the form of a lotus

Liao dynasty, 1081 or earlier
From the tomb of Boteben at Maiwanggou,
Ningcheng County
Silver
Length: 36.6 cm
Research Institute of Cultural Relics
and Archaeology of Inner Mongolia

Excavated from the tomb (dated 1081) of someone named Boteben (d. 1080) in Ningcheng County, where the Liao Central Capital was located, this censer was made in the form of a lotus flower.[1] The lotus stem is the handle, and the large full lotus blossom is the body of the censer, which is supported by the lotus leaf as a base. An additional lotus flower comes midway out of the stem. Because of its elegant and ingenious design, this censer is one of the finest examples of Liao metalwork.

In Buddhism, the lotus is a symbol of purity, and long-handled censers are ritual implements commonly used in Buddhist ceremonies. A bronze bowl-shaped censer with a long handle was found in the Buddhist relic deposit (dated 741) underneath the foundation of the pagoda at Qingshan Monastery in Lintong, Shaanxi Province. It is likely that it was used in a ceremony conducted in the relic deposit shortly before the deposit chamber was sealed. It is also likely that it was buried with the relic to ensure a perpetual offering of incense in the ages to come.[2]

On the basis of evidence from Buddhist silk paintings from Dunhuang, it is known that members of the laity and of monastic communities held long-handled censers in their hands to make offerings of incense to the Buddha. A silk banner in the Stein Collection at the British Museum depicts a bodhisattva holding a long-handled censer in his or her left hand; inside the censer is some blue material, from which smoke arises.[3]

The inclusion of such a censer in a tomb indicates the possible affiliation of the tomb's occupant with Buddhism. In a mural in the

tomb of Zhang Gongyou (died 1113, buried 1117) in Xuanhua, Hebei Province, a lotus-shaped censer and a case of scriptures are depicted sitting side by side on a table, confirming Zhang's involvement in Buddhist activities (fig. 102).[4]

HMS

1. Neimenggu wenwu kaogu yanjiusuo and Liao Zhongjing bowuguan (Ji Ping and Ta La), "Ningcheng xian Maiwanggou Liaodai mudi fajue jianbao" [Brief excavation report on the Liao tombs at Maiwanggou, Ningcheng] in Wei Jian, ed., Neimenggu wenwu kaogu wenji [Essays on the Archaeology of Cultural Relics in Inner Mongolia], vol. 2, pp. 609–30, pls. 15–17.

2. Comparable examples are found in the Tang tombs in Ruichang, Jiangxi Province, and in Changsha and Chifengshan, Hunan Province; and in the tomb (dated 765) of Monk Shenhui in Luoyang, Henan Province. See *Wenwu* 1992.3, p. 69, fig. 4; *Wenwu* 1960.3, p. 27, fig. 27; *Wenwu* 1992.3, pl. 7.3.

3. The silk banner is datable to the late ninth century. For reference to the banner, see Roderick Whitfield, *The Art of Central Asia*, p. 43. A similar pictorial representation of a bodhisattva holding a long-handled censer can be found in Whitfield, *The Art of Central Asia*, fig. 94. Other paintings in the Stein Collection show devotees making offerings of incense using similar censers. See Whitfield, *The Art of Central Asia*, pl. 23 (dated 864), pl. 26 (dated 892), figs. 73, 74.

4. Zhang Gongyou's involvement in various Buddhist activities is articulated in his epitaph. See *Xuanhua Liaomu* [*Liao tombs in Xuanhua*], vol. 1, pp. 286–87.

Fig. 102. Mural on the southeast wall of the tomb of Zhang Gongyou (buried 1117) in Xuanhua, Hebei Province

70a. Head of a bodhisattva

Liao dynasty, eleventh century
From Wanbu Huayanjing Pagoda, Baita
Village, near Hohhot, Inner Mongolia
Earthenware
Height: approximately 40 cm
Museum of the Inner Mongolia
Autonomous Region

70b. Head of a bodhisattva

Liao dynasty, eleventh century
From Wanbu Huayanjing Pagoda, Baita
Village, near Hohhot, Inner Mongolia
Earthenware
Height: 40 cm
Hohhot City Museum

These two bodhisattva heads are quite similar. The face of one (cat. 70b), however, is fuller, with ample cheeks and a slight extra roll of flesh under the chin. This head may be dated a bit earlier, closer to the rounded forms of the Tang era, than the longer, thinner head (cat. 70a.). The deep holes in the eyes probably held cone-shaped ceramic pupils, the tips inserted into the holes and a black glaze covering the rounded surface. This technique was developed by Liao sculptors to impart a life-like quality to sculptures of deities.[1]

The tall crowns fit against the high chignon of hair and are tied on at the base with prominent bows above the ears. Such crowns are typical of those worn by Liao bodhisattvas.[2] The remaining fragment of the central motif on the crown of one of the bodhisattvas (cat. 70b) retains the shape of a figure in a lotus pose, possibly an Amitābha Buddha, which would have identified this as Guanyin, bodhisattva of compassion and mercy.

Archaeologists discovered the heads in 1986 during the excavation of the foundations of the seven-story octagonal Wanbu Huayanjing Pagoda (fig. 103).[3] On the exterior of the first two stories, earthenware relief sculptures of guardian figures and heavenly kings face the cardinal directions. Pairs of bodhisattvas face the intermediate directions; on the first floor, they flank small Buddhas positioned above windows.[4] The two heads in the exhibition must have come from two bodhisattva sculptures that were replaced during an earlier restoration. Only one restoration was recorded before the recent one. An inscription, no longer extant, on the east wall of the seventh floor indicated a renovation by impe-

rial edict in Jin Dading second year (1162) or possibly Dading seventh year (1169).[5]

The pagoda stands in what was the northwest corner of the old Liao city of Fengzhou, a key military town of the Liao and Jin (1115–1234) periods. Although the Guisui County gazetteer dates the pagoda to the reign of the Liao emperor Shengzong (r. 982–1031), some scholars believe a date in the reign of Daozong (r. 1055–1101) is more likely.[6] The heads, however, especially the fuller one (cat. 70b), with its sweet expression, pleasing proportions, and placement of features, must date from relatively

early in the eleventh century, which would place it during the Shengzong reign.

MG

1. The eyes of the colossal Guanyin at Dule Monastery may be the earliest example of this technique. The Liao added such shining eyes to many of the Wei-dynasty sculptures at Yungang. Marilyn Leidig Gridley, *Chinese Buddhist Sculpture under the Liao*, pp. 72, 87.
2. For examples, see the crowns on attendant deities dating from 1038 on the altar of the sutra library at Lower Huayan Monastery in Datong, Shanxi. Ding Mingyi, *Huayansi* [*Huayan Monastery*], pp 39–57, 60–63; also Marilyn Gridley, *Chinese Buddhist Sculpture under the Liao*, pp. 57, 62, pls. 14, 26.
3. *Qidan wangchao* [*Khitan dynasty*], p. 345.
4. For a discussion of the relief sculpture now in place on the pagoda, see Zhang Hanjun, "Liaodai Wanbu Huayanjing ta fojiao diaosu yishi" [The art of the Buddhist relief sculpture on the 10,000 Huayan sutras pagoda], *Huhehaote wenwu* 1991.7, pp. 39, 41–45.
5. Gu Juying , "Wanbu Huayanjing ta" [Ten-thousand Huayan-sutras pagoda], in Lu Minghui et al. (eds), *Neimenggu wenwu guji sanji*, pp. 38–39.
6. For the argument that the city was too small for such a grand pagoda during the reign of Shengzong, and further that the pagoda, with its Huayan theme, could not have predated the Huayan Monastery at Datong, see Gu Juying , "Wanbu Huayanjing ta," pp. 38–40.

Fig. 103. Wanbu Huayanjing Pagoda (Pagoda of Ten Thousand Volumes of Huayan Sutras), located in the Baita Village (White Pagoda Village) eastern suburb of Hohhot

71a–c. Three miniature pagodas decorated with the Seven Buddhas of the Past (each with sutra scrolls and attached streamers)

Liao dynasty, 1049 or earlier
Excavated from the White Pagoda
in Balin Right Banner
Pagodas: painted wood, gold leaf;
height: 22.8 cm; diameter of base: 9 cm
Streamers: gauze
Scrolls: ink on paper
Museum of Balin Right Banner

These three miniature pagodas were discovered in the relic deposit inside the White Pagoda in Balin Right Banner. According to the archaeological report, the deposit comprises five rooms inside the cavity of the *chattra* parasols, at the pinnacle of the pagoda. Among the many objects excavated from the deposit, the most numerous were the pagoda-shaped containers, each of which housed three scrolls of sutra scriptures or *dhāranīs*. Of the 109 miniature pagodas, 104 were identical in size and were decorated with the same images of the Seven Buddhas of the Past.

The similarity in form and iconography of the miniature pagodas shows that a well-organized module system was in operation during their production. Each of the miniature pagodas is composed of three parts—a dome-shaped pedestal, a tubular body decorated in relief with images of the Buddha, and a roof-pinnacle lid. Simple colors were applied to limited areas on each of the pagodas (for example, red in the background, blue on the clouds, and gold on the tip of the pinnacle), leaving the Buddha images in unadorned cypress. The miniature pagodas were made in such a way that individuality seems almost completely absent, until one finds inscriptions, written in ink with the marks and names of individual artisans, on the bottoms of the pagodas.

The module system was also applied to the production of the enshrined Buddhist scriptures, which were made by woodblock printing. The earliest dated book surviving from China is a version of the Buddhist *Diamond Sutra* (dated 868), which was retrieved from the caves at Dunhuang, in the desert of Northwest China. Early on, the Chinese devised systems for assembling objects from standardized parts. Printing, which made it easy to produce multiple copies of texts in a fast and affordable fashion, gained popularity among Buddhists, given their concept of accumulating merit through duplication of Buddhist texts.[1]

HMS

---

1. For a discussion of the contribution of Buddhism to the dissemination of the technique of woodblock printing, see Lothar Ledderose, *Ten Thousand Things: Module and Mass Production in Chinese Art*, pp. 149–53.

72. Lotus Sutra

Liao dynasty, 1049 or earlier
Excavated from the White Pagoda
in Balin Right Banner
Sutra: ink on paper;
length: 20.54 meters; width: 27 cm
Wrapping cloth: ink on silk;
length: 21 cm; width: 23.5 cm
Museum of Balin Right Banner

The *Lotus Sutra* (Sanskrit: *Saddharmapundarīka-sūtra*; Chinese: *Miaofa lianhua jing*) is one of the most popular and influential of all the sutras of Mahāyāna Buddhism in East Asia. Among the several Chinese translations that have been produced, the version done in 406 by the Central Asian monk Kumārajīva (344–413) is the most well known and widely read.[1] This sutra gives instructions on the concept and usage of expedient means; vast merits are promised to those who uphold the tenets of the sutra. The Kumārajīva translation of the *Lotus Sutra* comprises twenty-eight chapters; three consecutive chapters are transcribed on the scroll exhibited here: "Devadatta," "Encouraging Devotion," and "Peaceful Practices."[2]

The long scroll, now damaged, was made up of eighteen sheets of paper, and each sheet had twenty-five columns. The text was written in ink in standard script. In addition to this handwritten version of the *Lotus Sutra*, there were also woodblock-printed scrolls of the sutra enshrined in the White Pagoda. One such scroll (printed in 1017; overall length 20.54 meters) was enshrined inside a large and elaborately decorated miniature pagoda, which was, in turn, placed in the middle room of the multichamber deposit built inside the top structure of the pagoda. Four other printed scrolls were placed inside four miniature pagodas, which were interred in a pit below the deposit (see cat. 64).

The *Lotus Sutra* was frequently deposited in Japanese sutra burials at about this time. Archaeological evidence shows that most Japanese sutra burials contained the *Lotus Sutra*, and that in most of them it significantly

珠若以與之玉諸臺屬必大驚怪文殊師利如來亦
復如是以禪定智惠力得法國土王於三界而諸魔
王不肯順伏如來賢聖諸將與之共戰其有功者
心亦歡喜於四衆中為說諸経令其心悅賜以禪
定解脫无漏根力諸法之財又復賜與涅槃之城
言得滅度引道其心令皆歡喜而不為說是法華
経文殊師利如轉輪王見諸兵衆有大功者心甚
歡喜以此難信之珠久在髻中不妄與人而今與
之如来亦復如是於三界中為大法王以法教化一
切衆生見賢聖軍與五陰魔煩惱魔死魔共戰有

outnumbered other sutras. Moreover, the locations of these Japanese sutra burials were often related to the cult centers for this particular sutra, showing a close connection between the *Lotus Sutra* and the practice of sutra burial in Japan. Interestingly, the *Lotus Sutra* was also the most favored sutra in relic deposits made in Southeast China during the Song dynasty (960–1279), testifying to the links between the scripture deposits of Liao territory, Japan, and the southeast of China.[3]

HMS

chapters 12 and 13 are in *juan* 4, and chapter 14 is in *juan* 5.
   3. For a discussion of the features shared by scripture deposits in Liao territory, Korea, Japan, and southeast China, and the connection established via the sea route between them, see Hsueh-man Shen, "Buddhist Relic Deposits from Tang (618–907) to Northern Song (960–1127) and Liao (907–1125)," pp. 175–89.

---

1. T262, 9.1c–62b. For an introduction to and an English translation of the sutra, see Burton Watson (trans.), *The Lotus Sutra*.
   2. The three chapters are numbered chapters 12 through 14, and they are grouped in *juan* 5 (scroll number 5) in the example in the exhibition. But in the modern standard canon, Taishō Daizōkyō (Taishō canon),

73a–c. Three mirrors

Liao dynasty, 1049 or earlier
Excavated from the White Pagoda
in Balin Right Banner
Bronze
a–b. Diameter: 50 cm
c. Height: 20 cm; width: 30 cm
Museum of Balin Right Banner

Archaeological surveys have shown that the exteriors of many Liao Buddhist pagodas were adorned with bronze mirrors. Over a thousand mirrors were attached to the exterior of the seven-story White Pagoda in Balin Right Banner, and many of them remain intact. According to the archaeological report for the pagoda, all circular mirrors came from the second, fourth, and sixth stories, while diamond-shaped mirrors adorned the first, third, fifth, and seventh stories of the brick pagoda. These three mirrors are from the White Pagoda. Perforations along the rim and multiple loops on the backs of the mirrors were designed to fasten the mirrors onto the wall.[1]

Unlike most Chinese mirrors, these mirrors were decorated on the reflective side instead of on the back. The function of these mirrors attached to the exterior of the pagoda was to catch light—a metaphor for Buddhist wisdom—as well as to add to the splendor of the building. Filling the circular surface of one of the mirrors (cat. 73a) is a frontal image of a Buddha seated on a lotus pedestal. Surrounded by three concentric halos around his body, the Buddha raises his right hand with the palm facing outward, while his left hand lies flat on his lap. Across the center of the mirror and at the waist level of the Buddha image are three horizontal lines dividing the remaining surface into two parts. An inscription above the horizontal lines and to the Buddha's left identifies the figure as Shakyamuni Buddha. Another inscription, on the lower part of the mirror, provides a date—the fifth month of the fifth year of the Qiantong era (1105)—indicating the fifth year of the reign of the Emperor Tianzuo (r. 1101–1125).

The other circular mirror (cat. 73b), which is incised with fine lines on the reflective surface, also bears the date of 1105, in addition to the personal names of a few carpenters and laymen. The calligraphic style of the incisions is much coarser than that on the other circular mirror (cat. 73a) and may have been done by a different hand. That both mirrors bear a date fifty-six years later than the completion of the pagoda indicates that the pagoda might have undergone renovations in 1105.

The reflection of images in a mirror represents a Buddhist analogy with the transient and is related to the notion of emptiness. In various Buddhist texts, the multitudes were instructed to view the phenomenal world as an image in a mirror and emptiness as the mirror itself.[2] Moreover, a great round mirror reflects all forms exactly as they are, as does the wisdom of the Buddha. The *great perfect mirror wisdom*, therefore, refers to the pure wisdom gained at Buddhahood by a qualitative transmutation of the eighth consciousness. Once this wisdom is attained, the mind and its various factors function in accordance.

Not many bronze mirrors incised with images on their reflective surface dating from the time of Liao dynasty have been found in Song China. However, one such mirror was discovered along with many other treasures inside the hollow body (deposit dated 985) of the wooden statue of the Shakyamuni Buddha now enshrined at Seiryōji Monastery in Kyoto, Japan.[3] Other examples include six incised mirrors found in the relic deposit inside the body of the West Pagoda in Lingshi Monastery in Huangyan, Zhejiang

Province. The dates incised along with the Buddhist images on these mirrors range from 966 to 998. An additional example was recently unearthed from the underground relic deposit (datable to the late tenth century) at Leifeng Pagoda in Hangzhou, Zhejiang Province.[4]

Mirrors incised with Buddhist images on the reflective side are called *kyōzō* in Japanese. Archaeological evidence shows that no later than the mid-Heian period (794–1185), *kyōzō* appeared in Japan in considerable number. Some scholars link them to the assimilation of Buddhism with the indigenous Shintoism, while others argue that they are related, in accordance with Esoteric Buddhism, to the moon disk in which Buddhist deities are manifest.

HMS

1. Three very brief reports about the finds have been published so far. See *Wenwu* 1994.12, pp. 65–72; *Wenwu* 1989.9, pp. 67–68; *Neimenggu wenwu kaogu* 2000.2, pp. 56–57.

2. For example, see T 1509, 25:104a–105a.

3. According to a gift inventory accompanying the mirror, two mirrors incised with the image of the Water Moon Guanyin Bodhisattva were offered to the Buddha and were consequently deposited inside the statue. See *Butsuzō: tainai no sekai* [*Buddha statues: The world inside their bodies*], p. 6, pl. 1.3. See also Namba Taakira (ed.), *Kyōzō to kakebotoke* [*Mirrors incised with Buddha Images, and suspended plaques with Buddha images*], Nihon no bijutsu 1990.284.

4. See *Dongnan wenhua* 1991.5, pp. 263–66, figs. 16–19; *Leifeng yizhen* [*Treasures from Leifeng Pagoda*], p. 189.

74. Great Perfection of Wisdom Sutra

Liao dynasty, 967
Excavated from the White Pagoda
in Balin Right Banner
Ink on paper
Length: 874 cm
Museum of Balin Right Banner

This scroll was among the many Buddhist scriptures retrieved from the relic deposit built on top of the White Pagoda in Balin Right Banner, Inner Mongolia. On it is transcribed *juan* 76 of the *Great Perfection of Wisdom Sutra* (Sanskrit: *Mahāprajñāpāramitā-sūtra*; Chinese: *Da banruo boluomiduo jing*). The sutra was translated into Chinese by the great monk Xuanzang (602–64) in the mid-seventh century. Comprising 600 *juan* fascicles in total, this sutra is a compilation of sixteen different sutras, which expound the doctrine of *prajñāpāramitā* or the supreme, perfect wisdom of emptiness.[1] It includes well-known works, such as the *Heart Sutra* and the *Diamond Sutra*, and is one of the most complete collections of *prajñāpāramitā* sutras available.

The text was written in ink on seventeen sheets of paper, on which fine lines were carefully drawn, that were pieced together to make a long scroll. Following the sutra text is an inscription indicating that the scripture was transcribed in the seventeenth year of the Yingli era (967) by the nun Huishen of Miaoyin Monastery, who wished to share with all others the merits gained through duplication of this sutra. Toward the end of the scroll, on the lower part, is a mark certifying that the transcription of the sutra text was officially proofread. Three stamps reading "*Miaoyin cang ji*," or Registration for the Collection of Miaoyin Monastery, can be found on the scroll.

On the back of the scroll is written a single Chinese character, *huang* (fig. 104), which refers to the eighth character of the *Thousand Character Essay* (*Qianzi wen*). The *Thousand Character Essay* comprises one thousand differ-

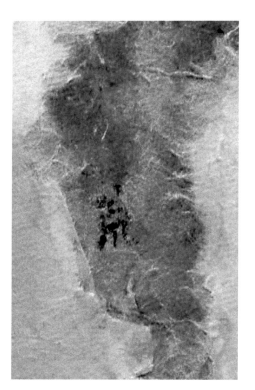

ent characters, which can be used, like an alphabet, to sort large quantities of items. By the late Tang dynasty, the *Thousand Character Essay* was used to number the bundles in which the texts of the Buddhist canon were counted. The first 480 characters of the essay were used to number the 480 bundles of the Kaiyuan canon (complied in 730). The *Great Perfection of Wisdom Sutra*, the very first sutra text included in the canon, was divided into sixty bundles (each contained ten scrolls on average), which were numbered from the first character, *tian*, through the sixtieth character, *nai*. The same numbering system was applied to the texts of the canon compiled during the Liao dynasty (the so-called Khitan canon),

as is evidenced by the eighth bundle number on the back of the scroll in the exhibition (*juan* 76 of the *Great Perfection of Wisdom Sutra*).

HMS

---

1. See T220, 600 *juan* in Taishō Daizōkyō, vols. 5–7.

Fig. 104. The character *huang* on the back of the scroll

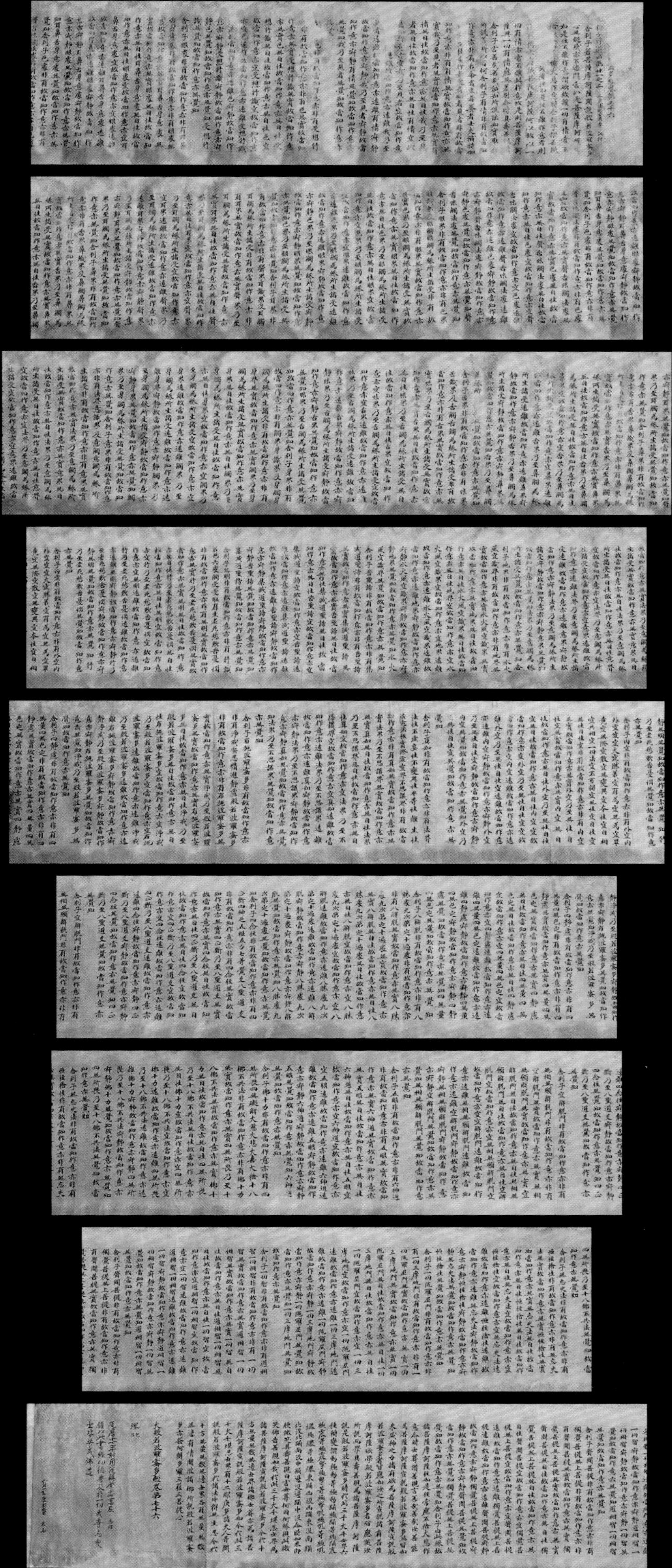
大般若波羅蜜多經卷第七十六

75. Shakyamuni Buddha

Liao dynasty, 957
Ningcheng County, Inner Mongolia
Stone
Height: 40 cm
Research Institute of Cultural Relics
and Archaeology of Inner Mongolia

This Shakyamuni Buddha sits in a lotus position, with his right foot bare. His left hand lies palm up on his lap; his right rests palm down on his right knee in the earth-touching (*bhūmisparsha*) mudra, indicating that this image represents the moment Shakyamuni calls the earth to witness his triumph over the temptations of the evil Mara. As is typical of many Liao images, his torso is long in proportion to his legs, and his eyes are long and large. A slight soft smile creates a benevolent expression. Damage to his midsection makes deciphering the eccentric arrangement of his robes difficult.[1] A square *sumeru*[2] throne supporting his lotus seat rests on a row of downturned lotus petals. Ropelike swirls representing flames surround the halos around his body and his head.

This image is extraordinarily important as it is the earliest dated Liao Buddhist sculpture. An inscription on the back dates it to the seventh year of the Yingli reign of the Liao emperor Muzong (r. 951–69), or 957 (fig. 105).[3] The sculpture was excavated in October 1956, in Ningcheng, Inner Mongolia, where the Shengzong emperor (r. 982–1031) established the Liao Central Capital (Zhongjing) in 1007.

While this sculpture has a provincial air, one can discern impressive cosmopolitan traces. Indian Pala-period (730–1250) stelae from the ninth and tenth centuries feature relief figures of Shakyamuni or Aksobhya, Buddha of the Eastern Paradise, sitting on a lotus-topped *sumeru* throne, his hands in the *bhūmisparsha* mudra.[4] Like the 957 Shakyamuni Buddha, the Pala images have squared halos around their bodies that resemble the back of a throne. The colossal sculptures of the Seven Buddhas of the Past dating from 1020 on the altar of Daxiongbaodian at Fengguo Monastery in Yixian, Liaoning Province, also have the squared halos around their bodies.[5] The halo surrounding the 957 image is valuable evidence of a link between Pala masterpieces and tenth- and eleventh-century Liao Buddhist sculpture in and around the Central Capital.

The inscription incised on the back of the sculpture reads,

> Master of Merit Wang Jinqing,
> [his wife]
> female disciple Zhangshi,
> [their first and second]
> sons Dashen and Ershen
> commissioned [this] Shakyamuni
> Buddha. All family members
> made offerings on a day of
> the first lunar month [*zheng yue*]
> of the seventh year
> of the Yingli [reign]. Tie shan
> [possibly the name of
> the carver].

Translation by Chang Qing.

MG

and under the right arm. Under the *kāshāya* is a sleeved robe and a *dhotī* (a length of cloth wrapped around like a skirt and worn as an undergarment), tied high across the chest. An elaborate knot beside his left arm appears to secure yet another garment.

2. The term *sumeru* refers to the pedestal's constricted waist, which represents the Buddhist world mountain, Mount Meru, connecting the base and platform, which represent earth and heaven.

3. Li Yiyou, "Neimenggu chutu wenwu gaishu" [General account of cultural relics excavated in Inner Mongolia], *Neimenggu wenwu xuanji*, p. 8, pls. 143, 144.

4. See the Buddha and the Eight Great Miracles, tenth–eleventh centuries, Bengal or Bihār. Museum of Fine Arts, Boston, in Heinrich Zimmer, *The Art of Indian Asia*, vol. 2, pl. 383.

5. See especially Kanakamuni (Chinese: *Junahanmuni*), one of the Seven Buddhas of the Past, 1020, Daxiongbaodian, Fengguosi, Yixian, Liaoning, in Sekino Tadashi and Takeshima Takuichi, *Ryō-Kin jidai no kenchiku to sono Butsuzō* [Liao-Jin architecture and its Buddhist sculpture], vol. 1, pl. 31.1. Though these halos are thought to date from later restorations, I believe their angularity retains characteristics of the originals. See Marilyn Leidig Gridley, *Chinese Buddhist Sculpture under the Liao*, p. 140, for a full discussion of this motif.

1. A.B. Griswold, "Prolegomena to the Study of the Buddha's Dress in Chinese Sculpture," *Artibus Asia*, 26.2 (1963), p. 91, describes the closest approximation of the disposition of his *kāshāya* (monk's robe): the fold curving back across his right shoulder and the one crossing from the lower right hip to the waist appear to represent the covering mode with opening inflection, which drapes over the right shoulder, then back around

Fig. 105. Inscription on the back of the sculpture

During the eleventh and twelfth centuries, the Liao dynasty was the most powerful regime in East Asia. It developed contacts with Korea and Japan, to the east; with Song China, to the south; and with the Uighur and Tangut peoples, to the west. Through extensive routes, both overland and via the sea, the Liao's trading network extended to India, West Asia, and the Baltic Sea. The broad exchange of goods and ideas contributed to the richness of Liao material culture.

The abundance of luxurious materials found in Liao tombs testifies to the international aspect of Liao culture. In the tomb of the Princess of Chen and her husband, Xiao Shaoju, seven glass vessels (among them, cat. 102, 103) and a large bronze basin (cat. 117) were imported from Iran or the Near East; amber, which was used to make various pieces of jewelry (cat. 34–37a–b, 45a–b, 77), came from the area around the Baltic Sea; rock crystal (cat. 33) came from South Asia or Southeast Asia; jade (cat. 44) came possibly from Inner Asia; fine green wares (cat. 109, 110) came from Song China. An amber plaque with a carving of a foreigner with a lion on a leash (cat. 77) shows vividly a Liao impression of a foreigner. In addition, several objects from the tomb of the Princess of Chen and her husband bear foreign influences. For example, C-shaped bracelets with animal terminates (cat. 31) were first developed in the Near East and later spread across Eurasia. Beaded necklaces strung with spacers (cat. 37a–b) were Indian in origin and were often seen on Buddhist statues of the Tang dynasty (618–907). They probably became known to the Liao people through the introduction of Buddhist iconography into Liao territory. Moreover, the style and craftsmanship involved in the making of the double-dragon headdress with leaf-shaped pendants (cat. 27) that adorned the head of the Princess of Chen are comparable with Korean examples. That Korean coins and celadon have been found at some Liao sites is evidence of the close connections between the Liao and Korea.

Plentiful textual sources show that the Liao had frequent contacts with the Jurchens, Tanguts, and Uighurs, from whom they acquired various resources, ranging from horses and falcons to Buddhist scriptures to jade and precious metals. As a result of the Treaty of Shanyuan in 1005 between the Liao and the Song, the Liao received annually from the Song large quantities of cash (cat. 118a–l) and silk. With this steady stream of wealth, the Liao could afford to buy luxurious items from the Song, including delicate Yue celadon wares from Zhejiang Province (cat. 110), fine white and green wares (cat. 105, 109, 111) from Shaanxi and Hebei provinces, and the *qingbai* (bluish-white) ware from Jingdezhen in Jiangxi Province.

While foreign materials and designs were adopted by the Liao, the associations attached to these materials or designs were absorbed as well. From the jade pendant set with decorations of the five poisonous animals (cat. 44) found near the corpse of the Princess of Chen, it is evident that the Liao fully understood the protective function of jade carvings in traditional Chinese tombs. Liao craftsmen excelled in fusing cultural elements of different origins, giving them a distinctive Liao flavor. Many gold and silver items discovered in Liao tombs look distinctly non-Chinese but were, nonetheless, made by Chinese craftsmen who worked according to Khitan specifications. Jade and rock-crystal carvings (cat. 13, 14a, 15, 38, 78, 79a–c, 100, 101a–c) show that the Liao also adopted the Han Chinese affection for hardstone carving. Yet characteristic Liao motifs, such as bears and horses, made these jade and rock-crystal carvings unmistakably Liao.

There was no tradition of producing high-fired ceramics in Northeast China prior to the Liao. However, soon after the Liao empire was established, kilns were built near the capital areas. While some of the ceramics produced in these kilns were in imitation of gold and silver vessels (cat. 91, 107a–d), others copied wood or leather prototypes (cat. 39–42) that were originally developed for use on horseback. Colorful lead glazes were applied to roof tiles and to the dragon heads and phoenixes that adorned the ends of the upper eaves and roof ridges of pagodas (cat. 60a–b), as well as to Buddhist statues and to some daily utensils. Unlike Tang-dynasty lead-glazed wares, which were low-fired and thus were only suitable for use as funerary figurines or models, the Liao lead-glazed wares were high-fired, which made it possible for them to actually be used in daily life (cat. 106, 108, 112a–e, 113, 114a–b, 115a–b, 116a–b).

A clear preference for the use of certain materials made Liao material culture distinct from that of the parallel Song dynasty. These materials included amber, agate (cat. 98–99a–b), and rock crystal. Amber and agate, in particular, were symbols of excellence for the Khitan, and were used extensively in making small vessels and articles for personal adornment (cat. 7a–b, 27, 32, 34–37, 45a–b, 77) during the Liao dynasty. Rock crystal was also highly valued by the Khitan, but it was hardly seen in Song China. In addition, anthropomorphic forms, including representations of mandarin ducks, turtles, cats, and parrots, as well as mythical creatures such as the phoenix (cat. 29) and *makara* (cat. 25, 26a–b, 87, 113)—were clearly favored by Liao craftsmen but were much less popular with the Song.

HMS

76. Vase with appliqué decoration

tenth century, before 942
From the tomb of Yelü Yuzhi and
Chonggun at Hansumu Township,
Aluke'erqin Banner
Lead-glazed earthenware
Height: 29.5;
diameter at widest point: 22.3 cm
Research Institute of Cultural Relics
and Archaeology of Inner Mongolia

This vase from the tomb of Yelü Yuzhi (890–941) and Chonggun (d. 942) represents a distinctive type of ceramics produced in tenth-century China. Although it is damaged above the shoulder, it can be inferred through comparison with similar vases excavated elsewhere that the vase originally had a mouth that broadened into a shallow dish shape and a long neck that widened toward the shoulder.[1] Three rows of appliquéd leaf shapes encircle the shoulder; six tassel-like forms connected by appliquéd beading decorate the tapered, finely textured clay body, which is covered with green glaze. According to the archaeological report, additional yellow glaze was applied to part of the foot-ring.

The most unusual feature of this vase is the carefully laid out system of lugs, indicating it was designed for a mobile life style. A groove runs in a straight line from the shoulder down the body, and a pair of lugs project from both ends of the groove. Further down, on the foot-ring, but still in line with the lugs, are two rectangular holes through which a rope could be fastened, so that the bottle could be transported.

In the tenth century, tassel design was not only seen on ceramics but also used as architectural decoration. For example, three balls with long red tassels were painted above a niche in the east side chamber of the tomb (dated 958) of Feng Hui in Xianyang, Shaanxi Province.[2]

HMS

1. A green-glazed *kundikā* ewer discovered in the Yexian Pagoda in Beijing (late tenth or early eleventh century) has a similar green glaze and appliqué of tassel-like forms. A *kundikā* is a vessel with a spout but without a handle. It is a Buddhist symbol of purification and distributor of compassion, and is often associated with the bodhisattva Avalokiteshvara. See *Wenwu* 1994.2, p. 58, figs. 1, 2. The body of a brown-glazed vase with a dish mouth discovered in Helinge'er, Inner Mongolia (tenth century) is decorated with a stamped-tassel design. See *Wenwu* 1961.9, pl. 2.1, p. 32.

2. *Wudai Feng Hui mu* [*The Five Dynasties tomb of Feng Hui*], pp. 60–62.

77. Amber plaque with a carving of a foreigner with a lion on a leash

Liao dynasty, 1018 or earlier
From the tomb of the Princess of Chen
and Xiao Shaoju at Qinglongshan Town
in Naiman Banner
Amber
Length: 8.4 cm; width: 6 cm
Research Institute of Cultural Relics
and Archaeology of Inner Mongolia

A lively scene in which a muscular man tries to subdue a lion held on a leash is depicted on the front of this carved amber plaque. The plaque was discovered lying low on the chest of the Princess of Chen in her tomb at Qinglongshan Town, Naiman Banner, in Southeast Inner Mongolia. The plaque is one-sided, with a hole drilled through it horizontally, so presumably it was one of the princess's ornaments.[1]

The man is obviously a foreigner—he appears to be neither Chinese nor Khitan. He wears a long-sleeved jacket with a sash, long trousers, a turbanlike cap, and soft boots, presumably made of leather. He is shown in front of the lion, bracing his feet against the counter-pull on the leash. The lion is shown in typical Liao fashion, his tail represented by three furry tufts. His head is turned backward and depicted full face, framed by a thick, curly mane.

The basic composition and animation of the scene recall an early Western Han (206 BC–AD 9) gilded-bronze belt plaque in which a foreigner attempts to subdue a bull.[2] The Khitan carving must represent a very meaningful tale for it to have been included among the personal ornaments of the Princess of Chen.

To date, no similar scenes have been discovered in extant Liao-dynasty paintings and tomb murals. However, there are references to this type of genre scene in two well-known Chinese texts that describe the historical events and sights of the period: the *Dongjing meng hua lu* (Record of a Dream of the Eastern Capital) and the *Songshi Yufuzhi* (Song History: Treatise on Chariots and Garments).[3]

The *Dongjing meng hua lu* is a kind of travelogue that notes numerous exotica of the period, among which was a lion tamer.

ECB

1. *Liao Chenguo gongzhu mu* [*Liao tomb of the princess of the state of Chen*], p. 100, fig. 64:13.
2. Jenny F. So and Emma C. Bunker, *Traders and Raiders on China's Northern Frontier*, pp. 93–94.
3. *Qidan wangchao* [*Khitan dynasty*], p. 163.

78. Pendant in the shape of a recumbent bear

Liao dynasty, eleventh century
Excavated in You'ai Village,
Baiyinhan Township, Balin Right Banner
Jade
Length: 6.8 cm; width: 3.8 cm
Chifeng City Museum and Ningcheng
County Museum

This delightful white-jade bear pendant was excavated from a tomb at You'ai Village in Baiyinhan Township, Balin Right Banner, Southeast Inner Mongolia, and dates to the eleventh century.[1] The bear is shown recumbent, with his head turned backward and in full face. The small piece of jade from which this pendant is carved probably came from Khotan, a city on the southern Silk Road in Xinjiang that was famous for high-quality white jade. Here, the artist has cleverly used the natural shape of the jade, with its slight brownish tinges, to mark the bear's ruff and short tail. Jade always had associations with immortality for both the Chinese and the Khitan, their northern neighbors. Since jade carving, which involves abrading and polishing, is a very special craft, it is possible that this bear pendant may have been made by a captive Chinese artisan to appeal to Khitan taste.

Bears were plentiful in the Dongbei (Northeast China) forests during the Liao period, and they were considered a symbol of bravery. According to the *Liaoshi* (History of the Liao), bears were among the animals hunted by the Khitan for both their meat and their fur.[2] Bear paws have long been considered an edible delicacy in China, and a Song envoy reported seeing a Liao emperor leaning against a bearskin during his investiture.[3] Bears were worshipped by Tungusic shamans, who considered them sacred.[4]

ECB

1. *Qidan wangchao* [*Khitan dynasty*], pp. 155, 168.
2. Karl A. Wittfogel and Fêng Chia-shêng, *History of Chinese Society: Liao, 907–1125*, p. 119.
3. Wittfogel and Fêng, *History of Chinese Society*, p. 275, note.
4. Jenny F. So (ed.), *Noble Riders from Pines and Deserts: The Artistic Legacy of the Qidan*, p. 224.

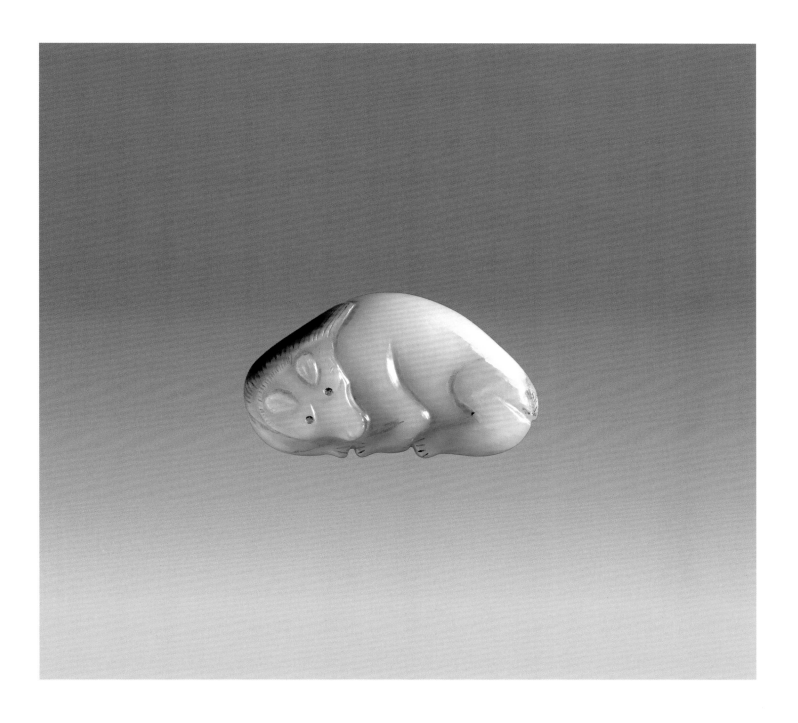

79a–c. Three rock-crystal pendants

Liao dynasty
Excavated in Jiwangyingzi, Guanjiayingzi
Rural Area, Kalaqin Banner
a. Fish: length: 3.6 cm; width: 1.7 cm
b. Rodent: length: 4 cm; width: 2.3cm
c. Lion: length: 3.6 cm; height: 2.5 cm
Museum of Chifeng City

These three rock-crystal zoomorphic-shaped pendants were recovered from a Khitan site in Jiwangyingzi at Guanjiayingzi Rural Area, Kalaqin Banner, in Southeast Inner Mongolia.[1]

The fish, which is quite realistically carved, has a hole that pierces its mouth, allowing it to be hung as a pendant. The fish was a symbol of abundance, an appropriate emblem for the Khitan, whose territory included major rivers and streams from which they fished at various times of the year. Fish and lotus flowers were popular Buddhist symbols for the Khitan and also frequently decorated amber plaques worn by the elite.

The large ears and the shape of the body of another one of the pendants suggest that it represents some kind of rodent. Due to the hardness of the material and the difficulty of carving it, deep cuts provide only an abstract image of the animal, with few details. A vertical perforation drilled behind the head of the creature allows the piece to be hung as a pendant.

The crouching lion has a vertical perforation, from which it could be suspended, just behind its head. The animal is carved in the round, with its head turned to the front and seen full face; its tail is represented as a furry tuft resting on its haunches. The facial features and anatomical details are rendered with deep broad incisions. Though not indigenous to China, lions were represented there as early as the middle of the second millennium BC, in small stone sculptures found near Erlitou in Henan Province.[2] The lion symbolizes bravery in China, as elsewhere, and, in addition, was considered especially important due to its association with Buddhism.

Rock crystal—transparent, perfectly white, macrocrystalline quartz—is readily available throughout China. Its hardness makes it difficult to carve. Rock crystal is not abraded but rather cut with a treadle-lathe that produces only straight lines, such as those that form the cross-hatching that simulates scales on the fish pendant.

Rock crystal appears to have been a popular material among the Liao, who used it for the manufacture of small personal objects, although the stone was very rarely used as an artistic medium in Song-dynasty China. Several rock-crystal animal images have been found buried in Liao temple crypts.[3] The enthusiasm for rock crystal continued during the Jin (1115–1234), another non-Chinese northern dynasty that was founded by the Jurchens.

ECB

1. *Qidan wangchao* [*Khitan dynasty*], pp. 169–170.
2. Edith Dittrich, "The Spread of the Lion Motif in Ancient Asia," paper presented at the International Academic Conference of Archaeological Cultures of the Northern Chinese Ancient Nations, Hohhot, 1992.
3. Jenny F. So (ed.), *Noble Riders from Pines and Deserts: The Artistic Legacy of the Qidan*, p. 189.

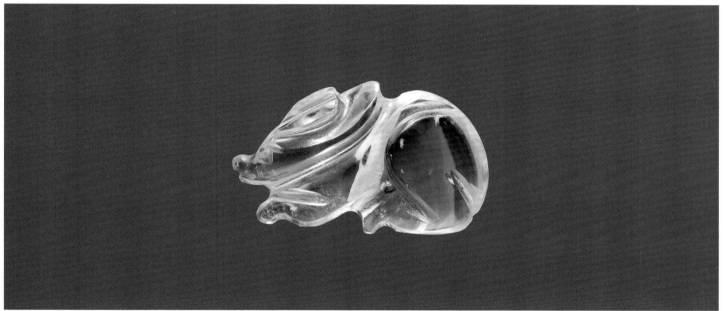

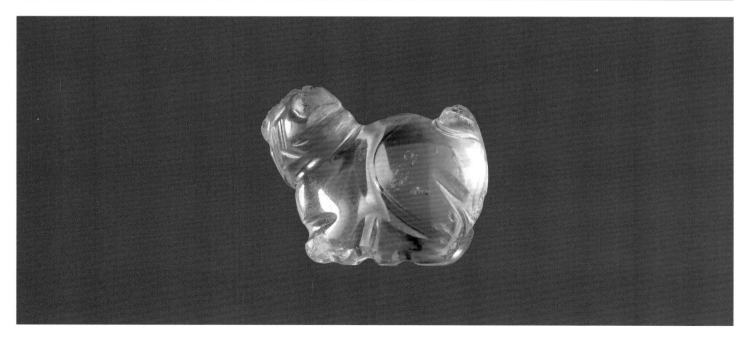

80. Silk gauze fan

Liao dynasty, early or mid-tenth century
From Tomb Number 3, Daiqintala
Township, Keyou Central Banner,
Xing'an League
Bamboo, silk gauze, pigments, gilding
Length of fan surface: 27 cm;
width of fan surface: 18.7 cm;
total length: 46 cm
Museum of the Inner Mongolia
Autonomous Region

This fan was excavated in 1991 from a looted tomb, which belonged to an unidentified couple of noble rank, in Daiqintala Township, Keyou Central Banner, Xing'an League.[1] Eight other tombs were part of the grave complex. The fan was found in the main chamber, in the rear of a small house in which both corpses were placed together on a wooden bed. The house is comparable to the one excavated from a Liao tomb in Wengniute Banner (cat. 46a).

This elliptically shaped fan is made of a bamboo frame in which a red gauze was inserted. A piece of bamboo divides the surface of the fan into two halves. The lower part serves as a handle over which another piece of gauze is wrapped.

On the surface of the fan, two birds with long tail feathers are delicately painted in gold and outlined with black ink. Together they form a confronting couple, each sitting on a rock set among a bush with white blossoms. Above them flutters a single small butterfly. Butterflies, flowering bushes, and a bizarre rock can also be seen on a wooden panel from a tomb at Zhanpu, Linxi County (cat. 49a). On several murals in tombs in Xuanhua, Hebei Province, dating from 1093 to 1117, the theme of birds standing among rocks, flowering bushes, butterflies, or dragonflies is repeated.[2] At the same site, in other murals, this type of fan is depicted in scenes of preparations for tea ceremonies;[3] an example of a fan similar in both shape and design to the one in the exhibition is held by a male attendant,[4] and undecorated fans are used to fan the fire.[5] In addition to their practical uses, such small fans also served as personal accessories for both men and women.[6] One of the oldest examples made out of bamboo wickerwork was found in 1972 in the tomb of the Marquise of Dai (d. 150 BC) in Mawangdui, Changsha, Hunan Province.[7]

SLG

1. See Meng Jianren and Piao Chunyue, "Keyouzhongqi Daiqintala Liao mu qingli jianbao" [Brief report on the clearing of a Liao tomb at Daiqintala, Keyou Central Banner], in Wei Jian (ed.), *Neimenggu wenwu kaogu wenji*, vol 2, pp. 651–67.

2. For information about the murals, see *Xuanhua Liaomu* [Liao tombs in Xuanhua], vol. 2, color pls. 75–78, color pls. 82–84; pls. 136–138.

3. For an example of a scene with preparations for serving tea, see *Xuanhua Liaomu*, vol. 2, color pls. 21–22.

4. For an example of a similar fan, see *Xuanhua Liaomu*, vol. 2, color pl. 78.

5. For an example of an undecorated fan, see *Xuanhua Liaomu*, vol. 2, color pl. 85; fig. 90.1.

6. Two comparable fans were found in the tomb of the scholar Zhou Yu (b. 1222) in Jintan County, Jiangsu Province, see *Kaogu Xuebao* 1977.1, pl. 2; figs. 1, 2. Two of the female court attendants depicted on the eastern wall of the antechamber of the tomb of Princess Yongtai, Li Xianhui (684–701), are holding similar fans, see *Tang mu bi hua zhen pin xuan cui* [The cream of original frescoes from Tang tombs], pls. 7, 8, pp. 7–9.

7. For an illustration of the fans, see *Changsha Mawangdui yihao Han mu fajue jianbao* [Brief report on a Han-dynasty Tomb Number 1 in Mawangdui, Changsha], pls. 229, 234.

81. Blue gauze embroidered with blossoms

Liao dynasty, 1049 or earlier
Excavated from the White Pagoda
in Balin Right Banner
Silk, gauze, tabby, embroidery with silk threads
Length: 65 cm; width: 50 cm
Museum of Balin Right Banner

This embroidered textile was among over one thousand items discovered in the relic deposit inside the *cha*, the top structure of the White Pagoda in Balin Right Banner, from 1988 to 1992, when it was undergoing restoration.[1] A commemorative stele found near the deposit reveals that Buddhist clerics and court officials constructed the pagoda between 1047 and 1049 under the patronage of Empress Dowager Zhangsheng.

The deposit contained a variety of objects. Among them were ritual and devotional artifacts (cat. 61a–b, 62–67, 71a–c, 72a–b), silver and lacquer wares, ceramics, medicines, and silk textiles. The 276 textiles that were found can roughly be divided into three major groups according to their function: sutra wrappers, either embroidered (cat. 59) or made from tabby or twill damask; decorative gauze that was either embroidered or patterned using a clamp-resist dyeing technique; and banners attached to miniature pagodas, which were made from gauze or twill damask —or, in one case, from a samite (cat. 65)— and were sometimes embroidered.

A large flowering stem forms the central motif of the embroidery on this dark-blue gauze, which is lined with green tabby on the back. The stem is surrounded by butterflies and clouds in almost symmetrical order. Bamboo stalks with intertwined flowering twigs grow from an imaginary ground. A chain of small white dots frames the whole composition, except for the upper part, like a string of pearls.[2] The same framing is also found on three embroideries on red gauze from the same relic deposit. One of them has a similar, but less strictly arranged composi-

tion of blossoming twigs, butterflies, and clouds.[3] On the other two, coiled dragons chasing flaming pearls are set in a roundel of white dots.[4] The dragon motif might indicate that those embroideries belonged to a member of the imperial family.[5] The well-preserved state of the embroideries suggests that they were not folded up, but were laid out flat in the deposit. Their purpose is not clear. Although none of the embroideries bear any Buddhist emblems, they were most likely used in a religious context.

SLG

---

1. See "Neimengu Balinyouqi Qingzhou baita faxian Liaodai fojiao wenwu" [Buddhist relics from the White Pagoda in Qingzhou, Balin Right Banner, Inner Mongolia], *Wenwu* 1994.12, pp. 4–33.

2. The use of beaded borders on metal and stone objects, on ceramics, and especially on textiles was widespread in Asia; the use of such borders had origins in Western metalwork and textiles. They were particularly popular during the sixth and seventh century in China. Jessica Rawson, *The Ornament on Chinese Silver of the Tang Dynasty (AD 618–906)*, pp. 2–3.

3. For an illustration, see Zhao Feng, *Treasures in Silk: An Illustrated History of Chinese Textiles*, no. 5.1, p. 159.

4. For an illustration, see *Qidan wangchao: Neimenggu Liaodai wenwu jinghua* [Khitan dynasty: Liao archaeological treasures from Inner Mongolia], pp. 176–77. The other embroidery with dragon-roundels is unpublished. It is not as well preserved and was discovered later than the others. *Wenwu* 2000.4, pp. 70–81, p. 78.

5. Yang Xiaoneng, *New Perspectives on China's Past: Chinese Archaeology in the Twentieth Century*, vol. 1, p. 477.

82. Small bowl decorated with bird pairs and fish

Five Dynasties, tenth century, before 942
From the tomb of Yelü Yuzhi and
Chonggun at Hansumu Township
in Aluke'erqin Banner
Gold
Height: 3 cm; diameter of mouth: 7.7 cm;
diameter of base: 4.2 cm
Research Institute of Cultural Relics
and Archaeology of Inner Mongolia

Until the discovery of the tomb of Yelü Yuzhi (890–941) and Chonggun (d. 942) in 1992, no golden cups or bowls from the tenth century had been excavated in China. The tomb yielded two such vessels, this bowl and a cup (cat. 83). Both were made in a style fashionable throughout China during the first decades of the tenth century. The bowl has five embossed grooves that structure its side into equal segments. Each panel is decorated on the outside with the same chased image of two birds facing each other, surrounded by a leafy frame. Although the birds are rendered in a rather stylized manner, they likely represent ducks or geese. The same design, albeit with more animately rendered birds, is seen on the silver spittoon excavated from the same tomb (cat. 90). The inside of the bowl shows two decidedly happy fish frolicking in

a pool. While the auspicious image of fish (see cat. 83) has been common in cups and bowls since the seventh century, smiling fish are less often seen and, like the stylized birds, probably reflect the personal preference of the artisan.

FL

83. Five-lobed cup decorated with ducks and fish

Five Dynasties, tenth century, before 942
From the tomb of Yelü Yuzhi
and Chonggun at Hansumu Township
in Aluke'erqin Banner
Gold
Height: 4.9 cm; diameter of mouth: 7.3 cm;
diameter of base: 4 cm
Research Institute of Cultural Relics
and Archaeology of Inner Mongolia

The flared foot-ring and the blossom-shaped body of this cup, which was discovered in 1992 in the tomb of Yelü Yuzhi (890–941) and his wife, Chonggun (d. 942), were each made from a piece of hammered gold sheet and then soldered together. The imagery on the cup evokes a lush garden pond. Ducks appear in various poses in the five medallions on the outside of the bowl; marsh grasses fill the spaces between the medallions; lotus leaves and stylized lotus petals cover the lower half of the bowl; and on the inside, below a band of ornamental waves, two carp cruise around the lotus pool. Because precious tableware in medieval China was mainly used to entertain honored guests and was often presented as a gift, the decorative imagery on it usually expresses flattering wishes for good luck. Long-whiskered fish, predecessors of modern-day koi, were easily recognized centerpieces of several verbal puns. Pictures of fish (yu) in a pool (tang) could be understood as yutang, or "Jade-Hall," the lofty academy at the imperial court to which only the most honored scholars had access. The image could thus express the wish for an exalted career in government service. Lotus (lian) and fish (yu) can also be a play on the words meaning "continuous abundance" (lianyu), and the friendly, playful ducks (ya), as a result of the widespread popularity of Buddhism in medieval China, evoked the homophonous crushing (ya) of bad karma. Duck motifs are, indeed, found on Buddhist artworks of the Tang (618–907) and Song (960–1279) eras and express this same auspicious symbolism.[1]

FL

1. A silver pagoda discovered in the treasure of the Jingzhi Monastery Pagoda of 977 is a tenth-century example; *Chika kyūden no ihō: Chūgoku Kahoku-shō Teishi Hokusō tōki shutsudo bunbutsuten* [*Treasures from the underground palaces: Excavated treasures from northern Song pagodas, Dingzhou, Hebei Province, China*], cat. no. 6.

84a–b. Two bowls decorated with dragon-fish

Five Dynasties or Liao dynasty,
tenth century, before 942
From the tomb of Yelü Yuzhi
and Chonggun at Hansumu Township
in Aluke'erqin Banner
Partly gilded silver
a. Height: 6.5 cm;
diameter of mouth: 20 cm
b. Height: 7.1 cm,
diameter of mouth: 23.3 cm
Research Institute of Cultural Relics
and Archaeology of Inner Mongolia

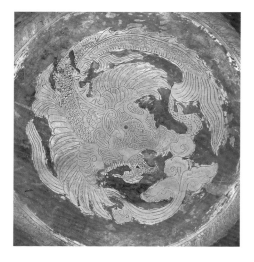

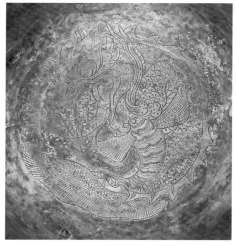

According to Chinese Buddhist tradition, there is a precious jewel that makes all wishes come true. The origin of this powerful gem was long a matter of intellectual debate, and some theories held that it came from the head of a mysterious sea creature (Sanskrit: *makara;* Chinese: *mojie*).[1] Since the third century AD, *makaras* had been depicted in the pictorial tradition of India as elephant-headed fish or snakes; a similar-looking sea monster is first found in Chinese imagery by the late sixth century.[2] In China, the image appeared in funerary and secular rather than monastic contexts, and in the course of the Tang era (618–907) a characteristic iconography developed, consisting of several types of fish with dragon heads.[3] Such dragon-fish were particularly popular between the ninth and twelfth centuries, and numerous examples have been discovered in Liao contexts (see cat. 25, 26, 87, 113). Because of the link to Indian imagery, Chinese dragon-fish are nowadays routinely identified as *makaras*. Yet in medieval times, they were hardly intended to depict the creatures of Buddhist scripture alone, if at all— so dominant was the traditional lore that recognized dragonlike beasts as the transformational protagonists of Chinese creation mythologies.[4] The two specimens depicted inside these silver bowls represent two separate iconographic types. One is hornless and has short arms with three claws (cat. 84b); the other has a single horn and wings and is shown in the air, next to a cloud, flying after a flaming gem. Both beasts look intimidatingly fierce—reminiscent of the divine scaly dragons (*jiao*) frequently mentioned in early Chinese literature.[5]

The two bowls, discovered in 1992 in the tomb of Yelü Yuzhi (890–941) and Chonggun (d. 942) at Hansumu Township in Aluke'erqin Banner, differ not only in the iconography of their ornament, but also in the quality of their manufacture. While one (cat. 84b) has thick walls and neat chasing and gilding, and its fish monster is rendered in convincing plasticity, the other (cat. 84a) has relatively thin walls and sloppy workmanship, and its dragon-fish appears flat. The bowls were likely made in different locations and at different times.

FL

1. *Foguang dacidian*, 2374.
2. The earliest datable image of this sea creature in China appears in the tomb of Li He (d. 583) in Sanyuan County, Shaanxi; see *Wenwu* 1966.1, pp. 27–42.
3. For a typological discussion of these beasts, see Qi Xiaoguang, "Yelü Yuzhi mu han yuwai wenhua yinsu zhi jinyinqi" [Gold and silver from Yelü Yuzhi's tomb showing foreign features], *Neimenggu wenwu kaogu wenji* 1997.2, pp. 561–66.
4. On early Chinese dragon mythologies, see John Hay, "The Persistent Dragon (*Lung*)"; Jean-Pierre Diény, *Le symbolisme du dragon dans la Chine antique* [The symbolism of the dragon in ancient China].
5. Edward H. Schafer, *The Vermilion Bird: T'ang Images of the South*, pp. 217–22; *Taiping yulan* [Imperial digest of the Taiping reign period] 930.4134–36.

85. Two cups with faceted sides

Five Dynasties, tenth century, before 942
From the tomb of Yelü Yuzhi and
Chonggun at Hansumu Township
in Aluke'erqin Banner
Gilded silver
Height: 6.4 cm; diameter of mouth: 7.3 cm;
diameter of base: 3.9 cm
Research Institute of Cultural Relics
and Archaeology of Inner Mongolia

These two wine cups, discovered in 1992 in the tomb of Yelü Yuzhi (890–941) and his wife, Chonggun (d. 942), are nearly identical in design and decoration. They are each gilded on the outside and across the rim, have a handle with a leaf-shaped thumb plate, and rest on a hexagonal foot, which is soldered to the cast and chased body. Beaded bands frame the seven main decorative fields, on each of which a bearded man seated out-doors on a leopard skin is depicted. The tableaux show the Seven Worthies of the Bamboo Grove, a standard pictorial theme in medieval China that celebrated the scholar's escape from the conformities of public life.[1] The sages, who were all historical figures of the third century, are shown enjoying the pleasures of leisure: drinking, playing music, reading, composing poetry, and engaging in intellectual discourse.

The same subject matter is depicted in greater detail on a scroll painting attributed to Sun Wei (active around 900 in Chengdu), now in the Shanghai Museum (fig. 106). Uncannily, two of the worthies in the painting are enjoying wine from angular gold cups very similar to the ones discovered in Yelü Yuzhi's tomb. Like many luxury items found in that tomb, these cups were most likely made in central or southern China and sent to the Khitan in the north.[2] Angular wine cups of this type first became fashionable at the Tang court around the seventh century, when their design held a distinctly exotic appeal and their sides were decorated with images of entertainers from Central Asia.[3] By the early tenth century, such cups had, how-ever, lost much of that exotic aura and were regarded, instead, as part of a Chinese her-itage, decorated most appropriately with imagery pertaining to Chinese antiquity.

FL

1. On this theme, see Audrey Spiro, *Contemplating the Ancients: Aesthetic and Social Issues in Early Chinese Portraiture.*
2. François Louis, "Shaping Symbols of Privilege: Precious Metals and the Early Liao Aristocracy," *Journal of Song-Yuan Studies* 33 (2003), pp. 85–87.
3. Carol Michaelson, *Gilded Dragons: Buried Treasures from China's Golden Ages*, p. 126.

Fig. 106. Detail from Seven Sages of the Bamboo Grove, after Sun Wei (active ca. 900). Shanghai Museum

86. Dish decorated with a pair of phoenixes

Five Dynasties, tenth century, before 942
From the tomb of Yelü Yuzhi
and Chonggun at Hansumu Township
in Aluke'erqin Banner
Gilded silver
Height: 3.5 cm; diameter: 18.4 cm
Research Institute of Cultural Relics
and Archaeology of Inner Mongolia

A pair of auspicious phoenixes (*fenghuang*) circling toward each other in a symmetric swirl has been a popular image in China since the eighth century. The male and female birds not only allude to a harmonious marriage but also, more universally, represent the *yang* and *yin* aspects of the generative cycles of nature. Platters such as this one, therefore, made fine wedding gifts, as well as flattering presents to influential people who—like the phoenixes—had the power to bring about beneficial change.

An older silver dish with a very similar phoenix motif corroborates this point (fig. 107). Its inscription explains that it was presented to Tang emperor Dezong (r. 779–805) around 800 by the prefect of what is now Shaoxing, in Zhejiang Province, in southern China;[1] it was just one of many such gifts bestowed to curry imperial favor.

The dish from the tomb of Yelü Yuzhi (890–941) and Chonggun (d. 942) appears to have reached the Khitan court in a similar fashion, as a gift from one of the courts of central or southern China. Although the iconography of the decorative imagery is very similar to that of the mid-Tang period, the vessel's shape points to a manufacture around the early tenth century. Characteristic design features of that time are the low foot-ring, the flat bottom, the thin ridge along the edge of the rim, and the steep, straight walls. Stylistically, this plate is closely related to the small gold bowl from the same tomb (cat. 82).

FL

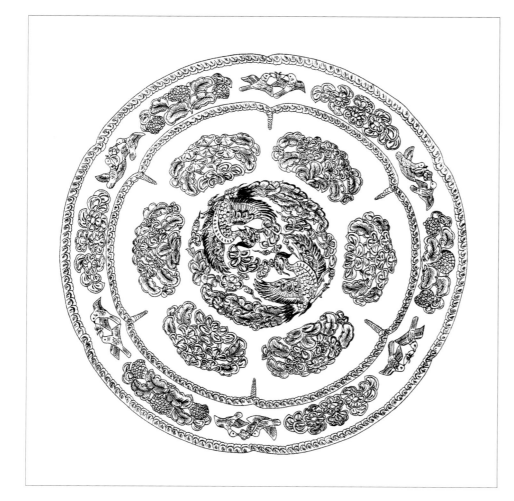

1. The vessel was discovered in Xi'an in 1962. Li Changqing and Hei Guang, "Xi'an beijiao faxian Tangdai jinhua yinpan" [A gilded-silver dish of the Tang dynasty discovered in the north of Xi'an] p. 60; Lu Zhaoyin, "Guanyu Xi'an beijiao suochu Tangdai jinhua yinpan" [A gilded-silver dish of the Tang dynasty from a northern suburb of Xi'an], *Kaogu* 1964.3, pp. 159–160; Carol Michaelson, *Gilded Dragons: Buried Treasures from China's Golden Ages*, pp. 97–98.

Fig. 107. Tang silver platter, late eighth century, discovered in 1962 in Kengdi, Xi'an (drawing after Lu Jiugao and Han Wei, *Tangdai jinyinqi* [*Tang dynasty gold and silver wares*], no. 154)

87. Jar with swing handle and lid

Tang or Liao dynasty, ninth or tenth century
Discovered in Dongshan Village, Chengzi
Township, near Chifeng City
Partly gilded silver
Height: 33 cm
Museum of Chifeng City

This jar was washed out of the ground during a heavy summer rain in 1979, along with a second, very similar jar and a silver bottle in the shape of a horseman's leather bag (fig. 108).[1] When archaeologists investigated the site, no tomb was found, and it became clear that the vessels had been hidden for safekeeping. None of the vessels showed signs of extensive use, but the time they had spent underground had left its marks. The bottom of the jar included in the exhibition had corroded, and the two handle attachments were missing. Perhaps the handles resembled those of the companion piece, which seem to represent water spouting from the heads of the sea creatures that form the jar's body. Known as *makaras*, such dragon-fish were popular throughout China between the ninth and twelfth centuries as images of transformational power.[2]

The three vessels found at Chengzi are unique within the current archaeological record, and their date of manufacture is still a matter of debate. Bold and unorthodox in design, the vessels modify Tang-era silver and textile designs from central and southern China. Scholars agree that they were made in the north and conventionally date them to the early Liao period (907–1125). In a little-noticed article, however, Zhang Songbai and Song Guojun of the Museum of Chifeng City have argued that the vessels were made much earlier, around the end of the eighth century.[3] At that time, the site where they were buried was still part of the Tang empire and lay within the grazing grounds of the Xi people, southern neighbors of the Khitan and, like the latter, tribute-paying nomadic allies of the Tang court. Zhang and Song suggest that the vessels were produced for

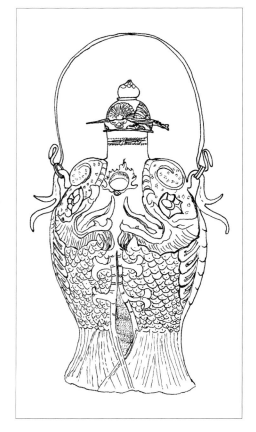

members of either the Xi or the Khitan elite in the Tang settlement of Yingzhou (modern-day Chaoyang in Liaoning Province), a burgeoning trading town located some 150 kilometers to the southeast of the site of the cache.[4] While Zhang and Song's explanation goes a long way to explain the "provincial" workmanship of the vessels, their dating requires further discussion, as stylistic parallels are found more readily in tenth-century contexts (see cat. 84).

FL

1. *Wenwu* 1985.2, pp. 94–96.
2. See also cat. 31, 32, 54, 89 in this catalogue.
3. Zhang Songbai and Song Guojun. "Chengzi jinyinqi yanjiu" [Research on the gold and silver objects from Chengzi], p. 75.
4. Zhang and Song, "Chengzi jinyinqi yanjiu," p. 78.

Fig. 108. The silver jar and bottle found at Chengzi along with the jar with swing handle and lid

88. Small ewer with lid

Liao dynasty, 1018 or earlier
From the tomb of the Princess of Chen
and Xiao Shaoju at Qinglongshan Town
in Naiman Banner
Silver
Height: 10.1 cm; diameter of mouth: 4.6 cm;
diameter of body: 9.2 cm;
diameter of base: 5.6 cm
Research Institute of Cultural Relics
and Archaeology of Inner Mongolia

Although it resembles modern-day tea pots, this small, stout ewer from the tomb of the Princess of Chen and Xiao Shaoju was intended for serving wine. Two wine cups made of white agate (cat. 99) were found near it, in the small eastern storage room of the tomb.[1] Brilliantly shiny in its original state, this silver ewer once made a fine visual complement to the white agate cups and an appropriate offering to the deceased couple. Its lid and thin spout indicate that it was apparently designed to contain a drink that was not only aromatic but also warm. The Khitan consumed various types of alcoholic beverages besides the traditional koumiss (made from fermented mare's milk) and its distillates. Millet wines were produced in the southern parts of the Liao state, while both rice and grape wines were imported. All these drinks were traded throughout the Liao empire. Not so, however, for the highly coveted chrysanthemum-flower wine, which was reserved for the imperial family and was shared with administration officials only on rare occasions.[2]

FL

---

1. *Liao Chenguo gongzhu mu* [*Liao tomb of the princess of the state of Chen*], pp 20, 42.
2. *Liaoshi* [*History of the Liao*], 10.116, 11.124, 53.879.

89. Cup stand

Liao dynasty, 1018 or earlier
From the tomb of the Princess of Chen
and Xiao Shaoju at Qinglongshan Town
in Naiman Banner
Silver
Height: 7.8 cm; diameter of mouth: 8.4 cm;
diameter base: 6.8 cm;
diameter of plate: 16 cm
Research Institute of Cultural Relics
and Archaeology of Inner Mongolia

This simple stand is composed of three pieces of hammered silver; the flared foot-ring and the high, cup-shaped receptacle are both soldered to the flat plate. Stands of this type were intended to hold a ceramic bowl; they became fashionable in China in the tenth century. While they mainly held tea bowls, such stands could also be used to present bowls containing cakes and the like, as seen in a painting from a Liao tomb discovered at Mount Yang in Aohan Banner (fig. 109).[1] As the enthusiasm for tea drinking spread, the stands, usually ceramic or lacquer, quickly grew popular, and by the twelfth century they were commonly used throughout East Asia. Silver stands are rare and are primarily associated with Khitan tombs.

This example is one of two discovered in the eastern storage room of the Princess of Chen's tomb (a third was found in the front hall of the tomb).[2] It features two large Khitan characters engraved on the outside of the foot-ring and a third engraved underneath the plate; their meaning remains unclear. Of the various ceramic bowls discovered nearby,

two pale-green Yue ware bowls imported from the tea-growing regions of southern China would have been the most suitable for use with the silver stands.[3]

FL

1. *Qidan wangchao* [*Khitan dynasty*], p. 196.
2. *Liao Chenguo gongzhu mu* [*Liao tomb of the princess of the state of Chen*], p. 42.
3. *Qidan wangchao*, p. 249; *Liao Chenguo gongzhu mu*, p. 20.

Fig. 109. Detail from a mural showing the preparation of tea and food; excavated in 1995 at Mount Yang, Sijiazi Township, Aohan Banner; Liao dynasty, eleventh century. Aohan Banner Museum

90. Spittoon

Five Dynasties, tenth century, before 942
From the tomb of Yelü Yuzhi and
Chonggun at Hansumu Township
in Aluke'erqin Banner
Partly gilded silver
Height: 14 cm; diameter of mouth: 18 cm;
diameter of base: 9.5 cm
Research Institute of Cultural Relics
and Archaeology of Inner Mongolia

Vessels of this shape, with a bulbous body, a short, narrow neck, and a wide, dishlike rim, are found most frequently in Tang, Liao, and Song tombs dating from the ninth to the thirteenth centuries. The majority of such vessels are made of glazed ceramics, but in tombs of the high nobility, there are occasionally examples made of silver and gold, as in this case.[1] Modern scholars have assigned various names to objects of this design, reflecting the uncertainty that exists about their original purpose. Most often such vessels are recognized as spittoons (*tuohu* or *tuoyu*), but more recently they have also been classified as refuse vessels (*zhadou*), on the presumption that they were used during meals or tea drinking to catch waste matter such as fish bones or tea dregs.[2] While no early textual evidence can be cited that convincingly supports the refuse vessel interpretation, some pictorial and archaeological evidence does link such vessels to the preparation and consumption of tea, wine, and food.[3] However, Liao and Song paintings never show the vessels on a table. Instead, they are always depicted conspicuously in the hands of a valet or maid servant, often along with a towel.[4] It is most probable, therefore, that they served as spittoons, and were held by attendants for their masters, who could cleanse their mouths with tea or water before and after eating and drinking. The tomb of Yelü Yuzhi (890–941) and his wife, Chonggun (d. 942), contained two silver spittoons, one for each of the tomb's occupants.[5]

As prominent sanitary objects, spittoons had become a curious kind of status symbol in China as early as the Six Dynasties period (220–589). Not only did members of the imperial court use elaborately decorated spittoons made of jade, gold, silver, glass, or rock crystal, but also emperors frequently presented such precious items as gifts to meritorious officials, and their use was regulated in sumptuary laws.[6] In one recorded case in the ninth century, a subaltern in the Tang capital was sentenced to death for using a golden spittoon and thereby infringing on imperial prerogative.[7]

FL

1. For Liao examples, see Lu Jing, *Liaodai taoci* [*Liao dynasty ceramics*], pp. 114–15

2. For a fine survey of Chinese spittoons, see Xie Mingliang, "Tuohu zaji" [Notes on the spittoon], *Gugong wenwu yuekan* 110 (May 1992), pp. 34–47.

3. See, for example, *Xuanhua Liaomu* [*Liao tombs in Xuanhua*], vol. 2, pl. 139; Su Bai, *Baisha Song mu* [*Song tomb at Baisha*], color pl. 5; *Liao Chenguo gongzhu mu* [*Liao tomb of the princess of the state of Chen*], p. 20.

4. *Liao Chenguo gongzhu mu*, color pl. 2.1; *Xuanhua Liaomu*, vol. 2, color pls. 63, 65, 81, pl. 94; Wen C. Fong and James C.Y. Watt, *Possessing the Past: Treasures from the National Palace Museum, Taipei*, p. 145.

5. The second spittoon is not mentioned in the preliminary excavation report but is published in *Caoyuan guibao: Neimenggu wenwu kaogu jingpin* [*Treasures on grassland. Archaeological finds from the Inner Mongolia Autonomous Region*], pp. 168–69.

6. *Taiping yulan* [*Imperial digest of the Taiping reign period*], 703.3138; *Xin Wudai shi* [*New historical records of the Five Dynasties*], 14.153.

7. *Jiu Tangshu* [*Old history of the Tang dynasty*], 173.4493.

91. Ewer decorated with a dragon in a lotus pond motif

Liao dynasty, second half of the
eleventh century or early twelfth century
From Songshan District, Chifeng City
Lead-glazed earthenware
Height: 18.8 cm;
diameter of mouth: 3.5 cm;
diameter of base: 7.8 cm
Museum of Chifeng City

This ewer has a long, narrow neck; a short, slanting spout; a flat, stepped handle; a globular body; and a vertical foot with a flat base. Identical molded designs of a dragon situated among waves, small fish, and blossoming lotus flowers topped by a flaming pearl decorate both the front and back of the globular body. Above the horizontal line that marks the shoulder is a circle of lotus leaves with thin veins; around the long neck floral and geometric patterns are impressed. Yellow and green glazes, which stop short of the base, were applied to the pink clay. Traces of a white slip underneath the glaze can clearly be seen on the foot.

It was common for Liao craftsmen to share their repertory of decorative motifs. The design of a dragon rising from a lotus pond on this ewer is very similar to the design on the gilded-silver inkstone case from the tomb (dated 942) of Yelü Yuzhi and his wife (cat. 93); it is also similar to the ornament on a piece of *kesi* silk tapestry approximately two meters long that was used to cover the corpse in Tomb Number 7 (Liao, datable to the second half of the tenth century) at Yemaotai in Faku, Liaoning Province. In addition, lotus leaves similar to those decorating the shoulder of this earthenware ewer can be found on the rim of the silver cups unearthed from You'ai Village in Balin Right Banner (cat. 92) and on the foot of the gold cup from Yelü Yuzhi's tomb (cat. 83). The meaning of a dragon rising from a lotus pond remains unclear; yet the flaming pearl—a Buddhist symbol of wisdom—atop the lotus flowers on the ewer suggests a possible Buddhist connection.

The shape of this ewer, like that of its stoneware counterpart covered with white glaze (see cat. 107a), was based on silver prototypes (see cat. 88), and it most likely had a lid. Silver ewers similar in shape have been recovered from a few tombs, including Tomb Number 1 at Qujiagou in Chifeng City, Inner Mongolia.[1] However, given the coarse surface of this lead-glazed ewer, it was probably not intended for actual use and was made for burial.

HMS

---

1. See *Beifang wenwu* 1991.3, p. 36, fig. 4, right.

92a–c. Three cups

Liao dynasty, eleventh or early twelfth century
Excavated in You'ai Village, Baiyinhan
Township, Balin Right Banner
Silver
a. Basket cup: height: 5.6 cm;
diameter of mouth: 10.4 cm
b. Lotus-leaf cup: height: 3.8 cm;
diameter of mouth: 10 cm
c. High-footed cup with lotus-petal
decoration: height: 6.4 cm;
diameter of mouth: 9.6 cm
Museum of the Inner Mongolia
Autonomous Region

These three cups were part of a treasure hoard discovered in the summer of 1978 during the plowing of a field. The hoard included eight silver cups, a silver tray, a finely decorated silver ewer with warming bowl, silver tassel fittings, one agate and two jade cups, a bronze mirror, bronze boxes, Buddhist devotional objects, and several ceramic vessels.[1] The items appear to have been the valuable belongings of a household that were buried for safekeeping during the late Liao era. The cache site lies about one mile to the east of a Liao settlement, as evidenced by a number of architectural remains, including roof tiles.

Each of these three cups has an identical companion piece. The silver cup that resembles a woven basket is the most unusual type. Only a handful of other examples are known in silver; more have survived in clay.[2] First produced in late-ninth-century Tang China and sometimes referred to as "reed baskets" (*pulan*) or "willow dippers" (*liudou*), these imitations in precious material of the most humble of all containers make a bizarre kind of understatement. In Song China, silver wares had become widely available luxury commodities by the early twelfth century, commercially produced and used even in fine winehouses. But in the Liao territories, where the traditional barter economy had barely become monetized, ownership of silver was a well-guarded prerogative of the ruling elites, even toward the end of the era and despite the fact that Liao silver wares followed the designs fashionable in Song China. At least two of the cups from the hoard of You'ai, including the high-footed cup with lotus-petal decoration exhibited

here, were once Khitan property, for two Khitan characters are engraved on the bottom of each.[3]

FL

1. *Wenwu* 1980.5, pp. 45–51.
2. For silver examples, see Qi Dongfang, *Tangdai jinyinqi yanjiu* [*Research on Tang gold and silver*], pp. 123–24. For Liao clay bowls, see *Xuanhua Liao mu* [*Liao tombs in Xuanhua*], vol. 2, pls. 145.3, 145.4. For a jade example now in the Sackler Gallery of Art in Washington, D.C., see *Bulletin of the Museum of Far Eastern Antiquities* 36 (1963), pl. 26.2.
3. *Wenwu* 1980.5, p. 48, fig. 9.

93. Inkstone in partly gilded silver case with lid

Liao dynasty, 942 or earlier
From the tomb of Yelü Yuzhi and
Chonggun at Hansumu Township
in Aluke'erqin Banner
Height: 7.6 cm; length: 18.4 cm;
width at deep end: 11 cm;
width at top: 13.6 cm
Research Institute of Cultural Relics
and Archaeology of Inner Mongolia

This black inkstone narrows slightly at its deep end, where the writing brush was dipped into the ink. The stone itself is encased in a custom-fitted silver box that rests on thirteen short feet. A small brush decorated with a dragon was found in fragmentary condition inside the silver case.[1] While the sides of the case are decorated with floral sprigs as well as scroll and rope patterns, the top of the lid shows a dragon rising from a lotus pond with an ornate retaining wall. The dragon winds around three long-stemmed lotus flowers; the central one, in full bloom, grows through the dragon's snout. The lotus blossom serves as the base for a cartouche inscribed with the three characters *wan sui tai* (Myriad Years Terrace). In the background, the sun rises from behind the distant mountains.

Myriad Years Terrace was the name given to one of the imperial altars on Mount Tai, China's Sacred Peak of the East, in Shandong Province. The name was chosen in 665 by the Tang emperor and empress to commemorate the auspiciousness of the *feng shan* rites they had just conducted there—the most extraordinary of all imperial legitimation rituals.[2] But the image on the lid of the inkstone case refers to this venerable site in a curious manner: with the central lotus flower growing precariously through the dragon's snout, are we to see the age-old ritual prerogatives of the Chinese empire being reborn, but at the mercy of a rising Khitan empire?

Qi Xiaoguang, one of the archaeologists who recovered the inkstone from the tomb of Yelü Yuzhi (890–941) and his wife, Chonggun (d. 942), interprets the inscription figuratively to mean "imperial inkstone" and speculates

that the object was bestowed on Yelü Yuzhi by the second Liao emperor, Taizong (r. 927–947).[3] Whatever its provenance, the inkstone implies that the deceased was a man of letters. In Yelü Yuzhi's case, we know from textual sources that he was endowed with extraordinary intellectual skills and a great desire for learning. A cousin of the first Liao emperor, Yuzhi was a brilliant strategist who spoke the languages of many of the allied tribes that fought with the Khitan during their early decades of conquest.[4] At the age of thirty-six, he was entrusted with one of four ministerial positions in the newly annexed Bohai kingdom in the east. Soon thereafter, he conceived of the founding of a new capital (the Eastern Capital), which he ably administered for the next two decades. Upon his death, he was eulogized as a shaper of early Khitan policy and given a lavish state funeral by Emperor Taizong.[5]

FL

1. Qi Xiaoguang, "Phönix in der Steppe. Das Kammergrab des Qidan-Prinzen Yelü Yuzhi in der Inneren Mongolei" [Phoenix in the steppe: The tomb of the Khitan prince Yelü Yuzhi in Inner Mongolia], *Antike Welt* 26 (1995), p. 440.

2. *Jiu Tangshu* [Old history of the Tang dynasty], 23.888. On the 665 *feng shan* sacrifices in general, see Howard J. Wechsler, *Offerings of Jade and Silk: Ritual and Symbol in the Legitimation of the T'ang Dynasty*, pp. 170–94.

3. Qi Xiaoguang, "Phönix in der Steppe," p. 440; cf. *Qidan wangchao* [Khitan dynasty], p. 206. For additional theories proposing that the inkstone may have come from Dongdan, see Gai Zhiyong, *Tanxun shiqu de wangchao: Liao Yelü Yuzhi mu* [Exploring a lost dynasty: the tomb of Yelü Yuzhi], p. 60.

4. *Liaoshi* [History of the Liao], 75.1238.

5. Karl A. Wittfogel and Fêng Chia-shêng, *History of Chinese Society: Liao, 907–1125*, p. 112; *Wenwu* 1996.1, pp. 30–32.

94. Box with relief decoration

Ninth and early-tenth century, before 942
From the tomb of Yelü Yuzhi and
Chonggun at Hansumu Township
in Aluke'erqin Banner
Gilded Silver
Height: 8.9 cm; diameter: 14.6 cm
Research Institute of Cultural Relics
and Archaeology of Inner Mongolia

The elaborately designed lid of this box was made by a truly accomplished Chinese silversmith, using both intricate chasing and bold repoussé techniques. A pair of galloping and fiercely roaring lions dominates the central frame. Small, puffy clouds line the outside of the frame and point at a variety of auspicious birds and cicadas amid vegetal scrolls. The side of the lid is decorated with lions, goats, and a long, continuous floral scroll. The lower half of the box shows a similar scroll, but in contrast to the one on the lid, this scroll is chased in an amateurish manner and surrounded by loosely scattered ring-punching with no spirited animals. Undoubtedly, the lower half of the box was made by a separate craftsman. While coarsely worked areas are sometimes found on the bottom of silver boxes from the late Tang era, that kind of workmanship is usually not in plain sight. Given how visible the qualitative difference between the lid and the bottom half is on this box, it seems likely that the bottom half was made at a later time, presumably to replace a damaged or lost original.

While bracketed silver boxes are an innovation of eighth-century Tang China, examples with a foot-ring became fashionable only during the ninth century.[1] Among the Tang examples discovered in recent years is a box, very similar in design to this one, found in the crypt of Famen Temple, near Xi'an.[2] It was one of the prime personal possessions of the Tang emperor Yizong (r. 859–873), who received it as a birthday gift from Hongzhou, a city in modern-day Jiangxi Province, in southern China. The emperor, in turn, presented it as an offering to the Buddha. The box from the tomb of Yelü Yuzhi (890–941)

and Chonggun (d. 942) most likely served as a precious gift, too. The close stylistic resemblance of its lid to silver objects from the mid-ninth century suggests that it, too, was made during the late Tang dynasty (618–907) and was passed along as a gift among the ruling elites for several decades before it eventually reached the Khitan court.[3] Its lower half was probably replaced in the early decades of the tenth century.

FL

---

1. Qi Dongfang, *Tangdai jinyinqi yanjiu* [*Research on Tang gold and silver*], pp. 84–86.
2. *Wenwu* 1988.10, p. 14; Lu Zhaoyin, "Guanyu Famensi digong jinyinqi de ruogan wenti" [Some problems concerning the gold and silver objects from the Underground Palace of Famen Temple], pp. 641–42.
3. Closely related in style are an incense burner discovered at Famen Temple (*Wenwu* 1988.10, p. 16) and several gold and silver pieces discovered on the Belitung shipwreck in Indonesia in 1998 and 1999 (cf. Zoi Kotitsa [ed.], *The Belitung Wreck: Sunken Treasures from Tang China*, forthcoming).

95. Jug decorated with scenes of filial piety

Five Dynasties, tenth century, before 942
From the tomb of Yelü Yuzhi and
Chonggun at Hansumu Township
in Aluke'erqin Banner
Gilded silver
Height: 14.8 cm; diameter of body: 12.2
cm; diameter of mouth: 7.6 cm;
diameter of base: 7.1 cm; weight: 364 gm
Research Institute of Cultural Relics
and Archaeology of Inner Mongolia

An ancient story has it that on an icy winter day the heartless stepmother of a young boy named Wang Xiang was feeling ill, and so she demanded that he find her fresh fish. Deeply committed to his parents' happiness, Wang went to the river, which was frozen over. There, he took off his clothes and lay on the ice so that it would melt. When a hole in the ice opened, two carp leaped out. He brought them home, and as his stepmother learned of this selfless act, her attitude toward Wang improved greatly.[1] This story of filial piety is one of eight illustrated on this exquisite vessel. Most of them are traditional tales of Chinese morality and featured regularly in the various sets of illustrations of *Twenty-Four Paragons of Filial Piety* popular during the past millennium.[2]

The jug, which once had a ring handle and a thumb plate, was used for serving wine, probably along with the two heptagonal cups recovered from the same tomb (cat. 85). Because looters discovered and vandalized this grave in 1992, we can only surmise that the original arrangement of the vessels was comparable to that of a very similar jug and cups in an undisturbed royal tomb at Tuerjishan, discovered in 2003.[3] There, the vessels were set on a small offering table in front of the deceased. The wine vessel from the tomb of Yelü Yuzhi (890–941) and his wife, Chonggun (d. 942), with its scenes of filial piety, would, therefore, appear to have been a carefully chosen offering, presumably by one or several of the couple's children, who were grieving the loss of both their parents, who died in quick succession. Yuzhi, buried in March 942, was survived by two daughters and thirteen sons; Chonggun, who died less than three weeks after her hus-

band's funeral, was the mother of nine of his sons.[4] She was buried in June.

Although the shape of this vessel is inspired by Turkic precedents, it is a Chinese product, likely made for the Later Tang (923–36) or the Later Jin dynasty (936–46), both of which were Turkic (Shato). The Later Jin, in particular, is known to have supplied the allied Khitan with a great number of Chinese luxury objects.[5] The early Khitan elite eagerly amassed Chinese exports and were sufficiently steeped in Chinese culture to recognize the iconography of moral tales such as those depicted here. Aside from the story of Wang Xiang, the scenes on the body of the vessel show Yuan Gu saving his grandfather from being abandoned by his father and converting the latter to filial behavior;[6] Zhong Zilu, the filial disciple of Confucius, presenting food to his parents after having carried it for a hundred miles;[7] and Cai Shun eating sour berries and saving the ripe ones for his mother, thereby impressing two rebel soldiers.[8] Those on the neck of the vessel include the destitute Guo Ju about to bury his three-year-old son, whose appetite made it impossible to feed Guo's mother, and later finding a pot of gold;[9]

Ding Lan leaving his wife in charge of a revered wooden image of his deceased mother, which would subsequently be desecrated, infuriating Ding;[10] Wang Pou protecting his mother's tomb during a thunderstorm, telling her to not be afraid;[11] and Yang Xiang, a fourteen-year-old farmer's daughter, jumping on the back of a wild tiger and strangling it to protect her father.[12]

FL

1. *Soushen ji* [*Records of ghosts*], 11.215; *Jinshu* [*Standard history of the Jin*], 33.987; *Taiping yulan* [*Imperial digest of the Taiping reign period*], 411.1895.

2. For a discussion of such illustrations up to the Yuan period, see Duan Pengqi, "Woguo gu muzang zhong faxian de xiaoti tuxiang" [Images of filial piety discovered in Chinese tombs], in *Zhongguo kaoguxue luncong*, pp. 463–71.

3. *Kaogu* 2004.7, pp. 50–53.

4. Another son and two daughters predeceased the parents; *Wenwu* 1996.1, p. 32.

5. François Louis, "Shaping Symbols of Privilege: Precious Metals and the Early Liao Aristocracy," *Journal of Song-Yuan Studies* 33 (2003), pp. 83–88.

6. *Taiping yulan*, 519.2360.

7. *Dunhuang bianwen ji* [*Compendium of Dunhuang transformation texts*], 8.903.

8. *Dunhuang bianwen ji*, 8.902.

9. *Soushen ji*, 11.219; *Taiping yulan*, 411.1898.

10. *Taiping yulan*, 396.1832, 414.1909.

11. *Soushen ji*, 11.222. The protagonist is sometimes called Wang Bao, and similar behavior is also recorded of Cai Shun; see *Hou Hanshu*, 39.1312; *Dunhuang bianwen ji*, 8.907; *Taiping yulan*, 13.65.

12. *Taiping yulan*, 415.1915.

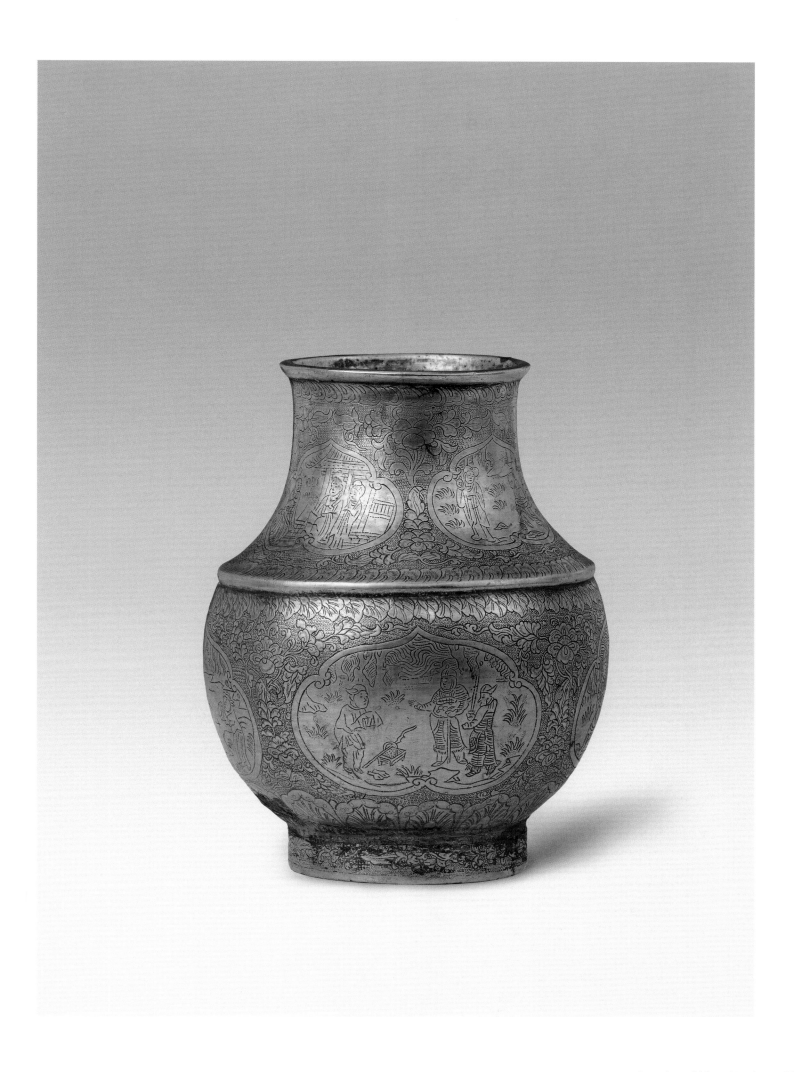

96a–f. Cosmetics case with three small boxes and two lidded jarlets

Liao dynasty, late tenth
or early eleventh century, before 1018
From the tomb of the Princess of Chen
and Xiao Shaoju at Qinglongshan Town
in Naiman Banner
Partly gilded silver
a. Cosmetics case: height 21 cm;
diameter: 25.4 cm;
diameter of base: 20.8 cm
b–d. Three small boxes: height 2.9 cm;
diameter: 5 cm
e–f. Two jarlets: height: 8.2 cm;
diameter of mouth: 5.4 cm
Research Institute of Cultural Relics
and Archaeology of Inner Mongolia

A magnificent golden dragon chases a flaming ball of essential energy on the lid of this silver cosmetics case, while flying phoenixes alternate with floral sprigs on the side of the case. As the most prestigious embodiments of cosmic creation, the dragon and the phoenix were standard images on silver cosmetics cases in both Liao and Song China.[1] Not only did these images bespeak the elite status of the women who used such boxes, but they also alluded to the theme of fertility. Women in medieval China were only too aware of the emphasis society placed on their role as child bearers. Cosmetics cases played their own small part in this complex system of idealizing social responsibilities. Since a well-groomed, seductive appearance could increase a woman's chances of becoming pregnant, the decoration of cosmetics cases with fertility symbols would appear appropriate. In the tomb of the Princess of Chen and Xiao Shaoju, however, the case becomes a particularly sad reminder of the tragic loss of a young life, for the princess died at the age of seventeen, already a widow and apparently before she had borne any children.[2] Her cosmetics case was found with two silver jarlets and three small silver boxes. One of the boxes still contained rouge (which had blackened with time), and another still held white powder makeup.[3] The cosmetics case was originally placed on the altar in front of the coffin of the deceased couple, in the main chamber of the tomb.[4]

FL

1. For Song and Yuan examples, see *Wenwu* 1959.11, pp. 19–24; *Wenwu* 1986.5, pp. 78–80; *Wenwu* 1990.9, pp. 1–13.
2. For her epitaph and biography, see *Liao Chenguo gongzhu mu* [*Liao tomb of the princess of the state of Chen*], pp. 114–16, 158–62.
3. *Qidan wangchao* [*Khitan dynasty*], p. 213.
4. *Liao Chenguo gongzhu mu*, p. 40.

97. Large basin

Late-ninth or tenth century, before 942
From the tomb of Yelü Yuzhi
and Chonggun at Hansumu Township
in Aluke'erqin Banner
Silver
Height: 7.2 cm; diameter of mouth: 34 cm;
diameter of base: 23.5 cm
Research Institute of Cultural Relics
and Archaeology of Inner Mongolia

This large, heavy, five-lobed silver washbasin
was hammered by a skilled silversmith in the
best Chinese tradition. It shows considerable
wear, which indicates that it was used extensively before its eventual burial in the tomb
of Yelü Yuzhi (890–941) and his wife,
Chonggun (d. 942). Three characters
scrawled on the bottom of the vessel read *zuo
xiang gong* (Minister Duke to the Left), an
honorific title given only to the most influential executive officials. It refers to Yelü
Yuzhi and designates him as the owner of the
vessel. Yuzhi, a leading strategist and a
visionary administrator in the early Khitan
empire, held the position of Grand
Councilor to the Left (*zuo xiang*) in the government of the eastern part of the Liao
empire from 927 on.[1] Instrumental in shaping the policies for that part of the empire,
he was promoted in 938 to the all-powerful
position of Grand Mentor of the Eastern
Capital (*Dongjing taifu*), which he held until
his death. Because Yuzhi's title changed in
938, this silver basin had, in all probability,
been among his personal belongings for several years. It is the largest and heaviest silver
object recovered from his tomb, weighing 1.4
kilograms.

FL

1. Qi Xiaoguang, "Yelü Yuzhi muzhi dui wenxian
jizai de kanbu" [Emendations of textual records based
on Yelü Yuzhi's epitaph], p. 43.

98. Bowl with high foot-ring

Liao dynasty, 1018 or earlier
From the tomb of the Princess of Chen
and Xiao Shaoju at Qinglongshan Town,
Naiman Banner
Agate
Height: 3.1 cm; diameter of mouth: 7.4 cm;
diameter of base: 4.4 cm
Research Institute of Cultural Relics
and Archaeology of Inner Mongolia

99a–bTwo small cups

Liao dynasty, 1018 or earlier
From the tomb of the Princess of Chen
and Xiao Shaoju at Qinglongshan Town,
Naiman Banner
Agate
Height: 3.1 cm; diameter of mouth: 4.3 cm;
diameter of base: 2.3 cm
Research Institute of Cultural Relics
and Archaeology of Inner Mongolia

Although these three undecorated agate vessels excavated from the tomb of the Princess of Chen and Xiao Shaoju are small in size, a great deal of effort was invested in the creation of their elegant shapes and highly polished surfaces. The flared, high foot-rings refer to a prototype in gold and silver. Similar examples came from Tomb Number 7 (Liao, datable to the second half of the tenth century), of a high-ranking individual, at Yemaotai in Faku, Liaoning Province.[1]

By the mid-Tang dynasty, vessels made of semiprecious stones, including agate, became more common than they had been before, yet they remained closely associated with people of high status. A lobed cup made of white jade, a plain rock-crystal bowl, an elongated oval cup made of agate, and an agate rhyton cup were retrieved from the large hoard of objects made of gold, silver and other precious materials found in 1970 at Hejia Village, outside Xi'an.[2] A reliquary box made of precious stones and adorned with strings of pearls was presented as a gift by the Tang emperor Yizong (r. 859–73) to the Buddha's relic, along with large quantities of textiles, fine ceramics, and gold and silver, all of which were buried underneath the pagoda at Famen Monastery (in modern Fufeng, Shaanxi Province) in 874.[3] An agate jar with a gold lid was used to hold relic grains at the North Pagoda in Chaoyang, Liaoning Province (deposit dated 1043), confirming the high status of agate in the Liao period.[4]

HMS

1. See *Wenwu* 1975.12, pl. 3.1.
2. A rhyton is a drinking vessel in the shape of an animal or an animal's head. Rhytons were favored ceremonial wine vessels in the Near East and Persia. For the excavation report on the Hejia Village hoard, see *Wenwu* 1972.1, pp. 30–42. See also Shaanxi lishi bowuguan, Beijing daxue kaogu wenbo xueyuan, Beida zhendan gudai wenming yanjiu zhongxin et al. *Hua wu Datang chun: Hejiacun yibao jingcui* [*Selected treasures from Hejia Village Tang hoard*].
3. See *Wenwu* 1988.10, p. 8, fig. 5.
4. See *Wenwu* 1992.7, color pl. 1.1. A hoard in Balin Right Banner yielded two agate bowls and one marble bowl among other treasures, including twenty-four silver vessels. See *Wenwu* 1980.5, p. 51, figs. 19, 20, 22. A few Liao tombs have yielded agate vessels, and all of these tombs belonged to high-ranking people. See *Kaogu xuebao* 1954.8, p. 193, fig. 23.1; p. 196, fig. 25.8; *Wenwu* 1975.12, pl. 3.1.

100. Four-lobed cup

Liao dynasty, 1018 or earlier
From the tomb of the Princess of Chen
and Xiao Shaoju at Qinglongshan Town,
Naiman Banner
Rock crystal
Height: 2.3 cm; diameter of mouth:
3.6–5.3 cm; diameter of base: 1.8–2.5 cm
Research Institute of Cultural Relics
and Archaeology of Inner Mongolia

101a–c. Three small cups

Liao dynasty, 1018 or earlier
From the tomb of the Princess of Chen
and Xiao Shaoju at Qinglongshan Town,
Naiman Banner
Rock crystal, gilded silver
Overall height: 3.5 cm; diameter of mouth:
2.8 cm; diameter of base: 1.8 cm
Research Institute of Cultural Relics
and Archaeology of Inner Mongolia

These small cups excavated from the tomb of the Princess of Chen and Xiao Shaoju were carved out of blocks of colorless rock crystal—a highly valued material in Liao culture. The four-lobed cup is decorated with an incised, patterned cloud motif. It is related in shape to Tang and contemporaneous gold and silver wares, which, in turn, took their form from metal prototypes that originated in West Asia. The three small cups are identical except that one is missing its lid and loop-in-loop chain by which it would have been attached to the princess's belt.[1] The simple shape of the cups and their fine polish show the translucency of the material.

Liao rock-crystal carvings fall into two categories—body ornaments (pendants and beads) and small vessels. Both types were found only in the tombs of high-ranking people and in Buddhist relic deposits, which indicates the rarity and high status of rock crystal during the Liao period.[2] Historical texts show that rock crystal was transferred as a precious gift among the lesser states that preceded the Song, Northern Song, and Liao dynasties. For example, a rock-crystal inkstone was presented to the Liao court as a gift by a Later Jin ruler to reinforce his alliance with the Liao.[3] Moreover, Buddhist statues and artifacts made of rock crystal were presented by the king of the Wuyue state (in present-day Zhejiang Province) to the Song court; the gifts were presented as a means of buying peace with the threatening Song, who later took over the Wuyue territory and united China.[4] Indian rock crystal had been imported into China long before the Liao era. It is likely that the rock crystal used to make these cups was imported from

India or perhaps from Sumatra, as is indicated in some textual sources.[5]

Given the rarity of rock crystal and the size of these vessels, the conspicuous consumption of rock crystal in the making of the cups must have made them far more precious gifts than small pendants or beads made of the same material.

HMS

---

1. The three cups were found by the waist of the body of the princess, indicating their original use as pendants. See *Liao Chenguo gongzhu mu*, pp. 61–62.

2. In addition to these four vessels made of rock crystal, 152 rock-crystal beads were retrieved from the tomb of the Princess of Chen and her husband. In addition to being found in tombs of the high-ranking, rock-crystal carvings have also been found in Liao Buddhist relic deposits, including the North Pagoda in Chaoyang, Liaoning Province (deposits dated 1043 and 1044), the White Pagoda in Balin Right Banner, Inner Mongolia (deposit dated 1049), and Dule Temple Pagoda in Tianjin (deposit dated 1058). See *Wenwu* 1992.7, pls. 4.1, 4.3–4.5; 1994.12, p. 13, fig. 21.7; *Kaogu xuebao* 1989.1, p. 105, fig. 27.

3. *Liaoshi, juan* 4, p. 50.

4. See *Songshi* [*History of the Song*], *juan* 480, pp. 13901, 13910.

5. See *Songshi, juan* 489, pp. 14088–89, and *juan* 490, p. 14103.

102. Ewer with boss decoration

Syrian or Egyptian, 1018 or earlier
From the tomb of the Princess of Chen
and Xiao Shaoju at Qinglongshan Town,
Naiman Banner
Glass
Height: 17 cm; diameter of mouth: 6 cm;
diameter of base: 8.7 cm
Research Institute of Cultural Relics
and Archaeology of Inner Mongolia

The seven glass objects excavated from the tomb of the Princess of Chen and her husband are one of the most important finds of Islamic glass in China. They include this ewer, a mallet-shaped flask with wheel-cut decoration (cat. 103), two bell-shaped bottles (fig. 110), two brown cups with handles (fig. 111), and a large bowl (fig. 112).

This colorless ewer has a long conical neck, a globular body supported by a wide flaring foot, and a stepped handle. Decorating the body of the ewer are five registers of bosses. The stepped handle, the most unusual part of the ewer, was made of horizontal looped trail patterns piled one on top of another. Scientific analysis of the glass shows a high sodium oxide component (20.66 percent), close to that of glass objects from Egypt or Syria; hence the ewer might have been a product of that area.[1]

HMS

1. See An Jiayao, "Chen guo gongzhu yu fuma hezangmu chutu de boli qimin ji youguan wenti" [Glass vessels unearthed from the joint burial of the princess of the state of Chen and her husband], *Liao Chenguo gongzhu mu* [*Liao tomb of the princess of the state of Chen*], pp. 179–86.

Fig. 110. Bell-shaped glass bottle; height: 31.2 cm; from the tomb of the Princess of Chen and Xiao Shaoju

Fig. 111. Brown glass cup; height: 11.4 cm; from the tomb of the Princess of Chen and Xiao Shaoju

Fig. 112. Glass bowl; diameter of mouth: 25.5 cm; from the tomb of the Princess of Chen and Xiao Shaoju

103. Mallet-shaped flask with linear decoration

Persian (Iranian), 1018 or earlier
From the tomb of the Princess of Chen and Xiao Shaoju at Qinglongshan Town, Naiman Banner
Glass
Height: 24.5 cm;
diameter of mouth: 7.4 cm;
diameter of base: 11 cm
Research Institute of Cultural Relics and Archaeology of Inner Mongolia

The body of this mallet-shaped flask with a tall tapering neck and broad flat lip curves outward at the shoulder and then inward to a broad flat base. The neck and the body are of approximately equal height. While the body is decorated with wheel-cut linear patterns, the neck is cut into vertical facets in geometric shapes.

This vase, which was excavated from the tomb of the Princess of Chen and Xiao Shaoju, was imported from Islamic Persia. Several glass flasks with similar shape and decoration have been unearthed from a number of contemporaneous sites, most of which were Buddhist relic deposits.[1] These glass artifacts bear witness to the trade contacts the Liao had with their neighbors in the West via the ancient Silk Road.

HMS

---

1. Similar mallet-shaped flasks have been found in the relic deposits in the pagodas at Xianyan Temple in Rui'an, Zhejiang Province (deposit dated 1043) and at Dule Temple in Jixian, Hebei Province (deposit dated 1058). See *Wenwu* 1973.1, p. 65, fig. 2; *Kaogu xuebao* 1989.1, pl. 24.5. For a list of glass artifacts found in Liao pagodas, see Hsueh-man Shen, "Luxury or Necessity: Glassware in *Sarira* Relic Pagodas of the Tang and Northern Song Periods," in Cecilia Braghin (ed.), *Chinese Glass: Archaeological Studies on the Uses and Social Context of Glass Artefacts from the Warring States to the Northern Song Period*, pp. 71–110; appendix, pp. 100–102.

104. Lidded jar with loop handles and rectangular lugs

Tenth century, 942 or earlier
From the tomb of Yelü Yuzhi and Chonggun at Hansumu Township, Aluke'erqin Banner
Stoneware with green glaze
Height: 34.2 cm;
diameter of mouth: 9.8 cm;
diameter of base: 10.5 cm
Research Institute of Cultural Relics and Archaeology of Inner Mongolia

This lidded jar from the tomb of Yelü Yuzhi (890–941) and Chonggun (d. 942) has a swelling ovoid body and a short neck. The jar reaches its maximum diameter at the midsection of the belly, tapers sharply below the belly, and flares slightly outward near the foot-ring. Its rather low center of gravity makes the curvature of the jar seem more rounded than most jars of similar type. The entire piece is covered with green glaze, except for a ring of spur marks on the foot-ring and the area where the lid rests on the shoulder of the jar.

The shoulder of the jar is embellished with two perforated rectangular lugs between which, on either side, are two loop-handles, set vertically. Projecting from the sides of the convex lid are two loops that, when the lid is in place, fall just between the two loop-handles. Thus, a string can be drawn through the lugs, loops, and loop-handles to fasten the lid firmly to the jar.

The yellowish-green, somewhat devitrified color of the jar's glaze and its warm, mellow texture are typical of the Yue green ware produced near Yuyao in Zhejiang Province during the tenth century. Similar tone and texture of glaze can be found on Yue green wares recovered from a number of late-ninth- and early-tenth-century sites, including a jar-shaped tomb epitaph, dated 887, from Shanglinhu in Cixi (fig. 113) and several celadon objects from the tomb (dated 901) of Lady Shui Qiu at Lin'an, near Hangzhou.[1]

So far, very few comparable examples have been found. Four smaller jars, each with six perforated rectangular lugs on the shoulder,

Fig. 113. Jar-shaped tomb epitaph, dated 887, from Shanglinhu in Cixi, Zhejiang Province

were unearthed from the tomb (dated 958) of Liu Cheng, king of the Nanhan kingdom (917–71), in Guangzhou, in southern China.[2] A lid with two protruding, perforated rectangular lugs survives from the tomb (dated 942) of Qian Yuanguan, king of the Wuyue kingdom (907–978), in Hangzhou, Zhejiang Province. Judging from the rarity of this particular type of jar and its association with the ruling families in the South, it can be inferred that this lidded jar was presented to the Liao by southerners as a extremely precious gift.

HMS

1. See Zhongguo Shanghai renmin meishu chubanshe, ed., *Zhongguo taoci quanji 4: Yue yao* [*Comprehensive collections of Chinese ceramics: 4 Yue ware*], pls. 134, 137, 149–51, 185.
2. See *Kaogu* 1964.6, pl. 10.5. See also Xie Mingliang, "Lue tan jiaerguan" [Brief discussion of *jiaer* jars], *Gugong wenwu yuekan* 16.4 (1998), pp. 16–31.

105. Vase decorated with loop handles

Tenth century, before 942
From the tomb of Yelü Yuzhi
and Chonggun at Hansumu Township,
Aluke'erqin Banner
Stoneware with transparent glaze
Height: 37.1 cm;
diameter of mouth: 12.8 cm;
diameter of base: 12.5 cm
Research Institute of Cultural Relics
and Archaeology of Inner Mongolia

This porcelaneous white vase with ovoid body, rounded shoulder, and a long neck with an inverted flattened mouth has a low foot and a recessed flat base. Three indented lines decorate the shoulder; on opposite sides of the body are raised double straps that extend from the shoulder to the bottom of the body. At the top and bottom of each pair of straps are two horizontal bridge-shaped loops. The entire vase is glazed except for the foot-ring.

Vases with ovoid bodies, high rounded shoulders, and long necks with shallow dish-shaped mouths have been identified as a distinctive ceramic type that exemplifies the stylistic transition between late Tang and early Liao wares.[1] The loops and raised ribs on the body are also signature elements of tenth-century ceramics. The impressed concentric circles at either end of the loops, which mimic metal bosses, suggest that the shape of the vase was borrowed from a leather, metal, or wood prototype.

By the seventh century, white wares produced in northern China were characterized by a compact and translucent body. By the mid-eighth century, as evidenced by *The Classic of Tea* (*Cha jing*), an analogy was drawn between fine white wares from the Xing kilns in Hebei Province and silver and snow, the former for its impressive thinness and brightness and the later for its whiteness. Excavations at Samarra in Iraq and Fustat (ancient Cairo) in Egypt show that large quantities of northern Chinese white wares, as well as lead-glazed wares and southern green wares, were exported to the west by the mid-ninth century. Among over ten thousand Chinese ceramic shards found in Fustat (site no later than 969), fragments of vases similar in form to this vase, decorated with loop handles, were found.[2]

HMS

---

1. For an example, see *Kaogu xuebao* 1956.3, pl. 8.3.
2. For an introduction to the discoveries of Chinese ceramics in South Asia and the Middle East, see Mikami Tsugio, *Tōji bōekishi kenkyū* [*Studies on the history of export ceramics*], vol. 2, pp. 29–70.

106. Vase decorated with a phoenix head

Liao dynasty, eleventh century
From the walled city of Qingzhou,
Suoboriga Township, Balin Right Banner
Lead-glazed earthenware
Height: 48.1 cm;
diameter of mouth: 12.5 cm;
diameter of base: 8.1 cm
Museum of Balin Right Banner

This tall vase has an ovoid body that tapers to a flared foot. Rising from the round shoulder is an elongated neck topped by a phoenix head with a foliate crest that flares into the dish-shaped mouth of the vessel. The entire body is covered with a lustrous amber-yellow glaze. The phoenix head is powerfully rendered, with bulging eyes and a sharp beak. Most Liao vases of this type are tall, usually ranging from thirty centimeters to fifty centimeters high.

Metal phoenix-head vases originated in Central Asia. The form was translated into ceramics in Tang China, and a handle was added for easier handling, turning the vase into a ewer (fig. 114). It is uncertain if the Liao phoenix-head vases were direct descendants of the Tang lead-glazed ewers. However, some archaeological evidence points toward a possible continuity in style and use. In the tomb of Zhang Shigu (d. 1108; buried 1117) at Xuanhua, Hebei Province, a mural depicting wine serving includes a white (possibly silver) phoenix-head ewer, indicating that the form existed at the end of the Liao dynasty (fig. 115). Three fluted lines decorate the shoulder of the ewer. Similar fluted lines can also be seen on the neck of a white phoenix-head ewer, which is identified as Xicun ware from Guangdong Province dating from the tenth to eleventh century, in the collection of the British Museum, indicating trade contacts between Liao territory and the far south of China via sea.[1]

Similar vases covered in green glaze have been recovered from several Liao tombs, including Tomb Number 2 (mid-eleventh century) at Qinghemen in Yixian, Tomb Number 1 (early

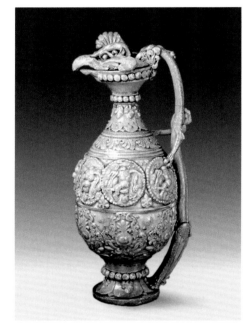

eleventh century) at Shuiquan in Beipiao, and a tomb (late tenth or early eleventh century) at Qianchuanghu Village in Chaoyang, Liaoning Province.[2] In the tomb in Chaoyang,

two phoenix-head vases, two bag-shaped flasks, and a lidded ewer with a globular body, all of them green-glazed, were found in the west side-chamber. In the east side-chamber of the tomb were two more flasks, a cup, and a basin, again all of them green-glazed. It seems that these green-glazed wares were meant to make a complete set for drinking or serving wine. Such grouping is further confirmed by the recent discovery of a mural painting in a tomb at Zhaoduba in Chaoyang. Instead of green, the set represented in the mural is yellow, like this vase.[3]

HMS

1. For a picture of the white ewer, see Shelagh J. Vainker, *Chinese Pottery and Porcelain: From Prehistory to the Present*, p. 131.
2. See *Kaogu xuebao* 1954.8, p. 177, fig. 10.4; *Wenwu cankao ziliao* 1958.2, p. 13, fig. 21, right; *Wenwu* 1980.12, p. 18, fig. 2; p. 20, figs. 6–7, 9, 11–14.
3. See *Beifang wenwu* 2002.2, pl. 3.2.

Fig. 114. Phoenix-headed ewer with moulded decoration; Tang dynasty (618–907); stoneware with celadon glaze; height: 41.9 cm. Collection of the Palace Museum, Beijing

Fig. 115. Southeast wall of the rear chamber of the tomb of Zhang Shigu (died 1108; buried 1117) in Xuanhua, Hebei Province

107a–d. Set of drinking vessels: ewer, bowl, cup, and cup stand

Liao dynasty, late tenth
or early eleventh century
Excavated in Beizifu Town, Aohan Banner
Stoneware with transparent glaze
a. Ewer: height: 22.5 cm;
diameter of mouth: 4.8 cm;
diameter of base: 8.6 cm
b. Bowl: height: 7.8 cm;
diameter of mouth: 19.6 cm;
diameter of base: 8 cm

c. Cup: height: 6 cm;
diameter of mouth: 8.8 cm;
diameter of base: 4.6 cm
d. Cup stand: height: 3.8 cm;
diameter of mouth: 15.2 cm;
diameter of base: 8.3 cm
Museum of Aohan Banner

This spouted ewer, large bowl, cup, and cup stand form a typical set of vessels for wine drinking. The ewer has a straight neck, a short curved spout, a stepped handle, and a globular body; it is decorated with two facing bands of lotus petals, one upright and one inverted, on its shoulder and body. The domed cover has a deep collar and an elegant bud-shaped finial. The base has an incised inscription reading *guan* (government official). The bowl is decorated with carved lotus petals on its exterior. The cup, embellished with matching lotus-petal motifs in low relief, has a deep curved belly and a somewhat tall foot-ring. A ring rises from the center of the cup stand, which has a foliate lip, to hold the foot of the cup firmly in place. All four objects are made of fine grayish-white stoneware that is covered with a transparent glaze. A slanting blade was used to carve or incise the decorative elements on these pieces, resulting in different thicknesses of glaze.

These drinking vessels took their form from silver prototypes (compare cat. 88, 89). A number of ceramic vessels similar in shape and grouping have been found in Liao tombs, including a set in green glaze from Tomb Number 3 (datable to the late tenth or early eleventh century) at Daiqintala Township in Keyou Central Banner, Inner Mongolia, and several Yue celadon wares found in the tomb of Han Yi (d. 995) in Beijing. One ewer that was also incised at the bottom with a *guan* character was found in the tomb (dated 959) of Xiao Qulie in Chifeng City, Inner Mongolia.[1] Such ceramic ewers continued to be popular, and examples have been recovered from tombs dating into the eleventh century.[2]

Fig. 116. South wall, rear chamber of the tomb (dated 1116) of Zhang Shiqing in Xuanhua, Hebei Province

Mural paintings in Liao tombs like those found in the Zhang family tombs in Xuanhua, Hebei Province, illustrate the occasions and settings in which such a group of vessels might have been used to serve wine (fig. 116).

HMS

1. See Wei Jian, ed., *Neimenggu wenwu kaogu wenji* [*Essays on the archaeology of cultural relics in Inner Mongolia*], vol. 2, p. 660, fig. 9; p. 661, figs. 10.2, 10.5; *Kaogu xuebao* 1956.3, pl. 7.1; *Kaogu* 1960.2, p. 20, fig. 3.

2. For example, see *Wenwu* 1980.12, pl. 3.3; p. 28, fig. 31; *Wenwu* 1983.9, p. 30, figs. 2.2–2.3.

108. Large basin decorated with floral patterns

Liao dynasty, eleventh century
Discovered in Tongliao City
Stoneware with transparent glaze
and green pigment
Height: 5.4 cm; diameter: 34.9 cm
Museum of Tongliao City

This large basin has an everted rim, slightly tapering sides, and a flat bottom. A lotus roundel with pointed petals and noticeable seed pods dominates the bottom of the interior, and four full peony flowers with leaves decorate the sides. Three tiny fish are interspersed at roughly equal intervals around the lotus. Executed in sgraffito—with the white slip cut away to expose the coarse, pink-brown body—these flowers and fish are accented with green glaze along their contours. The milky-white glaze has cracking throughout. An unrecognizable character is written in ink at the center of the exterior of the flat bottom.

Large white wares with decoration executed in sgraffito and accented with green pigments form a small but distinctive group among Liao ceramics; in addition to large basins like this one, this group also includes several tall vases (fig. 117).[1] It is likely that these vessels were products of the Nanshan kilns, situated to the south of the Supreme Capital in modern Balin Left Banner; the kilns specialized in firing glazed wares tinted in green.[2]

Since no extant examples of Liao sgraffito basins come from dated sites, it is difficult to establish their dates. Comparisons with the lotus motifs in the centers of the lead-glazed bowls excavated from the tomb (late tenth or early eleventh century) at Qianchuanghu Village in Chaoyang and Tomb Number 3 (late eleventh century) at Beiling in Kazuo, Liaoning Province, suggest that this large basin, which was discovered in Tongliao City in 1996, dates from the eleventh century.[3]

HMS

1. For extant examples, see *Wenwu ziliao congkan* 1987.10, p. 179, fig. 4, pl. 8.3; *Neimenggu wenwu kaogu* 2000.2, p. 87; 1996.2; p. 78, fig. 1; p. 80, fig. 2; *Kaogu yu wenwu* 1999.6, p. 18, fig. 5.5; Feng Yongqian, *Dongbei kaogu yanjiu* [*Essays on the archaeology of northeast China*], vol. 1, p. 299, fig. 13; *Wenwu* 1975.12, p. 34, fig. 10.

2. Lu Jing, *Liao dai taoci* [*Liao-dynasty ceramics*], p. 36, fig. 2.90; pp. 112–14.

3. See *Wenwu* 1980.12, p. 20, fig. 14; p. 28, fig. 32.

Fig. 117. Vase with long neck and foliate mouth, decorated with a flowering plant incised through white slip and touches of green glaze; Liao dynasty, eleventh century; height: 37.7 cm

109. Lobed Bowl

Song dynasty, 1018 or earlier
From the tomb of the Princess of Chen
and Xiao Shaoju at Qinglongshan Town,
Naiman Banner
Stoneware with green glaze
Height: 7 cm; diameter of mouth: 19 cm;
diameter of base: 6.4 cm
Research Institute of Cultural Relics
and Archaeology of Inner Mongolia

110. Lobed bowl decorated with chrysanthemums

Song dynasty, 1018 or earlier
From the tomb of the Princess of Chen
and Xiao Shaoju at Qinglongshan Town,
Naiman Banner
Stoneware with green glaze
Height: 4.6 cm; diameter of mouth: 17 cm;
diameter of base: 10.7 cm
Research Institute of Cultural Relics
and Archaeology of Inner Mongolia

In addition to ceramic forms closely linked with the Khitan lifestyle—such as the so-called cockscomb flask (cat. 39–41) and chicken-leg or ox-leg bottle (cat. 42)—ceramics produced by Song-dynasty potters existed in Liao territory. Fine Song ceramics were imported by the Liao as luxury items for the pleasure of those who could afford them. The imported ceramics ranged from Ding white ware to bluish-white (qingbai) ware to Yaozhou and Yue celadon wares; examples of all of these were found in the tomb (dated 1018) of the Princess of Chen and Xiao Shaoju.

By the end of the eighth century, the Yue celadon wares produced in present-day Zhejiang Province, in the area that was to become the Wuyue kingdom (907–978), had become the most celebrated type of ceramics in all of China. They were admired for the lustrous verdant green color of their glazes, their fine clay bodies, and their elegant shapes. The Shanglinhu kiln complex there, which had manufactured late-Tang "tribute porcelain," continued to produce large quantities of superb green ware thanks to demand for it and to attentive management on the part of the Qian clan, the ruling house of the Wuyue kingdom. Despite the Wuyue kingdom's pledge of allegiance to the Northern Song dynasty in 978, Yue celadon wares made there were not only presented to the imperial courts of the Latter Zhou (951–60) and the subsequent Northern Song (960–1127) but also exported overseas.

The Yue lobed bowl decorated with chrysanthemums (cat. 110) has thin sides and a somewhat tall foot-ring that curls outward in

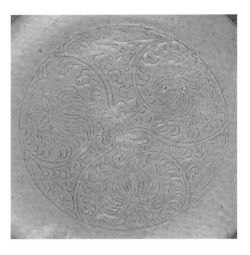

a manner evocative of metalwork. Incised at the center of the bowl are scrolls of chrysanthemums spreading out from a central flower. There is a guan (government official) mark on the base of the bowl. Only a few other Yue green wares bearing such marks have been discovered, and they are all associated with the imperial family of Wuyue.[1] Although the precise meaning of the guan mark is uncertain, it seems to be related to a court taste that developed out of an affection for gold and silver wares and copies of them made of fine ceramics.[2]

In the North, Yaozhou green ware emerged in the Shaanxi area during the late Tang period and flourished during the Northern Song era. It was known for the carving of decorative motifs with a slanting blade, showing contours in depth, and the subtle hue of the glossy, olive-green glaze. Yaozhou celadon wares have been discovered in a number of Liao tombs. That a Yaozhou lobed bowl (cat. 109) was included in the tomb of

the Princess of Chen and her husband indicates the high regard Yaozhou ware enjoyed in the Liao era.[3]

HMS

1. See Wenwu 1975.8, p. 71, figs. 6, 7; Mou Yongkang and Ren Shilong, "Guan, Ge jianlun" [Brief discussion of Guan and Ge wares], Hunan kaogu jikan 1986.3, p. 253.
2. Xie Mingliang, "Youguan 'guan' han 'xin guan' kuan baici guan zi hanyi de jige wenti" [On interpreting the meaning of the guan character in the guan and xin guan inscriptions seen on some white wares], Gugong xueshu jikan 5.2 (Winter 1987), pp. 1–38.
3. For comparable examples from the kiln site, see Wudai Huangpu yaozhi [Five Dynasties kiln site in Huangpu], p. 122, figs. 65.4, 65.6, pls. 55.4–55.6.

111. Pillow in the form of a tiger

Song or Liao dynasty, eleventh century
Excavated in Bayan'erdeng Township,
Balin Right Banner
Porcelaneous stoneware with transparent glaze
Length: 15.5 cm; width: 12.8 cm;
height: 9.4 cm
Museum of Balin Right Banner

The top of this small pillow is concave, and the base, in the form of a crouching tiger, is lobed at the four corners. One end of the pillow is modeled into the large, grinning face of the tiger. The appliquéd round eyes and dramatically raised eyebrows enhance the fierce look of the tiger. Made of fine grayish-white clay, the entire pillow, except for the base, is covered with transparent glaze. Traces of vermillion red color in the nostrils and on the eyes indicate that at least part of the piece was originally painted with cinnabar.

Ceramic pillows in animal forms appeared in China no later than the ninth century. Although extant examples have come primarily from tombs, what they might have been used for is unclear. Comparable examples in the form of a tiger include a Yue celadon pillow excavated in 1977 from Shangpu in Shangyu, Zhejiang Province (tenth century); a Jingdezhen bluish-white ware excavated in 1953 from Hanyang in Hubei Province (eleventh century);[1] and a brown pillow excavated from the Tang-dynasty port city of Yangzhou, Jiangsu Province (ninth to tenth century).

Historical texts and stories show that during the Tang dynasty, auspicious meanings were attached to pillows in animal forms. According to the *Jiu Tangshu* (Old History of the Tang Dynasty), in the early eighth century pillows in the form of a leopard head were used to ward off evil spirits, and pillows in the form of a crouching bear were used to promote fertility.[2] Besides, a Tang-dynasty story entitled "A Journey through a

Pillow" recounts the journey a person named Lu took while sleeping on a celadon pillow that was offered to him by a Daoist magician.[3] Therefore, it is plausible that the tiger pillow in the exhibition was offered to the dead because of its auspicious meaning. That the pillow was once painted with cinnabar, a primary ingredient used in the elixirs of Daoist Outer Alchemy, is in line with this theory.

HMS

1. For a picture of this find, see *Zhongguo wenwu jinghua da cidian: Taoci juan* [*Encyclopedia of Chinese cultural relics: Ceramics*], p. 310, pl. 475.
2. See *Xin Tangshu* [*New history of the Tang dynasty*], juan 37, p. 1377.
3. See *Tang ren xiaoshuo jiaoshi* [*Collated and annotated collection of Tang-dynasty stories*], vol. 1, pp. 23–25.

112a–e. Set of five nesting boxes

Liao dynasty, eleventh
or early twelfth century
From a tomb at Jiefangyingzi,
Wengniute Banner
Lead-glazed earthenware
Overall height: 21.9 cm;
diameter of mouth: 6.6–12.6 cm;
diameter of base: 8.5–14.7 cm
Museum of Chifeng City

This set of nesting boxes was excavated from a tomb in which two more sets of nesting boxes were found. The tomb, at Jiefangyingzi in Wengniute Banner, Inner Mongolia, is datable to the late Liao period.[3]

HMS

1. See Niigata kenritsu kindai bijutsukan, ed., *Tō kōtei kara no okurimono* [*Gifts of the Tang emperors: Hidden treasures from Famen Temple*], pp. 170–71.
2. See *Wenwu* 2000.2, p. 21, fig. 29; *Huaxia kaogu* 1988.3, p. 37, fig. 5.
3. For the excavation report, see *Kaogu* 1979.4, pp. 330–34.

Fig. 118. *Boluozi* boxes, gilded silver; from the relic deposit (dated 874) underneath Famen Pagoda in Fufeng, Shaanxi Province

Each of the five nesting boxes, covered in amber-brown glaze, in this set was made by a mould impression into an oblong shape with four lobes on the sides. Echoing the shape of the box is a four-lobed opening on the convex side of each box; on either side of the opening are diamond shapes and strings of pearls, all made in a style that mimics metal repoussé. While the shape of the boxes derives from Sasanian metalware, sets of nesting boxes have origins in China.

The relic deposit (dated 874) underneath Famen Pagoda in Fufeng, Shaanxi Province, yielded a luxurious set of five nesting boxes made of gilded silver (fig. 118). Scholars have suggested that these boxes might have been the *boluozi* that were listed on the accompanying inventory carved in stone. Because the *boluozi* were included in a sequence of vessels related to incense, it can be inferred that they were containers for precious incense and formed part of a larger set of vessels used for incense burning.[1]

A small number of nesting boxes made of fine celadon have been discovered in tombs of people of very high status, including the tomb (dated 939) of Queen Ma of the Wuyue kingdom and the tomb (dated 1000) of Empress Li of the Song dynasty.[2] All of these celadon nesting boxes were Yue ware from northern Zhejiang Province.

113. Ewer in the form of a dragon-fish

Liao dynasty, second half
of the eleventh century
From Kezuo Central Banner, Tongliao City
Lead-glazed earthenware
Height: 22.3 cm; length: 30 cm;
diameter of base: 9 cm
Museum of Tongliao City

This ewer is in the shape of a dragon-fish reclining on a lotus flower. Between the wings and the tail is a handle in the form of a flowing cloud; behind the creature's horn is a square opening, for pouring water into the ewer; the pearl in its open mouth is the spout. The vessel is made of two moulded halves, each of which is full of details, such as scales and raised eyebrows, rendered in relief. A round solid foot supports the lotus flower on which the dragon-fish reclines. The ewer is covered with white slip and glossy lead glazes.

Indian in origin, the image of the dragon-fish (*makara*) became popular in China during the

Tang dynasty, and its popularity continued through the twelfth century. It was a favored motif in the art of the Liao and appeared in various mediums, ranging from metalwork to ceramics to stone carvings (see cat. 25, 26, 84, 87). Comparable examples covered with lead glazes include an ewer from Fuxin in Liaoning Province and a flask from Yushulinzi in Ningcheng, Inner Mongolia.[1] A lamp in the shape of a dragon-fish, covered with fine celadon glaze, was found in Tomb Number 1 at Shuiquan in Beipiao, Liaoning Province (fig. 119).[2]

Vessels in anthropomorphic or animal shapes form a distinctive group among Liao lead-glazed wares and white wares. Motifs ranging from turtles, cats, and mandarin ducks to a mythical creature with a human head and the body of a winged fish (fig. 120) were adopted to make the sculptural body of a vessel.

HMS

1. Feng Yongqian, *Dongbei kaogu yanjiu* [*Essays on the archaeology of Northeast China*], vol. 1, p. 232, figs. 7, 9.
2. See *Wenwu* 1977.12, p. 51, fig. 19.1.

Fig. 119. Green lamp in the form of a dragon-fish, excavated from Tomb Number 1 at Shuiquan in Beipiao, Liaoning Province; collection of the Liaoning Provincial Museum

Fig. 120. White ewer in the form of a mythical creature with a human head; excavated in Balin Left Banner, Inner Mongolia; collection of the Museum of Chifeng City

114a–b. Two square dishes decorated with peonies

Liao dynasty, second half
of the eleventh century
Excavated from Xiaoliuzhangzi,
Ningcheng County
Lead-glazed earthenware
Height: 2.8 cm; diameter of mouth: 12.5 cm;
diameter of base: 8 cm
Museum of Chifeng City

Distinguished by scalloped rims, these two square dishes with flat bottoms were made of similar mould impressions with similar designs. At the center of the bottom of the interior of each dish is a peony in full bloom, and there is a leaf in each of the corners; on the four sides are more flowers, as well as cloud patterns. The pink clay of the body was covered with a white slip that was embellished with patches of green and amber-yellow glazes to give a design of three colors. Moulded vines along the rim, at the corners, and in the middle of each side are highlighted with yellow glaze. Three spur marks are on the bottom of each of the dishes.[1]

Square ceramic dishes, in imitation of wood or metal prototypes, were popular among the Liao during the eleventh and twelfth centuries. Similar pieces in three-color glaze have been found in the tomb (dated 1089) of Xiao Xiaozhong in Jinxi, Liaoning Province, and a late-Liao tomb in Fenning, Hebei Province.[2] White square dishes have also been recovered from the tombs of high-ranking individuals and from Buddhist relic deposits in pagodas.[3]

HMS

12.5, 12.6. Six white square dishes were retrieved from the relic deposit (dated 1043) on top of the North Pagoda in Chaoyang, Liaoning Province. Three more dishes were retrieved from the relic deposit (dated 1044) underneath the foundation of the same pagoda. See *Wenwu* 1992.7, p. 12, fig. 24; pls. 5.3, 5.4; p. 25, figs. 57, 58. Three intact dishes were found in the Yexian Pagoda in Miyun, Beijing; ten dishes were found in the Liao pagoda in Fangshan, Beijing. See *Wenwu* 1994.2, p. 60, figs. 5, 6; *Kaogu* 1980.2, p. 156, fig. 13.1, pl. 10.2. Nine square dishes white in color were found in Tomb Number 5 at Chuangjinfou in Balin Right Banner, Inner Mongolia; see *Wenwu* 2002.3, figs. 24.3, 24.5, 27, 28.

---

1. For an excavation report of the site where these dishes were found, see *Wenwu* 1961.9, pp. 44–49. Evidence of the mould impression method has been found at the Liao kiln site at Longquanwu in Beijing. See *Beijing Longquanwu yao fajue baogao* [*Excavation of the Longquanwu kiln site in Beijing*], p. 182, fig. 59; p. 183, pl. 57.1.
2. See *Kaogu* 1960.2, p. 35, fig. 1.3; 1993.10, p. 957, fig. 1.5.
3. For example, fragments were unearthed from Tomb Number 2 at Qinghemen in Yixian, Liaoning Province. See *Kaogu xuebao* 1954.8, p. 179, fig. 14.4; pls.

115a–c. Three inkstones

a. Drum-shaped inkstone
Liao dynasty, second half
of the eleventh century
Excavated in Shifo Village,
Ningcheng County
Lead-glazed earthenware
Height: 8 cm; diameter: 21.9 cm
Museum of Ningcheng County

b. Octagonal inkstone
and basin combined
Liao dynasty, 1070 or earlier
Excavated from a tomb in
Toudaoyingzi Village, Ningcheng County
Lead-glazed earthenware
Height: 12.6 cm; diameter: 22 cm
Research Institute of Cultural Relics and
Archaeology of Inner Mongolia

c. Round inkstone
Liao dynasty, second half
of the eleventh century
Excavated from the kiln site
at Gangwayao Village, Chifeng City
Earthenware
Height: 6.7 cm; diameter: 21.9 cm
Research Institute of Cultural Relics
and Archaeology of Inner Mongolia

The drum-shaped inkstone (cat. 115a) with a slanted, cloud-shaped ink pool in the middle is an extraordinary example of Liao lead-glazed ceramics in terms of the brilliant color of the glaze and the crisply moulded designs. The ink pool is rendered as a lotus pond in yellow against a green ground of waves. Surrounding the ink pool are auspicious motifs such as butterflies, clouds, and peonies. Four panels on which dragons are depicted alternate with columns of white flowers to decorate the sides of the inkstone. Bright green, brown, and transparent glazes were applied throughout, except at the high end of the ink pool, which was deliberately left unglazed so that the exposed clay body could be used for ink grinding. Interestingly, the concave base of the inkstone is also glazed, making it possible to convert the inkstone into a basin when it is flipped over.

The octagonal inkstone (cat. 115b) was excavated from a Liao tomb dated 1070 at Toudaoyingzi Village in Ningcheng County, Inner Mongolia. Similar to the drum-shaped inkstone, the top of the octagonal inkstone is decorated with a lotus pond and floral motifs. On the eight vertical sides of the inkstone are more flowers moulded in relief. The octagonal shape of the inkstone, along with the yellow-glaze border, is associated with gilded-silver vessels, on which this inkstone was modeled.

Unlike the drum-shaped inkstone, the octagonal inkstone is composed of two parts—an inkstone and a separate basin. It has been suggested that inkstones of two-part construction were forerunners of double-sided inkstones.

The unglazed earthenware inkstone (cat. 115c) was an unfinished piece retrieved from the Liao kiln site at Gangwayao Village in Chifeng City, Inner Mongolia, where large quantities of lead-glazed shards were found. It has a high-fired clay body that is finely modeled with crisply moulded designs. In other examples, white slip would have been applied to the inkstone to enhance the contrast of the glaze colors. After glazing, the inkstone would have been fired again at a lower temperature.[1]

HMS

---

1. See [Jia] Zhoujie, "Chifeng Gangwayaocun Liao dai ciyao diaocha ji" [Survey of the Liao-dynasty kiln site at Gangwayao Village in Chifeng], *Kaogu* 1973.4, pp. 241–43; Feng Yongqian, "Chifeng Gangwayaocun Liao dai ciyaozhi de kaogu xin faxian" [New archaeological discoveries at the Liao-dynasty kiln site at Gangwayao Village in Chifeng], *Zhongguo gudai yaozhi diaocha fajue baogaoji*, pp. 386–92.

116a–b. Two plates with foliate rim

Liao dynasty, second half
of the eleventh century
Excavated in Xiaoliuzhangzi,
Ningcheng County
Lead-glazed earthenware
Height: 2 cm; length: 26 cm
Research Institute of Cultural Relics
and Archaeology of Inner Mongolia

In these two shallow oblong plates with four bracket lobes along the rims, both the shape and surface decoration were formed and impressed from a mould before white slip was applied over the buff pink body. The flat bottom of the plates is unglazed, showing the rust color of the clay. While a moulded lotus pond with fish is the central motif of one of the plates, the other has a simple pond with three opened-up lotus flowers; both are popular decorative motifs on Liao artifacts (compare cat. 83, 115a–b).

Unlike the moulded decorations on the ink-stones (cat. 115a–c), which have a relief quality, these plates are decorated with patterns executed in fine lines. The lines are so thin that they risk being obscured by the white slip and opaque glazes applied on top of them.

The shallow oblong plate with foliate rim is a typical Liao shape. It is based on gold and silver prototypes; the shape, including the bracket rim, would have been relatively easy to produce in sheet metal, and less easy to produce in clay—as evidenced by the crooked edges of one of these plates (cat. 116b).[1]

These two plates were recovered from Tombs M2 and M4 at Xiaoliuzhangzi in Ningcheng County, Inner Mongolia (datable to the late eleventh century).[2]

HMS

1. A silver plate similar in shape and decoration came from a hoard in Balin Right Banner. See *Wenwu* 1980.5, p. 48, fig. 10.
2. See *Wenwu* 1961.9, p. 46, fig. 4.6; pl. 2.

117. Basin with inscriptions in Arabic

Persian (western Iranian), tenth century
From the tomb of the Princess of Chen
and Xiao Shaoju at Qinglongshan Town
in Naiman Banner
Bronze
Height: 19 cm; diameter of mouth: 57 cm;
diameter of base: 33 cm
Research Institute of Cultural Relics
and Archaeology of Inner Mongolia

This deep basin with flaring sides on a flat base, which was excavated from the rear chamber of the tomb (dated 1018) of the Princess of Chen and Xiao Shaoju, was an import from western Iran. The basin and seven other glassware vessels found in the tomb form a distinctive group of luxurious items imported from the Islamic world. Made of hammered bronze with sparse engraved decorations, the basin is notable for its large size and unusual decorations.

The main decorations engraved on the basin are a row of pseudowriting in fine lines along the interior of the rim and a six-pointed star on the bottom. Instead of transcribing a passage of a text, the Arabic inscription turns the word *Allah* into a decorative form that is repeated over and over to form a continuous band. The six-pointed star, or Solomon's seal, is composed of two overlapping triangles and dominates the center of the bottom of the basin. In the middle of the star is a circle, whose meaning is unclear. Surrounding the

star is a circlet of punched rings resembling fish roe. The background area of the star is filled with the same fish-roe rings. Similar six-pointed stars are seen on shards excavated from Nishapur and Susa in eastern Persia as well as from Samarra in Iraq.[1]

HMS

1. See Charles K. Wilkinson, *Nishapur: Pottery of the Early Islamic Period*, pp. 183, 194, figs. 1a, 1b.

118a–l. An ingot and eleven coins

a. Ingot
Song dynasty, eleventh or early
twelfth century
From Dayingzi Rural Area, Linxi County
Silver
Length: 14.8 cm; width: 9 cm;
thickness: 2.1 cm
Cultural Relics Management Institute
of Linxi County

b–l. Eleven coins
Liao dynasty, tenth through twelfth century
From Xinchengzi Town, Linxi County
Copper
Diameter: 2.2–2.51 cm;
thickness: 0.1–0.15 cm
Cultural Relics Management Institute
of Linxi County

The silver ingot has raised rims on its edges and an inscription engraved in Chinese on one side. Part of the inscription reads "forty-nine taels and seven," referring to the weight of the ingot. The eleven copper coins discovered in Xinchengzi Town, Linxi County, have a square opening in the middle surrounded by four Chinese characters written in clerical script. The coins date from different periods of the Liao era, the earliest from the Tonghe period (983–1012) of Emperor Shengzong's reign (r. 982–1031) and the latest from the Tianqing era (1111–21) of Emperor Tianzuo's reign (r. 1101–25), toward the end of the Liao dynasty. Copper coins were often found in Chinese tombs, and Liao tombs are no exception. They were also frequently found in relic deposits and hoards dating from earlier periods, possibly placed there for auspicious reasons. However, a majority of the coins found in Liao sites are Song rather than Liao in origin. For example, at the White Pagoda in Balin Right Banner 490 coins have been found within or near the deposit (dated 1049) on top of the pagoda, but none of them are Liao. Among the some 60,000 coins discovered in a hoard at the site of the Supreme Capital in Balin Left Banner, only 44 are of Liao origin.[1]

By the end of the tenth century, the circulation of money increased in the Liao state, thanks to the exploitation of the natural resource, copper. However, large quantities of Song copper coins entered the Liao empire, both in payment for Liao commodities and as part of the Song's annual tribute to the Liao. Su Che (1039–1112), who visited Liao territory during the later part of the Liao dynasty, was so astounded by the number of Song coins in use in the northern empire that he suggested iron coins be made available in the Song border regions as a protective measure.[2]

As a result of the Treaty of Shanyuan in 1005 between the Liao and the Song, the Liao received an annual payment of a hundred thousand taels of silver and two hundred thousand bolts of silk from the Song. In 1042, the amount increased to two hundred taels of silver and three hundred thousand bolts of silk. The silver ingot is, therefore, an example of the tribute items presented by the Song to the Liao.

HMS

---

1. A study of four hoards excavated in the area of Balin Right Banner and Balin Left Banner reveals that Liao coins were as few as 0.1 percent to 0.3 percent of the finds. See Wulanchabu bowuguan, "Chayouhouqi Shimenkou Jin dai yizhi fajue jianbao" [Brief report on the excavation of a Jin-dynasty site at Shimenkou in Chayou Rear Banner], in Li Yiyou and Wei Jian (eds.), *Neimenggu wenwu kaogu wenji* [*Essays on the Archaeology of cultural relics in Inner Mongolia*], vol. 1, pp. 585–95.
2. Karl A. Wittfogel and Fêng Chia-shêng, *History of Chinese Society: Liao, 907–1125*, p. 183.

119. Lined and padded pants

Early Liao dynasty
From a tomb in Xiaojingzi,
Aluke'erqin Banner
Pongee silk
Length: 112 cm
Museum of Aluke'erqin Banner

This pair of pants was found in a tomb in Xiaojingzi, Aluke'erqin Banner, dating from the early Liao dynasty.[1] The trousers are tied at the waist on the back with two broad attached sashes. A pair of attached suspenders provides additional support. The crotch is not sewn together.[2] Socks are sewn to the bottom of the legs.

So far, only one other pair of trousers with attached socks has been documented. Among the more than twenty textiles found in the tomb of an unidentified couple of noble rank in Daiqintala Township, Keyou Central Banner, there were three pairs of trousers.[3] They are fastened in the same way as the pair from Xiaojingzi: they are tightened at the back with two broad sashes and have additional suspenders for support;[4] one of them (height 144 cm, width 27 cm) also has socks sewn onto the bottom of the legs.[5] The three pairs of trousers found in the tomb in Daiqintala are less well preserved than the pair from Xiaojingzi. Through the creases and the damaged areas around the knees, it is possible to reconstruct how the trousers were folded when they were placed near the tomb's occupants. The Xiaojingzi trousers do not show any traces of being folded and therefore might have been used to dress the deceased. Of course, the many layers of garments worn by deceased members of the Khitan elite deteriorated over time, as did other textiles found in Liao tombs.[6]

Among the textiles found in the tomb at Daiqintala, there was also an undergarment made from gauze. It has slits for the thighs and a closed crotch and would have been worn underneath the trousers found in the tomb.[7]

SLG

1. Zhao Feng, *Liao Textiles and Costumes*, p. 27.
2. Zhao Feng, *Liao Textiles and Costumes*, p. 206.
3. For the excavation report, see "Keyou zhongqi Daiqintala liaodai qingli jianbao [Brief report on the investigations of the Liao-dynasty tombs in Daiqintala, Keyou Central Banner]," *Neimenggu wenwu kaogu wenji* 1997.2, pp. 651–67.
4. For an illustration of the pair of trousers with a straight-cut leg, see *Wenwu* 2002.4, fig. 19, p. 63; for the pair of trousers with a broad-cut leg, see Zhao Feng (ed.), *Recent Excavations of Textiles in China*, p. 125, no. 51.
5. For an illustration of the pair of trousers, see Zhao Feng, *Recent Excavations*, p. 124, no. 50. For a drawing of the cut of the trousers, see Zhao Feng, *Liao Textiles and Costumes*, p. 206, fig. 262. Measurements are taken from the upper part of the leg at the waistline. Zhao Feng, *Recent Excavations*, p. 124, no. 50.
6. For an example of a tomb in which the female occupant was lavishly dressed, in Tuerjishan, Kezuohou Banner, Tongliao, Inner Mongolia, see Cang Wangling, "Tuerjishan mu: Sheng yu si de mimi pei zang qidan nuzi" [The tomb in Tuerji Hill: The secret death and life as seen in a tomb of a Khitan-woman]," *Wenwu tiandi* 2003.3, pp. 20–27.
7. For an illustration of the undergarment, see Zhao Feng, *Recent Excavations*, p. 127, no. 53.

120a–b. Patchwork

Liao dynasty, early or mid-tenth century
From Tomb Number 3, Daiqintala
Township, Keyou Central Banner,
Xing'an League
Silk, satin, gauze, samite, tabby
Length: 90 cm; width: 46 cm
Museum of the Inner Mongolia
Autonomous Region

This patchwork was among more than twenty textiles found in the tomb of an unidentified couple in Daiqintala Township.[1] Its shape resembles a six-pointed star that has been extended vertically; originally, the lower and the upper halves were not separated. Small patches of different silk fabrics in shades of brown are sewn together in a symmetric pattern on both halves of the patchwork's front side The most prominent of them is made of satin samite[2] with a pattern of flying geese and flowers. This rectangular patch is in the center of each half and stands out in contrast to the two other main patches. The borders of these three patches are decorated with small knots with loops. From the damaged middle section and lower and upper points on the left-hand side, one can see that the patchwork was once folded. The only other patchwork similar in shape and design is in the collection of the Cleveland Museum of Art, in Cleveland, Ohio.[3] It is less well preserved and considerably smaller in size (53 cm by 25.7 cm), with no knots sewn onto it. Variations of the flying-geese motif are found on two jackets and one of the two robes discovered in Daiqintala.[4] Although the identity of the couple of noble rank buried in the tomb at Daiqintala is unknown, fragments of the same material used in these robes were found in the tomb of Yelü Yuzhi (dated 942) and help to date the Daiqintala tomb to the early or mid-tenth century.[5]

Patchwork is an economical way of using scraps of textiles left over from other projects to make a larger piece of decorative fabric. Often this method is used for banners, pouches, and face covers or other small articles.[6] The function and aesthetics associated

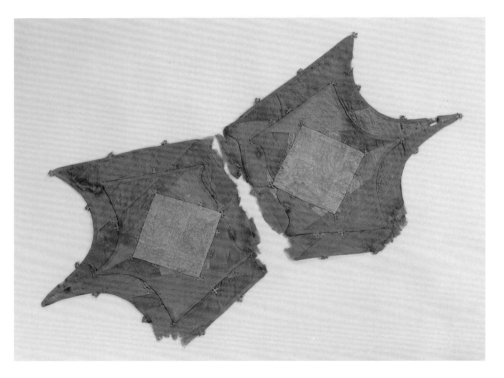

with this particular patchwork remain unclear. With its pointed ends, it seems likely to have been a banner rather than part of a robe, although close analyses of the patches and related texts will need to be done before its usage can be determined.

SLG

1. *Wenwu* 2002.4, p. 68. See Meng Jianren and Piao Chunyue, "Keyouzhongqi Daiqintala Liao mu qingli jianbao" [Brief report on the clearing of a Liao tomb at Daiqintala, Keyou Central Banner], *Neimenggu wenwu kaogu wenji*, vol. 2, pp. 651–67.

2. Zhao Feng uses this term, which corresponds to a weft-faced compound satin binding. Zhao Feng, *Recent Excavations of Textiles in China*, p. 130, no. 55. For a dis-

cussion of the development of weft-faced compound twill and satin binding during the Liao dynasty, see Zhao Feng, "Satin Samite: A Bridge from Samite to Satin," *CIETA-Bulletin* 76 (1999), pp. 46–63.

3. For an illustration of the patchwork, see Zhao Feng, *Liao Dynasty Costumes and Textiles*, p. 245, fig. 307.

4. For an illustration of the two jackets, see Zhao Feng, *Recent Excavations*, p. 121, no. 48; p. 122, no. 49.

5. *Wenwu* 2002.4, p. 79.

6. It has been suggested that a large patchwork (107 cm by 149 cm) dating from the eighth or ninth century, during the Tang dynasty, found in Cave Number 17 at the Mogao Caves in Dunhuang, Gansu Province, is a monk's robe (*kāshāya*). For an illustration of the patchwork, which is part of the Stein Collection in the British Museum, see Roderick Whitfield and Anne Farrer, *Caves of the Thousand Buddhas: Chinese Art from the Silk Route*, pp. 114–15, no. 89.

121. Dragon-fish and lotus patterned silk-tapestry cap

Liao dynasty, early or mid-tenth century
From Tomb Number 3, Daiqintala
Township, Keyou Central Banner,
Xing'an League
Silk, tapestry, gauze, damask,
silk floss padding
Height: 30 cm; width: 27 cm
Museum of the Inner Mongolia
Autonomous Region

The silk padded cap was, like the silk gauze fan (cat. 80), excavated in 1991 from the looted tomb of an unidentified couple in Daiqintala, Keyou Central Banner, Xing'an League.[1] Together with the textile patchwork (cat. 120a–b), it was among the six parcels of silk garments that lay inside a small house in front of the wooden bed on which the bodies of the couple were placed, a typical final resting place for members of the Khitan aristocracy.[2]

Whether the owner of the cap was a male or a female is not known, as no conclusions can be drawn from the main motif, a dragon-fish, or from the placement of the cap in the tomb. The cap was fastened under the chin with red damask ribbons.[3] The beige colored gauze ribbons were used to adjust the flaps.[4] Astonishingly, there was no lining.[5] Moreover, when the flaps were folded over on top of the cap, the padding would have been exposed.

The precious silk tapestry (*kesi*), with flat gold strips for the dragon-fish among the waves and for the lotus flowers, was purposely woven in the shape of the cap. The rarity of *kesi* pieces in the tombs of Liao nobles—most are smaller items like caps and boots[6]—indicates that *kesi* was a very costly textile, especially if gold strips or threads[7] were used.[8] *Kesi* was appreciated more for its artistic value than for the weaving technique. The motifs used in the *kesi* found in Liao tombs are repeatedly found in Liao gold and silver wares (see cat. 25, 26a–b, 84), providing evidence that Liao *kesi* was woven within Khitan territory.[9]

SLG

1. See Meng Jianren and Piao Chunyue, "Keyouzhongqi Daiqintala Liao mu qingli jianbao" [Brief report on the clearing of a Liao tomb at Daiqintala, Keyou Central Banner], in Wei Jian (ed.), *Neimenggu wenwu kaogu wenji*, vol. 2, pp. 651–67.

2. Dieter Kuhn, *How the Qidan Reshaped the Tradition of the Chinese Dome-shaped Tomb*, p. 60.

3. *Wenwu* 2002.4, p. 61.

4. A depiction of a cap with fur lining where the flaps covering the ears are tied back can be seen in a mural on the northern wall of the passageway at Tomb Number 1, Kulun Banner, Zhelimu Meng, Jilin Province. See *Wenwu* 1973.8, p.17.

5. Most of the published Liao caps have a lining. For an example of a Liao cap at the Abegg-Stiftung, Riggiberg, Bern, Switzerland, see Nikkibarla Calonder, "Documentation and Conservation of a Liao Dynasty Cap," *Orientations*, May 2004, pp. 44–47. Regarding the cap of an elaborate headdress found in the tomb of an unidentified female Khitan aristocrat in Yemaotai, Faku County, Liaoning Province, the excavation report states that the cap consisted of four layers of material. Presumably, this refers to an outer shell, followed by a protective lining, silk padding, and an inner lining. See *Wenwu* 1975.12, p. 29.

6. An exception is the shroud (length 200 cm, width 150 cm) found in the tomb of an unidentified female Khitan aristocrat in Yemaotai, Faku County, Liaoning Province. For an illustration of a fragment of the shroud, see *Heaven's Embroidered Cloths*, p. 316.

7. For a discussion of the use and composition of flat gold strips and gold threads in Liao textiles, see Krishna Riboud, "A Brief Account of Textiles Excavated in Dated Liao Dynasty Tombs (907–1125) in China," *CIETA-Bulletin* 74 (1997), pp. 28–49.

8. Tombs of nobles or high officials in Inner Mongolia include the tomb of Yelü Yuzhi, at Hansumu Township, Aluke'erqin Banner; the tomb of the king of the state of Wei, Dayingzi, Chifeng; the tombs of an unidentified couple in Daiqintala, Keyou Central Banner, and in Xiaonurimu, Kezuo Central Banner, Zhelimu; the tombs of an unidentified woman in Jiefangyinzi, Wengniute Banner, and in Yemaotai, Faku County, Liaoning Province. Zhao Feng, *Liao Textiles and Costumes*, p. 93.

9. James C. Y. Watt and Anne E. Wardwell, *When Silk Was Gold: Central Asian and Chinese Textiles*, p. 60.

Appendices

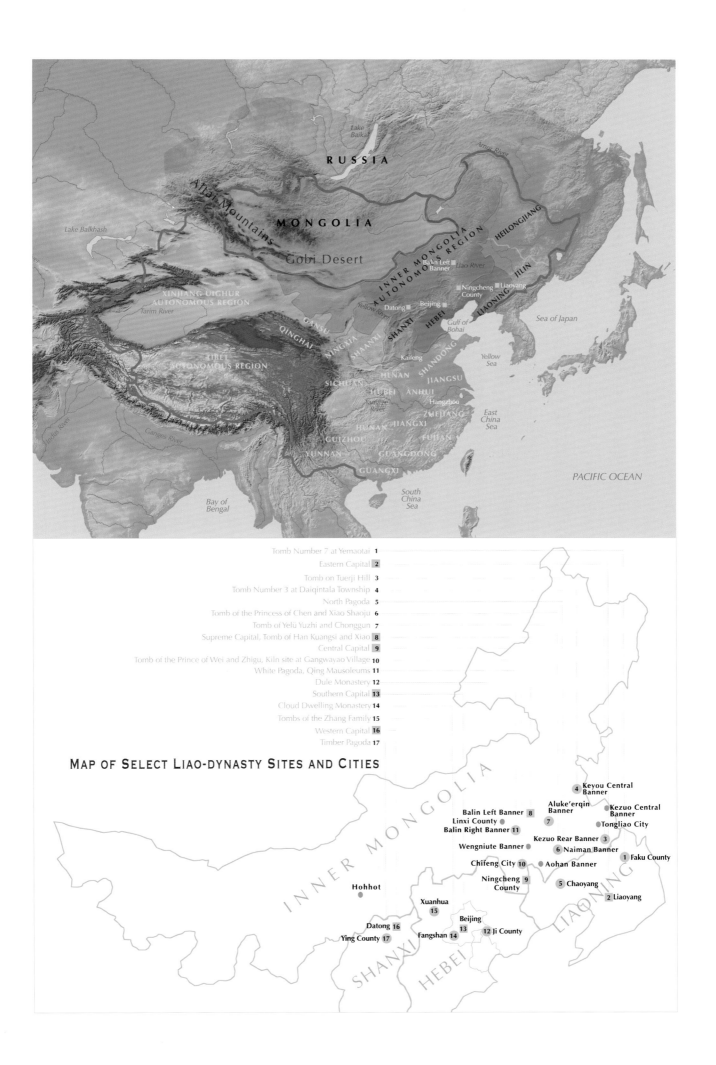

Tomb Number 7 at Yemaotai **1**
Eastern Capital **2**
Tomb on Tuerji Hill **3**
Tomb Number 3 at Daiqintala Township **4**
North Pagoda **5**
Tomb of the Princess of Chen and Xiao Shaoju **6**
Tomb of Yelü Yuzhi and Chonggun **7**
Supreme Capital, Tomb of Han Kuangsi and Xiao **8**
Central Capital **9**
Tomb of the Prince of Wei and Zhigu, Kiln site at Gangwayao Village **10**
White Pagoda, Qing Mausoleums **11**
Dule Monastery **12**
Southern Capital **13**
Cloud Dwelling Monastery **14**
Tombs of the Zhang Family **15**
Western Capital **16**
Timber Pagoda **17**

MAP OF SELECT LIAO-DYNASTY SITES AND CITIES

Copenhagen

Baltic Sea

Moscow

Ural Mountains

Venice

Rome

Adriatic Sea

Black Sea

Istanbul

Caspian Sea

Aral Sea

Syr Darya River

QAR

Tashkent

Samarkand

Amu Darya (Oxus) River

Mediterranean Sea

Damascus

Jerusalem

Cairo

Euphrates

Tigris

Baghdad

SELJUP SULTANATE

Zagros Mountains

Tehran

Kabul

New

Indus River

Nile

Riyadh

Mecca

Red Sea

Arabian Sea

Lake B

INDIAN O

MAP OF LIAO EMPIRE AND ITS NEIGHBORS, CA. 1120

Lake
Baikal

Amur River

LIAO DYNASTY

Great Khingan

Little Khingan

JURCHEN

Altai Mountains

Gobi Desert

Beiting (Besh Baliq)

Kucha

Khara Khojo (Turfan)

XIZHOU
UIGHURS

Supreme
Capital
(Balin Left Banner)

Liao River

Eastern
Capital
(Liaoyang)

Khara Khoto

TANGUT
XI XIA

Western
Capital
(Datong)

Central
Capital
(Ningcheng County)

Tarim River

Shazhou
(Dunhuang)

Khotan

Xingqingfu
(Yinchuan)

Yellow River

Southern
Capital
(Beijing)

Gulf of
Bohai

Dingzhou

Sea of Japan

KOREA
(Goryeo)

Heian Kyo (Kyoto)

TIBET

Bianjing (Kaifeng)

Yellow
Sea

JAPAN
(Heian)

Lhasa

Ganges River

Chengdufu
(Chengdu)

Yangtze
River

Lin'an (Hangzhou)

Mingzhou
(Ningbo)

East
China
Sea

NORTHERN
SONG
DYNASTY

BIHAR

Dali

DALI

Guangzhou

PACIFIC OCEAN

BENGAL

KHMER
(Angkor)

South
China
Sea

Bay of
Bengal

Yangon

Angkor

Phnom Penh

Kuala Lumpur

SUMATRA

Developments and Benchmarks of the Liao Dynasty and of World History (4th century–13th century)

4th century
The Khitan, a nomadic confederation from the eastern region of the Eurasian steppes, first appear in China.

313
Constantine and his fellow emperor, Licinius, meet at Milan and confirm Galerius's edict of 309, in effect making Christianity a lawful religion.

777
Charlemagne attempts to invade Islamic Spain but fails.

ca. 800–ca. 1000
On the African continent, stone monoliths, lost-wax casting, terracotta, and copper-alloy objects proliferate.

ca. 800–ca. 1200
In eastern India, Buddhism flourishes under Pala patronage.

907
In China, the Tang dynasty (618–907) falls; Abaoji (r. 907–26) becomes *kaghan* (supreme ruler) of the Khitan.

909
The Islamic Fatimid dynasty (909–72) begins its reign in Ifriqiya (now Tunisia).

912–61
Cordoba, Spain, is the greatest intellectual center in Europe.

918
The first walled city in Inner Mongolia—the Liao imperial capital at Huangdu (in present-day Inner Mongolia)—is established by the Khitan.

918
Wang Geon (r. 918–43) reunites Korea (Goryeo) under the new Goryeo dynasty (918–1392).

924–25
The Khitan adopt their dual writing system, consisting of a so-called large script and small script.

926
The Liao conquer the southern Manchurian kingdom of Bohai.

938
Liao emperor Deguang (Taizong, r. 927–47) acquires an area of northern China known as the Sixteen Prefectures; the Liao capital Shangjing (Supreme Capital), the first Khitan city where a palace is known to have been built, is established.

941
Liao-dynasty aristocrat and official Yelü Yuzhi (890–941) is buried in a tomb with a square-shaped burial chamber and a corbeled dome.

947
Liao emperor Taizong invades northern China and proclaims himself ruler.

ca. 950
Construction of Chan Chan—where one of the first royal palace compounds (*ciudadelas*) is Chayhuac—begins (located in what is now Peru).

957
Earliest known dated Liao-dynasty Buddhist sculpture, a carved stone image of a seated Shakyamuni Buddha (excavated in Ningcheng County, Inner Mongolia) is created.

959

The body of the Prince of Wei, Xiao Shagu, is placed in the tomb where he and his wife, Zhigu—the daughter of the first Liao emperor, Abaoji—are interred.

960

Song-dynasty founder Zhao Kuangyin (r. 960–76) reunifies and rules much of China, though the Liao continue to possess a stronghold in the north until 979.

1005

The Khitan invade Song territory and ultimately negotiate the Treaty of Shanyuan, ending a long period of conflict.

1018

The Princess of Chen (1001–18) dies and is then buried in a tomb with her husband, Xiao Shaoju.

1049

The White Pagoda, containing a major scripture deposit, with inscribed stone stele and 109 pagoda-shaped containers with scrolls inside, is built in present-day Balin Right Banner, Inner Mongolia.

1065

Yelü Yixin, a Liao-dynasty Khitan courtier, gains power, precipitating a period of great corruption and violence, until he is removed from power in 1081.

1092

Mongolian nomads, the Zubu, rebel and invade the northwestern pasturelands of the Liao empire.

1120

Aguda, leader of the Jurchen of eastern Manchuria, destroys the Liao dynasty's Supreme Capital, which eventually leads to the collapse of Liao political and military leadership.

1125

The Liao empire falls to the Jurchen, who also capture the Chinese capital at Kaifeng (formerly Bianliang), forcing the Song court south.

960

King of Denmark, Harald Bluetooth, unifies Norway and Denmark and adopts Christianity.

969

Cairo founded as the new capital of the Fatimid dynasty, ruling areas in Africa and the Middle East.

1002

Leif Eriksson explores the coast of North America.

ca. 1015

A combined fleet from Genoa and Pisa evicts Arabs from Sardinia and Corsica.

1053

The Byōdōin temple, a major example of Japanese Buddhist architecture, is established in Kyoto Prefecture, Japan.

ca. 1050–66

Baphuon, a major Hindu temple-mountain at Angkor, Cambodia, is constructed.

1066

At the Battle of Hastings, the Normans defeat the English and become the new rulers of the English mainland.

1084

Basilica of San Marco in Venice is consecrated.

ca. 1095

The First Crusade begins; Christians led by Pope Urban II undertake a campaign to recapture Mediterranean territory from Muslim rule, conquering Jerusalem in 1099.

ca. 1100

Carving of first colossal stone figures (*moai*) on Easter Island.

1122

The compromise known as the Concordat of Worms is arranged between Pope Calixtus II and the Holy Roman emperor Heinrich V, settling the struggle between the empire and the papacy over the control of church offices.

1127

Southern Song dynasty is established in China.

early 13th century
Cast-metal movable type is invented in Korea (Goryeo).

1215

King John signs the Magna Carta in Runnymede, England.

Chronology of Dynastic China

Xia Period (protohistoric)	ca. 2100–ca. 1600 BC
Shang Dynasty	ca. 1600–ca. 1050 BC
Western Zhou	ca. 1050–771 BC
Eastern Zhou	771–256 BC
Spring and Autumn Period	722–481 BC
Warring States Period	403–221 BC
Qin Dynasty	221–210 BC
Han Dynasty	206 BC–AD 220
Western Han	206 BC–AD 9
Wang Mang interregnum	9–23
Eastern Han	23–220
Three Kingdoms	220–80
Wei	220–65
Shu Han	221–63
Wu	222–80
Western Jin	265–316
Eastern Jin	317– 420
Northern Dynasties	
Sixteen Kingdoms	310–439
Northern Wei	386–534
Eastern Wei	534–50
Western Wei	535–56
Northern Qi	550–77
Northern Zhou	557–81
Sui Dynasty	581–618
Tang Dynasty	618–907
Five Dynasties	907–60
Liao Dynasty	907–1125
Song Dynasty	960–1279
Northern Song	960–1127
Southern Song	1127–1279
Xi Xia Kingdom	ca. 997–1227
Jin Dynasty	1115–1234
Western Liao	1125–1211
Yuan Dynasty	1279–1368
Ming Dynasty	1368–1644
Qing Dynasty	1644–1911

Glossary of Words and Names

The following Chinese administrative divisions below the provincial level are referred to in English translation throughout the catalogue.

cheng (city) 城
cun (village) 村
meng (league) 盟
qi (banner) 旗
sumu (township) 蘇木
tun (village) 屯
xian (county) 縣
xiang (rural area) 鄉
zhen (town) 鎮

Abaoji (Liao emperor) 阿保機
Aluke'erqinqi 阿魯科爾沁旗
Anyang 安陽
Aohanqi 敖漢旗

bajiao dian 八角殿
Balinyouqi (Balin Right Banner) 巴林右旗
Balinzuoqi (Balin Left Banner) 巴林左旗
Bayanerdeng 巴彥爾登
Bayanguole 巴顏郭勒 (Baiyinguole 巴顏郭勒) he 河 (Bayan-gol River)
Bayankuren 巴顏庫仁
baimu 柏木
Baitacun 白塔村
Baiyinhansumu 白音漢蘇木
Baiyinwulasumu 白音勿拉蘇木
Banruo boluomiduo xin jing 般若波羅蜜多心經
Bencheng 本城
Bian Chengxiu 邊成修
Baoshan 寶山
Beita 北塔
Bohai 渤海
boluozi 波羅子

Cai Shun 蔡順
cha 刹
Chayouqianqi (Chayou Front Banner) 察右前旗 (abbreviated form of Chahaer youyi qianqi 察哈爾右翼前旗)
Chanyuan 澶淵
Changsha 長沙
Chaoyang 朝陽
Chen (Princess of) 陳
Chenba'erhu 陳巴爾虎
Chenggou 程溝
Chengtian (Liao empress dowager) 承天
Chengzi 城子
Chifeng 赤峰
chiwei 鴟尾
Chonggun (wife of Yelü Yuzhi) 重袞
chunshui 春水

Da banruo boluomiduo jing 大般若波羅蜜多經
Datong 大同

Daxiongbaodian 大雄寶殿
Daiqintalasumu 代欽塔拉蘇木
Daoyin 道殷
Daozong (Liao emperor) 道宗
Deguang (Liao emperor) 德光
Dezong (Tang emperor) 德宗
diba 帝玾
dianli 奠礼
diexie 蹀躞
Ding Lan 丁蘭
Dongbei 東北
Dongjing meng hua lu 東京夢華錄
Dongjing taifu 東京太傅
Dulesi 獨樂寺
Dunhuang 敦煌

Enshi 恩施

Faku 法庫
Famensi 法門寺
Fasheli zhenyan 法舍利真言
Fan wang jing 梵網經
Fengguosi 奉國寺
fenghuang 鳳凰
feng shan 封禪
Feng Yongqian 馮永謙
Fengzhou 豐州
Foding zunsheng tuoluoni jing 佛頂尊勝陀羅尼經
fokan 佛龕
Foshuo gaowang guanshiyin jing 佛說高王觀世音經
Foshuo molizhitian jing 佛說摩利支天經
Fo xingxiangzhong anzhi fasheli ji 佛形象中安置法舍利記
fubo 覆鉢
fugu 復古
Fushun 撫順
Fuxin 阜新

Gaojuli (Goguryeo) 高句麗
Genben tuoluoni 根本陀羅尼
Geng Yanyi 耿延毅
gou 韝
guduo 骨朵
Guyingzi 姑營子
Guanyin 觀音
Guisui 歸綏
Guixian 貴縣
Guo Ju 郭巨

Hadayinggexiang 哈達英格鄉 *haidongqing* 海東青
Han (dynasty) 漢
Han (Mme) 韓 (氏)
Hancheng 漢城
Han fu 漢服
Han Kuangsi 韓匡嗣
Hansumusumu 罕蘇木蘇木
Han Yanhui 韓延徽
Haoqianying 豪欠營

Hongji (Liao emperor)　洪基
Huhehaote (Hohhot)　呼和浩特
Huayan　華嚴
huang　荒
Huangcheng　皇城
Huangdu　皇都
Huitong　會同

Jixian　薊縣
jialingpinjia　迦陵頻伽
jiao　蛟
Jiefangyingzi　解放營子
Jin (Later Jin dynasty)　晉
jin fa sheli　金法舍利
Jin'gang banruo boluomi jing　金剛般若波羅蜜經
Jinguangming zuishengwang jing　金光明最勝王經
jinshi　進士
Jing (Liao emperor)　璟
Jingzong (Liao emperor)　景宗
Junahanmuni　拘那含牟尼

Kaitai　開泰
Kang Moji　康默記
kesi　緙絲
Keyouzhongqi (Keyou Central Banner)　科右中旗
(abbreviated form of Ke'erqin youyi zhongqi　科爾沁右翼中旗）
Kezuohouqi (Kezuo Rear Banner)　科左後旗
(abbreviated form of Ke'erqin zuoyi houqi　科爾沁左翼後旗）
Kezuozhongqi (Kezuo Central Banner)　科左中旗
(abbreviated form of Ke'erqin zuoyi zhongqi　科爾沁左翼中旗）
Kengdi　坑底
Kudi Huiluo　庫狄迴洛
Kulunqi　庫倫旗

Lamagou　喇嘛溝
lifang　里坊
Liji　禮記
Li Wenxin　李文信
Li Yiyou　李逸友
lian　蓮
lianyu　連餘
Liao　遼
Liaoshi　遼史
Liaoxi　遼西
Linxixian　林西縣
lingzhi　靈芝
liudou　柳斗
Longxu (Liao emperor)　隆緒
lu　虜
luo　絡

mamian　馬面
Ma Zhiwen　馬直温
Maiwanggou　埋王溝
mianju　面具
Miaofa lianhua jing　妙法蓮華經
mofa　末法
Mogao (caves)　莫高
mojie　摩羯
muguo　木椁

Murong Xianbei　慕容鮮卑
Muye (mountain)　木葉
muzhang　木帳
muzhiming　墓誌銘
Muzong (Liao emperor)　穆宗

nabo　捺钵
nai　奈
Nailingao　奈林稿
Naimanqi　奈曼旗
Nanyang　南陽
Ningcheng　寧城
Ningjiang　寧江
Ning Mao　寧懋

Pingnan　平南
Pingquan　平泉
pulan　蒲籃

Qidan (Khitan, Kitan)　契丹
qilin　麒麟
Qianshou qianyan guanshiyin pusa dabeixin tuoluoni
千手千眼觀世音菩薩大悲心陀羅尼
Qianwulibugecun　錢勿力布格村
Qianzi wen　千字文
Qinde　勤德
qingbai　青白
Qingzhou　慶州
qionglu　穹廬

ruyi　如意

Shanhaijing　山海經
Shangjing　上京
Shang Wei　尚暐
Shaozong (Northern Song emperor)　紹宗
Shengzong (Liao emperor)　聖宗
shier shengxiao　十二生肖
shi fang fo　十方佛
Shijing　詩經
Shizong (Liao emperor)　世宗
shuiyu　水玉
shun　楯
Shun'an　順安
Siling　四靈
Sishen　四神
Song (dynasty)　宋
Songshi Yufuzhi　宋史輿服志
Su Che　蘇轍
Suniteyou　蘇尼特右
Su Tianjun　蘇天鈞
Sun Wei　孫位

Taizong (Liao emperor)　太宗
Taizong (Tang emperor)　太宗
Taizu (Liao emperor)　太祖
tang　塘
Tang (dynasty)　唐
Tang Yulin　湯玉麟
Tengchong　騰衝

tian 天
tianguan 天官
Tianjin 天津
Tianzan 天贊
Tianzuo (Liao emperor) 天祚
Tieli 鐵驪
Tongliao 通遼
tongsi luo 銅絲絡
Tuerjishan 吐爾基山
Tujue 突厥
tuohu 唾壺
tuoluoni 陀羅尼
tuoyu 唾盂

Wanbu Huayanjing ta 萬部華嚴經塔
wan sui tai 萬歲臺
Wang Bao 王褒
Wang Pou 王裒
Wang Xiang 王祥
Wei (dynasty) 魏
Wei (Prince of) 衛
Wen Weijian 文惟簡
Wengniuteqi 翁牛特旗
woshou 握手
Wugou jingguang da tuoluoni jing 無垢淨光大陀羅尼經

Xi (people) 奚
Xilinguolemeng 錫林郭勒盟
Xi Xia 西夏
Xiabalicun 下八里村
Xian (Liao emperor) 賢
Xian mi yuantong chengfo xin yao ji 顯密圓通成佛心要集
Xianglun 相輪
Xiangluntang zhong tuoluoni 相輪樘中陀羅尼
Xiao 蕭
Xiao Jin 蕭僅
xiaomuzuo 小木作
Xiaonurimu 小努日木
Xiao Paolu 蕭袍魯
Xiao Qulie 蕭屈列
Xiao Shagu 蕭沙姑
Xiao Shaoju 蕭紹矩
Xiao Yi 蕭義
xiaozhang 小帳
Xinkai 新開
Xing'anmeng 興安盟
Xingzong (Liao emperor) 興宗
Xiongnu 匈奴
Xiongwu 雄武
Xuanhua 宣化
Xuanzang 玄奘
Xuanzong (Liao emperor) 宣宗

ya (crushing) 壓
ya (duck) 鴨
Yan (kingdom) 燕
Yanxi (Liao emperor) 延禧
Yang Xiang 楊香
Yelü 耶律
Yelü Guanyinnü 耶律觀音女

Yelü Longqing 耶律隆慶
Yelü Xiezhen 耶律斜軫
Yelü Yuzhi 耶律羽之
Yemaotai 葉茂台
Yijing 易經
Yiqie Rulai xin mimiquanshen sheli baoqie yin tuoluoni jing
一切如來心秘密全身舍利寶篋印陀羅尼經
Yixian 義縣
Yizhou 懿州
Yizong (Tang emperor) 懿宗
Yingfenggou 英風溝
Yingli 應曆
Yingluo 瓔珞
Yingtian (Liao empress) 應天
Yingxian 應縣
Yingzhou 營州
yongdao 甬道
You'ai 友愛
yu 魚
Yu Hong 虞弘
yutang 玉堂
Yutian 于闐
Yuan (Liao emperor) 阮
Yuan Gu 原穀

zaisheng shi 再生室
zaisheng yi 再生儀
zhadou 渣斗
zhanggan 帳竿
zhanggan tuoluoni 帳竿陀羅尼
Zhang Gongzhu 長公主
Zhang Guan (wife of Ma Zhiwen) 張館
Zhanghuai (Tang crown prince) 章懷王
Zhang Kuangzheng 張匡正
Zhang Qiao 張嶠
Zhangsheng (Liao empress dowager) 章聖
Zhang Shiqing 張世卿
Zhao Dejun 趙德鈞
Zhelimumeng 哲里木盟
zhentong 針筒
Zhenzong (Northern Song emperor) 真宗
Zheng Long 鄭隆
Zheng Shaozong 鄭紹宗
Zhigu 質古
Zhiju rulai xin po diyu tuoluoni 智炬如來心破地獄陀羅尼
Zhongjing 中京
Zhong Zilu 仲子路
Zongzhen (Liao emperor) 宗真
zu 族
Zuzhou 祖州
zuo xiang 左相
zuo xiang gong 左相公

Bibliography

An Jiayao. An Jiayao. "Chen guo gongzhu yu fuma hezangmu chutu de boli qimin ji youguan wenti" [Glass vessels unearthed from the joint burial of the princess of the state of Chen and her husband]. In *Liao Chenguo gongzhu mu* [*Liao tomb of the princess of the state of Chen*] (edited by Neimenggu zizhiqu wenwu kaogu yanjiusuo and Zhelimumeng bowuguan). Beijing: Wenwu chubanshe, 1993, pp. 179–86.

Aohanqi Fanzhangzi Liao mu. "Aohanqi Fanzhangzi Liao mu" [Liao tomb at Fanzhangzi, Aohan Banner]. *Neimenggu wenwu kaogu* 1984.3, pp. 75–79.

Aohanqi Lamagou Liaodai. "Aohanqi Lamagou Liaodai bihua mu" [Liao mural tomb at Lamagou, Aohan Banner]. *Neimenggu wenwu kaogu* 1999.1, pp. 90–97.

Ariès. Philippe Ariès. *Geschichte des Todes* [*History of death*]. Munich: Deutscher Taschenbuchverlag, 1982.

Aruz et al. Joan Aruz, Ann Farkas, Andrei Alekseev, and Elena Korolkova (eds.). *The Golden Deer of Eurasia: Scythian and Sarmatian Treasures from the Russian Steppes*. New York: Metropolitan Museum of Art, 2000.

Baisigou Xi Xia fangta. *Baisigou Xi Xia fangta* [*The square Xi Xia pagoda in Baisigou*]. Beijing: Wenwu chubanshe, 2005.

Baiyinhan shan Liaodai. Neimenggu zizhiqu wenwu kaogu yanjiusuo et al. "Baiyinhan shan Liaodai Han shi jiazu mudi fajue baogao" [Excavation report of the Liao-dynasty Han family cemetery in Baiyinhan Mountain]. *Neimenggu wenwu kaogu* 2002.2, pp. 19–42.

Barrett and Gray. Douglas Barrett and Basil Gray. *Painting of India*. Ascona: Skira, 1963.

Beijing Longquanwu. Beijing shi wenwu yanjiusuo (ed.). *Beijing Longquanwu yao fajue baogao* [*Excavation of the Longquanwu kiln site in Beijing*]. Beijing: Wenwu chubanshe, 2002.

Bei Song huangling. Henan sheng wenwu kaogu yanjiusuo (ed.). *Bei Song huangling* [*Imperial mausoleums of the Northern Song*]. Zhengzhou: Zhongzhou guji chubanshe, 1997.

Beiwei Luoyang Yongningsi. Zhongguo shehui kexueyuan kaogu yanjiusuo (ed.). *Beiwei Luoyang Yongningsi* [*Northern Wei Yongning Monastery in Luoyang*]. Beijing: Zhongguo da baike quanshu chubanshe, 1996.

Biran. Michal Biran. "Sinicization Out of China: The Case of the Western Liao (Qara Khitai)." Paper presented at the 51st meeting of the Association for Asian Studies, Boston, 1999.

Bivar. A.D.H. Bivar. "The Stirrup and its Origins." *Oriental Art*, Summer 1955, pp. 61–65.

Bol. Peter K. Bol. *"This Culture of Ours": Intellectual Transitions in T'ang and Sung China*. Stanford: Stanford University Press, 1992.

Bunker. Emma C. Bunker. "Gold Wire in Ancient China." *Orientations*, March 1997, pp. 94–95.

Bunker, White, and So. Emma C. Bunker, Julia M. White, and Jenny F. So. *Adornment for the Body and Soul: Ancient Chinese Ornaments from the Mengdiexuan Collection*. Hong Kong: University Museum and Art Gallery, University of Hong Kong, 1999.

Butsuzō: tainai no sekai. Shiga kenritsu Biwako bunkakan (ed.). *Butsuzō: tainai no sekai* [*Buddha statues: The world inside their bodies*]. Shiga: Shiga kenritsu Biwako bunkakan, 1999.

Calonder. Nikkibarla Calonder. "Documentation and Conservation of a Liao Dynasty Cap." *Orientations*, May 2004, pp. 44–47.

Cang Wangling. Cang Wangling. "Tuerjishan mu: Sheng yu si de mimi pei zang qidan nuzi" [The tomb in Tuerji Hill: The secret death and life as seen in a tomb of a Khitan-woman]. *Wenwu tiandi* 2003.3, pp. 20–27.

Cao Xun. Cao Xun. "Yemaotai Liao muzhong de guanchuang xiaozhang" [The small-scale "container" and coffin-bed in a Liao tomb at Yemaotai]. *Wenwu* 1975.12, pp. 49–62.

Caoyuan guibao. Shanghai bowuguan (ed.). *Caoyuan guibao: Neimenggu wenwu kaogu jingpin* [*Treasures on grassland: Archaeological finds from the Inner Mongolia Autonomous Region*]. Shanghai: Shanghai shuhua chubanshe, 2000.

Chayouhouqi Shimenkou. Wulanchabu bowuguan. "Chayouhouqi Shimenkou Jin dai yizhi fajue jianbao" [Brief report on the excavation of a Jin-dynasty site at Shimenkou in Chayou Rear Banner]. In *Neimenggu wenwu kaogu wenji* [*Essays on the archaeology of cultural relics in Inner Mongolia*], vol. 1 (edited by Li Yiyou and Wei Jian). Beijing: Zhongguo dabaike quanshu chubanshe, 1994, pp. 585–95.

Chayouqianqi Haoqianying. "Chayouqianqi Haoqianying di liu hao Liaomu qingli jianbao" [Excavation of the Liao-dynasty Tomb Number 6 at Haoqianying in Chayou Front Banner]. *Wenwu* 1983.9, pp. 1–8.

Chan. Hok-lam Chan. "Chinese Official Historiography at the Yüan Court: The Composition of the Liao, Chin, and Sung Histories." Chapter 2 of *China under Mongol Rule* (edited by John D. Langlois, Jr.). Princeton: Princeton University Press, 1981, pp. 56–106.

Chang'an zhi. Song Minqiu (1019–79). *Chang'an zhi* [*Record of Chang'an*], dated 1075. Taipei: Shangwu yinshuguan, 1983.

Changsha Mawangdui yihao. Hunan Sheng bowuguan, Zhongguo kexueyuan kaogu yanjiusuo, Wenwu bianji weiyuanhui. *Changsha Mawangdui yihao Han mu fajue jianbao* [*Brief report on Han-dynasty Tomb Number 1 in Mawangdui, Changsha*]. Beijing: Wenwu chubanshe, 1972.

Chaoyang Shi'ertaixiang. Liaoningsheng wenwu kaogu yanjiusuo. "Chaoyang Shi'ertaixiang zhuanchang 88 M1 fajue jianbao [Brief excavation report of Tomb 88 M1 in a brickyard at Shi'ertai Rural Area, Chaoyang]. *Wenwu* 1997.11, pp. 19–32.

Chen Fengshan et al. Chen Fengshan, Wang Cheng et al. "Neimenggu Chenba'erhuqi Bayankuren Liaodai muzang qingli baogao" [Excavation report of the clearing of the Liao tombs at Bayankuren, Chenba'erhu Banner, Inner Mongolia]. *Kaoguxue jikan* 2004.14, pp. 267–279.

Chen Mingda. Chen Mingda (ed.). *Yingxian muta* [*Ying County Timber Pagoda*]. Beijing: Wenwu chubanshe, 1980.

Chen Xiangwei and Wang Jianqun. Chen Xiangwei and Wang Jianqun. "Jilin Zhelimumeng Kulunqi yihao Liao mu fajue jianbao" [Brief excavation report on Liao Tomb Number 1 at Kulun Banner, Zhelimu League, Jilin]. *Wenwu* 1973.8, pp. 2–18.

Chengjisi han. Zhonghua shiji tan and Neimenggu bowuguan (eds.). *Chengjisi han: Zhongguo gudai beifang caoyuan youmu wenhua* [*Chingghis Khan: The ancient nomadic culture of northern China*]. Beijing: Beijing chubanshe, 2004.

Chifengxian Dayingzi. Qian Rehe sheng bowuguan choubeichu. "Chifengxian Dayingzi Liao mu fajue baogao" [Excavation report on the Liao-dynasty tomb at Dayingzi, Chifeng County]. *Kaogu xuebao* 1956.3, pp. 1–26.

Chika kyūden no ihō. Idemitsu Bijutsukan (ed.). *Chika kyūden no ihō: Chūgoku Kahoku-shō Teishū Hokusō tōki shutsudo bunbutsuten* [*Treasures from the underground palaces: Excavated treasures from northern Song pagodas, Dingzhou, Hebei Province, China*]. Tokyo: Idemitsu Bijutsukan, 1997.

Crossley. Pamela Crossley. "The Rulerships of China." *American Historical Review* 97.5 (1992), pp. 1468–83.

de Rachewiltz et al. Igor de Rachewiltz, Hok-lam Chan, Hsiao Ch'i-ch'ing, and Peter W. Geier (eds.). *In the Service of the Khan: Eminent Personalities of the Early Mongol-Yüan Period*. Wiesbaden: Harrassowitz, 1993.

De Xin et al. De Xin, Zhang Hanjun, and Han Renxing. "Neimenggu Balinyouqi [Qingzhou Baita] faxian Liaodai Fojiao wenwu" [Liao Buddhist relics discovered in the White Pagoda at Qingzhou, Balin Right Banner, Inner Mongolia]. *Wenwu* 1994.12, pp. 4–33.

Deydier. Christian Deydier. *Imperial Gold from Ancient China*. London: Oriental Bronzes Ltd., 1990.

Di Cosmo. Nicola Di Cosmo. "State Formation and Periodization in Inner Asian History." *Journal of World History* 10.1 (1999), pp. 1–40.

Diény. Jean-Pierre Diény. *Le symbolisme du dragon dans la Chine antique* [*The symbolism of the dragon in ancient China*]. Paris: Collège de France, 1987.

Ding Mingyi. Ding Mingyi. *Huayansi* [*Huayan Monastery*]. Beijing: Wenwu chubanshe, 1980.

Dittrich. Edith Dittrich. "The Spread of the Lion Motif in Ancient Asia." Paper presented at the International Academic Conference of Archaeological Cultures of the Northern Chinese Ancient Nations, Hohhot, 1992.

Dong Gao. Dong Gao. "Gongyuan san zhi liu shiji Murong Xianbei, Gaogoli, Chaoxian, Riben maju zhi bijiao yanjiu" [A comparative study on third-century to sixth-century horse trappings of Murong Xianbei and Gaogouli in Korea and Japan]. *Wenwu* 1995.10, pp. 34–42.

Du Xianzhou. Du Xianzhou. "Yixian Fengguosi Daxiongdian diaocha baogao" [Report on the investigation of Daxiong Hall of Fengguo Monastery in Yi County]. *Wenwu* 1961.2, pp. 5–13.

Duan Pengqi. Duan Pengqi. "Woguo gu muzang zhong faxian de xiaoti tuxiang" [Images of filial piety discovered in Chinese tombs]. In *Zhongguo kaoguxue luncong* [*Collected papers on Chinese archaeology*] (edited by Zhongguo shehui kexueyuan kaogu yanjiusuo). Beijing: Kexue chubanshe, 1993, pp. 463–71.

Dunhuang bianwen ji. Wang Zhongmin et al. (ed.). *Dunhuang bianwen ji* [*Compendium of Dunhuang transformation texts*]. Beijing: Renmin wenxue chubanshe, 1957.

Eberhard. Wolfram Eberhard. *Times Dictionary of Chinese Symbols: An Essential Guide to the Hidden Symbols in Chinese Art, Customs and Beliefs*. Singapore, Kuala Lumpur, and Hong Kong: Federal Publications, 1997. Originally published as *Lexikon Chinesischer Symbole* (Cologne: Eugen Diederichs Verlag, 1983).

Egami. Namio Egami. *The Grand Exhibition of Silk Road Civilizations. The Oasis and the Steppe Routes*. Nara: Association for Silk Road Exposition, 1988.

Faku Yemaotai Liao mu. Liaoningsheng bowuguan. "Faku Yemaotai Liao mu jilue" [Brief report on the Liao tomb at Yemaotai, Faku]. *Wenwu* 1975.12, pp. 26–36.

Feng Bingqi and Jia Tian. Feng Bingqi and Jia Tian. "Xin faxian de Liaodai jianzhu: Laiyuan Geyuansi

Wenshudian" [A newly discovered Liao building: Mañjushrī Hall of Geyuan Monastery in Laiyuan]. *Wenwu* 1960.8/9, pp. 66–67.

Feng Enxue (a). Feng Enxue. "Diexiedai: Qidan wen-hua zhong de Tujue yinsu" [Diexie belts: Turkic influence in Khitan culture]. *Wenwu jikan* 1998.1, pp. 65–69.

Feng Enxue (b). Feng Enxue. "Liaodai Qidan maju tansuo" [Exploring Liao Khitan horse gear]. *Kaoguxue jikan* 2004.14, pp. 441–64.

Feng Yongqian (a). Feng Yongqian. "Chifeng Gangwayaocun Liao dai ciyaozhi de kaogu xin fax-ian" [New archaeological discoveries at the Liao-dynasty kiln site at Gangwayao Village in Chifeng]. In *Zhongguo gudai yaozhi diaocha fajue baogaoji* [A collection of excavation reports on ancient Chinese kiln sites] (edited by Wenwu bianji weiyuanhui). Beijing: Wenwu chubanshe, 1984, pp. 386–92.

Feng Yongqian (b). Feng Yongqian. *Dongbei kaogu yanjiu: yi* [Essays on the archaeology of northeast China]. Vol. 1. Zhengzhou: Zhongzhou guji chubanshe, 1994.

Feng Yongqian (c). Feng Yongqian. "Jianguo yilai Liaodai kaogu de zhongyao faxian" [Important archaeological discoveries of the Liao dynasty since the founding of the People's Republic of China]. In *Liao Jin shi lunji* [Collection of articles on the history of the Liao and Jin] (edited by Chen Shu). Shanghai: Shanghai guji chubanshe, 1987, vol. 1, pp. 295–334.

Feng Yongqian (d). Feng Yongqian. "Liaoning Faku Qianshan Xiao Paolu mu" [Xiao Paolu's tomb of the Liao dynasty at Qianshan in Faku, Liaoning]. *Kaogu* 1983.7, p. 624–35.

Feng Yongqian (e). Feng Yongqian. "Liaoningsheng Jianping Xinmin de san zuo Liao mu" [Three Liao tombs in Xinmin, Jianping, Liaoning Province]. *Kaogu* 1960.2, pp. 15–24.

Foguang dacidian. Foguang dacidian [Foguang dictionary]. 8 vols. Kaohsiung, Taiwan: Foguang chubanshe, 1998.

Fong, Mary. Mary Fong. "Tomb-Guardian Figures: Their Evolution and Iconography." In *Ancient Mortuary Traditions of China: Papers on Chinese Funerary Sculptures* (edited by George Kuwayama). Los Angeles: Los Angeles County Museum, 1991, pp. 84–105.

Fong, Wen C. Wen C. Fong. "Images of the Mind." Chapter 1 of Wen C. Fong, Alfreda Murck, Shou-chien Shih et al., *Images of the Mind*. Princeton: Art Museum, Princeton University, 1984, pp. 1–212.

Fong and Watt. Wen C. Fong and James C.Y. Watt. *Possessing the Past: Treasures from the National Palace Museum, Taipei.* New York: Metropolitan Museum of Art, 1996.

Franke. Herbert Franke. "The Forest Peoples of Manchuria: Khitans and Jurchens." Chapter 15 of *The Cambridge History of Early Inner Asia* (edited by Denis Sinor). Cambridge: Cambridge University Press, 1990, pp. 400–423.

Franke and Chan. Herbert Franke and Hok-lam Chan. *Studies on the Jurchen and the Chin Dynasty.* Variorum Collected Studies Series. Aldershot, U.K.: Ashgate Publishing, 1997.

Franke and Twitchett. Herbert Franke and Denis Twitchett (eds.). *Alien Regimes and Border States, 710–1368* (volume 6 of *The Cambridge History of China*). Cambridge: Cambridge University Press, 1994.

Fu Lehuan. Fu Lehuan. *Liao shi cong kao* [Anthology of the history of the Liao]. Beijing: Zhonghua shuju, 1984.

Fuxin Chenggou Liao mu. Fuxin wenwu danhui et al. "Fuxin Chenggou Liao mu qingli jianbao" [Brief report on the clearing of the Liao tomb at Chenggou, Fuxin]. *Liao Jin shi yanjiu* 1995.2, pp. 25–28.

Fuchs. Walter Fuchs. *Beiträge zur Mandjurischen Bibliographie und Literatur* [Contributions to Manchu bibliography and literature]. Tokyo: Deutsche Gesellschaft für Natur-und Völkerkunde Ostasiens, 1936.

Gai Zhiyong (a). Gai Zhiyong. *Neimenggu Liaodai shikewen yanjiu* [Research on Liao stone inscriptions in Inner Mongolia]. Hohhot: Neimenggu daxue chubanshe, 2002.

Gai Zhiyong (b). Gai Zhiyong. *Tanxun shiqu de wangchao: Liao Yelü Yuzhi mu* [Exploring a lost dynasty: The tomb of Yelü Yuzhi]. Hohhot: Neimenggu daxue chubanshe, 2004.

Gai Zhiyong (c). Gai Zhiyong. "Yelü Yuzhi muzhiming kaozheng" [Some remarks on the memorial tablet inscription of Yelü Yuzhi]. *Beifang wenwu* 2001.1, pp. 40–48.

Geng Tiehua. Geng Tiehua. "Gaogouli bingqi chulun" [Preliminary discussion of Koguryo weapons]. *Liaohai wenwu xuekan* 1993.2, pp. 100–111.

Geschichte der Großen Liao. Geschichte der Großen Liao aus dem Mandschu übersetzt von H. Conon von der Gabelentz [History of the Great Liao Dynasty, translated from the Manchu by H. Conon von der Gabelentz] (edited by H. A. von der Gabelentz). St. Petersburg: Eggers & Co, 1877.

Ghose. Rajeshwari Ghose (ed.). *In the Footsteps of the Buddha: An Iconic Journey from India to China.* Hong Kong: University Museum and Art Gallery, University of Hong Kong, 1998.

Goepper. Roger Goepper. "Dressing the Temple: Textile Representations in the Frescoes at Alchi." In *Asian Art: The Second Hali Annual* (edited by Jill Tilden). London: Hali Publications, 1995, pp. 110–17.

Gridley (a). Marilyn Leidig Gridley. *Chinese Buddhist Sculpture under the Liao (Free Standing Works in Situ and Selected Examples from Public Collections).* New Delhi: Aditya, 1993.

Gridley (b). Marilyn Gridley. "Images from Shanxi of Tejaprabha's Paradise." *Archives of Asian Art* 51 (1998–99), pp. 7–15.

Gridley (c). Marilyn Gridley. "Three Buddhist Sculptures from Longquanwu and the Luohans from Yi Xian." *Oriental Art,* Winter 1995/96, pp. 20–29.

Griswold. A. B. Griswold. "Prolegomena to the Study of the Buddha's Dress in Chinese Sculpture (Part 1)." *Artibus Asiae* 26.2 (1963), pp. 85–131.

Gu Juying. Gu Juying. "Wanbu Huayanjing ta" [Ten thousand Huayan sutras pagoda]. In *Neimenggu wenwu guji sanji* (edited by Lu Minghui et al.). Hohhot: Neimenggu renmin chubanshe, 1987, pp 38–40.

Han Zhao. Han Zhao. "Nanbeichao Sui Tang shidai tong ping 'tong chi' yongtu bianxi: jiantan yu riben zuopoli qi zhi guanxi" [Analytical study on the usage of bronze bottles and spoons of the Northern and Southern Dynasties, Sui, and Tang: Also on their relations with the Japanese *Sapoli* bronzes]. In *Yuan wang ji: Shaanxi sheng kaogu yan-jiusuo huadan sishi zhounian jinian wenji* [Looking for-ward: Anthology in honor of the fortieth anniversary of the Research Institute of Archaeology of Shaanxi Province]. Xi'an: Shaanxi renmin meishu chubanshe, 1998, pp. 768–81.

Harrist. Robert E. Harrist, Jr. *Power and Virtue: The Horse in Chinese Art.* New York: China Institute Gallery, 1997.

Hasegawa. Hasegawa Michitaka. "Ryō, Kin, Gendai no nagatsubo" [Slender vases in the Liao, Jin, and Yuan dynasties]. *Tōyō tōji* 1987–89.17, p. 48.

Hay. John Hay. "The Persistent Dragon (*Lung*)." In *The Power of Culture: Studies in Chinese Cultural History* (edited by Willard J. Peterson, Andrew H. Plaks, and Ying-shih Yü). Hong Kong: Chinese University Press, 1987, pp. 119–49.

Heaven's Embroidered Cloths. Urban Council, Hong Kong; Oriental Ceramic Society of Hong Kong; in asso-ciation with the Liaoning Provincial Museum and the Hong Kong Museum of Art (eds.). *Heaven's Embroidered Cloths: One Thousand Years of Chinese Textiles.* Hong Kong: Urban Council, 1995.

Huaman lu. Zhang Shunmin. *Huaman lu* [Record of Zhang Shunmin]. In *Shuofu* [Florilegium of (unofficial) literature] (edited by Tao Zongyi). Vol. 2. Beijing: Zhongguo shudian, 1986; Shanghai: Shanghai guji chubanshe, 1988; pp. 855–73.

Hua wu Datang chun. Shaanxi lishi bowuguan, Beijing daxue kaogu wenbo xueyuan, Beida zhendan gudai wenming yanjiu zhongxin et al. *Hua wu Datang chun: Hejiacun yibao jingcui* [Selected treasures from Hejia Village Tang hoard]. Beijing: Wenwu chubanshe, 2003.

Huayansi. Shanxi Yungang shiku wenwu baoguansuo (ed.). *Huayansi* [Huayan Monastery]. Beijing: Wenwu chubanshe, 1980.

Huang Nengfu. Huang Nengfu and Chen Juanjuan. *Zhongguo sichou keji yishu qiqiannian* [Seven thousand years of Chinese silk technology and craftsmanship]. Beijing: Zhongguo fangzhi chubanshe, 2002, pp. 132–44.

Jett et al. Paul Jett, Janet G. Douglas, Blythe McCarthy, and John Winter. *Scientific Research in the Field of Asian Art: Proceedings of the First Forbes Symposium at the Freer Gallery of Art.* Washington D.C.: Archtype Publications and Freer Gallery of Art, Smithsonian Institution, 2003.

Jilin Zhelimumeng. "Jilin Zhelimumeng Kulunqi yihao Liao mu fajue jianbao" [Report on the excavation of Liao Tomb Number 1 at Kulun Banner, Zhelimu League, Jilin Province]. *Wenwu* 1973.8, pp. 2–18.

Ji Ping. Ji Ping. "Aohanqi Pijiangou Liaodai muzang" [A Liao-dynasty tomb at Pijiangou, Aohan Banner]. In *Neimenggu wenwu kaogu wenji* [Essays on the archaeology of cultural relics in Inner Mongolia], vol. 2 (edited by Wei Jian). Beijing: Zhongguo da baike quanshu chubanshe, 1997, pp. 639–50.

Ji Ping and Ta La. Ji Ping and Ta La. "Ningcheng xian Maiwanggou Liaodai mu de fajue jianbao" [Brief excavation report on the Liao tombs at Maiwanggou, Ningcheng County, Inner Mongolia]. In *Neimenggu wenwu kaogu wenji* [Essays on the archaeology of cultural relics in Inner Mongolia], vol. 2 (edited by Wei Jian). Beijing: Zhongguo da baike quanshu chubanshe, 1997, pp. 609–30.

Ji Ruoxin. Ji Ruoxin. "Shuo 'Liao yan'" [Liao ink-stones]. *Gugong wenwu yuekan* 2000.6, pp. 37–49.

Ji Shaoguang. Ji Shaoguang et al. "Neimenggu Chifeng Baoshan Liaomu bihuamu fajue jianbao" [Excavation report on Liao tombs with murals in Baoshan, Chifeng, Inner Mongolia]. *Wenwu* 1998.1, pp. 73–95.

[Jia] Zhoujie. [Jia] Zhoujie. "Chifeng Gangwayaocun Liao dai ciyao diaocha ji" [Survey of the Liao-dynasty kiln site at Gangwayao Village in Chifeng]. *Kaogu* 1973.4, pp. pp. 241–43.

Jinshu. Fang Xuanling (578–648). *Jinshu* [Standard history of the Jin]. Beijing: Zhonghua shuju, 1974.

Jintan Nan-Song Zhou. "Jintan Nan-Song Zhou Yu Mu" [The tomb of Zhou Yu from the Southern Song dynasty in Jintan]. *Kaogu Xuebao* 1977.1, pp. 105–32.

Jiu Tangshu. Liu Xu (888–947). *Jiu Tangshu* [Old history of the Tang dynasty]. Beijing: Zhonghua shuju, 1975.

Kamio. Kamio Kazuharu. *Kittan Bukkyō bunka shi kō* [Historical researches on the history of Khitan Buddhism]. Tokyo: Daiichi Shobō, 1982.

Kara. György Kara. "Kitan and Jurchin." In *The World's Writing Systems* (edited by Peter T. Daniels and William Bright). New York: Oxford University Press, 1986, pp. 230–38.

Karetzky. Patricia Eichenbaum Karetzky. "Engraved Designs on the Late Sixth Century Sarcophagus of Li Ho." *Artibus Asiae* 47.2 (1986), pp. 81–106.

Kessler. Adam T. Kessler. *Empires Beyond the Great Wall: The Heritage of Genghis Khan*. Los Angeles: Natural History Museum of Los Angeles County, 1993.

Kinoshita (a). Hiromi Kinoshita. "Burial Practices of the Liao (907–1125) Khitan Elite: A Reflection of Hybrid Culture." Ph.D. dissertation, University of Oxford, 2006.

Kinoshita (b). Hiromi Kinoshita. "Hybridity and Conquest: Patterns of Liao (AD 907–1125) Khitan Tomb Burial." Chapter 8 of *Cultural Interaction and Conflict in Central and Inner Asia* (edited by Michael Gervers, Uradyn E. Bulag, and Gillian Long). Toronto: University of Toronto Asian Institute, 2004, pp. 129–44.

Kleeman. Terry Kleeman. "Land Contracts and Related Documents." In *Chūgoku no shūkyō shisō to kagaku* [Chinese religious thoughts]. Tokyo: Kokusho Kankōkai, 1984, pp. 1–34.

Kotitsa. Zoi Kotitsa (ed.). *The Belitung Wreck: Sunken Treasures from Tang China*. Forthcoming.

Kuhn (a). Dieter Kuhn. *How the Qidan Reshaped the Tradition of the Chinese Dome-shaped Tomb*. Heidelberg: Edition Forum, 1998.

Kuhn (b). Dieter Kuhn. *Die Kunst des Grabbaus. Kuppelgräber der Liao-Zeit (907–1125)* [The art of tomb building: Dome-shaped tombs of the Liao period (907–1125)]. Heidelberg: Edition Forum, 1997.

Kuhn (c). Dieter Kuhn. "Liao Architecture: Qidan Innovations and Han-Chinese Traditions?" *T'oung Pao* 2000.86, pp. 325–62.

Kuhn (d). Dieter Kuhn. *A Place for the Dead: An Archaeological Documentary on Graves and Tombs of the Song Dynasty (960–1279)*. Heidelberg: Edition Forum, 1996.

Kuhn (e). Dieter Kuhn. *Die Republik China von 1912 bis 1937. Entwurf für eine politische Ereignisgeschichte* [Republican China from 1912 to 1937: Draft for a narrative history of political events]. 2 vols. Heidelberg: Edition Forum, 2004.

Laing. Ellen Johnston Laing. "Auspicious Motifs in Ninth- to Thirteenth-Century Chinese tombs." *Ars Orientalis* 33 (2003), pp. 33–75.

Lamouroux. Christian Lamouroux. "Geography and Politics, The Song-Liao Dispute of 1074–75." In *China and Her Neighbours: Borders, Visions of the Other, Foreign Policy, 10ᵗʰ–19ᵗʰ Century* (edited by Sabine Dabringhaus and Roderich Ptak). Wiesbaden: Harrassowitz, 1997, pp. 1–28.

Laufer. Berthold Laufer. "Historical Jottings of Amber in Asia." In *Memoirs of the American Anthropological Association*, vol. 1, part 3 (1907), pp. 215–44.

Ledderose (a). Lothar Ledderose. "Changing the Audience: A Pivotal Period in the Great Sutra Carving Project at the Cloud Dwelling Monastery near Beijing." In *Religion and Chinese Society* (edited by John Lagerwey). Hong Kong and Paris: Chinese University of Hong Kong and École française d'Extrême-Orient, 2004, pp. 385–409.

Ledderose (b). Lothar Ledderose. "Massenproduktion angesichts der Katastrophie" [Mass production in view of catastrophe]. *Asiatische Studien/Études Asiatiques* 44.2 (1990), pp. 217–33.

Ledderose (c). Lothar Ledderose. *Ten Thousand Things: Module and Mass Production in Chinese Art*. Princeton: Princeton University Press, 2000.

Leifeng yizhen. Zhejiang sheng wenwu kaogu yanjiusuo. *Leifeng yizhen* [Treasures from Leifeng Pagoda]. Beijing: Wenwu chubanshe, 2002.

Lei Runze and Yu Cunhai. Lei Runze and Yu Cunhai. *Xi Xia Fota* [Xi Xia Buddhist pagodas]. Beijing: Wenwu chubanshe, 1995.

Leung. Harold Mok Kar Leung. "Ceramic Flasks of the Liao Dynasty." *Oriental Art*, Autumn 1989, pp. 150–62.

Li Changqing and Hei Guang. Li Changqing and Hei Guang. "Xi'an beijiao faxian Tangdai jinhua yinpan" [A gilded-silver dish of the Tang dynasty discovered in the north of Xi'an]. *Wenwu* 1963.10, p. 60.

Li Jinyun. Li Jinyun. "Liushi haiwai de yipi Liaodai jinyin qi" [A group of gold and silver artifacts of the Liao dynasty now scattered abroad]. *Shoucangjia* 1999.14, pp. 12–15.

Li Yiyou (a). Li Yiyou. "Liaodai chengguo yingjian zhidu chutan" [Preliminary discussion on building formulas and systems in city construction of the Liao dynasty]. In *Liao Jin shi lunji* [Collection of articles on the history of the Liao and Jin] (edited by Chen Shu). Vol. 3. Beijing: Shumu wenxian chubanshe, 1987, pp. 45–94.

Li Yiyou (b). Li Yiyou. "Liaodai Qidanren muzang zhidu gaishuo" [Introductory remarks on the burial system of the Khitan in the Liao period]. In *Neimenggu Dongbuqu kaoguxue wenhua yanjiu wenji* [Research essays on archaeological culture of the eastern region of Inner Mongolia] (edited by Neimenggu zizhiqu wenwu kaogu yanjiusuo). Beijing: Haiyang chubanshe, 1991, pp. 80–102.

Li Yiyou (c). Li Yiyou. "Liao Qingling" [Imperial tombs of the Liao]; "Liao Shangjing yizhi" [The remains of the Liao Supreme Capital]; and "Liao Zhongjing yizhi" [The remains of the Liao Central Capital]. *Zhongguo dabaike quanshu: kaoguxue* 1986, pp. 277–79

Li Yiyou (d). Li Yiyou. "Lielun Liaodai Qidan yu Hanren muzang de tezheng he fenxi" [Special features and analysis of Khitan versus Han Chinese tombs in the Liao dynasty]. In *Zhongguo kaogu xuehui diliuci nianhui lunwen ji* [Collection of papers presented at the sixth annual meeting of the Chinese Institute of Archaeology]. Beijing: Wenwu chubanshe, 1987, pp. 187–95.

Li Yiyou (e). Li Yiyou. "Neimenggu chutu wenwu gaishu" [General account of cultural relics excavated in Inner Mongolia]. In *Neimenggu wenwu xuanji* [Selected relics of Inner Mongolia] (edited by Neimenggu zizhiqu wenwu gongzuo dui). Beijing: Wenwu chubanshe, 1963, pp. 3–10.

Li Yiyou (f). Li Yiyou. "Zhaowudameng Ningchengxian Xiaoliuzhangzi Liao mu fajue jianbao" [Excavation report on Liao tombs at Xiaoliuzhangzi, Ningcheng County, Zhaowuda League]. *Wenwu* 1961.9, pp. 44–49.

Li Yiyou and Wei Jian. Li Yiyou and Wei Jian (eds.). *Neimenggu wenwu kaogu wenji* [Essays on the archaeology of cultural relics in Inner Mongolia]. Vol. 1. Beijing: Zhongguo dabaike quanshu chubanshe, 1994.

Li Yufeng. Li Yufeng. "Fuxin Hailiban Liao mu" [A Liao tomb in Hailiban, Fuxin]. *Liaohai wenwu xuekan* 1991.1, pp. 106–19 and 123.

Li Yufeng and Yuan Haibo. Li Yufeng and Yuan Haibo. "Liaoning Fuxin Liao Xiao Jin mu" [The Liao tomb of Xiao Jin in Fuxin County, Liaoning Province]. *Beifang wenwu* 1988.2, pp. 33–36.

Liang Shuqin. Liang Shuqin. "'Guduo' shixi" [Elucidating and analyzing 'guduo']. *Liaohai wenwu xuekan* 1989.1, pp. 254–61.

Liang Sicheng (a). Liang Sicheng. "Baodixian Guangjisi Sandashidian" [Hall of the Three Great Buddhas at Guangji Monastery, Baodi County]. *Zhongguo yingzao xueshe huikan* 3, no. 4 (1932), pp. 1–50.

Liang Sicheng (b). Liang Sicheng. "Jixian Dulesi Guanyinge, Shanmen kao" [Research on Guanyin Pavilion and the gatehouse at Dule Monastery, Ji County]. *Zhongguo yingzao xueshe huikan* 3, no. 2 (1932), pp. 1–92.

Liang Sicheng (c). Liang Sicheng. "Jixian Guanyinsi Baita ji" [Notes on the White Pagoda of Guanyin Monastery, Ji County]. *Zhongguo yingzao xueshe huikan* 3, no. 2 (1932), pp. 93–99.

Liang Sicheng and Liu Dunzhen. Liang Sicheng and Liu Dunzhen. "Datong gujianzhu diaocha baogao" [Report on the investigation of ancient architecture in Datong]. *Zhongguo yingzao xueshe huikan* 4, nos. 3 and 4 (1934), pp. 7–76.

Liao Chenguo gongzhu mu. Neimenggu zizhiqu wenwu kaogu yanjiusuo and Zhelimumeng bowuguan (eds.). *Liao Chenguo gongzhu mu* [Liao tomb of the princess of the state of Chen]. Beijing: Wenwu chubanshe, 1993.

Liaoning Chaoyang Beita. "Liaoning Chaoyang Beita tiangong digong qingli jianbao" [Brief excavation report on the aboveground and underground palaces of the North Pagoda at Chaoyang, Liaoning]. *Wenwu* 1992.7, pp. 1–28.

Liaoning Faku Qianshan. "Liaoning Faku Qianshan Xiao Paulu mu" [The tomb of Xiao Paolu at Qianshan in Faku, Liaoning]. *Kaogu* 1983.7, pp. 624–35.

Liaoning kaogu wenji. Liaoningsheng wenwu kaogu yanjiusuo (ed.). *Liaoning kaogu wenji* [Collected works on Liaoning archaeology]. Shenyang: Liaoning minzu chubanshe, 2003.

Liao Shangjing chengzhi. Neimenggu zizhiqu wenwu kaogu yanjiusuo. "Liao Shangjing chengzhi kancha baogao" [Survey and excavation of the Liao Shangjing city site]. In *Neimenggu wenwu kaogu wenji* [Essays on the archaeology of cultural relics in Inner Mongolia], vol. 1 (edited by Li Yiyou and Wei Jian). Beijing: Zhongguo da baike quanshu chubanshe, 1994, pp. 510–36.

Liao Shangjing yizhi jianjie. Liao Shangjing yizhi jianjie [Brief introduction to the remains of the Liao Supreme Capital]. Balinzuoqi: Balinzuoqi wenhuaguan, 1983.

Liaoshi. Tuo Tuo (1313–55) et al. *Liaoshi* [History of the Liao]. Beijing: Zhonghua shuju, 1974.

Liao Yelü Yuzhi. Neimenggu zizhiqu wenwu kaogu yanjiusuo. "Liao Yelü Yuzhi mu fajue jianbao" [Brief report on the excavation of the Liao tomb of Yelü Yuzhi]. *Wenwu* 1996.1, pp. 4–32.

Linquan gaoshi. Guobao zaixian. *Linquan gaoshi* [Scholars in reclusion]. Shanghai: Shanghai shuhua chubanshe, 2003.

Little and Eichman. Stephen Little and Shawn Eichman. *Taoism and the Arts of China*. Chicago and Berkeley: Art Institute of Chicago and University of California Press, 2000.

Liu Bing. Liu Bing. "Qian tan Liaodai gongjian" [Brief discussion on Liao bows and arrows]. In *Neimenggu wenwu kaogu wenji* [Essays on the archaeology of cultural relics in Inner Mongolia], vol. 2 (edited by Wei Jian). Beijing: Zhongguo da baike quanshu chubanshe, 1997, pp. 556–60.

Liu Bing and Zhao Guochen. Liu Bing and Zhao Guochen. "Chifengshi Aluke'erqinqi, Wenduo'er Aoruishan Liao mu qingli jianbao" [Brief report on a Liao tomb at Aoruishan, Wenduo'er, Aluke'erqin Banner, Chifeng City]. *Wenwu* 1993.3, pp. 57–67.

Liudingshan yu Bohaizhen. Zhongguo shehui kexueyuan kaogu yanjiusuo (ed.). *Liudingshan yu Bohaizhen* [Liudingshan and Bohai Town]. Beijing: Zhongguo da baike quanshu chubanshe, 1997.

Liu Dunzhen (a). Liu Dunzhen. "Hebeisheng xibu gujianzhu diaocha jilüe" [Notes on the investigation of ancient architecture in western Hebei Province]. *Zhongguo yingzao xueshe huikan* 5, no. 4 (1935), pp. 9–15.

Liu Dunzhen (b). Liu Dunzhen. *Zhongguo gudai jianzhu shi* [*History of ancient Chinese architecture*]. Beijing: Zhongguo jianzhu gongye chubanshe, 1980 edition.

Liu Laixue. Liu Laixue (ed.). *Neimenggu kaogu wushi nian* [*Fifty years of archaeology in Inner Mongolia*]. Hohhot: Neimenggu zizhiqu wenwu kaogu yanjiusuo, 2004.

Liu Shufen. Liu Shufen. "Foding zunsheng tuoluoni jing yu Tangdai Zunsheng jingchuang de jianli—jingchuang yanjiu zhi yi" [The *Dhāraṇī of the Jubilant Corona* and the Tang-dynasty Zunsheng sutra-pillar: Series of the study on sutra-pillars, part 1]. *Zhongyang yanjiuyuan lishi yuyan yanjiusuo jikan* 67.1 (1996), pp. 145–93.

Lopez. Donald S. Lopez, Jr. *Elaborations on Emptiness: Uses of the Heart Sutra*. Princeton: Princeton University Press, 1996.

Louis. François Louis. "Shaping Symbols of Privilege: Precious Metals and the Early Liao Aristocracy." *Journal of Song-Yuan Studies* 33 (2003), pp. 71–109.

Lu Jing. Lu Jing. *Liaodai taoci* [*Liao-dynasty ceramics*]. Shenyang: Shenyang huabao chubanshe, 2003.

Lu Sixian. Lu Sixian. "Shi 'guduo'" [Explaining 'guduo']. *Kaogu yu wenwu* 1982.5, pp. 98–101.

Lu Sixian and Du Chengwu. Lu Sixian and Du Chengwu. "Chaoyouqianqi Haoqianying di liuhao Liao mu qingli jianbao" [Brief report on Liao Tomb Number 6 at Haoqianying, Chaoyou Front Banner]. *Wenwu* 1983.9, pp. 1–8.

Luting shishi. Wen Weijian (Song dynasty). *Luting shishi* [*Veritable facts from the caitiffs' court*]. In *Shuofu* [*Florilegium of (unofficial) literature*] (edited by Tao Zongyi). Vol. 2. Beijing: Zhongguo shudian, 1986; Shanghai: Shanghai guji chubanshe, 1988; pp. 172–73.

Lu Zhaoyin (a). Lu Zhaoyin. "Guanyu Famensi digong jinyinqi de ruogan wenti" [Some problems concerning the gold and silver objects from the Underground Palace of Famen Temple]. *Kaogu* 1990.7, pp. 638–43.

Lu Zhaoyin (b). Lu Zhaoyin. "Guanyu Xi'an beijiao suochu Tangdai jinhua yinpan" [A gilded-silver dish of the Tang dynasty from a northern suburb of Xi'an]. *Kaogu* 1964.3, pp. 159–60.

Luo Shiping. Luo Shiping. "Liao mu bihua shidu" [A tentative understanding of the murals in Liao tombs]. *Wenwu* 1999.1, pp. 76–85.

Meng Jianren and Piao Chunyue. Meng Jianren and Piao Chunyue. "Keyouzhongqi Daiqintala Liao mu qingli jianbao" [Brief report on the clearing of a Liao tomb at Daiqintala, Keyou Central Banner]. In *Neimenggu wenwu kaogu wenji* [*Essays on the archaeology of cultural relics in Inner Mongolia*], vol. 2 (edited by Wei Jian). Beijing: Zhongguo da baike quanshu chubanshe, 1997, pp. 651–67.

Michaelson. Carol Michaelson. *Gilded Dragons: Buried Treasures from China's Golden Ages*. London: British Museum Press, 1999.

Mikami (a). Mikami Tsugio (ed.). *Ryō, Kin, Gen* [*Liao, Jin, Yuan*] (volume 13 of *Sekai tōji zenshū* [*Catalogue of the world's ceramics*]). Tokyo: Shogakukan, 1981.

Mikami (b). Mikami Tsugio. *Tōji bōekishi kenkyū* [*Studies on the history of export ceramics*]. Vol. 2. Tokyo: Chūō kōron bijutsu shuppan, 1987.

Mino. Yutaka Mino. *Ceramics in the Liao Dynasty North and South of the Great Wall*. New York: China House Gallery, 1973.

Mo Zongjiang. Mo Zongjiang. "Laiyuan Geyuansi Wenshudian" [Mañjushrī Hall of Geyuan Monastery in Laiyuan]. *Jianzhushi lunwen ji* 1979.2, pp. 51–71.

Mou Yongkang and Ren Shilong. Mou Yongkang and Ren Shilong. "Guan, Ge jianlun" [Brief discussion of Guan and Ge wares]. *Hunan kaogu jikan* 1986.3.

Mu Yi. Mu Yi. "Liao mu chutu de jinshu mianju, wangluo ji xiangguan wenti" [Metal facemasks and netting excavated from Liao tombs and other questions]. *Beifang wenwu* 1993.1, pp. 28–34.

Müller. Shing Müller. *Yezhongji: Eine Quelle zur materiellen Kultur in der Stadt Ye im 4. Jahrhundert* [*Record of Ye: A source on the material culture of the city of Ye in the fourth century*]. Münchener Ostasiatische Studien 65. Stuttgart: Franz Steiner, 1993.

Mullie. Joseph Mullie. "Les anciennes villes de l'empire des grands Leao au Royaume Mongol de Bârin" [On the ancient cities of the Great Liao empire in the Mongol kingdom of Bârin]. *T'oung Pao* 1922.21, pp. 106–231.

Namba. Namba Taakira (ed.). *Kyōzō to kakebotoke* [*Mirrors incised with Buddha images and suspended plaques with Buddha images*]. *Nihon no bijustu* 284, 1990.

Nattier. Jan Nattier. *Once Upon a Future Time: Studies in a Buddhist Prophecy of Decline*. Berkeley: Asian Humanities Press, 1991.

Neimenggu Balinyouqi. "Neimenggu Balinyouqi Qingzhou baita faxian Liaodai fojiao wenwu" [Buddhist relics from the White Pagoda in Qingzhou, Balin Right Banner, Inner Mongolia]. *Wenwu* 1994.12, pp. 4–33.

Neimenggu chutu. Neimenggu zizhiqu gongzuodui (ed.). *Neimenggu chutu wenwu xuanji* [*Collected relics excavated in Inner Mongolia*]. Beijing: Wenwu chubanshe, 1963.

Neimenggu Tongliao shi. Neimenggu zizhiqu wenwu kaogu yanjiusuo. "Neimenggu Tongliao shi Tuerji shan Liao dai muzang" [The Liao-period grave at Tuerji Hill, Tongliao City, Inner Mongolia]. *Kaogu* 2004.7, pp. 50–53.

Neimenggu Xing'anmeng. "Neimenggu Xing'anmeng Daiqintala Liaomu chutu sichou fushi" [Silk garments from a Liao-dynasty tomb in Daiqintala, Xing'an League, Inner Mongolia]. *Wenwu* 2002.4, pp. 55–80.

Ningcheng xian Liwanggou. Neimenggu zizhiqu wenwu kaogu yanjiusuo and Liao Zhongjing bowuguan. "Ningcheng xian Liwanggou Liaodai mudi fajue jianbao" [Brief report on the discovery of a Liao tomb at Liwanggou, Ningcheng County. In *Neimenggu wenwu kaogu wenji* [*Essays on the archaeology of cultural relics in Inner Mongolia*], vol. 2 (edited by Wei Jian). Beijing: Zhongguo da baike quanshu chubanshe, 1997, pp. 609–30.

Ningcheng xian Maiwanggou. Neimenggu zizhiqu wenwu kaogu yanjiusuo and Liao Zhongjing bowuguan (Ji Ping and Ta La). "Ningcheng xian Maiwanggou Liaodai mudi fajue jianbao" [Brief excavation report on the Liao tombs at Maiwanggou, Ningcheng]. In *Neimenggu wenwu kaogu wenji* [*Essays on the archaeology of cultural relics in Inner Mongolia*], vol. 2 (edited by Wei Jian). Beijing: Zhongguo da baike quanshu chubanshe, 1997, pp. 609–30.

Owen. Elisabeth M. Owen. "A Stitch in Time: The Pearl-bordered Medallion, from Persia to Japan." Paper presented at the Third Silk Road Conference at Yale University, New Haven, Dec. 1998.

Pearlstein. Elinor Pearlstein. "Pictorial Stones from Chinese Tombs." *Bulletin of the Cleveland Museum of Art* 71, no. 9 (1984), pp. 304–31.

Porada. Edith Porada. *The Art of Ancient Iran: Pre-Islamic Cultures*. New York: Crown Publishers, 1965.

Qidan guozhi. Ye Longli (d. after 1267). *Qidan guozhi* [*History of the Khitan*] of 1247. 2 vols. Han yun zhai cong shu Bai bu cong shu ji cheng 43. Taipei: Yi wen yin shu guan, 1969.

Qidan nushi. Wumeng wenwu gongzuo zhan and Neimenggu wenwu gongzuo dui. *Qidan nushi* [*The remains of Khitan females*]. Hohhot: Neimenggu renmin chubanshe, 1985.

Qidan wangchao. Neimenggu zizhiqu wenhua ting and Zhongguo lishi bowuguan. *Qidan wangchao: Neimenggu Liaodai wenwu jinghua* [*Khitan dynasty: Liao archaeological treasures from Inner Mongolia*]. Beijing: Zhongguo zangxue chubanshe, 2002.

Qi Dongfang. Qi Dongfang. *Tangdai jinyinqi yanjiu* [*Research on Tang gold and silver*]. Beijing: Zhongguo shehui kexue chubanshe, 1999.

Qi Xiaoguang (a). Qi Xiaoguang. "Guanyu 'Yelü Yuzhi muzhi dui wenxian jizai zhi kanbu' yi wen de jidian buchong" [Some additions to the paper "Emendations of textual records based on Yelü Yuzhi's epitaph"]. *Wenwu* 1996.6, pp. 69–70.

Qi Xiaoguang (b). Qi Xiaoguang. "Phönix in der Steppe: Das Kammergrab des Qidan-Prinzen Yelü Yuzhi in der Inneren Mongolei" [Phoenix in the steppe: The tomb of the Khitan prince Yelü Yuzhi in Inner Mongolia]. *Antike Welt* 26 (1995), pp. 437–43.

Qi Xiaoguang (c). Qi Xiaoguang. "Yelü Yuzhi mu han yuwai wenhua yinsu zhi jinyinqi" [Gold and silver from Yelü Yuzhi's tomb, showing foreign features]. In *Neimenggu wenwu kaogu wenji* [*Essays on the archaeology of cultural relics in Inner Mongolia*], vol. 2 (edited by Wei Jian). Beijing: Zhongguo da baike quanshu chubanshe, 1997, pp. 561–66.

Qi Xiaoguang (d). Qi Xiaoguang. "Yelü Yuzhi muzhi dui wenxian jizai de kanbu" [Emendations of textual records based on Yelü Yuzhi's epitaph]. *Wenwu* 1996.3, pp. 41–44.

Qi Xiaoguang and Wang Jianguo. Qi Xiaoguang and Wang Jianguo. "Liao Yelü Yuzhi mu fajue jianbao" [Short report on the tomb of Yelü Yuzhi of Liao times]. *Wenwu* 1996.1, pp. 4–31.

Qi Xiaoguang et al. Qi Xiaoguang et al. "Neimenggu Chifeng Baoshan Liao bihuamu fajue jianbao" [Brief report on the wall paintings from a Liao tomb in Baoshan, Chifeng, Inner Mongolia]. *Wenwu* 1998.1, pp. 73–95.

Qi Yingtao. Qi Yingtao. "Hebeisheng Xinchengxian Kaishansi Dadian" [The main hall of Kaishan Monastery in Xincheng County, Hebei Province]. *Wenwu cankao ziliao*, 1957.1, pp. 23–29.

Qiao Yun and Sun Dazhang. Qiao Yun and Sun Dazhang (eds.). *Ancient Chinese Architecture*. Beijing and Hong Kong: Joint Publishing Company, 1982.

Qingdai fushi zhanlan tulu. Gugong bowuguan, Taipei. *Qingdai fushi zhanlan tulu* [*Catalogue of the exhibition of Qing-dynasty costume accessories*]. Taipei: Gugong bowuguan, 1986.

Quan Liaowen. Chen Shu (ed.). *Quan Liaowen* [*Complete Liao writings*]. Beijing: Zhonghua shuju, 1982.

Ratchnevsky. Paul Ratchnevsky. "Über den mongolischen Kult am Hofe der Grosskhane in China" [On the Mongolian "ritual" at the court of the great khans in China]. In *Mongolian Studies* (edited by Louis Ligeti). Amsterdam: B. R. Grüner, 1970, pp. 417–43.

Rawson (a). Jessica Rawson. *Chinese Jade from the Neolithic to the Qing*. London: British Museum Press, 1995.

Rawson (b). Jessica Rawson. "Creating Universes: Cultural Exchange as Seen in Tombs in Northern China between the Han and Tang Periods." In *Between Han and Tang: Cultural and Artistic Interaction in a Transformative Period* (edited by Wu Hung). Beijing: Wenwu chubanshe, 2001, pp. 113–49.

Rawson (c). Jessica Rawson. *The Ornament on Chinese Silver of the Tang Dynasty (AD 618–906)*. London: British Museum, Department of Oriental Antiquities, 1982.

Rawson (d). Jessica Rawson. "The Power of Images: The Model Universe of the First Emperor and Its Legacy." *Historical Research* 75, no. 188 (2002), pp. 123–154.

Reckel (a). Johannes Reckel. *Bohai: Geschichte und Kultur eines mandschurisch-koreanischen Königreiches der Tang-Zeit.* [*Bohai: History and Culture of a Manchu-Korean kindgom of the Tang period*]. Aetas Manjurica 5. Wiesbaden: Harrassowitz, 1995.

Reckel (b). Johannes Reckel. "Das Kitan-Volk im Spiegel seiner Gräber" [The (material culture) of the Khitan people as mirrored in the findings from their tombs]. *Zentralasiatische Studien des Seminars für Sprach- und Kulturwissenschaft Zentralasiens der Universität Bonn* 22 (1989/1991), pp. 18–141.

Riboud. Krishna Riboud. "A Brief Account of Textiles Excavated in Dated Liao Dynasty Tombs (907–1125) in China." *CIETA-Bulletin* 74 (1997), pp. 28–49.

Rossabi. Morris Rossabi (ed.). *China Among Equals: The Middle Kingdom and Its Neighbors, 10th–14th Centuries.* Berkeley: University of California Press, 1983.

Rudenko. Sergei Ivanovich Rudenko. *Frozen Tombs of Siberia: The Pazyryk Burials of Iron Age Horsemen* (translated by M. W. Thompson). London: J. M. Dent & Sons, 1970.

Schafer (a). Edward H. Schafer. *The Vermilion Bird: T'ang Images of the South.* Berkeley and Los Angeles: University of California Press, 1967.

Schafer (b). Edward H. Schafer. "The Yeh Chung Chi" [The record of Ye]. *T'oung Pao* 1990.76, pp. 147–82.

Schulten. Caroline Schulten. "Ancient Chinese Mirrors and Their Legacies in the Tang (AD 618–906), Liao (AD 907–1125) and Song (AD 960–1279) Periods." Ph.D. dissertation, University of Oxford, 2000.

Seidel. Anna Seidel. "Traces of Han Religions: In Funeral Texts Found in Tombs." In *Dōkyō to shūkyōbunka* [*Daoism and religious cultures*] (edited by Akitsuki Kan'ei). Tokyo: Hirakawa Shuppansha, 1987, pp. 678–714.

Sekino. Sekino Tadashi. "Manshū Giken Hōkokuji Daiyūhōden" [Daxiongbao Hall of Fengguo onastery in Yi County, Manchuria]. *Bijutsu kenkyū* 1933.14, pp. 37–49.

Sekino and Takeshima. Sekino Tadashi and Takeshima Takuichi. *Ryō-Kin jidai no kenchiku to sono Butsuzō* [*Liao-Jin architecture and its Buddhist sculpture*]. 2 vols. Tokyo: Toho bunka gakuin Tokyo kenkyujo, 1934–35.

Sen. Tansen Sen. "Astronomical Tomb Paintings from Xuanhua: Mandalas?" *Ars Orientalis* 29 (1999), pp. 29–54.

Shao Fuyu. Shao Fuyu. "Fengguosi" [Fengguo Monastery]. *Wenwu* 1980.12, pp. 86–87.

Shao Guotian (a). Shao Guotian. "Aohanqi Baitazi Liao mu" [Liao tomb at Baitazi, Aohan Banner]. *Kaogu* 1978.2, pp. 119–21.

Shao Guotian (b). Shao Guotian. "Aohanqi Xiawanzi Liao mu faxian jianbao" [A brief report on the excavation of Liao tombs at Xianwanzi, Aohan Banner]. *Neimenggu wenwu kaogu* 1999.1, pp. 67–84.

Shao Guotian (c). Shao Guotian. "Aohanqi Yingfenggou 7 hao Liao mu chutu yinzhi wenju kao" [The writing utensils excavated in Liao Tomb Number 7 at Yingfenggou, Aohan Banner]. *Neimenggu wenwu kaogu* 2003.2, pp. 71–77.

Shao Qinglong. Shao Qinglong. "Liaodai baici foxiang" [Liao-dynasty white ware Buddhist images]. *Neimenggu wenwu kaogu* 1981.1, pp. 143–44.

Shen (a). Hsueh-man Shen. "Body Matters: Manikin Burials in the Liao Tombs of Xuanhua, Hebei Province." *Artibus Asiae* 65.1 (2005), pp. 99–141.

Shen (b). Hsueh-man Shen. "Buddhist Relic Deposits from Tang (618–907) to Northern Song (960–1127) and Liao (907–1125)." Ph.D. dissertation, University of Oxford, 2000.

Shen (c). Hsueh-man Shen. "Liao yu Beisong shelita nei cang jing zhi yanjiu" [Scripture deposits of the Liao and Northern Song]. *Meishushi yanjiu jikan* 2002.12, pp. 169–212.

Shen (d). Hsueh-man Shen. "Luxury or Necessity: Glassware in *Sarira* Relic Pagodas of the Tang and Northern Song Periods." In *Chinese Glass: Archaeological Studies on the Uses and Social Context of Glass Artefacts from the Warring States to the Northern Song Period* (edited by Cecilia Braghin). Orientalia Venetiana 14. Venice: Leo S. Olschki, 2002, pp. 71–110.

Shen (e). Hsueh-man Shen. "Realizing the Buddha's *Dharma* Body during the *Mofa* Period: A Study of Liao Buddhist Relic Deposits." *Artibus Asiae* 61.2 (2001), pp. 263–303.

So (a). Jenny F. So (ed.) *Noble Riders from Pines and Deserts: The Artistic Legacy of the Qidan.* Hong Kong: Art Museum of the University of Hong Kong, 2004.

So (b). Jenny F. So. "The Ornamented Belt in China." *Orientations*, March 1997, pp. 70–78.

So (c). Jenny F. So. "Tiny Bottles: What a Well-dressed Qidan Lady Wears on her Belt." *Orientations*, October 2004, pp. 75–79.

So and Bunker. Jenny F. So and Emma C. Bunker. *Traders and Raiders on China's Northern Frontier.* Seattle: Arthur M. Sackler Gallery, Smithsonian Institution, in association with University of Washington Press, 1995.

Songmo jiwen. Hong Hao (1088–1155). *Songmo jiwen* [*Records of hearsay on the pine forests north of the desert*]. [China]: Wu Guan, Ming [between 1465 and 1620].

Songshi. Tuo Tuo (1313–55) et al. *Songshi* [*496 juan*] [*History of the Song (496 fascicles)*]. Beijing: Zhonghua shuju, 1977.

Soushen ji. Gan Bao (early 4th century). *Quanben Soushen ji pingyi* [*Complete and translated edition of Records of Ghosts*] (edited and translated by Zhang Su, Chen Tijin, and Zhang Jue). Shanghai: Xuelin chubanshe, 1994.

Spiro. Audrey Spiro. *Contemplating the Ancients: Aesthetic and Social Issues in Early Chinese Portraiture.* Berkeley: University of California Press, 1990.

Steinhardt (a). Nancy S. Steinhardt. "Chinese Architecture, 963–66." *Orientations*, February 1995, pp. 46–52.

Steinhardt (b). Nancy S. Steinhardt. *Chinese Imperial City Planning.* Honolulu: University of Hawai'i Press, 1990.

Steinhardt (c). Nancy S. Steinhardt. "A Jin Hall at Jingtusi: Architecture in Search of Identity." *Ars Orientalis* 33 (2003), pp. 76–119.

Steinhardt (d). Nancy S. Steinhardt. "Liao Archaeology: New Frontiers on China's Frontier." *Asian Perspectives* 37, no. 2 (1998), pp. 224–44.

Steinhardt (e). Nancy S. Steinhardt. *Liao Architecture.* Honolulu: University of Hawai'i Press, 1997.

Steinhardt (f). Nancy S. Steinhardt. "A Response to Dieter Kuhn, 'Liao Architecture: Qidan Innovations and Han-Chinese Traditions?'" *T'oung Pao* 2001.87, pp. 456–62.

Strong. John Strong. *Relics of the Buddha.* Princeton: Princeton University Press, 2004.

Su Bai (a). Su Bai. *Baisha Song mu* [*Song tomb at Baisha*]. Beijing: Wenwu chubanshe, 1957.

Su Bai (b). Su Bai. "Dulesi Guanyinge yu Jizhou Yutian Hanjia [Guanyin Pavilion of Dule Monastery and the Han family of Yutian, Ji Prefecture]. *Wenwu* 1985.7, pp. 32–48.

Su Bai (c). Su Bai (ed.). *Zhonghua renmin gongheguo zhongda kaogu faxian* [*Great archaeological discoveries of the People's Republic of China*]. Beijing: Wenwu chubanshe, 1999.

Sun Dawei. Sun Dawei. *The Art in the Caves of Xinjiang.* Xinjiang: Xinjiang Photographic Art Publishing House, 1989.

Sun Ji (a). Sun Ji. "Tangdai de maju yu mashi" [Tang-dynasty horse gear and ornaments]. *Wenwu* 1981.10, pp. 82–88 and 96.

Sun Ji (b). Sun Ji. "Yi zhi Liaodai ci'e zhui" [A Liao-dynasty swan-piercing awl]. *Wenwu* 1987.11, pp. 36–37.

Sun Jianhua et al. Sun Jianhua et al. "Balinyouqi Zhuangjingou 5 hao Liao mu fajue jianbao" [Brief report on the Liao Tomb Number 5 at Zhuangjingou in Balin Right Banner]. *Wenwu* 2002.3, pp. 51–64.

Ta La. Ta La. "Jiekai muzhu shenfen zhi mi: Tu'erjishan Liao mu fajue jishi" [Unveiling the identity of the tomb occupant: A record of the excavation of a Liao tomb at Tuerji Hill]. *Zhongguo guojia dili* 2004.9, pp. 132–43.

Taiping yulan. Li Fang (925–996) et al. *Taiping yulan* [*Imperial digest of the Taiping reign period*]. Beijing: Zhonghua shuju, 1960.

Takeshima. Takeshima Takuichi. *Ryō-Kin jidai no kenchiku to sono Butsuzō* [*Liao-Jin architecture and its Buddhist sculpture*]. Tokyo: Ryū bun shokyoku, 1944.

Tallgren. A.M. Tallgren. "The South Siberian Cemetery of Oglakty from the Han Period." *Eurasia Septentrionalis Antiqua* 9 (1937), pp. 69–90.

Tamura. Tamura Jitsuzō. *Keiryō no hekiga: kaiga, chōsoku, tōji* [*Murals in the Qing Mausoleums: Paintings, carvings, ceramics*]. Kyoto: Tōhōsha, 1977.

Tamura and Kobayashi (a). Tamura Jitsuzō and Kobayashi Yukio. *Keiryō* [*Qingling*]. 2 vols. Kyoto: Kyoto Daigaku bungakubu, 1953.

Tamura and Kobayashi (b). Tamura Jitsuzō and Kobayashi Yukio. *Tombs and Mural Paintings of Ch'ing-ling: Liao Imperial Mausoleums of 11th Century A.D. in Eastern Mongolia.* 2 vols. Kyoto: Department of Literature, Kyoto University, 1952.

Tamura and Kobayashi (c). Tamura Jitsuzō and Kobayashi Yukio. "Tombs and Mural Paintings of Ch'ing-ling: Liao Imperial Mausoleums of 11th Century A.D. in Eastern Mongolia." *Japan Quarterly* 1954.1, pp. 34–45.

Tangdai jinyin qi. Zhenjiang shi bowuguan (Lu Jiugao) and Shaanxi sheng bowuguan (Han Wei) (eds.). *Tangdai jinyin qi* [*Tang-dynasty gold and silver wares*]. Beijing: Wenwu chubanshe, 1985.

Tang mu bi hua zhen. Shanxi lishi bowuguan, Li Xixing, and Yin Shengping (eds.). *Tang mu bi hua zhen pin xuan cui* [*The cream of original frescoes from Tang tombs*]. Xi'an: Shaanxi renmin meishu chubanshe, 1991.

Tang ren xiaoshuo jiaoshi. Tang ren xiaoshuo jiaoshi [*Collated and annotated collection of Tang-dynasty stories*]. 2 vols. Taipei: Zhengzhong shuju, 1983.

Tanii. Tanii Toshihito. "Kittan bukkyō seijishi ron" [A study of the Buddo-political history of the Khitans]. In *Chūgoku Bukkyō sekkei no kenkyū: Bōzan Unkyoji sekkei wo chūshin ni* [*Essays on Chinese Buddhist stone sutras: Principally the stone sutras at Cloud-Dwelling Monastery in Fangshan*] (edited by Kegasawa Yasunori). Kyoto: Kyōto Daigaku Gakujutsu Shuppansha, 1996, pp. 133–91.

Tao. Jingshen Tao. *Two Sons of Heaven: Studies in Sung-Liao Relations.* Tucson: University of Arizona Press, 1988.

Tian Caixia. Tian Caixia. "Liao Qingzhou Baita zang shijiafo niepan shi xiang" [The stone sculpture of the parinirvana of Shakyamuni from the depository of the Liao White Pagoda in Qingzhou]. *Wenwu* 2002.11, p. 93.

Tianjin Jixian Dulesi ta. Tianjin lishi bowuguan. "Tianjin Jixian Dulesi ta" [The Pagoda of Dule Monastery in Jixian, Tianjin]. *Kaogu xuebao* 1989.1, pp. 83–119.

Tian Li and Qi Xiaoguang. Tian Li and Qi Xiaoguang. "Aluke'erqinqi Chaidamu Liao mu" [Liao tomb at Chaidamu, Aluke'erqin Banner]. *Neimenggu wenwu kaogu* 1981.4, pp. 77–79.

Tian Likun and Li Zhi. Tian Likun and Li Zhi. "Chaoyang faxian de San Yan wenhua yiwu ji xiangguan wenti" [Three Yan cultural relics excavated from Chaoyang and related questions]. *Wenwu* 1994.11, pp. 20–32.

Tietze. K. Tietze. "The Liao-Sung Border Conflict of 1074–1076." In *Studia Sino-Mongolica: Festschrift für Herbert Franke* (edited by Wolfgang Bauer). Wiesbaden: Franz Steiner, 1979. pp. 127–51.

Tō kōtei kara. Niigata kenritsu kindai bijutsukan (ed.). *Tō kōtei kara no okurimono* [Gifts of the Tang emperors: Hidden treasures from Famen Temple]. Niigata: Niigata kenritsu kindai bijutsukan, 1999.

Torii (a). Torii Ryūzō. *Kōkogakujō yori mitaru Ryō no bunka: zufu* [Illustrations of archaeology supplementary to the culture of the Liao dynasty from the viewpoint of archaeology]. Tokyo: Tōhōbunka gakuin, Tokyo kenkyusho, 1936.

Torii (b). Torii Ryūzō. "Ryōdai no hekiga ni tsuite" [On Liao-dynasty wall paintings]. *Kokka* 1931.490, pp. 272–80; 1931.491, pp. 283–89; 1931.492, pp. 313–17; 1931.493, pp. 343–50.

Torii (c). Torii Ryūzō. *Sculptured Stone Tombs of the Liao Dynasty.* Peping: Harvard Yenching Institute, 1942.

Vainker. Shelagh J. Vainker. *Chinese Pottery and Porcelain: From Prehistory to the Present.* London: British Museum Press, 1991.

Wang Changwui and Jia Yunpo. Wang Changwui and Jia Yunpo. "Chen guo gongzhu yu fuma hezang mu bufen jinyinqi de fenxi" [Scientific analysis of some of the gold and silver wares from the joint burial of the Princess of Chen and her husband]. In *Liao Chenguo gongzhu mu* [Liao tomb of the princess of the state of Chen] (edited by Neimenggu zizhiqu wenwu kaogu yanjiusuo and Zhelimumeng bowuguan). Beijing: Wenwu chubanshe, 1993, pp. 166–70.

Wang Jianqun and Chen Xiangwei. Wang Jianqun and Chen Xiangwei. *Kulun Liaodai bihua mu* [Liao mural tombs at Kulun]. Beijing: Wenwu chubanshe, 1989.

Wang Renbo. Wang Renbo. "Xi'an diqu Beizhou Sui Tang muzang taoyong de zuhe yu fenqi" [Chronology and typology of pottery tomb figurines in Northern Zhou, Sui, and Tang tombs in the Xi'an area]. In *Zhongguo kaoguxue yanjiu lunji: Jinian Xia Nai xiansheng kaogu wushi zhounian* [A collection of the research articles on archaeology in China: In memory of Xia Nai on his fiftieth anniversary in archaeology] (edited by Zhongguo kaoguxue yanjiu lunji bianweihui). Xi'an: Sanqin chubanshe, 1987, pp. 428–56.

Wang Zhihao and Wu Zhanhai. Wang Zhihao and Wu Zhanhai. "Yijinhuoluoqi Shihuigou faxian de E'erduosi shi wenwu" [Ordos-style cultural relics discovered at Shihuigou, Yijinhuoluo Banner]. *Neimenggu wenwu kaogu* 1992.1–2, pp. 91–96.

Watson. Watson, Burton (trans.). *The Lotus Sutra.* New York: Columbia University Press, 1993.

Watt. James C.Y. Watt et al. *China: Dawn of a Golden Age, 200–750 AD.* New York: Metropolitan Museum of Art and Yale University Press, 2004.

Watt and Wardwell. James C.Y. Watt and Anne E. Wardwell. *When Silk Was Gold: Central Asian and Chinese Textiles.* New York: Metropolitan Museum of Art, 1997.

Wechsler. Howard J. Wechsler. *Offerings of Jade and Silk: Ritual and Symbol in the Legitimation of the T'ang Dynasty.* New Haven and London: Yale University Press, 1985.

Wei Jian. Wei Jian (ed.) *Neimenggu wenwu kaogu wenji* [Essays on the archaeology of cultural relics in Inner Mongolia]. Vol. 2. Beijing: Zhongguo dabaike quanshu chubanshe, 1997.

Wen Lihe. Wen Lihe. "Liaoning Fakuxian Yemaotai Liao Xiao Yi mu" [The Liao tomb of Xiao Yi near Yemaotai Village in Faku County, Liaoning Province]. *Kaogu* 1989.4, pp. 324–30.

White and Bunker. Julia M. White and Emma C. Bunker. *Adornment for Eternity: Status and Rank in Chinese Ornament.* Denver and Hong Kong: Denver Art Museum and University of Hong Kong, 1994.

Whitfield. Roderick Whitfield. *The Art of Central Asia.* Tokyo: Kodansha, 1982.

Whitfield and Farrer. Roderick Whitfield and Anne Farrer. *Caves of the Thousand Buddhas: Chinese Art from the Silk Route.* London: British Museum Press, 1990.

Wilkinson. Charles K. Wilkinson. *Nishapur: Pottery of the Early Islamic Period.* New York: Metropolitan Museum of Art, 1973.

Wittfogel and Fêng. Karl A. Wittfogel and Fêng Chia-shêng. *History of Chinese Society: Liao, 907–1125.* Philadelphia: American Philosophical Society, 1949.

Wudai Feng Hui mu. Xianyang shi wenwu kaogu yanjiusuo (ed.). *Wudai Feng Hui mu.* [The Five Dynasties tomb of Feng Hui]. Chongqing: Chongqing chubanshe, 2001.

Wudai Huangpu yaozhi. Shaanxi sheng kaogu yanjiusuo. *Wudai Huangpu yaozhi* [Five Dynasties kiln site in Huangpu]. Beijing: Wenwu chubanshe, 1997.

Wudai Wang Chuzhi mu. Hebei sheng wenwu yanjiusuo and Baoding shi wenwu guanlichu. *Wudai Wang Chuzhi mu* [The Five Dynasties tomb of Wang Chuzhi]. Beijing: Wenwu chubanshe, 1998.

Wu Hung. Wu Hung. "House-shaped Sarcophagi." Paper presented at the conference "Between Han and Tang: Visual and Material Culture in a Transformative Period," University of Chicago, October 2001.

Wu Jiachang. Wu Jiachang. "Kazuo Beiling Liao mu" [Liao tomb at Beiling, Kazuo, Liaoning]. *Liaohai wenwu xuekan* 1986.1, pp. 32–51.

Xiari ji. Liu Qi. *Xiari ji* [Days of leisure record]. In *Wuchao xiaoshuo* [Novels of the Five Dynasties]. 6 vols. Taipei: Guangwen shuju, 1979.

Xiang Chunsong (a). Xiang Chunsong. *Liaodai bihua xuan* [A selection of Liao-dynasty mural paintings]. Shanghai: Renmin meishu chubanshe, 1984.

Xiang Chunsong (b). Xiang Chunsong. *Liaodai lishi yu kaogu* [History and archaeology of the Liao dynasty]. Hohhot: Neimenggu renmin chubanshe, 1996.

Xiang Chunsong (c). Xiang Chunsong. "Liaoning Zhaowuda diqu faxian de Liao mu huihua ziliao" [Materials on the mural paintings found in a Liao-dynasty tomb at Zhaowuda, Liaoning Province]. *Wenwu* 1979.6, pp. 22–32.

Xiang Chunsong (d). Xiang Chunsong. "Neimenggu Jiefangyingzi Liao mu fajue jianbao" [Excavation report of the Liao tomb in Jiefangyingzi, Inner Mongolia]. *Kaogu* 1979.4, pp. 330–34.

Xiang Chunsong (e). Xiang Chunsong. "Neimenggu Wengniuteqi Liaodai Guangdegong mu" [The Liao tomb at Guangdegong, Wengniute Banner, Inner Mongolia]. *Beifang wenwu* 1989.4, pp. 41–44.

Xiang Chunsong (f). Xiang Chunsong. "Zhaomeng diqu de Liaodai muzang" [Liao tombs in Zhaomeng]. *Neimenggu wenwu kaogu* 1981.1, pp. 73–79.

Xie Mingliang (a). Xie Mingliang (Ming-liang Hsieh). "Ji pinang shi hu" [Research notes on bag-shaped flasks]. *Gugong wenwu yuekan* 18.1 (2000), pp. 46–63.

Xie Mingliang (b). Xie Mingliang (Ming-liang Hsieh). "Lue tan jiaerguan" [Brief discussion of *jiaer* jars]. *Gugong wenwu yuekan* 16.4 (1998), pp. 16–31.

Xie Mingliang (c). Xie Mingliang (Ming-liang Hsieh). "Tuohu zaji" [Notes on the spittoon]. *Gugong wenwu yuekan* 10.2 (1992), pp. 34–47.

Xie Mingliang (d). Xie Mingliang (Ming-liang Hsieh). "Xila meishu de dongjian?" [Transmission of Greek art to the East?]. *Gugong wenwu yuekan* 15.7 (1997), pp. 32–53.

Xie Mingliang (e). Xie Mingliang (Ming-liang Hsieh). "Youguan 'guan' han 'xin guan' kuan baici guan zi hanyi de jige wenti" [On interpreting the meaning of the *guan* character in the *guan* and *xin guan* inscriptions seen on some white wares]. *Gugong xueshu jikan* 5.2 (1987), pp. 1–38.

Xin Tangshu. Ouyang Xiu (1007–72) et al. *Xin Tangshu* [New history of the Tang]. Beijing: Zhonghua shuju, 1975.

Xin Wudai shi. Ouyang Xiu (1007–72). *Xin Wudai shi* [New historical records of the Five Dynasties]. Beijing: Zhonghua shuju, 1974.

Xiong. Victor Cunrui Xiong. "Ritual Architecture under the Northern Wei." In *Between Han and Tang: Visual and Material Culture in a Transformative Period* (edited by Wu Hung). Beijing: Wenwu chubanshe, 2003, pp. 31–95.

Xu Bingkun and Sun Shoudao. Xu Bingkun and Sun Shoudao. *Dongbei wenhua* [Northeast culture]. Shanghai and Hong Kong: Shanghai yuandong chubanshe and Shangwu yinshuguan, 1995.

Xu Pingfang. Xu Pingfang. "Liaodai muzang" [Liao Burials]. *Zhongguo dabaike quanshu: kaoguxue* 1986, p. 274.

Xu Xiaodong (a). Xu Xiaodong. "East-West Connections and Amber under the Qidans." In *Noble Riders from Pine and Deserts: The Artistic Legacy of the Qidan* (edited by Jenny F. So). Hong Kong: Art Museum of the Chinese University of Hong Kong, 2004, pp. 34–37.

Xu Xiaodong (b). Xu Xiaodong. *Liaodai yuqi yanjiu* [Research on Liao jades]. Beijing: Zijincheng chubanshe, 2003.

Xu Zhiguo and Wei Chunguang. Xu Zhiguo and Wei Chunguang. "Faku Yemaotai di 22 hao Liao mu qingli jianbao" [Brief report on the clearing of Tomb Number 22 at Yemaotai, Faku County]. *Beifang wenwu* 2000.1, pp. 48–51.

Xuanhua Liaomu. Hebei sheng wenwu yanjiusuo. *Xuanhua Liaomu: 1974–1993 nian kaogu fajue baogao* [The Liao-dynasty tombs in Xuanhua: Reports on archaeological excavations from 1974 to 1993]. 2 vols. Beijing: Wenwu chubanshe, 2001.

Xuanhua Liaomu bihua. Hebei sheng wenwu yanjiusuo (ed.). *Xuanhua Liaomu bihua* [Liao-dynasty murals in tombs in Xuanhua]. Beijing: Wenwu chubanshe, 2001.

Yanshi Xingyuan. Zhongguo shehui kexueyuan kaogu yanjiusuo (ed.). *Yanshi Xingyuan Tang mu* [Tang tombs at Xingyuan in Yanshi]. Beijing: Kexue chubanshe, 2001.

Yang. Lien-sheng Yang. "A 'Posthumous Letter' from the Chin Emperor to the Khitan Emperor in 942." *Harvard Journal of Asiatic Studies* 10.3/4 (1947), p. 418–28.

Yang Renkai. Yang Renkai. *Yemaotai di qi hao Liao mu chutu guhua kao* [Investigation of the old paintings excavated from the Liao Tomb Number 7 at Yemaotai]. Shanghai: Shanghai renmin meishu chubanshe, 1984.

Yang Shusen. Yang Shusen. "Liaodai shixue shulue" [A brief summary of Liao-dynasty historiography]. In *Liao Jin shi lunji* [Collection of articles on the history of the Liao and Jin] (edited by Chen Shu). Vol. 3. Beijing: Shumu wenxian chubanshe, 1987, pp. 187–202.

Yang Xiaoneng (a). Yang Xiaoneng. *New Perspectives on China's Past: Chinese Archaeology in the Twentieth Century* (volume 2 of *Major Archaeological Discoveries in Twentieth Century China*). New Haven: Yale University Press, 2004.

Yang Xiaoneng (b). Yang Xiaoneng. "Unearthing Liao Elite Art and Culture: An Empire in Northern China from the 10th to the 12th Century." *Orientations,* October 2004, pp. 66–74.

Yingxian Muta Liaodai. Shanxi sheng wenwu ju and Zhongguo lishi bowuguan. *Yingxian Muta Liaodai micang* [Liao hidden relics in the Ying County Timber Pagoda]. Beijing: Wenwu chubanshe, 1991.

Yü. Chün-fang Yü. *Kuan-yin: The Chinese Transformation of Avalokiteśvara*. New York: Columbia University Press, 2001.

Yuan Hairui and Tang Yunjun. Yuan Hairui and Tang Yunjun. "Huayansi" [Huayan Monastery]. *Wenwu* 1982.9, pp. 78–91.

Yuan Junqing. Yuan Junqing. "Nanjing Xiangshan wuhao liuhao qihao mu qingli jianbao" [Brief report on the clearing of Tomb Numbers 5, 6, and 7 at Xiangshan, Nanjing]. *Wenwu* 1972.11, pp. 23–41.

Zhang Bozhong. Zhang Bozhong. "Neimenggu Tongliaoxian Erlinchang Liao mu" [Liao tomb at Erlinchang, Tongliao County, Inner Mongolia]. *Wenwu* 1985.3, pp. 56–62.

Zhang Hanjun. Zhang Hanjun. "Liaodai Wanbu Huayanjing ta fojiao diaosu yishi" [The art of the Buddhist relief sculpture of the 10,000 Huayan sutras pagoda]. *Huhehaote wenwu* 1991.7, pp. 39, 41–45.

Zhang Hongbo and Li Zhi. Zhang Hongbo and Li Zhi. "Beipiao Quanjuyong Liaomufaxian jianbao" [Excavation of a Liao tomb in Quanjuyong, Beipiao]. *Liaohai wenwu xuekan* 1990.2, pp. 24–28.

Zhang Songbai and Song Guojun. Zhang Songbai and Song Guojun. "Chengzi jinyinqi yanjiu" [Research on the gold and silver objects from Chengzi]. In *Neimenggu dongbuqu kaoguxue wenhua yanjiu wenji* [Essays on archaeological and cultural research in the eastern region of Inner Mongolia] (edited by Neimenggu zizhiqu wenwu kaogu yanjiusuo). Beijing: Haiyang chubanshe, 1991, pp. 73–79.

Zhang Songbai. Zhang Songbai. "Guanyu jiguan hu yanjiu zhong de jige wenti" [Several issues concerning the research on cockscomb flasks]. In *Neimenggu wenwu kaogu wenji* [Essays on the archaeology of cultural relics in Inner Mongolia], vol. 2 (edited by Wei Jian). Beijing: Zhongguo da baike quanshu chubanshe, 1997, pp. 584–91.

Zhang Yu. Zhang Yu. "Liao Shangjing chengzhi kancha suoyi" [Notes on the excavation of remains of the Liao city of Shangjing]. *Neimenggu wenwu kaogu wenji* [Essays on the archaeology of cultural relics in Inner Mongolia], vol. 2 (edited by Wei Jian). Beijing:

Zhongguo da baike quanshu chubanshe, 1997, pp. 525–30.

Zhang Yuhuan and Luo Zhewen. Zhang Yuhuan and Luo Zhewen. *Zhongguo guta jingcui* [The cream of Chinese pagodas]. Beijing: Kexue chubanshe, 1988.

Zhao Fangzhi. Zhao Fangzhi (ed.). *Caoyuan wenhua* [Grassland culture]. Shanghai: Shangwu Yinshu Guan, 1995.

Zhao Feng (a). Zhao Feng. "Liao Qingzhou Baita suochu sizhou de zhi ran xiu jiyi" [The craftsmanship of woven, colored, and embroidered Liao-dynasty textiles found in the White Pagoda in Qingzhou]. *Wenwu* 2000.4, pp. 70–81.

Zhao Feng (b). Zhao Feng. *Liao Textiles and Costumes*. Hong Kong: Muwen Tang Fine Arts Publication, 2004.

Zhao Feng (c). Zhao Feng (ed.). *Recent Excavations of Textiles in China*. Hong Kong: ISAT/Costume Squad, 2002.

Zhao Feng (d). Zhao Feng. "Satin Samite: A Bridge from Samite to Satin." *CIETA-Bulletin* 76 (1999), pp. 46–63.

Zhao Feng (e). Zhao Feng. *Treasures in Silk: An Illustrated History of Chinese Textiles*. Hong Kong: ISAT/Costume Squad, 1999.

Zhao Songling and Chen Kangde. Zhao Songling and Chen Kangde. *Zongguo bao yu* [Precious jades of China]. Taipei: Shu xin chubanshe, 1991.

Zhao Wengang. Zhao Wengang. "Tianjinshi Jixian Yingfangcun Liao mu" [Liao tomb in Yingfang Village, Jixian, Tianjin]. *Beifang wenwu* 1992.3, pp. 36–41.

Zhao Xiaohua. Zhao Xiaohua. "Liaoningsheng bowuguan zhengji rucang yitao Liaodai caihui muguo" [A painted wooden coffin chamber from the Liao dynasty preserved in the Museum of Liaoning Province]. *Wenwu* 2000.11, pp. 63–71.

Zhejiang jinian ci. Zhejiang sheng bowuguan (ed.). *Zhejiang jinian ci* [Zhejiang chronological porcelain]. Beijing: Wenwu chubanshe, 2000.

Zhejiang Lin'an Banqiao. Zhejiang sheng wenwu guanli weiyuanhui (Yao Zhongyuan). "Zhejiang Lin'an Banqiao de Wudai mu" [A Five Dynasties tomb in Banqiao, Lin'an, Zhejiang Province]. *Wenwu* 1975.8, pp. 66–72.

Zheng Shaozong (a). Zheng Shaozong. "Chifengxian Dayingzi Liao mu fajue baogao" [Excavation report on a Liao tomb at Dayingzi, Chifeng County]. *Kaogu xuebao* 1956.3, pp. 1–25.

Zheng Shaozong (b). Zheng Shaozong. "Qidan Qin Jin guo dachanggongzhu muzhiming" [The epitaph of the Khitan princess supreme of Qin and Jin]. *Kaogu* 1962.8, pp. 429–35.

Zhongguo meishu quanji (a). Zhongguo meishu quanji bianji weiyuanhui (ed.). *Zhongguo meishu quanji, Huihua bian* [Complete treasury of Chinese fine arts, Painting series]. Vol. 12, *Mu shi bihua* [Tomb mural paintings]. Beijing: Wenwu chubanshe, 1989.

Zhongguo meishu quanji (b). Zhongguo meishu quanji bianji weiyuanhui and Dunhuang yanjiusuo (eds.). *Zhongguo meishu quanji, Huihua bian* [Complete treasury of Chinese fine arts, Painting series]. Vol. 14, *Dunhuang bihua (shang)* [Dunhuang murals (first part)]. Shanghai: Shanghai renmin meishu chubanshe, 1985.

Zhongguo meishu quanji (c). Zhongguo meishu quanji bianji weiyuanhui (ed.). *Zhongguo meishu quanji, Jianzhu yishu bian* [Complete treasury of Chinese fine arts, Architectural art series]. Vol. 4, *Zongjiao jianzhu* [Religious architecture]. Beijing: Zhongguo jianzhu gongye chubanshe, 1991.

Zhongguo taoci quanji. Zhongguo Shanghai renmin meishu chubanshe (ed.). *Zhongguo taoci quanji* [Comprehensive collections of Chinese ceramics]. Vol. 4, *Yue yao* [Yue ware]. Shanghai: Shanghai renmin meishu chubanshe, 1984.

Zhongguo wenwu jinghua. Guojia wenwuju (ed.). *Zhongguo wenwu jinghua da cidian: taoci juan* [Encyclopedia of Chinese cultural relics: Ceramics]. Vol. 1. Shanghai: Shanghai cishu chubanshe, 1995.

Zhou Hanxin and Ha Si. Zhou Hanxin and Ha Si. "Keyouzhongqi chutu Liaodai muguoshi ji shichuang qianxi" [Brief analysis of the Liao wooden outer coffin and coffin-bed excavated at Keyou Central Banner]. In *Neimenggu wenwu kaogu wenji* [Essays on the archaeology of cultural relics in Inner Mongolia], vol. 2 (edited by Wei Jian). 1997, pp. 567–79.

Zhu Tianshu. Zhu Tianshu. *Liaodai Jinyinqi* [Liao gold and silver wares]. Beijing: Wenwu chubanshe, 1998.

Zhu Zifang and Xu Ji. Zhu Zifang and Xu Ji. "Liaoning Chaoyang Guyingzi Liao Geng shi mu fajue baogao" [Report on the Geng family tombs of the Liao in Guyingzi, Chaoyang, Liaoning]. *Kaoguxue jikan* 1983.3, pp. 168–95.

Zimmer. Heinrich Zimmer. *The Art of Indian Asia* (edited by Joseph Campbell). 2 vols. Princeton: Princeton University Press, 1968.

Catalogue Contributors

Emma C. Bunker is research consultant to the Asian art department of the Denver Art Museum.

Nicola Di Cosmo is the Henry Luce Foundation Professor of East Asian Studies in the School of Historical Studies at the Institute for Advanced Study.

Lynette Sue-ling Gremli is a faculty member and doctoral candidate in Chinese art history at the University of Zurich. She specializes in the study of Chinese textiles of the medieval period, with a particular focus on Liao-dynasty textiles.

Marilyn Leidig Gridley is a research associate at the Center for East Asian Studies at the University of Kansas.

Hiromi Kinoshita is a doctoral candidate at Somerville College, Oxford University. Her area of specialized study is the hybridization of Liao Khitan tombs.

Dieter Kuhn is professor of sinology in the Department for Cultural Studies of East and South Asia at the University of Würzburg.

François Louis is associate professor at the Bard Graduate Center for Studies in the Decorative Arts, Design, and Culture, New York.

Hsueh-man Shen is a lecturer in Chinese art at the University of Edinburgh.

Nancy Shatzman Steinhardt is professor of East Asian art at the University of Pennsylvania and curator of Chinese art at the University of Pennsylvania Museum of Archaeology and Anthropology.

Sun Jianhua is a dean, professor, and curator at the Research Institute of Cultural Relics and Archaeology of Inner Mongolia.

Ta La is the director of and a professor at the Research Institute of Cultural Relics and Archaeology of Inner Mongolia.

Zhang Yaqiang is a staff member of the Research Institute of Cultural Relics and Archaeology of Inner Mongolia.

Index

Photo Credits

Fig. 1: after Xiang Chunsong [d], *Kaogu* 1979.4, pl. 7.1; Fig. 2: after *Wenwu* 1983.9, p. 5, fig. 12, pl. 1.1; Fig. 3: after Qi Xiaoguang and Wang Jiangu, *Wenwu* 1996.1, fig. 2; Fig. 4: after Qi Xiaoguang et al., *Wenwu* 1998.1, fig. 2; Fig. 5: after Tamura Jitsuzō and Kobayashi Yukio, *Japan Quarterly* 1954.1, p. 38; Fig. 6a: Xiang Chungsong, *Kaogu* 1979.4, p. 331, fig. 2; Fig. 6b: Xiang Chunsong, *Kaogu* 1979.4, pl. 6.2; Fig. 7: after Feng Yongqian, *Kaogu* 1983.7, fig. 2; Fig. 8a: after *Liao Chenguo gongzhu mu*, p. 7, fig. 3; Fig. 8b: after *Liao Chenguo gongzhu mu*, p. 21, fig. 12; Fig. 9: after Xiang Chunsong [c], *Wenwu* 1979.6, fig. 8; Fig 10: after *Wenwu* 1975.12, p. 28, fig. 4; Fig. 11: after *Wenwu* 1975.12, p. 28, fig. 5; Fig. 12: after *Wenwu* 1975.12, color pl. 1; Figs. 13, 14, 15b, 15d, 15f, 15i, 15j, 23: photograph by Nancy S. Steinhardt; Fig. 15a: after Mo Zongjiang, *Jianzhushi lunwen ji* 1979.2, fig. 4; Fig. 15c: after *Zhongguo meishu quanji* 4, pl. 49; Fig 15e: after Liang Sicheng [a], *Zhongguo yingzao xueshe huikan* 3, no. 4 [1932], pl. 10; Fig 15g: after Qiao Yun and Sun Dazhang, p. 89; Fig 15h: after Liang Sicheng and Liu Dunzhen, *Zhongguo yingzao xueshe huikan* 4, nos. 3 and 4 [1934], pl. 10; Fig 15k: after "Shanhua Temple, a Historic Site in Shanxi," Beijing Slide Studio set, slide 6; purchased by author in 1986; Fig. 15l: after "The Huayan Temple," Beijing Slide Studio set, slide 2; purchased by author in 1986; Fig. 15m: after Liu Dunzhen [a], *Zhongguo yingzao xueshe huikan* 5, no. 4 [1935], pl. 5, *ding*; Fig. 15n: after Liu Dunzhen [a], *Zhongguo yingzao xueshe huikan* 5, no. 4 [1935], pl. 4, *bing*; Fig. 15o: after Liu Dunzhen [a], *Zhongguo yingzao xueshe huikan* 5, no. 4 [1935], pl. 2, *ding*; Fig. 16: after Liu Dunzhen [a], *Zhongguo yingzao xueshe huikan* 5, no. 4 [1935], pl. 4, *jia*; Fig. 17: after "The Huayan Temple," Beijing Slide Studio set, slide 10; purchased by author in 1986; Fig. 18: after Qiao Yun and Sun Dazhang, p. 82; Fig. 19: after Liu Dunzhen [b], p. 207; Fig. 20: after Sekino Tadashi and Takeshima Takuichi, vol. 1, pl. 18; Fig. 21: after *Xuanhua Liaomu*, vol. 2, color pl. 15; Fig. 22: after Zhou Hanxin and Ha Si, p. 567; Figs. 24–71, 86, 89–90, 110–112: courtesy of the Cultural Bureau of Inner Mongolia Autonomous Region; Fig. 72: after *Wenwu* 1992.7, p. 14, fig. 30; Fig. 73: after *Wenwu* 1994.12, cover page, color pl. 1; Fig. 74: after Su Bai [c], p. 466; Fig. 75: drawing by Hsueh-man Shen, based on *Wenwu* 1982.6, p. 2, fig. 2; Fig. 76: after Su Bai [c], p. 467; Fig. 77: after Chen Mingda, drawing 2; Fig. 78: after Chen Mingda, pl. 59; Fig. 79: after Chen Mingda, pl. 62; Fig. 80: after *Xuanhua Liaomu* [*Liao tombs in Xuanhua*], vol. 2, color pl. 34; Fig. 81: after *Xuanhua Liaomu*, vol. 2, pl. 46.1; Fig. 82: after *Xuanhua Liaomu*, vol. 2, color pl. 62; Fig. 83: after *Xuanhua Liaomu*, vol. 2, color pl. 33; Fig. 84: after *Xuanhua Liaomu*, vol. 1, p. 89, fig. 69; Fig. 85: after *Wenwu* 1992.7, p. 22, fig. 51; Fig. 87: drawing after *Liao Chenguo gongzhu mu*, p. 109, fig. 69; Fig. 88: after *Kaogu xuebao* 1958.2, p. 107, fig. 7; Fig. 91: after *Tō kōtei kara no okurimono* [*Gifts of the Tang emperors: Hidden treasures from Famen Temple*], pp. 82–83; Fig. 92: courtesy of the Museum of Balin Left Banner; Fig. 93: after *Xuanhua Liaomu* [*Xuanhua Liao tombs*], vol. 1, pp. 31–32, figs. 24–25, figs. 27–28; p. 41, fig. 30; Fig. 94: after *Neimenggu wenwu kaogu*, 2002.2, color pl., back cover; Fig. 95: after Shanxi Yungang shiku wenwu baoguansuo, ed., *Huayansi* [*Huayan Monastery*], pl. 33; Fig. 96: after *Wenwu* 1994.12, p. 70, fig. 8; Fig. 97: after *Wenwu* 1994.12, p. 71, figs. 10.1–10.3; Fig. 98: courtesy of the Museum of Balin Right Banner; Figs. 99, 101, 103: photograph by Marilyn Gridley; Fig. 100: after *Wenwu*, 1994.2, color plate inside front cover; Fig. 102: after *Xuanhua Liaomu* [*Liao tombs in Xuanhua*], vol. 2, color pl. 81; Fig. 104: photograph by Hseuh-man Shen; Fig. 105: after Li Yiyou [f], pl. 144; Fig. 106: after Guobao zaixian, *Linquan gaoshi* [*Scholars in reclusion*] p. 7; Fig. 107: drawing after Lu Jiugao and Han Wei, *Tangdai jinyinqi* [*Tang dynasty gold and silver wares*], no. 154; Fig. 108: drawing by François Louis; Fig. 109: after *Qidan wangchao* [*Khitan dynasty*], p. 196; Fig. 113: after Zhejiang sheng bowuguan, ed., *Zhejiang jinian ci* [*Zhejiang chronological porcelain*], pl. 170; Fig. 114: after James C.Y. Watt et al., p. 323; Fig. 115: after *Xuanhua Liaomu* [*Liao tombs in Xuanhua*], vol. 2, color pl. 74; Fig. 116: after *Xuanhua Liaomu*, vol. 2, color pl. 61; Fig. 117: after Mikami Tsugio [a], pp. 14–15, pl. 5; Fig. 118: after *Tō kōtei kara no okurimono* [*Gifts of the Tang emperors: Hidden treasures from Famen Temple*], p. 92; Fig. 119: after *Zhongguo wenwu jinghua da cidian: taoci juan* [*Encyclopedia of Chinese cultural relics: Ceramics*], p. 318, pl. 502; Fig. 120: after *Zhongguo wenwu jinghua da cidian: taoci juan* [*Encyclopedia of Chinese cultural relics: Ceramics*], p. 315, pl. 491.

All entry images courtesy of the Cultural Bureau of Inner Mongolia Autonomous Region.